Vagabond
Memoirs

Other books by Phil Karber

Postmarks from a Political Traveler

*Fear and Faith in Paradise:
Exploring Conflict and Religion in the Middle East*

*The Indochina Chronicles:
Travels in Laos, Cambodia and Vietnam*

*Yak Pizza to Go:
Travels in an Age of Vanishing Cultures and Extinctions*

Vagabond Memoirs

Phil Karber

COTTAGE STREET PRESS

Copyright © 2024 by Phil Karber.

All rights reserved. No part of this book, whether text or imagery, may be reproduced in any form or by any means without express permission from the publisher, except for brief quotations used in reviews.

>Cottage Street Press
>Fayetteville, Arkansas
>cottagestreetpress@gmail.com

ISBN: 979-8-218-40363-8

Front cover photographer—Harry Schwartz, bail bondsman. Taken in Fort Smith across the street from the city jail the night of my first marijuana bust in 1972.

Back cover photo: Phil Karber and Syrian driver. Taken in Palmyra, Syria in 2006

Cover art and design: Randal Dickinson

Book design and layout: H. K. Stewart

Printed in the United States of America

For my granddaughters,
Parker, Suzi, Lila *and* Mabyn,
the next generation of sojourners

Contents

Introduction 11

I. The Early Years
1. Roots 17
2. Playful Childhoods 51
3. Doctoritis 73
4. Whiskers, Pimples, and Rock 'n' Roll 80

II. Rebellion and Disillusion
5. Hell Raisin' 91
6. A Moveable Feast 105
7. The Judge's Grudge 121
8. The Age of Aquarius Rocks On 154
9. The Road to Perdition 171

III. Sojourns and Wanderings
10. California Dreaming 187
11. Kissing the Joy on the Fly 208
12. Hemingway's Key West 222
13. A Big Easy Social Call 237
14. Furry Sang the Blues 256

IV. Wild Country to Be Young In
15. On the Lam 281
16. Swan Songs 339

Epilogue 357
Acknowledgments 381
About the Author 383

I was wise enough never to grow up,
while fooling people into believing I had.

—**Margaret Mead**
author of *Coming of Age in Samoa*

I had an inheritance
from my father,
it was the moon and the sun.
And though I roam all
over the world,
the spending of it is never done.

—**Ernest Hemingway**
For Whom the Bell Tolls

Portrait of the author's family in 1956. (Author is bottom left.)

Introduction

A DECADE AGO, my wife Joellen Lambiotte and I visited our friends Leon Lancaster and Lynn Fiedler at their small Cape Cod home on Nantucket. Leon had worked as a carpenter on the island for forty years, and Lynn managed a bowling alley. Between the two of them, they knew everyone on the island. Leon's best friend is Allen Baker, a cinemaphotographer, whose father, Russell Baker, was a renowned *New York Times* columnist and host of *Masterpiece Theatre*. Joellen and I had read Russell's humorously irreverent *Times* column, "Observer," but didn't fathom the national treasure he was.

Thanks to Leon, that changed for us one fine sunny August morning when we joined Allen and Russell for tea on the garden patio of a rental near Brandt Point. Joellen and I had only recently returned to our home in Cambridge, Massachusetts, after living in Nairobi, Hanoi, Bangkok, and East London, South Africa. Slightly stooped at eighty-seven years old, Russell was all ears that morning, genuinely interested in our Arkansas childhoods and where and why we had lived abroad and what travel books I had written, from *Yak Pizza to Go* in the '90s to more recently *Postmarks from a Political Traveler*.

From his Washington days as a political reporter for the *Times*, Russell had covered Vietnam and had had more than a passing acquaintance with Senators J. William Fulbright and John L. McClellan from Arkansas. At some point, in his kind, soft voice, he brought up the Southern Manifesto, written in 1956 by several racist Deep South senators, which pledged to overturn the *Brown v. Board of Education* (1954) decision that called for the desegregation of schools. He liked Fulbright, his grace of mind and particularly the international scholarships he established and his eventual stance against President Lyndon Johnson over using the Gulf of Tonkin Resolution to escalate the Vietnam War. He said the Southern Manifesto had made Fulbright squirm. In the end, though, Fulbright had caved for political reasons back in Arkansas.

Our conversation circled back to Arkansas and one of the immediate consequences of the Manifesto. On September 4, 1957, Arkansas's governor Orval Faubus ordered the Arkansas National Guard to prevent black students from entering Little Rock Central High School. The Guard was later nationalized by President Eisenhower and, together with the 101st Airborne, was called upon to escort the students known as the Little Rock Nine into Central. Russell knew his political history and all the players. Joellen and I were mesmerized at what a delightful, self-effacing raconteur he was.

Joellen and Russell talked about Nixon and Watergate briefly, before the conversation drifted to the early sixties and the Kennedy White House. "One last story before you take off," Russell said, chuckling to himself. I wasn't taking notes, but my best recollection of the story went like this:

"I was with *Times* photographer George Tames the day he snapped the iconic shot of President Kennedy standing over his desk in the Oval Office with his back to the door, three weeks after his inauguration, seemingly bearing the weight of the world on his shoulders. What happened was much different. We were all on a first-name basis, so when Tames walked into the Oval Office he quickly snapped the shot and said something like, 'Jack, how's it going?' Kennedy turned and looked up from reading the *New York Times* and responded with, 'That fucking asshole can't write for shit.'"

Russell didn't say who the "fucking asshole" was, but Joellen and I never looked at that photo the same again.

The next week, back in Cambridge, I stopped by the Harvard bookstore, bought Russell's Pulitzer Prize–winning memoir, *Growing Up*, and read it in two days. Russell suddenly became the bell cow for me to chronicle my coming-of-age travels. His early years in the backwoods of Loudoun County, Virginia, resonated with my family's roots in the piney hinterlands of Arkansas, and our political conversations that morning on Nantucket fairly sketched out the context in which I grew up: Jim Crow South, Kennedy assassination, Vietnam, and Watergate.

While I've written several travel books, this book combines travel and memoir, a much different endeavor than, say, describing a train journey from Beijing to Amsterdam. The art of travel memoir writing—in this case the linear, horizontal travels to another geographic space and the vertical one through my coming of age interior life—is a tricky thing, in that it relies on self-recollection, recall of others, photos and diaries if available, and unavoidably the imagination. When summoning memories from half a century ago, my mind, like many, is like an air filter: It's random what sticks to it. Once an image, such as an idyllic upbringing, imagined or real, is excavated, it must be built out and amplified with recollections and the historical landscape of the world that once was.

Russell's book *Growing Up* ended when he was in his mid-twenties. No need to tell more, he was a popular journalist, a public intellectual. This book ends in the same way, but not being so famous, I felt the need for an epilogue capsulizing the next five decades.

Long ago I had consciously muted all the bells and whistles of my family (and my personal) drama. Now it was time to draw out my coming-of-age story from its interior hiding place and into the light. As poet and fellow Arkansan Maya Angelou once said, "There is no greater agony than bearing an untold story inside you." So it is, with each and all of us. My story begins on a family road trip in rural Arkansas.

The Early Years

Part One

Roots

Chapter One

BASKING ON A WHITE-SAND BEACH before some impossibly vast ocean blue was an indulgence I would not enjoy until I paid for it myself a few months before turning sixteen. In the 1950s and early '60s, my family—Mom, Dad, and five boys: John, Stan, myself, Greg, and Kent the toddler—had no money for hotel rooms or cross-country beach vacations. Mom was a homemaker and Dad a county extension agent, agricultural educator, and facilitator, earning the equivalent of a teacher's salary. He picked up extra income as a weekend pilot in the Air National Guard, flying single-engine planes. Simple paycheck economics and post-Depression-era spending values dictated the where and how our school breaks and summer excursions came down. Camping at Dad's old homeplace, near Alpine, Arkansas, down in the Piney Woods on the banks of the Caddo River, was a freebie. A fringe benefit was calling on our country kinfolk, from both sides of the family, a daily double. Look no further—the choice made perfect sense to Dad and Mom.

For us "citified" boys raised on concrete and not in barns, playing sports year-round, ensconced in the rhythms of school, church, and neighborhood, a trip to the country was something of a forced family adventure. Our lack of enthusiasm for a sojourn with our rustic relatives was seemingly at odds with our fascination with television Westerns, wagon trains, stagecoaches, and the whole shebang of America's settler history that Dad's old homeplace recalled.

On our drives down to Alpine, while scenes of our family's rural past and the more familiar present unscrolled in colorful vignettes, we usually acted out like a bunch of Mexican jumping beans, kids throwing off tension after being cooped up in the old Mercury station wagon for three hours. With Dad as trail boss, the pit stops, family lore, competitive counting of cows, and familiar points of interest took off some of the edge.

Checking off the one-stoplight towns of Jenny Lind, Greenwood, Witcherville, and Huntington, south of Mansfield on U.S. 71, Dad's windshield tour on shimmering blacktop included directing our attention to baseball greats Dizzy and Paul Dean's birthplace at the Lucas turnoff, a cue for John to tune up and sing "The Wabash Cannonball," Dizzy's favorite song to belt out in the broadcast booth during rain delays. Dizzy was a folk hero in the South, with the St. Louis Cardinals being the most southern and western team during the '30s reign of the Gashouse Gang. After retirement from baseball, his cocklebur twang as he mangled and made up words while plugging and chugging Falstaff beer on the "Game of the Week" made watching television baseball an existential joy. It traveled well with a carload of Cardinal fans, kids replaying the old hurler's funny bits: "He slud into third"; "It ain't braggin' if you can back it up"; "Son, what kind of pitch would you like to miss?"; and a Niagara more of Dizzy's colorful sayings.

Lucas existed as a dirt road crossing of poor farms, more as a state of mind than an actual town. We always kept our ears cocked during Dizzy's broadcasts, but we never once heard him mention his childhood days in Lucas, Arkansas, shoeless and picking cotton. Didn't matter. The Lucas thread spooled out like a lasso all the way to wherever Dizzy's broadcast booth was, around his neck and back again, as we passed the sign for the Lucas turnoff. He was our cotton pickin' homeboy.

On a clear day, near the community of Needmore, the ramparts of the Ouachita Mountains came into view as rolling blue waves of shortleaf pine forests. Some gumption-filled, seventeenth-century

Frenchman in buckskins came up with the name Ouachita, a translation derived from the Indian word "Washita," meaning good hunting grounds. Wending down the mountainside, into a broad valley and the ramrod-straight backwoods of bluish plumes, the highway crossed the Fourche La Fave River, once the wildlife-rich home of Caddo Indians and French trappers, bear hunters, and traders. Black bear skins and bear fat oil (favored for illumination and cooking) from Arkansas were big sellers in the early nineteenth-century markets of New Orleans. Small wonder, in the day, that the popular portrayals of Arkansas generated nicknames such as the "Bear State" and the "Toothpick State," a reference to the custom of backwoodsmen carrying large knives on belts.

The Midway Park Restaurant announced the turnoff at Y City. The city, frustrated in the fulfillment of its aspirations, now only marked the halfway point between Fayetteville and Texarkana and served as a convenient stopover for those forking southeast off of U.S. 71 to Hot Springs. Bored with counting cows, on arrival at the Midway we made a contest out of counting the out-of-state license plates, including those of Greyhound buses using the restaurant as a scheduled rest stop. Illinois, Missouri, and Kansas popped up the most. More often than not, Detroit's finest metal ferried in a gabby mashup of funny-accented geezers and amateur gamblers, or both, to and from the curative, mineral-rich waters of Hot Springs coupled with its casinos, marquee nightclub acts, and thoroughbred horse racing. Bird Vines, Midway's owner, who lived in the nearby community of Boles, often greeted Dad by name at the front door beneath the mounted head of a bull elk that he had killed in Colorado. Long before Bird purchased the property in the mid-1950s and put in a one-pump gas station across the street, it had been a time-worn waypoint for travelers: first a wagon and tent camp and then a tourist court with a popular swimming hole beneath a series of waterfalls on Mill Creek.

We only made it to the swimming hole once before it was judged off limits after two kids drowned below the waterfalls. Unrelated to the drownings, but around the time Bird purchased the property, the former owner shuttered the tourist cabins. From then on, Midway became everyone's favorite pit stop, known by all passersby for its cheeseburgers, meat-and-three lunches, fresh coconut pies, and clean restrooms, as well as the whitewashed trunks of the surrounding pine trees (code for a recreational area stopover in those days). A treasure trove of curios—hard candy, Silly Putty, snow globes, birthstone rings, and hexagonal quartz crystal rocks and Arkansas Razorback souvenirs, equally possessed of energy-enhancing powers—lined the counters and shelves of the gift shop.

From Y City, for the next thirty-five miles down U.S. Route 270, as Dad kicked the Merc into passing gear, blasting out the carbon up Blowout Mountain and around Vista Point, the Ouachita National Forest (originally the Arkansas National Forest) engulfed the highway in a shaded corridor of greenery and south-facing exposed rock. In 1907, President Theodore Roosevelt established the national forest out of cutover woodlands once owned by timber companies and farmers. Seen through the hungry eyes of daily necessity—legacy being a bridge too far—these small-farm-owning Paul Bunyans, mostly of English and Scots-Irish stock, settled in single-pen log homes; cleared the forests by ax, crosscut saws, fire, plow, and dynamite; and drained the lands. River otter, muskrat, black bear, and other over-hunted wildlife disappeared. With nothing left to exploit, like our Aunt Pearl's tribe, many of these farmers picked up lock, stock, and barrel and left for California, gone with the wind. Once Roosevelt established the national forest and pine trees were replanted on the slash-and-burn farms, Arkansas adopted the pine as the state tree and the Ouachita National Forest, "taking in more acreage than Delaware," rose from the ashes to become a conservation symbol of an Arcadian past: land and humans striking a chord of harmony.

Dad was fast to point out that the piney ridges of the Ouachita Mountains were the only ones to trend east-west in the United States. In the heart of those oddly turned mountains, by no surprise, was a yokeldom called Pine Ridge (originally named Waters), home to *Lum and Abner*, the fictional characters in the hillbilly-loafers versus city-slickers syndicated radio sitcom popular nationwide from the mid-1930s to the mid-'50s. The show's creators, Chester Lauck and Norris Goff, grew up in nearby Mena before getting their start doing blackface comedy. Set at the Jot 'Em Down Store in Pine Ridge, Dad said the sitcom probably set Arkansas back a few decades, image-wise, in the eyes of outsiders. Still, there was plenty of truth in its hillbilly humor. My paternal grandmother, Myrtle Pierce (aka Maw), was born to Ed and Tinny Pierce in a logging camp near Pine Ridge, and any one of them, Dad asserted, could have been mined as a primary source for the inspiration of *Lum and Abner*.

Before turning off of U.S. Route 270, which ran a New-Age-before-New-Age-was-cool gauntlet of hexagonal quartz crystal shops all the way to Hot Springs, we took a break at our Uncle Carroll Pierce's Mt. Ida Courtyard Motel. Located near Lake Ouachita, newly created by the Blakely Mountain Dam (the third of its kind on the Ouachita River), the motel did a brisk business with the summer stampede of recreational boaters and fishermen. At his first sight of us roaring out of the station wagon, Uncle Carroll, our very own Daddy Warbucks, hurriedly fished out a "silver series" quarter apiece from his coin-heavy pockets before some paying customer arrived and witnessed the unleashed chaos of five boys. After a few pleasantries about our growth spurts, heights, and foot sizes, and Dad cleaning the splattered insects from the windshield with a hose he pulled from beneath the neon "No Vacancy" sign, we were back in the car, our worn silver Washington quarters burning holes.

Farther along on Arkansas 27, Dad detoured at Caddo Gap, a wide spot in the road on the banks of the upper Caddo River. The river surfaced from an aquifer in the nearby Potato Hills and meandered from there for eighty-two miles before it joined the Ouachita River below a prominent bluff north of Arkadelphia. The Caddo Gap detour lasted no more than five minutes, time to circle the Indian statue and Hernando de Soto marker memorializing the Spanish gold-seeker's arrival in the area over 400 years before, circa 1541. For a few moments outside the car, we stood in awe of the unfathomable reach of time and of this Spanish explorer popping off the pages of our primary school history books.

In a compilation of essays and other nonfiction writing titled *Escape Velocity*, Charles Portis describes what might have been "the forest primeval that de Soto saw when he came crashing through these woods...with some 600 soldiers, 223 horses, a herd of hogs, and a pack of bloodhounds. He was looking for another Peru, out of which he had taken a fortune in gold, more than enough to pay, from his own pocket, for this very costly expedition. As it turned out there was no gold or silver here in [Arkansas]. What he found was catfish."

Here, at the westernmost point of his historic expedition, in a nearby mountain pass, de Soto encountered the Tula tribe, which rolled novaculite boulders onto the hostile invaders. Armed with arquebuses, crossbows, swords, and lances, the Iberians retreated down the Caddo. "The best fighting people that the Christians met with," de Soto's chronicler wrote of the Tula. Dad told us it was malaria and Tula resistance that convinced de Soto to take his sham posturing as the immortal "son of the sun" in search for gold back to the Mississippi River, but not before taking a break for a month-long dip into the magic waters of Hot Springs. By the following year, fate proved not to be on de Soto's side; he died of a fever near Ferriday-Natchez on May 21, 1542. In the dark of night, so as not to give away his mortality to the local Indians, de Soto's soldiers commended his soul to God and dropped him to the depths of the Mississippi River.

As we stood all those times below his statue and memorial, Dad recited how the militant Catholics left in their wake a swath of hostile Indians, a host of communicable diseases, and, not least, runaway domestic hogs. In time, those hogs turned feral and became colloquially known as razorbacks; the University of Arkansas later adopted it as its mascot. The football team's outstanding performance in 1908 reminded the coach of a bunch of hogs running wild.

Giddy-upping back into the car, we could smell the barn. This sometimes literally meant a stop on the outskirts of Glenwood at our Aunt Melba and Uncle Willard's small horse farm, where our cousin Sandy would saddle up her blazed-face sorrel for us to ride. We soon crossed the Caddo River at Glenwood's low water bridge, below the Missouri Pacific railroad trestle, and turned onto Highway 8, tracking the meander of the Caddo past the abandoned sawmill town of Rosboro. Seven miles on, across the spur tracks and beyond the Barksdale mill, Dad tooled the bottle-green Merc wagon into the city square of Amity, Arkansas.

With the completion of the Gurdon and Fort Smith Railroad (later acquired by the Missouri Pacific), sleepy towns like Amity, Glenwood, and Rosboro gained a lifeline and turned into hubs for the timber industry. The Big Cut, as historians called the boom period, saw 95 percent of Arkansas's virgin timber harvested, financed mostly by out-of-state investors and speculators. Almost overnight, forested hilltops took on the appearance of barren haycocks. It was boom or bust, extractive capitalism at its worst, resembling the European colonialist model for Third World exploitation. Once the timber was exhausted at one location, the sawmillers moved to another, a time and practice that became widely known as "the epoch of cut out and get out."

During the boom, lumber companies employed up to 75 percent of Arkansas wage earners. On the banks of the Caddo River, between Glenwood and Amity, the mill town of Rosboro—a shortened spelling of the Kansas City owner's surname, Rosborough—at its peak, had a population of 500 (some say twice that), all employed by the Caddo River Lumber Company. At the height of its development, Rosboro flourished as a full-fledged town, boasting a train depot, a single-men's boardinghouse, segregated schools and churches, a turbine for electricity, a theater, a water tower, several stores, a commissary, and company offices. As the Great Depression ground on, however, the Caddo River Lumber Company ceased to be profitable.

Whit Rosborough had been drawn to the promise of depressed stumpages in Oregon since his first visit to the Pacific Northwest twenty years before. Calculating that an acre of shortleaf pine would produce only 5,000 board feet, while Oregon's Douglas fir would yield 225,000 feet, his decision was easy. By January of 1939, he had removed valuable machinery, auctioned the Rosboro mill to salvagers, sold cutover land to the National Forest Service, hauled company houses away, and paid off bondholders. He departed Arkansas in his chauffeur-driven car, while most of his remaining employees, picked up lock, stock, and barrel and traveled to Springfield, Oregon, for jobs at his new mill.

A mere fifteen years after the mill's closing, the town's welcome sign read: Rosboro, Arkansas, Population 8. "It's a ghost town—everyone's gone to Oregon or California," Dad trumpeted, as we vied for who could spot the novel sign first. He pointed to empty spaces, identifying former landmarks and the vanished spirit of things: the commissary here, the "colored" quarters there, a brush arbor yonder in which a coiled copperhead had once scattered a congregation of writhing Holy Rollers. Toddler to teenager, he had witnessed Rosboro teeming with life and commerce. Then one day it was no more, like a bosky Pompeii with only sawdust heaps as reminders.

Although the ranks of sawyers, filers, doggers, and blocksetters had thinned, the timber heyday left in its tracks a new means for local farmers to make money. By the late '50s, most of the small farms that once grew cotton or corn in the Caddo bottoms had been completely cleared of hardwoods and replanted in pine seedlings. From Caddo Gap all the way down Highway 8 south and east of Amity, every roadside pine forest was a field of enterprise for the few remaining out-of-state paper companies and a handful of local timber titans, the Dierks, Barksdales, and Beans. Most stands over fifteen years old weren't safe from the pulp mill, though sustained-yield forestry was gaining currency. Slim pickings were the more valuable stands, say with trees having a ten-inch diameter or more, and that had survived to thirty-five years, the age at which growth of a pine tree slows.

As kids, it made us dizzy to show up and discover that our chosen woodsy playground had been flattened into clean-cut rectangles, with the birds, snakes, insects, and white-tail deer evicted. What we came to think of as a magical realm—nature's unchecked exuberance, sacred as any religious sanctuary—the piney woods were worth no more sentimentality to the small farmer than a bale of hay or a bushel of snap beans. They were just another commodity, a piece of the small pie called eking out a living. The pine monoculture was their tobacco road.

My mother, Joyce Fincher, grew up in the drowsy Caddo River town of Amity, six miles from Dad's homeplace in Alpine (even drowsier). Drawn by the fertile bottomland, surveyor William F. Browning settled Amity in 1846 and soon formed the Caddo Valley Baptist Church of Christ. Other settler groups gamely followed, establishing competing denominations in the wake of America's transition from its Second to Third Great Awakening, from hell-fire-and-damnation revivalists to disciples of social justice. Once the first shots were fired at Fort Sumter, Amity townsmen divided, some going north to Springfield, Missouri, to join the Union army, others choosing the Confederacy.

By the 1950s, with no fewer than twenty preachers and two Methodist Episcopal churches, North and South, Amity's population had reached around 500 souls, mostly of Scots-Irish descent but transplanted in the nineteenth century from states such as Georgia, Alabama, Tennessee, and Kentucky. Neither Alpine nor Amity were the kinds of places folks pitched up in by mistake. The nearest stoplight was twenty-five miles away.

Fayette Fincher, my maternal grandfather, a soft-spoken gent among gents, who valued character over money, preferred the South Methodist Episcopal Church because that's where "the little people worshipped," he told us. "The Amity Methodist Episcopal Church North was where the big shots gathered." Aunt Carrie Maddie, a Biggs, the first woman to attend Arkansas Methodist College (1890), was fond of pooh-poohing the South Methodists as nothing more than Catholics. The A-list, wealthier wing of the extended Fincher family—the Hays, the Biggs, the Olds—attended North Methodist and are buried in the church's private cemetery. The Wagners and Finchers shared their boot hill with the South Methodists in Jones Cemetery, where the whole kit and kaboodle of Karber ashes and bones are also buried, in the popularly priced plots, downslope, in the sun-bleached, pale red dirt.

Not so many years before we arrived in Fort Smith and joined the First Methodist Church, North and South in Amity had buried the hatchet. At least on paper, our family and we Methodists were all on the same page.

Our camping weekend arrival in Amity signaled it was time to make a brief blitz of the Fincher Cafe (and skating rink). Owned by my maternal grandparents, Fayette and Alsia, the café and rink occupied a barnlike-premises across the town square from the WPA-built native stone movie theater, with Sodi's Barbershop to one side facing (Great Uncle) Hall Fincher's hardware store and the Bank of

Amity, owned by three spinster aunts, the Olds sisters. The sisters, who gave off an air of gentility, were known for their sharp elbows and steady faith in the small-town banker's guiding principle: never make a loan to anyone who needs it.

On Saturday nights, the bench-high stone wall circling the theater teemed with restless country girls and good ol' boys. As I would later discover, when the petting turned heavy, couples fanned out to a back seat or a Caddo River sandbar or the nearest corn crib. And more than a few of those good ol' boys were guilty of slugging back too much of Amity bootlegger Johnathan Cox's aqua vitae, turning rowdy, choosing hot-rodding or recreational head bashing over romance. An enterprising feller, Cox doubled as a pickup-truck taxi service, ferrying home many of his moon-barking customers. It was the quaint hub of a friendly named sawmill town.

There was plenty to recommend Amity as a model for the peaceful, white-picket-fenced, fictional community of Mayberry. That is, if it weren't for a couple of half-cocked (and crocked) hayseeds coming to town and whupping out their special brand of crazy. Hanky-panky was behind it all, burning white hot as fresh-cooked corn juice in their backwoods brains. In June of 1948, Dossie Cox, a farmer and father of six children, and his wife Almadale, walked fifteen miles over mountain trails from Kirby to Amity to settle differences over an alleged affair between Almadale and South Street hotel owner Oscar Wheeler. When Dossie Cox spotted Wheeler on the street talking to Doyle Buck, an Amity businessman, he riddled him with eight rounds from a .22 caliber rifle before fleeing to the hills. Wheeler bled out that day near his hotel, while Cox was arrested the next day and later convicted of first-degree murder. A year and a half on, in December of 1950, Slim Garret, a former deputy sheriff and father of five children, made advances on twenty-year old Catherine Dorsey Simpson, a waitress at Mom's Café across the street from Wheeler's hotel and next door to the Ice House. After the "shapely" Mrs. Simpson, whose husband was away in the army, laughed him off one evening with four tables of customers looking on, the fat was in the fire. Garret stormed out the door, retrieved his German rifle from his pickup, and, at point-blank range, fatally shot Mrs. Simpson before turning the gun on himself. By the late '50s, the remembrance of those barbarians-at-the-gates on South Street had been firmly notched into the otherwise quaint lore of Amity. Cox and Garret, however, were not the first ruffians, nor would they be the last, to make their feral, often bottle-inspired, mark on the somnolent sawmill town named for its friendliness.

Given finger-wagging warnings not to sow havoc, once we disgorged from the car, Uncle Carroll's quarters flew out of our pockets for sweets either at the café counter, Hays Drug Store across the street, or three doors down at Sorrell's Country Store, where we checked out the ample hard candy selection one by one as if each were an object of revelation. On slow days at the roller rink and café, Grandmother Fincher, powdered and perfumed with the smell of rising dough, with a full apron on to protect one of her three cotton print dresses, would have us line up on counter stools, by turns telling us we were cute as a bug's ear, and, amid shrieks of delight, serve each of us apple crumble or peach fried pie with a scoop of ice cream. Unbeatable among sweet-toothed descendants of *homo habilis*. Time permitting, we were fitted out with skates; someone plugged the jukebox with Hank Williams, Kitty Wells, or whoever; and off we went like a pack of simians slipping on banana peels.

In late summer, four or five miles southeast of Amity on Highway 8, Dad turned in at Claudia Dwiggins's family peach orchard and open-air shed, where he and John (who off and on was a paid picker for the Dwiggins) sorted through half a bushel of Elberta or Red Globe peaches for our camping weekend. The leftovers went to all the family piemakers—aunts, grandmothers, and Mom (who usually stayed back in Amity).

A mile on Pick Jones's lean-to–sized cabin set up against the piney woods. When Dad was ten years old or so, and Pick was a full-grown man of thirtysomething, he gave Dad a bee swarm he'd found in a hollow oak, endearing the two for life. Many believed that Pick had "toys in the attic" as a result perhaps of a combination of suffering from mustard gas exposure on the Western Front in World War I, working the cinnabar mines and furnaces at nearby Jacks Mountain, and being jailed by Sheriff Piggy Widener on trumped-up bootlegging charges. Dad knew different. Feared by some as a mean-spirited, armed to-the-teeth misanthrope, Pick was merely uncomfortable around people, spending most of his time fading into the piney woods to prowl and roam free with the coons and deer and critters.

As we approached Pick's cabin, with a flutter of anticipation, Dad pulled off on the shoulder of the road, drew a package from beneath his seat, sauntered up to an unthreatening distance from Pick's cabin door, and coaxed him out. "Pick, it's Junior. Brought you something," he said. Pick at some point stuck his head out the latched door, his skin etiolated and hair whiter than a ghost, eyes dark, sunken and squinting to life with a strained discomfort as if just awakening from yet another shitty night of the soul. Dad and Pick exchanged a few words and then Dad handed him the small jug of Ozark mountain dew.

Dad said the only adornment on his walls was a campaign sign for G. W. Luckidew, a judicious Clark County prosecutor who helped Pick beat the bootlegging rap. Pick had a wife, Nora, but we never laid eyes on her. We imagined him to have all the makings of an old and dotty hermit, wandering the piney woods as solitary as a bobcat and tamping down his demons with a daily dose of corn, the old-fashioned way. Dad admired all war veterans and certainly knew his quirky country characters. If we weren't waiting in the car, he stayed awhile.

Beyond a couple of wide swings down the road, the (Buck) Country Store and Service Station, a dead ringer for *Lum and Abner's* Jot 'Em Down Store, announced the blink-in-the-road burg of Alpine, Arkansas, population fifty or so. If open, the Buck Mall, as Dad came to know it, was usually fronted by a slow-talking quorum of tobacco-spitting sages of the sawmills, which on any late afternoon might have included Uncles Mark, James, and Billy. Almost uniformly attired in clodhopper shoes, bib overalls, and puffed-up railroad caps, they perched there daily atop a row of Coca-Cola crates like a fence line of over-the-hill bulls chewing the cud (never to be confused with chattering magpies). Other than an unverified sighting of a monkey of unknown species leaping out of the pines and crossing the highway, the most ordinary comings and goings—an out-of-state tag, a convertible whooshing by, a woman driver, a wayfaring "fur-riner" staying too long—inspired a fulcrum of idle whittling, down-home humor and folklore, chuckles, and slack jaws of surprise. The same boom-time, good-ol'-days stories were told and retold, and true to Dizzy and Lum and Abner, were often filled with deliberate malaprops, anachronisms, and the ubiquitous word endings with a dropped "g." Around Alpine, where time has always hung heavy in the air, it didn't take a wise old Mississippi literary genius to come up with the maxim, "The past is never dead. It's not even past."

As we drew closer, Dad slowed it down to a crawl, waved wildly, and called out by name Jesse or Clarence or Claude or whoever he laid eyes on first. Wary of outsiders by nature, once the old timers recognized Junior, as Dad was known in Alpine, they, as was their custom, rallied for a moment, shook their cow-staring-at-a-new-gate expressions, poked at one another, choked back a har-de-har, and calmly nodded or put up a dead-fish, welcome-back wave, mimicking the intrinsic pace of life in the pines.

Forget that their potatoes came from the Andes; their tomatoes from Mexico; their corn from the Indians; their pigs, cattle, horses, mules, surnames, and genes from Europe; their tractors from Peoria; and trucks from Detroit, settler family descendants around Alpine in the '50s and '60s wore their yeoman farmer roots like a tribal totem (or a redneck stigmata), proudly different, the real thing, no falseness or fakery, free of hang-ups, authentic and inward-looking, never out of character. The old timers had held ground in their piney woods Promised Land while the rising tide of the post-war "River Progress" surged ahead. As during the Great Depression, they never lost their free will, or the ability to stay the course and avert washing up on some alien soil. Although they might dabble in the cultural doings of Amity, six miles to the northeast, they shied away from getting too caught up in the hurly-burly of Arkadelphia, nineteen miles to the southeast. And Little Rock and Dallas may not have actually been Sodom and Gomorrah, but they were surely as phony as a two-headed cow.

Uncle Billy, a lifelong resident of Alpine but for a few months at Uncle Guy's sawmill in Grass Valley, California, and Uncle Sam's training center at Fort Polk, was a hard man to pull the wool over as well. Slightly tongue in cheek, as if coming off a *Lum and Abner* set and when drawn out of his inborn shyness, he liked to drill down to the core definition and meaning of local character, if not his own self-identity: "Ain't no shame in being a drawlin' redneck from Alpine. Honest to god, it's a badge of honor." Pausing, kicking up some dirt, eyes cast downward, saying more than he normally did: "Workin' this rocky red clay is where true rednecks thrive. Shore 'nuff that's the way it is, has been, and will be till hell freezes over. I'll be a monkey's uncle if it ain't so."

Dad was the ideal expression of his generation's rural-to-urban migration—the second wave of Steinbeck's sons of the soil seizing the future. In Arkansas, the demise of the timber industry and the rise of mechanized farming, among other things, fueled this movement, freeing up labor for other enterprises. It was a time when no one gave a hoot about where you came from; the sky was the limit. Stepping aboard the slipstream of this changing social order, "have nots" became "haves." Dad had gone off and gotten educated, served two years in the Aleutian Islands in World War II, and later trained to pilot single engines and B-17s. He married the belle of Amity High School, started a family, landed a government job as county agent, became a 32nd-degree Mason, and took his showers before work, no more toiling by the cycles of the sun. In spite of all that, not least his membership in a secret men's society and occasionally letting slip their handshake or special prayer language—Oh Architect of the Universe—he never got above his raisin', a Southern thing of a certain era, I'm told. As with most of those sons of the soil, Dad became a proud storyteller of his agrarian youth.

With the assistance of a white midwife and a black nursemaid, his mother brought Dad into the world on January 28, 1920, in a logging railroad camp where his father worked, near Graysonia, on a bend of the Antoine River. The whistling of trains and whining of sawmills would have been among the first sounds he registered. Thanks to the generosity of the Homestead Act, the family soon settled on a small farm, among the pine forests, beyond Alpine and below Cleavet Mountain (a hill). Like many farm boys of his elemental world, he grew to be a skillful hunter and fisherman and to have the tutored eye of a first-rate naturalist. He came by it honestly, understanding the grain of the land in ways that only hard work on a hardscrabble farm can teach. Strapping on bib overalls, plowing fields, planting corn, chopping and picking cotton, castrating and birthing cattle, harvesting the fescue hay meadow, praying for sunshine and rain as seasons shifted. Nothing was false on the farm—it was either chicken or feathers, some years better than others. But all years demanded donkey-hard work. That much was certain.

If there wasn't enough money, someone was off to harvest wheat in Kansas or tomatoes in Indiana, or like Dad, to the CCC

(Civilian Conservation Corps) camps to build forest roads, ranger stations, and fire towers. Every able-bodied boy or man did their share in the off season (if such a time existed), repairing fences, putting up a corncrib, expanding the hog pen, fixing the chicken coop, shoveling out the barn, butchering the porkers, selling calves, and mending the steel. The girls and women had it no easier, pickling, combing blueberries, canning, shucking, darning, washing, waxing, milking, sewing, quilting, pumping the treadle, tending to the flower garden, snapping beans, and slaving over a hot potbelly. The old saw, "A man works from sun to sun, but woman's is never done," was a common refrain in the piney woods.

For every pause on the farm there was an upfront price to be paid. Breakfast was served after the (sulfur-tasting) water was hand drawn, kindling and fresh-split firewood fed the potbelly stove, the cow was milked, the butter was churned, the hogs were slopped, the (orange-yolk) eggs were gathered (often in Maw's apron), the squirrels and rabbits were shot, and the peaches and strawberries were picked and preserved. Betty Crocker was three decades away. The Alpine supper menu was stick-to-your-ribs Southern peasant fare (or "soul food" as they say at Sylvia's up in Harlem). Staples were fresh skint squirrel, turnip greens, collards and pole beans in bacon fat, crackling corn bread, butter beans and hog jaw, ham hocks, head cheese, sowbelly, souse, stewed ears and neckbone, barbecued shoat, and pickled pig's feet, everything but the squeal. Soft biscuits and all conceivable brews of gravy were served three meals a day: red eye gravy, milk gravy, water gravy, giblet gravy, sawmill gravy. A stringer of crappie or gunnysack of bullfrogs was not uncommon. Beef, even the tripe, was a delicacy. Alpine foodways were of a holistic piece, understanding the farm ecology, making the most of the fat of the land, eating gratefully and sleeping well.

So, when Dad returned to the piney woods and the barnyard stomping grounds of his youth, he still belonged and always would—

the thread was golden. And, because of the Karber name and my very countrified drawl, a sort of cloaking device for acceptance, they treated me as one of theirs. Once the center of his longing, Dad now saw Alpine through the lucid eye of experience born of travel, more culturally whole than when he left and less likely to return other than for short visits. Home had taken on an internal address, not a roadside dwelling. Alpine lived inside his soul just as the Karbers were embodied in the essence of Alpine.

Jesse, Clarence, Claude, Hollis, the Boyds, the Bucks, and all of Alpine were proud of him and never forgot the day he and co-pilot Leland Duncan buzzed low over the store when flying on a weekend with the Air National Guard, dropping a message in a bottle: Junior says hello. The old birds were, however, as cultured up as they ever wanted to be right there lolling on the Coca-Cola crates, in the bosom of the piney woods. People, culture, and cone-bearing conifer farms inseparable as bacon grease and collard greens. For those who weren't laid to rest in the Alpine cemetery across from the Buck Mall, the boots they would be buried in would travel almost as far to the Jones or Thompson cemeteries, five to seven miles away, as they would have traveled in the last twenty years of their lives. If they had been farther afield, it had happened so rarely that they talked about it the rest of their lives as if shipwrecked with Gulliver among talking horses when in fact they had only ventured as far as the county fair in Arkadelphia.

Claude and Maude Faulkner's home lay shouting distance from the Buck Mall, at the fork with Old Fendley Road. Whether shucking peas with my grandmother (Maw) on her wide front porch or reading a new book, Maude stood out in Alpine, incongruous as a lone daisy in a harrowed field. Dad said she dressed like a gypsy, wearing long homemade dresses, colorful headscarves, and dangling earrings. But mostly what set her apart was that she was smart as a whip and read everything she could get her hands on. "There's Maude,"

he'd remark, drawling extra, reverting to character, as he gave the horn a light tap, breaking the Sunday afternoon stillness of Alpine. "She's right smart. Darn tootin'. Got the curiosity of a librarian."

A short stretch beyond Maude's, we approached the old homeplace at the foot of Cleavet Mountain, taking the back entrance to Palmer Loop, turning east off the pavement at McAnally's red barn. We dodged the deep ruts as dust powdered the trees and clouded in the air behind us. Named for a family with a reputation for moonshining, you could churn butter on that bumpy, dusty forest road. The Karbers, not opposed to some moon themselves, didn't want the road paved, or even graded or smoothed. If they did, Uncle Billy maintained, the "pooleece" would patrol it and be in everyone's business like the Revenuers in the '30s.

The Palmers, whom Dad often accused of squatting on a corner of Karber land, were an ill-tempered bunch and poor as sawmill rats, going whole hog at all the bad behaviors: drinking, neglect of family, and, after a snoot full, prone to pull a knife or a gun. Pat Palmer, the oldest son and always a family friend, was well known for his knee-walking public rants, bearing a striking resemblance to Boggs in the chapter "An Arkansas Difficulty" from Mark Twain's *Adventures of Huckleberry Finn*.

Ed, the youngest Palmer, was born in 1940 with cerebral palsy, and by the time he reached his teens, his parents had exiled him into a doll-house sized outbuilding in the pocket forest behind their four-room shack. His drooling, grunting speech and spastic carriage scared the bejesus out of kids, including me. Until I was around him with Dad by the sody pop cooler at the Alpine store a time or two, I couldn't get over thinking he was touched in the head. Or as the locals whispered: "his cornbread ain't done in the middle." Red blood, it eventually occurred to me, as he munched down on a Moon Pie by the cooler, ran in Ed's veins, too. Dad knew how to handle Old Man Page Palmer and his boys, but when on our own, we were told to steer clear. (Years later, a local boy named Billy Bob Thornton, Claude and Maude Faulkner's grandson, made an Oscar-winning movie about Ed, *Sling Blade*.)

In spite of the antics, the Palmers and Karbers were always neighborly, pitching in to feed the cows, fence a pasture, cut a hog, bail hay, thresh corn, or show up for a barn raising. When the Karber water well dried up in 1951, Maw hauled by mule a *warsh* pot, set upon a travois, to the Palmers' spring-fed well. She took a tin cup sup or two, filled up the pot, and did the laundry.

By '54, Granddaddy Karber dug a new well. Things went back to normal, heating the water in the warmth of the sunshine. Three years on, the Karbers installed running water, their first indoor tub and toilet. Granddaddy was seventy-three years old, Maw fifty-eight.

Maw always had a sixth sense of when her son Junior would arrive. She'd be perched outside on the down-sloping screened-in porch, snapping peas, cracking pecans, and just settin' a spell, with ears pricked and eyes peeled, as we turned in next to a berm of earth that was the storm cellar, the family's second home during tornado season, and came to a stop under a twisted old cedar, the car and tree and everything else finely powdered in Palmer Loop dust. The familiar front yard landscape, fenced with a prim garden of daffodils and other perennials, spread from there like a rusty graveyard to the bosom of the piney woods: a cannibalized tractor and propane tank to one side and to the other a two-holer outhouse, a discarded bull-tongue plough and ringer washer, and a slumping tool shed filled with mason jars, traps, mule collars, mule shoes, traces, axes, adzes, crosscut saws, sharpening files, carborundum stones, nineteenth-century hand tools, and a heap more of magpie'd things a farmer would never throw away.

Maw, known by the Arkansas expression as a "good woman," was the heart and soul of the family, as well as its bell cow. She missed having Dad around; he was the only Alpine-raised Karber who went off to World War II and didn't come back to live out his days. Uncles Mark and Cable boarded the crowded troop trains west and served four years in the navy in the Pacific before returning to their nearby piney woods' farms. Aunt Maxine worked in an airplane factory at Long Beach, circling back to Alpine after the war. Uncle James, a blithe spirit known by everyone as Screw, short for Screwdriver (suggesting he might not have all his buttons), enlisted in the army but never completed basic training. Among other challenges, he dropped a live pine-cone grenade during his practice run at Fort Polk. A gamely drill sergeant reacted in time and tossed it in the grenade pit. That was Screw's last day in the army before coming home.

Maw was so short it was hard to tell when she stood up and hollered with unrestrained happiness over her shoulder for Granddaddy to come on out, the screen door clacking behind him: "Look who the cat's drug up. Junior's home!" Predictably, at that point we would fly out of the car, John with a book heading in the opposite direction, dumping the rest of us like dirty shirts. Maw and Granddaddy often took a minute to admiringly circle the Merc wagon as if it were the Batmobile, curiously amused by the power windows, factory air-conditioning, and hideaway third seat. After a cold, wet-nosed greeting from Uncle Billy's bluetick coonhound (Buddy), Stan, Greg, and I beelined to the milk barn, hog wallow, and corral fence, crawled atop it, and, no less than the skulking or slinking arrivals of coons, chicken snakes, or foxes, set off a barnyard conniption fit of bellowing bulls (Hereford), bleating gilts (Yorkshire), and a clucking harem of hens (Rhode Island Reds).

The sound of Maw's voice warned us away from causing more havoc. In a heartbeat, her mood could go from sweet and accommodating to madder than a box of frogs. Out of sight, chucking fresh-laid eggs at each other, climbing the hay ricks, tap dancing on the salt lick, or trying to mount a bawling young bull in the pen awaiting castration, when we heard her yell, we'd whoop and make a mad dash through an obstacle course of cow chips to the front pasture cover-cropped in clover where Uncle Billy kept his fighting cocks, Kelsos and Clarets, mostly of the straight-comb red breed, tethered by a rope next to small mesh cages. If home, he would join us and spar a couple of cocks as we watched goggle eyed. Instinctively combative toward each other, they needed no prompting to let loose an aerial buzz-saw flurry of natural spurs. Much to our relief, like any good "rooster man" protecting his birds, Billy would pull them apart before blood was drawn.

Besides, Greg got queasy and was known to barf at the sight of too much blood. But we knew the whole point in raising gamecocks was to engage in blood sport, as it had been going back eight thousand years into the folds of time when Asians first domesticated junglefowl. On scheduled weekends throughout the summer, Uncle Billy would put the metal spurs on his better feathered warriors, cage them separately in the back of his pickup, and head south across the Red River to Louisiana, home to the big cockpits and the best prize money east of the Rio Grande.

Beyond the field of gamecocks, up against the piney woods by a hollow oak, Uncle Billy kept his white-painted box hives, which smelled of its melliferous dwellers. If lucky, we might convince him to don his veil, light the pine needle smoker, pump the bellows, and fetch with his hive stick some "liquid sunshine," to be passed around and licked clean like a popsicle (as if we needed more of a sugar high).

When nature called, we steered clear of the slop jars but didn't mind walking the well-trodden path to the outhouse, which was piled with old newspapers and a Sears catalogue. More than a few times, however, Maw would caution us that she had sprayed it with DDT (or something) for dirt daubers and yellowjackets. The thought of dirt daubers on our privates in the half-darkness would often set off a wave of wisecracking, eventually sending us to the right side of the front door where the sharp odor of ammonia rose out of the ground. The "piss field" Dad called it, where all Karber men and boys relieved themselves, mostly at night, country style, staring up at the stars.

On our camping trip weekends, we never burned too much daylight around the nineteenth-century plain, practical, and unadorned homeplace, spic and span to a fault. In the kitchen, which often smelled of ham hocks, butter beans, and crackling cornbread, a potbelly stove sat near the back wall and an icebox in the opposing corner that held two twenty-five-pound blocks. In rooms without doors, iron beds were piled high with homemade quilts, and gun racks fashioned from deer antlers adorned the walls. The grandparents' bed was bracketed by two nightstands, each topped with a jar of water for their false teeth and Granddaddy's also with a rabbit's foot that he had rubbed since he was a toddler before falling asleep. In the narrow hallway, a hand-cranked Singer sewing machine took root with enough thread, yarn, needles, buttons, bobbins, patterns, and cloth to stock a notions shop. As a family, we often gathered with forced reverence, minding our P's and Q's, on the sloping-with-age linoleum floors in the living room around Granddaddy Karber in his rickety oak wood rocker, a Maxwell House coffee can spittoon at his side and idle wood-burning stove opposite.

Hanging above the stove, next to a gimme clock from the Elkhorn Bank in Arkadelphia, where Aunt Maxine had worked, was a grainy photo of a dark-haired Granddaddy Karber standing in front of a tool shed, circa 1915, accoutered Paladin-like in all black, a slouch hat askew and cocked backward, bandoliered with a scabbarded knife and shotgun shells, with the stub of a stogie in his mouth and a cavalry-style, butt-forward Colt .38 Special revolver tucked into his wide waist belt. What resembled an old Remington 16-gauge was slung over his right shoulder. With his left hand, he held two wild turkeys by their feet. Hamming it up or not, the photo convincingly evoked a nineteenth-century woodsman.

Granddaddy Karber was born in Independence County on August 26, 1884, more than eight months after his father, William Henry, who served in Arkansas's Dobbins brigade in the Civil War, had died on December 10, 1883. His mother, Martha Youngblood, who was half Cherokee, remarried and by the time he was thirteen years old, his stepdad had run him out of the house. He proved his mettle in the logging camps, cutting skid trails through the wilderness to move timber onto steamboats, from the White River Basin to Texarkana and the Red River. This wasn't a mere tree-thinning enterprise: he was in the vanguard of the Big Cut, which also made him one of the last witnesses to the region's old-growth forests. These rough-and-ready Paul Bunyans teamed up on two-man crosscut saws to girdle and chop down old-growth forests, clearing the natural abundance for more cotton and cane plantations, pastures, and steam engines. Rattlesnakes, water moccasins, and other reptile malefactors were only slightly less common than flies, chiggers, and mosquitoes. Wearing a sidearm just made good sense in his fresh-faced world in which survival and responsibility transcended ideals.

While still a teenager, he had hired on as a straw boss in the cypress swamps of northern Louisiana, supervising mostly black men and a few white bindle stiffs laying tracks for a sawmill spur and loading logs. Delirious from malarial fevers, he hopped an empty boxcar on an Illinois Central freight train highballing north to Arkansas and left behind his five-string banjo (an instrument introduced into the U.S. via the slave trade route from West Africa and picked up by southern whites in the 1830s). Like so many loggers, farmers, railroaders, sailors, and slaves in this time before radio, records, and movies, he used banjo and fiddle music and work songs to reduce the boredom of a repetitive task and elevate the mood and efficiency of the work day. When he and other sick and exhausted loggers, two of whom were black, were discovered by the railroad "bulls," rather than arresting or throwing the young stowaways off the train, the conductor sent them a jug of ice water to go with their gunnysack of two-day-old corn dodgers and salt pork; it was a kindness never forgotten. After none other than Homer Plessy had had his day in court and Jim Crow was the law of the land, it was an unsensational story Granddaddy delighted in telling that seemed to spring from pages of Jack London's turn-of-the-century tramp diaries, *The Road*.

By his mid-twenties, Granddaddy Karber had saved enough money to buy an Indian motorcycle and soon landed a logging railroad job near Graysonia, Arkansas, where he met my grandmother. Myrtle Pierce was a rural postmistress, carrying the mail by horseback to the railroad camp. Granddaddy was twenty-nine years old and Myrtle was fifteen when they married. In that railroad camp, they had four kids, and four more came later in Alpine, over a span of twenty-seven years, one who died at birth and another as a four-year-old. From day one, life was a struggle defined by two stages, work and death. In between, John Karber and Myrtle Pierce Karber lived a love story. Not a fifty-year-long sit on the couch cooing type, but of two imperfect, archetypical Arkies equally yoked in a shared vision, improving the family's prospects. Theirs was a daily matching of generosities, defined by personal and practical roll-up-the-sleeves considerations. The older they grew, the passage of time etched in fluent lines like road maps across their faces, the closer they stood, the more they laughed.

Tall and barrel-chested, now with ashen hair encircling a bald pate, Granddaddy Karber only had an eighth-grade education, but was no slouch at reading, writing, and doing sums. He also oozed horse sense when he spoke, one of many traits of a well-used life that advantaged him as Alpine's representative on the Amity school board for three generations of students. In the mid-'50s, as president of that board (and Maw head of the Alpine PTA), he oversaw the building of a modern new high school and agriculture building. When neighbor Lola Walker called him on the party line they shared with half of Alpine about Jack Kirksey (an agriculture teacher) not allowing her (or any other girls) to attend the state fair in Little Rock, he told her he would have Jack stay at home and have someone else take her. Jack got the word before the conversation was finished from Fanny Langston, who had listened in on the call.

Dad told us Granddaddy had a soft spot for girls. He and Maw had lost two, Geraldine and Dorothy Helen, to pneumonia before penicillin came around. Granddaddy never talked much about those things, though; not his style, too personal and he also was never one to toot his own horn about helping people.

Because his father, William Henry, had gone to his heavenly reward before he was born, superstition in the backwoods of Arkansas had it that, on top of his folksy, uncomplicated wisdom, Granddaddy had magical powers that were closely akin to the healing wonders ascribed to the seventh son of the seventh son. That he could blow three times in a baby's mouth and rid them of evil or ill health, or bless them as a baptismal rite. Modern medicine was not available around Alpine. Death was a common visitor. Every disease known to man carried off kids, who died at home as Geraldine and Dorothy Helen had and not in some distant hospital. Granddaddy, like most traditional healers in his day, thought it taboo to take payment for his services. Dad told me that he had witnessed many a mother who brought her child to his boyhood home for three blows of Granddaddy's magical breath, the success of which Dad said was roughly equal to one's faith in the success of the ritual. Belief is everything. Sounds like voodoo, but it was a medieval Christian practice known as insufflation that migrated across the centuries (and oceans) into a low-key spiritualism in backwoods Arkansas.

Maw nurtured a superstitious temperament, too. Viewing owls in daylight forebode something unusual; hanging horseshoes on the porch promised good luck; follow the moon signs when weaning a baby. She also ministered to all comers a medicine chest of folk remedies that ranged from wild raspberry roots (for hives), oak bark tea (stomach disorders), Jimson weed oil (boils), pleurisy root (congestion), and nightshade (poison ivy) to steam infusions, herbal poultices, purgatives, homemade horse lineament, and the store-bought panacea, Carter's Little Liver Pills. On one occasion, when the nightshade and calamine lotion weren't relieving a bad case of poison ivy, she had me bathe outdoors in a No. 3 wash tub of well water diluted with turpentine and kerosene, which burned my inflamed pink skin to a scorched pale gray and sent me yelping around the yard like a scalded dog, naked as the day I was born. It worked. No more itch to scratch.

On those sloped floors of the living room, as a rule, Granddaddy and Dad would saucer their coffee while they discussed, in earthy, backwoods tones and a vocal cadence equivalent to pouring cold molasses, the price of steers and hogs on the hoof, a board-foot of timber, a bushel of bumblebee cotton, detasseling corn, flying airplanes, or other more far-reaching topics. Dad always asked for the latest news from two of Maw's sisters, aunts Pearl Jones and Corrine Busby, who packed up their families during the Depression and caravanned down Tom Joad's "mother road" to California's Imperial Valley. They survived as crop pickers in the early years alongside dark-skinned migrants before Pearl's husband, Fred, found work as a welder and Corrine's husband, Guy, hired on at a sawmill in Grass Valley. More than once, after hearing Pearl and Corrine's news, Dad asked us if we knew the difference between an Arkie and an Okie. "An Arkie going west has two mattresses on his car," was the answer, a humorous jibe thought up to make Arkies feel better.

In the late '40s, Granddaddy made his last trip out of Clark County on a family outing with his brother Mark. Driving up the 1,200-foot-high Petit Jean Mountain, he got dizzy half way to the top, turned around, and drove home to Alpine. He lived another twenty years staying put, never darkening the door of our Fort Smith home.

The rest of our Caddo River vacation was wire-to-wire woodsbound fun, with us boys smelling of the barnyard pungency we had just brushed through in our mischief-making arrival. At the Caddo-Brushy Creek camp, down Fendley Road, we were never any farther than a few miles from Palmer Loop, making it convenient for Granddaddy and all the other Karber men and cousin Jimmy to join us around the campfire.

For reasons that remain a mystery, we rarely camped in the colorful explosion of fall fireworks or in the early clear spring air and the openness as trees broke their caterpillar green buds and the dogwoods bloomed. It was almost always late May and June, the river a dull shade of jade, the air heavy, the woods dense, concealed, droning and humming like a tropical jungle. We were all fair game to the voracious appetites of ticks, chiggers, gnats, horse flies, fleas, leeches, giant water bugs, and salvos of mosquitoes the size of hummingbirds. A well-aimed rock or single-shot, bolt action .22 short or the high-tension release of five baby boomer boys, usually scattered the estivating cottonmouths, snapping turtles, and river otters below our camp.

The honey hole, jumping with green sunfish and small-mouth and spotted bass, the source of many a well-spun fishing escapade, was a fine stretch of foam-tipped milky jade a few hundred yards from where Brushy Creek flowed into the Caddo. A soft and springy pine needle deer trail, scalloped with small gravel and sand bars, often scratched in a maze of muskrat, deer, and racoon tracks (each identified by Dad), traced the Caddo upriver. Farther along was our swimming hole with a bag swing roped to the whitened bough of a sycamore, the banks below shaded by its mask-sized leaves and willow thickets. On the opposite shore, we hurled our parboiled bodies off a rock wall and sandstone boulders as big as cars and swam beneath clear blue waters to the sandy, pebbly bottoms, occasionally surfacing with a harvest of freshwater mussels whose iridescent blue shells we collected.

Once, I was trip-trapping along on that springy pine needle trail and came upon a cottonmouth coiled and puffed as thick as a man's thigh. I jumped two feet high and three feet forward. The snake let go an evil hiss at my landing spot, where I froze astride a pile of raisin-like white tail deer scat. Dad heard me screech and hurried down to dispatch the snake. A solid memory: the venomous viper, with its evil cat eyes, cottony mouth, and hissing glottis left splattered with birdshot and deflated like a pricked balloon on the generations-worn trail; a reminder of what could happen to keeled creatures that lay in wait.

All around, thick stands of loblolly pine and brakes of bottomland hardwood advanced up the mast-laden littorals and abounded in white-tailed deer browsing on young pines and wild turkey pecking the ground for seeds, insects, and berries. In the fall, the forest floor was sprinkled with prickly sweetgum balls and hickory nuts as big as plums, fodder to fatten Bambi for winter's dinner table. Two whoops and a holler west of the river, through tall stands of sweet-scented forest and out into a clearing, an unclipped fence line propped up a bushy profusion of briars, honeysuckle, and blackberries we foraged by the pail. A maze of rabbit getaways scored the ground beneath the thicket. Beyond the fence line, in a fallow cornfield, once lush in Native American crops known as the Three Sisters (corn, beans, and squash), we could almost always count on flushing quail and doves, and with enough grubbing around that cornfield, we might come up with an arrowhead or two.

Dad brought along cane poles, spinning rods, fly fishing gear, and a full tackle box. He'd have us dig for worms, filling a Folger's coffee can. At the time, Greg, Stan, and I were not gifted with a fisherman's patience and discipline, but we occasionally got lucky with a sun perch, crappie, bream, or small-mouth lunker. By the end of our weekend adventure, with all the hooks, lines, leaders, lures, sinkers, bobbers, and plastic and real worms lodged in the trees, it looked as if we had been trying to snag osprey or eagles or some other high-flying birds. Patience poor, full of Huck Finn innocence, we were the polar opposite of Hemingway's young Nick Adams.

John, the oldest and wisest of us all, picked up Dad's (and Nick's) woodsmanship. He believed in paddling his own canoe, Dad would brag. We counted on him to be our go-to hunter-gatherer who could fill a creel or bag a squirrel, Peter Rabbit, deer, or cote of doves, putting food on our plates around the fire. The usual protein fare in our Caddo River camp was squirrel or rabbit and eggs for breakfast and then fresh-caught and finger-licking fried channel catfish for dinner (nostalgia being the best-tasting fish of all).

For Dad, the Caddo had personal and practical meaning. It was the bloodstream of the land, a timeless silt-laden thread in a water cycle that wove together the family farms in the pines on a lazy but true course, shoal-to-pool-to-shoal, tributary by tributary, south toward the sea. The river's intrepid journey ran a motley gauntlet of towering sycamores and sweetgum, corn and cotton fields, old grist mills and thriving whiskey stills, baptism pools and bayous, fern-laden duck sloughs and alligator-infested cypress swamps, pump jacks and bar ditches, and beyond the canebrakes and floodway levees of Louisiana until its drink water changed into salt water and frothed with redfish, moaned and wailed with fog horns at the Mississippi and Atchafalaya estuaries. My hardy and hearty piney-woods' ancestors, de Soto's gold-happy Iberians, the sedentary, mound-building Caddo Indians, the footbound and feared fighters of the Tula tribe, the feral goats precariously perched on Cave Mountain's limestone ledges, the biannual hegira of ducks, geese and passenger pigeons, and what have you, had either fished the river's eddies, farmed its fertile lowlands, drank its waters, drawn a bowstring or blasted a musket on its banks, or merely marveled at the hypnotic motion of the aquatic landscape…back through seasons lost in time.

"You never step in the same river twice," Dad was fond of saying. As his father had done before him, he told us of the river's lore and natural history and of those who had threshed the same ground he had. Sometimes our ears were pricked, other times he was casting pearls before swine, but always the life-affirming river and its riparian buffer of forests and fertile fields ran bone deep as an ancestral memory in his sensory world.

Hard to imagine that a few properly placed sticks of dynamite could put the quietus on all that Edenic wonder and its long chain of being. But it did. The Army Corps of Engineers, authorized by the Congressional River and Harbor Act of 1950, invoked the power of eminent domain to confiscate our land of milk and honey, dam the Caddo River, and christen the new body of water Lake DeGray, after a French fur trader. John Graves wrote about the landowner and river lover's helplessness to fight the '50s-and-'60s-era dam-craze in *Goodbye to a River.* "When someone official dreams up a dam, it generally goes in. Dams are *ipso facto* good all by themselves, like mothers and flags." As with Graves's Brazos River in Texas, they turned our slice of the Caddo into a 100-foot-deep, treeless thoroughfare for a blitzkrieg of sports crafts. Overnight, half the Karber land, 225 acres, and not least the blood, sweat, sandbar memories, Indian artifacts, and settler homesteads, were flushed under to decompose like raw sewage in a septic tank.

Granddaddy didn't live to see the government shakedown or desecration of his Caddo land, though I suppose he watched restlessly from above, having dropped by the Alpine Presbyterian chapel to be baptized at seventy-nine years old by Brother Basil Hicks, a month before he shuffled off this mortal coil. I doubt that he knew of Pascal's wager, just running late on squaring things up for the Big Trip.

Maw, sharpened with a flinty resolve and hands of sandpaper, was as powerless as her small-farm-owning neighbors. They all took the government pencil whipping and the paltry check that came with it. As for Maw, who was getting near the outer edge of the onion, she bought the old McAnally place and built a modest all-brick house with an indoor privy on a new slash of blacktop. The resinous smell of plastic-wrapped couches and fresh-laid carpet, a do-not-touch zone, all to be avoided more than sat or walked upon, replaced the airy, organic scent of the farmhouse floor on up the weathered walls that spoke to us.

For the most part, it should be said that I had been all but sequestered from the wild earthly realities of Arkansas. Certainly, we did not fully comprehend the wilderness regions far beyond our campsite. Until our Eden and the Tiffany-blue-soaked skies and the cotton candy sunsets were gone and "progress" began, I took for granted the Caddo River farm as our disposable amusement park and shooting gallery. Armed with a sling, bow, the trusty Red Ryder BB gun or Crosman air rifle on up to the single-shot .22, a blue jay or robin red breast here (for our feather collections), cottontail rabbit or a gray squirrel there…ping, ping, bang, bang. Kid's play, nostalgic masculinity, proof of courage, everyone's a little Hemingway: some feathered, furry, or scaly creature must die daily.

Within a few years, the decomposition and absolute absence of the farm made me relish what I had kept at arm's length. Raised on concrete, we citified Karber boys thought the farm was "the sticks," the sad scope of my ecological vision for too long. The only saving grace was that our myopia and generational landscape amnesia were arrested once our "postage stamp of dirt" disappeared. Absence absolutely made the heart grow fonder.

Somewhere between vivid imagination and memory's monkeyshine, those camping trips are now reified as powerful childhood inflection points, viewed as a lyrical painting hung exclusively for my mind's eye.

Floating the pools atop a twenty-pound, Crimson Sweet watermelon before cracking it open for dessert (or on the shoals). The flush and glide and cranky cry of a blue heron stalking the small bream. The passerines' afternoon song fest: wrens, whippoorwills, robins, cardinals, kingfishers, finches, sparrows, chickadees, woodpeckers, mockingbirds, meadowlarks. The cicadas giddily buzzing their summer symphony. Choruses of bullfrogs gently throbbing in the night air. Wood smoke curling off a blazing campfire of chopped driftwood and cleared deadfall. The council of elders circled up. Mark and James in bib overalls, rolling Prince Albert. Jerry in Brylcreem-shiny ducktails, Elvis sideburns, rolled jeans. Billy chewing on Red Man, boots to brim a cowboy. Dad and Granddaddy Karber, in Stetsons, puffing on full-bent cherrywood pipes. Salty storytelling, spur-of-the-moment country fiddling, corn mash sipped from a mason jar. A well-spun spooky yarn as a nightcap. Granddaddy juddering off home to Maw in the candy-apple-red '51 Ford pickup. The barred owl's ghoulish hooting. Pulling a catfish (or turtle) off a trotline at three a.m. The glittering firmament of the Milky Way crosshatched in the tree tops. Sleeping like a log on an aural cushion of rushing water. The cheery avian medley of predawn proclamations. Dewy sunrises creeping through a pillared wall of darkness. Morning fresh textures and mourning doves fluting. Sun perch top-feeding on midges. The aquatic ballet of Dad in waders playing out coils of line, casting into fast-moving waters gilded by the fresh light. The rising heat drying the moisture from the daddy longlegs, mayflies, bumblebees, butterflies, lady beetles, whirligigs, walking sticks, stink bugs, katydids, aphids, millipedes, and mantises; the forest floor and river banks bursting to life.

    The banal transforming into the sublime. Those are the collected dew-fresh brushstrokes of memory I have of the Brushy Creek-Caddo River camp before the dam-building ghosts of Arkansas Power and Light founder Harvey Couch showed up and it was no more. As much as the passage of time shifted those memories to an abode in my grown-up heart, taking on the specter of allegory, the sad upshot of those growing-up years is that some of us denied the ordinary profoundness and laudable authenticity of Dad's roots in the rural wilds. His storehouse of farm and field skills and professional duties as county agent, including starting half a dozen 4-H clubs, failed to map onto our daily, coming-of-age realities.

His was a dichotomy of urban and rural, as old as the first mud-walled settlement. In *Goodbye to a River*, Graves addressed why such denials of our family's piney woods past might be ill-advised: "It's not necessary to like being a Texan, or a Midwesterner, or a Jew, or an Andalusian, or a Negro, or a hybrid child of the international rich. It is, I think, necessary to know in that crystal chamber of the mind where one speaks straight to oneself that one *is* or *was* that thing, and for any understanding of the human condition it's probably necessary to know a little about what the thing consists of."

I have been through a lot of trouble to remember that "thing," and to embrace the song of the Caddo River and the ballast it provides in a turbulent world.

Playful Childhoods

Chapter Two

A DEFINING CHARACTERISTIC of every generation is to think of themselves as new, unique, different from or even better than our antecedents. Baby boomers are no exception. Aside from our sheer numbers, we were the first generation to broadly enjoy truly playful childhoods.

Harrison, Arkansas, always brought on a rush of would-be remembrances. It was my natal turf. It's where those black-and-white photos were taken of Sunday-dressed, handsome parents and cute, perfectly coiffed and outfitted kids, John, Stan, myself, and Greg, lined up on our Chestnut Street front porch. They became our family avatars, the mnemonic tools—not the actual memories, which are fuzzy at best—that seared the idea of Harrison and Ozzie-and-Harriet values and unity into our family psyche.

In April of 1955, we said goodbye to Harrison and arrived the same day at 2815 Pendell Lane, Fort Smith, Arkansas. Dad had accepted the Sebastian County Agent's job and would fly with the army reserves at the municipal airport on weekends. As a family, we had a tail wind on life. While we unpacked our 1955 Mercury, two rowdy tow-headed kids, Jimmy and Jackie Gilker (a lefty like me), greeted us. Ranging in age from three to seven, most of us were just over the cusp of preconscious memory. The Gilker boys seemed to already know the ropes in our new garage. So, we followed them.

Up the work bench and onto the rafters, soon swinging from the garage door carriage, up and into the secret scuttle hole to the attic.

Within months, Jimmie, next-door neighbor Phillip Dovall, and Patrick Davis across the alley, all seven years old, were showing Stan and me how to cuss, spit, strike matches, and start fires. Two years later, to our disappointment, pals Jimmy and Jackie moved to a bigger house off Free Ferry Road, by St. Scholastica Monastery. It was 1958, the year of the pitiless Great Flood of Kelly Creek. Knee-deep water flowed from the creek and covered the ballparks and the adjoining forest, a place of boyish enchantment. When the water receded, left behind in the dying rivulets and flood pools of trapped treasure were enough tadpoles, frogs, turtles, and crawdads to fill all of Noah's Ark and several mason jars at our house. Knowing the Gilkers, they probably got their share of the bounty out of another creek.

In those carefree days, every street had at least one sheriff. Ours was Arthur Blake, a drooling man-child. He wore a crushed straw cowboy hat and farmer's overalls pinned with a tin badge. Arthur, who had fallen off a truck and banged his head at five years old, never evolved cognitively beyond that age. He was relentless in joining our daily affairs—and also harmless. In our GI Joe war games, where we all dressed like our World War II fathers in helmets, fatigues, combat boots, ammo belts, and canteens, he always played the out-of-dress commando who charged the hill, the first to get picked off in a volley of cap gun fire. Same storyline in the cowboy and Indian battles. He never just died, but roared and huffed like a wounded beast, then resurrected himself from his foxhole with one plastic-pistol-waving banzai charge after another. Some kids were cruel to him. Although fairness and favoring the underdog were frequent dinner table, church, classroom, and playing field discussions, Arthur was our everyday trial by fire. We came to think of him as a gift to the neighborhood like a unicorn, rare and out of context, an object lesson in proper empathy for those who are different and less capable.

During the counting-sheep-in-the-sky summers of the early years, three or four late afternoons a week, the Pinky Dinky ice cream truck rounded the Old Greenwood Road corner by the ballparks playing "Pop Goes the Weasel." The tune signaled the end-of-the-day wrap, whether to yard work, kickball play, hide-and-go-seek tag, or pickup basketball or baseball games. By the time five or six iterations of the catchy tune had played and we had been successful in persuading Mom to give up white knuckling a nickel a piece, the truck arrived in front of our house. Funds disbursed, we scrambled around the mimosa tree and leapt the ditch to the street for our share of fudgesicles and banana, strawberry, and grape popsicles.

Cooling down, our gritty, scratched up legs, freckled with bug bites, and weather-beaten bodies, lean as the privet hedge switches we fetched for our own whippings, smelled of the salty tang of a full day's sweat and all that we had grubbed up. Barefoot and buck wild, our summer days were a gauntlet of double dog dares and the sweet drone of earthy exploits: climbing the Goodman's Indian Cigar Tree to the highest perch, suspended between heaven and earth; shimmying up the Mark's crab apple tree to cross on branches over the white picket fence to the Wheeler's mulberry tree; digging foxholes on Parker's ridge; flying down the Q Street hill on a '57 model Schwinn Tiger; trekking up Big Goatie and Longfellow to overlook the beehive kilns of the brick plant; walking into a BB gun sniper attack by Audie Murphy and Davy Crockett lookalikes breaching neighborhood lines; sliding into bases at Kelly and Higgins Fields; mucking out Honey's manure from Skokos's barn; digging like hogs for truffles, those hidden treasures in the ground; catching crawdads, dragonflies, frogs, turtles, tadpoles, and garden snakes; and stepping in dog shit all over Hell's half acre.

By the time the sounds of the Pinky Dinky Man faded away and the tangerine-tinted glow over Christ the King turned to dusk, always slightly tinged with a fun-is-over melancholy, a widening chorus of crickets and tree frogs began to arise. Webworms chimed in, rattling and shaking the leaves and branches of their silken cocoons. With moonrise, bats jinked above the privet hedge, scooping bugs out of the burnished air. Like a bird's harsh warning call, ringing up and down Pendell, Garner, and Q Streets, parents shouted and whistled messages from front and back stoops for the tardy ones to hightail it home. Or in my dad's case, imitating Tennessee Ernie Ford, "Come and get it or we'll pour it in the trough." As we made our way home, with Jip, our German shepherd and chief protector, yipping in the lead, fireflies often filled the emptiness of the cooling air as did a bouquet of fragrant smells from the honeysuckled back hedge and street-side southern magnolias.

About this time, every home's gas streetlight flickered on in concert, an unspoken cue to circle around the kitchen table, pipe down, and say grace over supper. Windows open, the attic fan furnished a cooling draft as we took our designated seats. Dinner time was family time. Shirts on, television off, hands washed, eat your beets, talk in turn, and chew with your mouth closed were but a few of the ground rules. Had each home in the neighborhood been wired with Tannoy speakers, our chorus of grateful voices—Father in heaven, we thank you for this food...Amen—would have echoed across the valley like the evening call to prayer in the lands of Scheherazade.

The American ethos of the time, a legacy of "the Kingfish" Huey P. Long, may have promised "every man a king" and "a chicken in every pot," but dinner at the Karber house was a competitive sport if not uncivil. When Mom or Dad cooked fried chicken, one bird for all, we moved, as a family of seven, hastily through grace. John, a juvenile diabetic and the oldest sibling, rarely delighted in a popsicle but always had first dibs on the wish bone (pulley)—as it should have been. That left the rest of us ignoring the house rule of taking what's in front of you first. We instead reverted to what our boarding house reaches could clutch and consume fastest, always in hopes of capturing a "leg" for seconds and not a back, neck, or gizzard—as was the norm. No one ever went to bed hungry, but when who-got-what came up, we often settled it with taunts and a spontaneous knock-down-drag-out, followed by our parents' wholesale warming of rear ends.

I wasn't born standing up and talking back, as the song says. On most days, I came off as if I had lockjaw, a condition I contracted by having two older brothers who talked a blue streak and spoke for me. Shyness made muteness worse, brought on by Stan and Greg and others poking fun at my buckteeth and mocking my lisp (a slow tongue mostly). But still waters run deep: they paid for it, often at the dinner table. That's how I got to the top of the pecking order at an early age.

Due to Dad's county agent status, his farmer friends were generous about parting with a side of a well-fattened steer for next to nothing. Once those same friends harvested what their families needed from their fields of produce, they invited us to take what remained. Dad oversaw the picking of strawberries and boysenberries and Mom the making of jams and jellies, sealing the mason jars with paraffin. Every September, under Dad's supervision, we all spread out in Siegenthaler's corn field and picked and shucked as if in an old-fashioned, harvest moon husking bee. We had corn galore, a whole garage deep freeze full. Which, at the risk of sounding like the Bubba Blue of sweet corn, wound up on our plates as corn on the cob, creamed corn, corn fritters, crushed corn grits, and, occasionally, popcorn.

We also made frequent trips out to Cavanaugh Dairy to catch fat perch in George Combs's stock pond in a pasture of tall fescue and fresh cow chips. Black and white patched Holstein cattle foraged until evening milking time, and their chilled and sweet bottled product magically showed up on our doorstep, free of charge, two mornings a week. Additionally, there was always ample venison in the larder from Dad's annual deer hunt and week-long camp with Jim Charles and Clarence Higgins.

Dog food, for the most part, was the same as our food. Out the garage door to Jip went the evening scraps or a personal soup bowl of brown gravy and white Wonder Bread. Never making a complaining whimper, Jip was an intelligent, overprotective city dog—who, short on social capital, would instinctively back up a stranger or a snarling cur. Indeed, his short fuse blew up many a chance meeting with our friends and the better bred dogs of our neighbors. Free from millennia of hereditary herding skills or anything other than protective aggression, for fifteen years Jip was our very own Rin Tin Tin.

Every year, in late May, in the 1950s and '60s, at least one of our television Western heroes would appear on horseback at the Arkansas-Oklahoma Rodeo. On the afternoon before opening night, often spiffed up in Nudie of Hollywood glitz, they rode their prancing steeds in the rodeo parade down Garrison Avenue. In a grand manner, the parade customarily featured a cavalcade of buckaroos on Shetlands, ox-drawn buckboards, hay rides, stagecoaches, antique cars, the all-black Lincoln High band, Rotarians, Masons, Kiwanians, trick rope artists, formations of Fort Chaffee soldiers, the county sheriff's mounted patrol, make-believe Indians, a host of riding clubs sporting their sponsors' flags, and much more. For young and old, nostalgia rose to a higher power. At night, the parade's glory played on, as the ground shuddered with the concussion of a thousand hoofs in the Grand Entry at Harper Stadium. Riding clubs and rodeo royalty burst out of the main chute, quirting their mounts, rearing in caprioles, waving and hat tipping while caracoling right and left, amplifying the small stadium to a pitch of rolling thunder. As kids, we sat edgewise, gaping wide-eyed, and breathlessly drank it all in.

Daddy, using his county agent connections—more like good friends—always came up with opening night box seats at the stadium. From our perches on the fence, we watched and heard up close the clowns, cowboys, cowgirls, and Western stars, with the pounding hoofs of the fast-moving and often high-mettled steeds whooshing by, showering us cowboy wannabes with clods of churned up, barnyard-steeped debris. The complex aroma of the arena, the popcorn and burnt sugar smells of cotton candy mixed with the reek of manure and sweaty horses, grew on our cowlicked herd of five like hot corn bread in the oven, permeating everything.

Clowns, also known as "barrel men," produced more than comic relief with their baggy pants, painted faces, sad empty eyes, bulbous red noses, bandanas, and lariats. "Matadors in clown costumes," Dad would say. "They have a sixth sense for what a Mexican fighting bull might do next." Full of poised indifference, in the heat of the chase they beat a retreat to the fence next to us when their escape route to the large padded barrel in the center of the arena wasn't closer. The booming voice of legendary rodeo announcer Pete Logan, often synchronized with drum rolls from Ruby Nance's Rodeo Band, never failed to gin up crowd excitement and deliver play-by-play action. Once the bucking chute flung open in the bull riding competition, Dad turned our attention to the clown's steps and stunts. He knew at any moment these American matadors might be saving a fellow cowboy's cajónes. Unarmed, the clown's dangling red bandanas served as *muletas*, or capes. Once they got the eye of the bull, their ducking, dipping, and diving in a kind of dodgeball ballet played out, breathtakingly so at times. Dad had seen and met them all: Stillwell Shorty, the Clarke Brothers, Bunky Boger, Chuck Henson, Emmett Kelly, Duane Stephens, and, of course, Ken Bowman with his Old Grey Mare. I came to think of rodeo clowns as the Navy Seals of cowboys.

The Hollywood heroes who made the promotional schlepp to Arkansas, year after year, imprinted their marquee brand on us for at least the life of our childhoods (and often beyond): Cochise (Michael Ansara) from the show *Broken Arrow*, Zorro (Guy Williams) from the eponymous movies and serial, Charlie Wooster (Frank McGrath) and

Bill Hawks (Terry Wilson) from *Wagon Train*, Doc Adams (Milburn Stone) and Festus (Ken Curtis) of the popular *Gunsmoke*, and Daniel Boone (Fess Parker) of the namesake show *Daniel Boone*. Many of these actors further endeared themselves to the community by giving talks at elementary schools and the Kiwanis Club, or by vaulting over the rump to mount a neighbor's paint horse (Michael Ansara).

By 1959, television featured thirty prime-time Westerns. On Thursday nights in the '50s, when the *Lone Ranger* came on, we hummed or tapped out the *William Tell Overture*. At school we sang "Home on the Range" in choir practice. We religiously tuned in to the celluloid West, hanging on every word from our high-wattage, existential heroes Rowdy, Matt, Wishbone, Festus, Cochise, Chester, Hoss, and Josh.

Catching our Hollywood heroes in the flesh only enhanced their black and white messages of good, evil, and righteous self-reliance. On *Gunsmoke*, the main characters never married, too wise and world-wary to make a wrong move. They were in Dodge to keep the riff-raff out, not to exemplify some idealized version of domesticity. It was post–World War II, the Red Scare was real, the Cold War had hotspots, and our Hollywood heroes drew the sharp lines of right and wrong for our inexperienced minds.

Western movies and television shows are innately a form of American storytelling, a rabbit hole to the imagined simpler, romantic times of the nineteenth-century Frontier Movement. The heroes wanted nothing of government, unless there was a hitch. In that case, in rolled the cavalry to save the day. Every night of the week, these simple television dramas served up the latest popular portrayal of our American identity. We, in turn, dressed in cowboy costumes, rode horses (both real and stick), and carried those honor-bound, celluloid black-and-white cultural symbols out into our neighborhoods and lives.

By the late '60s, however, television programming moved on from its frontier era of cowboy ephemera. Once it was out of fashion, the genre became easy to misremember, over-romanticize, and mythologize, particularly among the anti-government ranks. Nostalgia for simpler times remained a feel-good emotion, but we liked our indoor toilets and city water. TV commercials that hawked new Westinghouse appliances, Chevy Super Sports, and Pontiac GTOs caught our attention. The future, going to the moon, was surely full of romantic promise.

Once Hollywood dropped the Hays Code, which dictated good and evil content in television and movies, the industry caught up with the complexity of the times. My celluloid enthusiasms matured in synch with the rest of me. Mel Brooks's Western spoof *Blazing Saddles* and its all-star cast—the Teutonic Titwillow (Madeline Kahn), Taggart (Slim Pickens), the Waco Kid (Gene Wilder), and Sheriff Bart (Cleavon Little), all pulling our lariats, so to speak—pushed the envelope to spotlight our society's changing attitudes.

Hollywood had moved on; the sun had set on Matt, Kitty, and the boys. But that was not true for our beloved Old Fort Parade and Rodeo. Cowboys, cowgirls, clowns, the parade, and the Grand Entry are still bedazzling kids (and adults) just as the Greatest Show in Town did my cow-licked herd over six decades ago. The Old Fort Rodeo is embedded culture, our fun and rowdy place in the sun, stubborn as old Festus, who might say of the rodeo's fate: Safer than chitlins on a city folk's supper plate.

The rodeo was a once-a-year happening, whereas Fort Smith's Wheeler Avenue Boys Club was a year-round home away from home. The regulars who passed beneath the blasted-in-concrete front door greeting, *Enter Ye Men of Tomorrow*, ranged from shoeless or sole-flapping Coke Hill squatter camp kids to country club dandies with new Keds for every season. Class constructs, thanks in large part to the venerable, pipe-smoking director Clarence Higgins, were left at the door. He created an energy that had a strong regression to the middle—a class of equals.

My parents and Clarence Higgins, known as Hig to adults, his wife "Ope," and their son, Billy, already a teenager when we arrived in Fort Smith, became family friends. The fringe benefits of such a friendship were invaluable for kids, young boys especially. The parents got on well, and John, Stan, Greg, and I were awestruck at the doors that opened for us. Mr. Higgins not only managed the Boys Club, he also oversaw Hunt's Park, an American Legion on up to semi-pro baseball field less than four blocks from our home on Pendell Lane. When he had paperwork to do on Sundays when the Boys Club was closed, he'd pick us up in his Chevrolet station wagon and let us loose in both gyms, the Olympic-size swimming pool, and the boxing room. If we were lucky, an old African American sparring partner of Jack Dempsey's, Arthur Davis (better known as Shifty in New Jersey boxing circles), would show us a few of his old moves. He lived in the boiler room beneath the big gym bleachers.

We all played baseball at the church league fields at the bottom end of our street. A few blocks north, at Hunt's Park, managed by Mr. Higgins and the Boys Club, we had worked our way into standing jobs before and after our church league games, slinging cones, Cokes, and hot dogs; shagging balls; posting the scoreboard; mowing, raking, and chalking the field; and cleaning up trash. As the oldest, John always got the concession gig, tracking the inventory and handling the cash box. As ball shaggers, we received 25 cents a game. On weekend nights, we got a bump to 35 cents. Fringes included a round or two a day of free hot dogs, snow cones, and ice-cold Nehi grape sodas; dropped coins found beneath the bleachers while cleaning up the trash; and all we wanted of the broken bats and partial packages of loose-leaf Red Man chewing tobacco left in the dugouts. The pay per game, the finders-keepers rule on dropped coins, and the other fringes were unnecessary, though. There was no other place on earth I'd rather have been. It was a racket, a back-gate key to a Field of Dreams.

Most foul balls that didn't climb up home plate's sloped-screen backstop went high, straight back, and crashed on the tin top of the bleachers like a cannon shot. I'd pick them up when they rolled off the backside and throw them to the ump. Retrieving out-of-play baseballs, that's what ball shaggers do. But some, myself on occasion, did it with panache.

One July evening during the district American Legion Tournament, I was working the hill behind home plate when a foul ball came down on top of four or five "scouts" sitting in a half-circle of lawn chairs. At the last second, as the scouts scrambled, I dove into the middle of those chairs and caught the ball on a measured roll with my homemade first baseman's glove. As I held it high in the air for all to see, Lester Johnson of the Los Angeles Dodgers ripped a "team calling card" from his wallet, reached my way, and said, "Take this, kid, and call me in a few years." For the next several weeks, I showed that card off to everyone as if it were Mickey Mantle's rookie Topps.

In the summer of '59 (at not quite eight years old), I worked behind the plate managing the stock of foul balls to be returned to the umpire at his command. Between innings I would sprint 100 yards down the first base fence line and hook a right turn to the thirty-foot-high black scoreboard, an excellent radiator of Arkansas's July heat. I'd hit the ladder on the run (as people watched), scurry up to the platform, and do a card-like shuffle for the correct black tin plates numbered in white, ranging from goose eggs to ten. During the heat of the day, the trick was to keep the likely numbers, the zeros and ones, covered from the sun on this manually operated monster scoreboard.

After yet another of those sweltering afternoons, as the sky darkened on July 31, 1959, Ray Seaman, the centerfielder for Midwest Hardware, stepped up to the plate with two outs and no men on. The infield was humming with the usual fast chatter: "last batter," "easy out," "let him have it." Behind home plate, I squared up in a folding metal chair, a few feet to the left of the backstop fence. Down the third base line, in front of the cinder-block field house, positioned like a panel of judges, were my Dad, Clarence Higgins, and several other baseball buffs, evoking a '50s-era respectability in which pipes were smoked, and white shirts and fedoras were standard dress.

Above me in the bleachers, next to the radio announcer, I heard old Cephus Peters, who had cerebral palsy, yak-yakking in his slurring speech. "Coach, you got to hold the bat steady," he said, while shaking his cane at Greenwood's coach Jeep Sadler. Cephus and Coach Sadler were at Hunt's Park most days when the gates opened.

Larry "Vinegar Ben" Wright and his ballpark buddy Gerald "Doody" Prince, whose mother was known by all as the waitress in the pink uniform and hairnet who rolled the hot dogs at Coney Island on Garrison Avenue, leaned on the fence over my left shoulder. As was his custom, Vinegar Ben had his transistor radio in his shirt pocket, plugged into one ear listening to the St. Louis Cardinals game.

On this steamy Friday evening, Vinegar Ben, Doody, and I shared the same line of sight as a high fast ball came out of nowhere—and bam. It made a dull thud on Ray Seaman's head, at the left temple area, unprotected by the plastic skull cap he wore. Ray's legs buckled, and he crumbled to the ground, out cold. In the same instant, Vinegar Ben and Doody screamed, almost in unison, "Get a doctor, get a doctor!"

Meantime, Coach Herman Whitson and Umpire Bill Norvel hovered over Ray for no more than a minute. The crowd hushed, time crawled. Vinegar Ben stood funeral silent. Doody turned off his transistor. Even Cephus quieted down. And, then, Lazaruslike, Ray Seaman came to, eyes hooded, slowly raising his head, saying, "I'm all right, I'm all right."

Coach Whitson helped him to his feet. Ray gathered himself a minute before walking to first base on his own. He received a standing ovation. "Go Ray, shake it off," Doody shouted. After a quick out,

Billy Howell, a teammate, threw Ray his glove, and Ray walked slowly to his place in centerfield. He played two more innings, but as he took the field in the bottom of the sixth, he complained of feeling sick. Once he was in position, before play began, Ray's legs crumpled forward, and he hit the ground face down. His mother watched it all, bereft, screaming over and over, "Ray, my baby, Ray, my baby…"

Teammates helped him back to his feet, and Ray's dad rushed him to the hospital. Dr. J. P. Shermer, a volunteer general practitioner, who had conducted many summer camp physicals for the Boys Club, met the Seamans at the Sparks Hospital emergency room. Ray's sixteen-year-old brain bled out on the operating table. We got the news the next afternoon.

I'd seen corpses of old people in coffins on display in living room wakes where Granddaddy and Maw lived in the piney woods of Arkansas, but I'd never fully registered the whimsical way death could repose just anybody at any age at any time. Now I did, in a more vivid way, at not quite eight years old. It gave me a sick feeling, the thought of dying someday.

A year later, plastic helmets with earflaps became common gear in the major leagues, replacing the skull caps. At the same time, a flagpole honoring Ray, dedicated by his Midwest Hardware teammates, went up at Hunt's Park. In seasons to come, whenever I covered the hill shagging balls, I perched at the ready waiting on a fly ball next to the flagpole, feeling the ghostly spirit of the departed on hallowed ground. Sixteen-year-old Ray Seaman was nowhere and yet everywhere.

Clarence Higgins raised money for the Boys Club every way he could shake a gourd. He often partnered in shoestring fundraisers with sponsors such as the Kiwanis, Sertoma, and Optimist clubs. He rounded up the cow-licked Karber herd on any given Saturday or Wednesday, an eager, one-stop-shopping work force, whenever the call came. We might go to Fayetteville to a University of Arkansas basketball game at Barnhill Arena or the *circus maximus* of screaming football fans at Razorback Stadium to sell Cokes, hot dogs, and popcorn. Or it might be the Golden Gloves, where we hawked concession goods, handled the trash, and got to see and do things that money couldn't buy.

At the '59 Golden Gloves in Fort Smith, Mr. Higgins elevated me to designated ring boy. That was me, the goofy kid, in an unfitting black suit and matching bowtie, holding up a numbered placard and circling the ropes, announcing each round. "You got it upside down, you stumblebum," goaded the hecklers until I flipped it and they'd really get their jollies.

My brother Greg was born with a funny bone and knew how to use it, especially when confronted with the amusingly eccentric. Mr. Higgins tapped Greg and me to work Wednesday nights on a Boys Club fundraising mission at Jimmy Lott's wrestling matches, at an abandoned factory on Towson Avenue. On Pat Porta's early Wednesday news segment, sponsored by Stag beer, Lott—a Damon Runyon–type promoter with a five o'clock shadow—presented the evening's lineup. The Scuffling Hillbillies didn't wrestle, he clarified, they scuffled. The Great Matsuda, Lott explained with a straight face, was the master of the Japanese Sleeper, a Vulcan Super Hold. The lineup and *sui generis* set of talents went on: Great Bolo, Gorgeous George, Danny Hodge, Haystacks Calhoun, Grizzly Smith, Scandor Akbar, Dr. X. As the newscast wrapped up, Lott warned fans in attendance that night to "watch out for flying chairs."

Jimmy Lott was my first encounter with full-tilt blue-collar fantasies. "Kayfabe" they called it, the practice of presenting staged performances as authentic. "Grown-ups screaming at the wrestlers and the referees with more venom than a pit of snakes, never letting up until the fight was over," wrote my brother Greg in a memoir. "The spit from the fanatical gathering made the smoke clouds appear to emit rain. It was an atmosphere unknown to us, where adults were out of control and into fights among themselves, where people would shout at and curse us, shove us from their view, or hug us as the fight went their way, and where food was available to eat or be thrown." Greg wrapped up our madcap evenings at Jimmie Lott's with: "My parents seemed to have assumed our safety in an environment, I still think, insofar as games of recreation are concerned, was as close to mindless chaos, generally harmless, I suppose, but certainly mindless, as humans could get or I'd ever want to see. My parents did not attend, nor did anyone else we knew."

On Sunday, October, 29, 1961, Mr. Higgins picked us up after church and took us to the Municipal Airport, a mile south down Old Greenwood. President John F. Kennedy was arriving in two hours on the first Boeing 707 to ever land in Fort Smith. The navy's Blue Angels performed aerial acrobatics while I loop-de-looped through an ecstatic crowd of 15,000 onlookers selling Cokes, popcorn, and hot dogs on behalf of the Boys Club.

Fans and curiosity seekers had arrived for the presidential razzle-dazzle from eastern Oklahoma and small communities across Arkansas, spreading out on blankets and in folding chairs. Kennedy emerged from the plane to a cheering crowd. Introduced by our Wolfe Lane neighbor Mayor Bob Brooksher, Kennedy began by thanking Arkansas for the eight electoral votes cast for him. I'd never sold so much popcorn and hot dogs as I did that day. My basket would empty out in ten minutes.

Key to Fort Smith officials—Mayor Brooksher, Governor Faubus, and Senators Fulbright and McClellan—all in attendance, was that Kennedy re-open—and keep open—Fort Chaffee, a couple of miles from Fort Smith. In his short speech, Kennedy assured everyone that the World War II–era base would be re-opened and that Fort Smith and Fort Chaffee were important to America's defense.

He was preaching to the Cold War choir. I had no problem clapping eyes on Kennedy but was too busy to catch everything he said that day, much less get into his magic space for a handshake. I was bent by the force field of printing money that afternoon, probably made four bucks. Two years later, the Pentagon closed Fort Chaffee as an active duty post and then on November 22, 1963 Kennedy was assassinated in Dallas, searing the day and his youthful visage in our collective memories forevermore.

For better or worse, the post–World War II segregated, class-free neighborhoods in which we baby boomers came of age stand out as much as the sex, drugs, and rock 'n' roll of the 1960s and all that milieu encompassed.

In the 1950s, mega-mansions were almost nonexistent. On Pendell Lane, Carrier window units and central heat and air had not replaced open windows and attic fans in the summer and floor furnaces and fireplaces in winter. Healthy hands washed the dishes. Clothes were scrubbed by hand in a wringer washing machine and pinned on the clothesline or laid atop a shrub to dry in the sun. By the next decade, it was no secret that consumerism, as opposed to hollow consumption, was on the upswing. The TV advertisers touted indulgence. Within a few years of arriving in Fort Smith, the Karbers had the full complement of appliances and monthly payments to Sears and Roebuck. Mom's many hours of household toil were sharply reduced.

The everyday joys of pre-adolescent boys were cheap, simple, and status free: penny candy, nickel soda pops, pocket yo-yos, marble shooting, and chin-wagging about Mantle, Musial, and Mays. For households, bargain shopping was a way of life, a necessity even. In my mother's case, assuming the '55 Nash Rambler was cranking, she beat a path to Piggly Wiggly on Tuesday for S&H Green Stamp double-stamp day, to Shipley's Bakery for day-old bread on Friday, and three times a week for advertised sales at Yutterman's Market, "Right on the Corner, Right on the Price." Gibson Discount Center and Bercher Mart offered tag sales, and frequently Mom prowled the second-hand stores for clothes and someone else's junk. For women in our neighborhood, marriage was an economic proposition that often included having babies like hens in a brooder house. Their career ambitions played out through their husband's work life. The few who had paid jobs did so because they were divorced or their husbands didn't make enough money. Apart from that, relative "income equality" in our community was real, an undistorted fact of life.

A young doctor made $16,000 a year, while a plumber, a teacher, a factory worker, or a county agent did half as well. In the dollars and cents and hours and inches of everyday life, the band of income separating the least from the most was hardly noticeable. Pendell Lane, our modest street of $15,000 to $20,000 houses, was home to a wide range of occupations, among them a Harding Glass factory worker (Dovall), real estate agents (Sagely and Schultz), insurance brokers (Ross and Hatcher), a plumber (Blake), a lawyer and judge (Langston), a Boys Club director (Charles), a county agent (Karber), doctors (Goodman and Kramer), a dentist (Skokos), a Jewish haberdasher (Marks), a famous sportscaster (Jones), and a pilot (Duncan).

No one in my family had ever met a millionaire. Of course, we had heard and read about the fabulous wealth of Daddy Warbucks zillionaires like the Rockefellers, the Hunts, or Howard Hughes. All were as far removed and unfathomable as a man on the moon…but for one local curiosity. A couple of Sundays a year we'd pack up in the Mercury station wagon and go for a catfish lunch at the foot of Log Town Hill in Van Buren. Afterward Dad would drive by the Palmer House at 515 Washington Street, said by friends-once-removed to have a swimming pool spattered like confetti with silver dollars on its concrete bottom. Sounded too good to be true. Greg wanted to climb a tree and see for himself, to explore the maze of hallways and inner mysteries of such an eccentric lifestyle that consciously closed out our kind. Word even had it that the owner was a country cousin to the Chicago Palmer family, heirs to the Palmer House hotel chain. We never saw this talked-about spendthrift personage, much less the swimming pool or silver dollars. In fact, he was as mysterious as John Beresford Tipton on the weekly Colgate-Palmolive-sponsored TV show *The Millionaire*. No one ever clapped eyes on Tipton either. Only his arm was revealed as he gave away the lordly sum of a million bucks to his secretary, Michael Anthony, to deliver to some unsuspecting lucky-duck.

We were Republicans and Democrats, Catholics and Protestants, two Jewish families, and one Hispanic—and no blacks, Buddhists, Hindus, or Muslims. There were no out-of-the-closet KKK members, maybe a few John Birchers, and absolutely no radical lefties or communists. Sightings of stray drifters and hobos, irrelevant curiosities at best, on the railroad spur behind the ballparks were not uncommon. But the whistle of the ballpark train signaled there was another world out there somewhere with all different kinds of people.

One of those different ones was Bobby Joe Burns, a twenty-eight-year old neighbor living at 2203 South L Street who marked to the marrow every kid for miles around. Bobby Joe blew the top off of the horror norms of Rod Serling's *Twilight Zone*, inviting us into "a dimension not only of sight and sound but of mind."

On Sunday evening, January 26, 1957, Bobby Joe decapitated his mother, Edna Burns, removed her eyes, nose, and tongue, and left her severed head, wrapped in a white sheet, in the vestibule of the Immaculate Conception Church in downtown Fort Smith. Altar boys Fred Miller and Willard Smith found the bundled head of Edna, a fellow worshipper at the church. "It is a story of mental illness, delusion and matricide," reported the local *Southwest American* newspaper.

Dad was out of town when the grisly murder occurred, so while the local police searched desperately for Bobby Joe, my mother, brothers, and I secured all the windows, drew the curtains, double-locked the doors, and jumped at shadows. A rapt city, spooked like a cat up a tree, tuned in to the hourly radio news, crackling with tension.

The television repeatedly showed a prior mug shot of Bobby Joe, revealing a scruffy, saturnine face and deep-set dark eyes with a liberated lock of coal black hair falling to his eyebrows. It was easy to conjure his mug as the personification of the demonic. Mercifully, local police captured him a day later in Oklahoma. When interviewed, while eating candy bars and drinking soda, he said that he was enacting an Aztec-style sacrifice and, quoting verses of Revelations 20: 9-11, claimed that the orders had come from God. The authorities carted the diagnosed schizophrenic off to the state's mental hospital, never to depart, not physically anyway.

The goblins were loose. This was no ordinary dark and scary cellar staircase. It was the first time I remember things going bump in the middle of the night and feeling vulnerable and alone. That's when my sleepwalking and nightmares started—and maybe others' too. The contours of the hair-prickling dream are always the same. After hearing footfalls—the intrusive clanging about of someone surely psychotic—a faceless stranger climbs through a window or keys an easy door, creeps up in the dark, and stands over my sleeping, frozen-with-fear body with a knife drawn, poised to waste me. My struggling moans grow louder as the odious dream progresses and my pulse quickens until I am jolted awake, usually in a sweat, threatened only by what's in my head: Bobby Joe Is Back!

The murder threw an ominous shadow across the neighborhood. After Bobby Joe, everyone had to tamp down their terrors and fears. But the taunts, the sightings, and the campfire stories that were bandied about had legs: "You got snakes in your head like Bobby Joe

Burns. Bobby Joe put her tongue in the toaster and ate it. Bobby Joe peeked in my mama's window last night." Imaginations had free rein. For a few weeks, every kid with a pulse developed an overactive amygdala, the frisson normally reserved for ghouls and demons and other paranormal meddlers.

Around that time, at the end of our first-grade year, Charlie Goodman and I were miraculously cured of our Huck Finn tendencies to pack a bandana full of apples, a box of matches, and his two silver dollars to run away from home. If we did, it was not after dark and we went straight to Byron Ware's back stoop, seeking shelter for the night in his basement.

No black people lived in our neighborhood. White Catholics made up half of the residents and attended Christ the King school. We white Protestants and Jews went to Ballman, the neighborhood public primary school. Protestants (and Jews I assume) didn't openly dislike Catholics, or vice versa. We did, however, rigidly attend separate schools and churches (or synagogues) and, if sick, went to separate clinics and hospitals: St. Edwards for Catholics and Sparks for white Protestants. And, when the grim reaper struck, if you were Catholic or Jewish, interment likely took place in separate sections of the Calvary Cemetery on Lexington Avenue. At the north end of Calvary, headstones were scored in crosses and imagery of Jesus and bore surnames like Sharum, Udouj, Schneider, Bercher, Borengasser, and Schwartz. To the south, accessed by a separate entrance, ground stones bore the Star of David and memorialized last names like Goldman, Cohn, Tilles, Marks, Katzer, and Mendelsohn. At one time or another, I knew or was aware of all those pioneering families, along with well-known Protestants buried in nearby Oak Cemetery. Less known to me were the people of color, most of whom were descendants of emancipated slaves, buried in Washington Cemetery, closer to their section of town on the north side.

The Karbers were never active or open haters of any group. Segregated as our community was, my brothers and I just thought it ended up that way naturally, the human ecosystem at work. Being nice to Arabela, the black maid, was about the extent of our racial socialization. Racism wasn't an event, however, it was and is a system infused across society and all its institutions: religious, educational, economic, criminal justice, and so on. We were the opposite of woke, sort of like the story about the fish that asked another fish about the water and the answer was: What's the water? For sure, though, no one in our house doubted that all souls met God, who we assumed was white, in the same room in heaven and that we were all bound by degrees to the American political theology of meritocracy.

Once a year, in the neighborhood, we came together for the Christ the King Carnival. As Protestant boys, it was in our nature to keep a few penguin jokes going about the nuns' habits. The purple-faced priests, sometimes sporting their Eucharist chasubles, partying it up, were also a constant source of amusement. In a matter of years, our amusement turned to admiration for the Catholics' boozy openness and lack of "Blue Law" hypocrisy. Then again, when our Catholic neighbors whipped out those Five-Decade Rosaries and let rip the Glory Bes and Hail Marys, it was easy to be blown away by their mysterious practices. In some ways, we were jealous that they all had personal saints and could pray directly for divine intervention. They seemed to have a leg up. But other than in 1960 when John Kennedy ran for president (and my parents supported him), there wasn't much for Catholics and Protestants to disagree on.

Birth control certainly was not an issue; everyone bred like hamsters. Summertime, we faced off with all denominations at the church league ballparks. Living seven houses away from those dusty diamonds was like standing in the on-deck circle, a swell place and time, which was destined to become our *hiraeth*, a Welsh word for yearning, a homesickness, a nostalgia for where your spirit lives.

It wasn't until the mid-'60s that the neighborhood began to reshape, a natural next-phase to the aspirational lifestyles we lived. Kids grew up, dogs died, marriages matured, Arthur's parents sent him off to a special needs school in Conway, and the memory of Bobby Joe faded along with the halcyon pleasures of earthy escapades. The Parkers sold their home to a black retired army major. Professional incomes rose sharply. Mega-mansions and gated communities became the new greener pasture. the more prosperous moved away. The pre-prosperous world had turned, and into this flux, our utopic household was about to be upended. As certainty gave way to uncertainty, a fierce awareness of Weberian class, the fixities of social station, and power suddenly insinuated itself like an unwanted relation.

Doctoritis

Chapter Three

HARVARD STUDENT QUENTIN COMPSON, William Faulkner's neurotic character in *The Sound and the Fury*, committed suicide by jumping off a bridge and drowning in the Charles River. He was distraught over his sister Caddy's sexual conduct. The perceived impurity and dishonor of it all disturbed him. Love, they say, inverts order, makes things change places, reveals the sexual and moral customs of an era, and leads lovers to ruin or redemption. As Faulkner advised, the South is not so much a geographical place as an emotional idea.

In the way of the fictional Compsons, the Karbers have never thought it a good idea for our mentally vexed to air their dirty laundry, much less check into a booby hatch. We didn't even counsel with our Methodist minister, the venerable Dr. Fred G. Roebuck, in the full howl of family darkness when our Rockwellian model-of-a-1950s-mother, Joyce, belly-crawled, no shit, in the middle of the night, out my oldest brother John's bedroom window. Just like that, snap-click-whoosh, she flew the coop from four of her five boys with a man who we thought of as the crabby old Fred Mertz on *I Love Lucy*. Visually it was all a mismatch, and troubling to watch unfold in a mid-'60s, morally conservative burg. My dad, John Karber, was a highly respected county agent, World War II vet, weekend pilot in the National Guard, and host of a Friday TV show on agriculture. He displayed Errol Flynn–like dash when swing dancing with my mother at Billy Garner's Supper Club. As *Übermensch* to a houseful of boys, Dad was left holding the bag—to explain things, to try his best to pick up the pieces of a broken home and shattered family ethos, which, like Humpty Dumpty, once broken were impossible to put back together.

The sourpuss character joining Mom on the shadowy edges of that bedroom window—a difficult image to unsee or rinse from our minds—was a pretentious shirttail cousin and professed Catholic who preferred being addressed by family, and the rare friend, as Dr. (Ralph) Wilson. Doc wasn't just conspiring that evening to burst our milk-delivered-to-the-doorstep, Cleaver family bubble, he was bailing on nine children and a German immigrant wife, Rosemary. She was not amused—and was fairly armed with all the secrets of the gun closet and a gumshoe's custom of surveillance.

It was chilling to have her park at the top of our street for hours awaiting the return of Mom and Doc from yet another indiscreet tryst. One such evening, Dad flashed the porch lights several times, walked to the street, and waved Rosemary down to our house. When she approached the front door, as we all watched from the picture window, he talked her into giving up her .38 Special revolver. Love lost, pride punished, and Catholic family dictates desecrated were certainly the crosscurrents of Rosemary's corrosive anger. We were all relieved that she surrendered the gun to Dad. Fleeting as it was, it felt like a long overdue act of peace.

Small towns, they say, can be a vast hell. Rather than face the community-wide condemnation that, for a fact, turned downright nasty, Mom and Doc fled to Oklahoma City. The truth of their Judas kiss had crucified their former incarnations. They became people with a vague past, reinventing themselves no less than the guiltless expatriate seeking freedom in some faraway colony. Their lives became abstract, like characters in fiction. Out of fourteen kids, Doc and Mom scrammed with one, my six-year-old brother Kent. He never had a choice or a chance. Chop, chop, lawyers sealed the deal; Mom and Doc were good to go. Vacating the moral high ground they once held over thirteen other kids was never inked in the decree. It wasn't necessary. It dwelt in the baggage they carried with them no less than some deft Irish shape-shifter…menacingly and transformatively.

Kent took some of the stink off. The token salve that soothed Mom and Doc's public personae, washing over their past, the makeup on the melanoma. It was at best a fraught role to be foisted on a six-year-old. Over time, Kent's fantasies, his need to fabricate, to tell tall tales of courageous feats or precocious rites of passages, to impress his much older brothers in Arkansas and to dazzle his new friends in OKC, were not at odds with the thin line of denial and dissembling that Mom and Doc walked. "Making it up" became a survival mechanism, the virtue of airbrushing, of trying on masks until one fit.

Kent, bright as a button, was always the ham, a necessity for attention as the youngest of the flock. His older brothers (John, Stan, Greg, and myself) played the impresario role. The youngest in the family has to be funny to get attention. We taught him, as a pot-bellied toddler, to entertain a room full of friends and family. With him in his tighty-whities, as we hovered around the television for the Gillette Friday Night Fights, we would have him affect a Charles Atlas, classic body builder's double-bicep pose, and crow, "I am the champion." As that closeness and brotherly fabric frayed, in a thousand ways, he would become an only child. At the time, though, it felt like an embarrassment of riches for him. We applauded his new financial leg up. It was his due, we thought, not foreseeing the bitter harvest to come of such a family food chain.

Kent's extracurricular activities soon fell somewhere between the Quail Creek fairway, country club swimming pool, and skiing in Colorado. He received a first-rate education at the city's estimable preparatory schools: Casady and Heritage Hall. Before long, Doc became "Dad" and Kent began kowtowing to his possessions and a paid-for façade of class. No sharing the Schwinn Speedster, so to speak, among bros anymore. Everything was proprietary and fiercely protected—his bedroom, his books, his basketball, his Jeep, and so on. That Cleaver family value of reciprocity back on Pendell Lane had been finely shredded, verboten even, no longer the currency of the realm. "I am the franchise," he learned to gloat. It was funny, certainly if you weren't listening.

Mom never offered any justification or atonement for her sudden departure, for sullying the family name, or for the caste system she later cultivated among brothers. And I never asked. I'm sure Dad did, though. He likely felt his honor had been besmirched. As several of my friends' virtuous-minded mothers often and indelicately reminded me, it all amounted to "trading up." That old-as-time art of a well-wooed woman of beauty giving up the family struggles and snagging a gilded passport to the future. The end of innocence for the Karber family was as plain to see as the noses on our faces.

Hell of a year 1965–66 turned out to be. The derangement of the Pendell Lane Karbers' cosmos had the star-seeing punch of an old-fashioned dry-gulching, leaving us without a plan; four loosely tethered huskies and the musher skipped town. We adjusted, more or less, sort of, and maybe not, as little pitchers have big ears. Time would tell…and it did. For the most part, we leathered up with moments in which we wished ourselves somewhere else.

Dad was soon returning from a day's work with a bag of groceries under his arm. He cooked dinner, tried to be the hard ass disciplinarian, and supervised a household of adolescents. He had lost the whistle in his step, though. More wooden than upbeat, a stranger in his own house. Before, when he entered a room in which we were gathered, he entertained us in a tongue-in-cheek way, stepping out a do-si-do move, jauntily singing his favorite stanzas from "Won't

You Come Home, Bill Bailey" or a Glenn Miller tune or whatever chimed in his head at the moment. He especially liked to keep the beat with mocking military steps as he belted out a march tune like the Caisson song, "Over hill, Over dale / As we will hit the dusty trail / And those caissons go rolling along."

The music in his head had died, strangled by the knot in his guts. He could fill a stadium with all his friends, but for now he shut most of them out. As the weeks turned to months and years, the weekend beers to daily bourbons, his stops by the mailbox yielded, among a stack of bills, periodic postcards from my mother checking in from Paris, Budapest, Prague, or London. Those postcards felt more like calculated cruelties heaped on my dad than meaningful missives to me and my brothers. If anything, they alienated us all from her and her side of the family. After a few trips to Merry Old, weird as it sounded during our infrequent visits and periodic phone calls, Mom, who had once poked fun at the pretentious fronts of the silk-stocking crowd, started affecting a highfalutin' British-style accent like Katharine Hepburn and Ingrid Bergman in their older movies. Dad often scoffed that she was a queen looking for a country. He mocked her phony voice. Meantime, the brothers and I kept twanging away, tapped out most of the time.

If not old-fashioned heartfelt romantic love, money bought Mom something more priceless than the family, honor, and loyalty she had had. Dad called it *doctoritis*. He even proposed a home remedy called a "blanket party," which involved getting the jump on Doc, wrapping him up mummy tight in an army-issue blanket, and pounding him like children taking turns hitting the piñata. In principle, we were all for it, but the plan foundered when they fled to Oklahoma City. Their departure was timely. Things were starting to boil over. Dad had delivered a personal threat to air Doc out with the ol' army .45, a crime of passion for which the sheriff, whose office was across the hall from Dad's, might have turned a blind eye.

As the months and years stacked up, Dad reckoned that our Pendell Lane pad and his oat-sowing boys needed some order. The wages of sin were plain to see everywhere. Old-school hell-raising had set in as a guiding condition, a way of being the best of the worst and worst of the best we had become.

The Karber family stag party had also become a sore subject with our neighbors. Naughty girls had begun crawling through our bedroom windows at all hours. Four testosterone-sated, overstimulated teenage boys and a middle-aged, handsome bachelor for a custodial parent had begun passing each other in the night, the rhythms of a flophouse. What a bash we were having…if only Thanksgiving and Christmas, family reunions, and every other household call to muster for some scheduled happiness could have been crossed off the calendar. Still raw and unreconciled, some were hanging in there better than others, and truth be told, freedom is just another word…

One Sunday afternoon, Dad jokingly remarked that he had arrived home at three in the morning from dancing to the swing music of the Paul Lewis Band at Billy Garner's Supper Club and was the first one in. We thought that was kind of cool. Rollick on, Pops, kindred spirits, one for all and all for one. He wasn't feeling the same.

My threshold for surprise in family matters, putting it mildly, had been diminishing for some time. Not long after that Sunday afternoon conversation, Dad announced his plans to remarry. His chosen bride was a paycheck-to-paycheck legal secretary at the Warner law firm by the name of Sara Shifflete. She had three children: two late-teenaged girls and an eight-year-old boy. Her ex was off in a Texas prison for white-collar fraud—land swindles on new homebuyers, I believe. In my sixteen-year-old noggin, Dad was doubling down on his own despair.

Dad called upon our long-time neighbor, Dr. R. C. Goodman, a family friend and fellow reservist, to make sure we boys showed up for the wedding. Reluctantly, responding in early-teen monosyllabic fashion, wearing a blue blazer and a rebellious snarl, I played along. Everyone agreed it was high time for me to get off the dime, to straighten up or hit the road.

In what seemed like a lightning flash, our nuclear family of five brothers had spread like bed bugs to seventeen siblings and steps. Perfect strangers were horning in on our sacred turf. Heads spun, bodies bounced off walls, the blue lights of bad luck haunted. It all had the Friday night cadence and character of the Fort Smith drunk tank. Get me the fuck out of this miasma of melancholy, was all I could think. Judge Cloninger would soon accommodate me on that one.

Years later, my brother Greg sure enough got it right when he sullenly invoked a Taj Mahal lyric to describe Mom's parting: "She caught the Katy and left him a mule to ride." For sure, getting the horns put on him took the starch out. Family and his pact of love with Mom were his pride and joy. And whatever it was Mom had—and would die with—plainly begged a name. Having the home life flipped ass over teakettle felt like a dream fraught with way too much truth, the opening act of a Faulknerian kind of drum roll of tragic characters and twisted plotlines. All the trust we had given to her as a mother and disciplinarian was now torn, disappearing bits and pieces at a time until there was nothing left. Greg cried and cried; Stan raged and ran off several times; John tried to reason with her. I didn't talk about it, but, sure as puberty's onset, delinquency and dropping out came easier than ever before. I felt older than I should have, as if I'd fallen through some hole in the universe, living in some strange space where I didn't want to be, bereft of ways to make things whole again.

Whiskers, Pimples, and Rock 'n' Roll
Chapter Four

ALAN FREED, a Cleveland radio disc jockey, coined the term *rock and roll* in the early 1950s to describe the black rhythm and blues recordings he played. He later defined the genre as "a river of music which has absorbed many streams: rhythm and blues, jazz, ragtime, cowboy songs, country songs, folk songs. All have contributed greatly to the big beat." Surprise, surprise, Bob Dylan added a curlicue or two in his interpretation of the ascendant music. When asked if rock 'n' roll—the even cooler way to spell it—was an extension of '30s music such as Duke Ellington's hit "Braggin'," he replied, "Rock and roll was indeed an extension of what was going on—the big swinging bands—Ray Noble, Will Bradley, Glenn Miller, I listened to that music before I heard Elvis Presley. But rock 'n' roll was high energy, explosive and cut down. It was skeleton music, came out of the darkness and rode in on the atom bomb and the artists were star-headed like mystical Gods."

The popularization of television and the electric guitar in the '50s, coupled with the baby boomer generation enjoying more leisure time, set the stage for rock 'n' roll music to develop and define the '60s. Like every other household on our street and in our broader neighborhood, the Karbers took the plunge at Ben Jack's Guitar Center out on Zero Street and invested in a right-handed Fender MusicMaker electric guitar and Junior Fender amplifier. I was a southpaw, so it didn't work for me. Besides, my childhood was one deep, unbroken kowtow to the altar of sports. All else was anticlimactic.

Stan, on the other hand, took lessons, learned three chords, and earned an appearance at the junior high talent show backing up Donna Matthews who sang the Peter, Paul and Mary hit "500 Miles." After those two chords and that three minutes of celebrity, he was finished. We retired the guitar and amp to the hall closet (where things of value were stored, later to be pawned). Beyond the Karber house, however, many neighborhood friends heard the clarion call, practiced hard, whacked and twanged away, became proficient on their chosen instruments, and eventually played in bands.

Brother John had a limited record collection, which included Elvis's early 45s "Hound Dog" and "Don't Be Cruel," Tennessee Ernie Ford's "Sixteen Tons," the Kingston Trio's "Tom Dooley," and the Ramsey Lewis Trio's album recorded at the Blue Note in Chicago. Beyond that peephole, the local radio, and Dad's collection of Singing Cowboys and swing bands, *The Ed Sullivan Show* was our touchstone for pop music. Most memorably, on February 9, 1964, as if they had just come down riding a meteorite, the Beatles made their first appearance in the States. The Fab Four opened with "All My Loving" and ended with "I Saw Her Standing There" and "I Want to Hold Your Hand." The cat was out of the bag.

Now, it is true that I am a non-musician. Can hardly read the phone book on key. Don't know a doorbell ring from the right note. Couldn't carry a tune with a bucket. Not even the "Clementine" refrain, "Oh my darling..." For all that, rock 'n' roll would become the original sin from which all other offbeat behaviors of mine would evolve. My tin ear aside, I loved the emotion of the music, and what I know deep down is that I am blessed with bones and attitude that can boogaloo to any rhythm when the spirit lifts me.

As the '60s hotted up, having fun and dancing became all about the larger theme of the decade: *freedom*. Standing apart from your dance partner, you could let rip with any ol' self-expressive thing that might resemble walking the dog, the twist, the mashed potato, the jerk, the Watusi, the locomotion, the swim, the hitchhike, the pony, the boogaloo, the Freddie, the frug, or the funky chicken, or just fall down and gator on till the sun came up. A sort of higher consciousness often took hold, a live-in-the-moment reprieve from our mundane and mortal pains. For me it was like blowing down an open highway, driving as if the car were stolen, and someone else was in charge of making the pistons pump. It was only for me to turn a key, accelerate, lie back, feel the wind, with music as my companion—the wind itself.

With music came sex, like whiskers and pimples in the same adolescent explosion. Education about the birds and the bees, however, was not something that happened at school or on a car ride with Dad. Instead, it literally came straight out of the gutter, the roadside ditches where many a neighborhood dad tossed his *Playboy* or other pornographic magazine out the window before arriving home, an unsafe hidey-hole for a family man. Stealthily, we, mostly Bruce Barnes and I, retrieved those dirty mags from the ditches. After a few peeks at, let's say, Jayne Mansfield's D-cup glory, accompanied by an alien flush of sexual arousal, we might tear out a saucy page or two and stash the rest like a pirate's buried treasure in the crawl space under my house for future consumption. In time, our vocabularies took on words to describe sex and the glossy vulgar poses revealed in the magazines. Bruce's older brother Bobby even taught us to boldly walk right up to the counter at our neighborhood convenience store, the Quickie, plop down a dollar bill, and tell Mr. Beasley, the six-foot-six-inch-tall owner, or his manager, Leroy, who was also our postman, the dirty little lie that Dad had sent us to pick up the current issue of *Playboy*. Change was 40 cents, our payola, with which we stocked up on Sour Grapes and Fruit Stripe gum. Bruce and I were eleven years old.

Two years on, after observing dozens of foxy lasses on *Ed Sullivan* screaming and crying with joy over four cheeky, mop-headed teddy boys, who could in fact sing and play and perform, it occurred to me that the least I could do to get closer to the adulating attentions of the opposite sex was give up the Butch wax and burr-cut-cum-flat-top and grow my own mop top. Only recently had I quit allowing Dad to cut my hair on the back porch in the only style he knew how to cut. One of life's less cosmic decisions, but costly nonetheless at four bucks a trim at Ernie Earp's Holiday Lanes barbershop. My stock went up right away among the girls who liked something dangerous. So, I started dressing slightly more idiosyncratically, shaking a leg at house parties and junior high sock-ups, making one small proclamation of emancipation after another. Copped an attitude, added an "L" to my name as a minor rebellion (Philip became Phillip), smoked "grits" between classes, played the payoff pins, shot a solid nine-ball game at Lola's on Texas Corner, chugged a 14-ouncer in the cornfields south of town, spiced up my language skills by injecting "fuck" into conversations as often and in as many ways as possible. Squares beware, born on Halloween among the goblins and ghouls, I was somebody who'd toss a brick through a window. It was a coming-of-age space I had never thought of inhabiting, caught completely unawares by the seduction of being more rebel than role model, more law breaker than law abider. Overnight, the guarded Rubicon became the doable rivulet, easier by the dozen. Or as singer/songwriter Billie Joe Shaver aptly put it: *Yeah, the devil made me do it the first time / The second time I done it on my own.*

It was all a groundbreaking, anti-authoritarian adventure down the steps on the road to juvenile perdition: the worldwide Beatlemania, a moon tide of well-written-and-performed pop music, the early-birth-control-era chick fans, and the Brando-cum-British brand of spontaneous cheekiness and class warfare. It was a first, young people determining the course of events no less than Kennedy had taken America to modernity from the old fogey era of Eisenhower. The Beatles kept getting better, grittier, pushing the bar higher, turning music into an art form: *Rubber Soul, Revolver, Sgt. Pepper's.* The Rolling Stones were close behind, notching it up more than a few bars from "(I Can't Get No) Satisfaction" with the release of *Beggars Banquet*, featuring "Street Fighting Man" and "Sympathy for the Devil." Lucy in the sky, I get high with a little help, Satan, Who killed the Kennedys?—a crossfire hurricane it was, from the civil rights movement and the Cold War to Vietnam and the counterculture. Plainly, my latching on to that avant garde, anti-establishment, free and easy fun hurt me with coaches, counselors, athletics and academics. That's the way it went. Juking the rules, Rebel Comes of Age 101. That the adults in the room objected only validated the behavior all the more. My emotional algorithms feeding back, "fuck the tight asses," made it the zero-sum game it was meant to be. The shifting cultural trade winds blew hard. So hard in fact, with some help, I sawed off the branch I had been sitting on, chucked it to the wind, and landed in another time zone on some magic carpet to nowhere. Like Brando in the 1953 outlaw biker film *The Wild One*, I sure didn't know what it was I stood for, if anything. In the movie, a fun-loving bleach blonde Mildred (Peggy Maley) asks gang leader Johnny Strabbler (Marlon Brando), "Hey Johnny, what are you rebelling against?" The sullen-faced, streetwise Johnny looks her straight in the eyes and says, "What've you got?"

One early evening in September of 1964 my brother John, four years my elder, took me out in the backyard to scan the sky in the crepuscular hour when bats darted overhead. He was confident we could catch sight of the Beatles' private plane cruising high over Fort Smith, Arkansas. John had calculated (or triangulated) that the Fab Fours' flight path from Kansas City to Dallas had to cross our Pendell

Lane axis. It was on his mind. His old neighborhood friend, Buzz Laughlin, had left that day to drive to that Beatles concert in Dallas, at the Memorial Auditorium. Buzz being there brought it all close to home, peer pressurized.

That late summer night John and I thought we heard a plane that could have been ferrying the Beatles. Otherwise, our attempt to edge tangentially closer to Beatlemania was a bust, a Haley's Comet fly-by not to circle back anytime soon. Rock concerts were yet to be an affordable leisure of the Karbers, but things were stirring in the bushes.

Two years on, shortly after Mom and Doc absconded to Oklahoma City, in 1966, that changed. Concerts became a destination for my fourteen-year-old self. I rat holed my paper route money for a month, and joined friends Mark Stouffer, Doug Rogers, and Billy Ward for a supervised road trip to Little Rock to take in the Animals and Herman's Hermits at War Memorial Stadium. Mark Stouffer's mother, Agnes, drove us. She was a switched-on parent, taking a room next to ours at the Markham Inn. We had loaded our suitcases with Coors, a watery 3.2 percent beer, procured from a motorcycle beer run to a juke joint in Shady Grove, Oklahoma, the night before. Agnes was wise to our shenanigans.

The Markham Inn sat directly across the street from War Memorial Stadium. It was the height of the British Invasion—and a worthy introduction to the pomp and live-and-let-live delirium of stadium circuit concert-going that came to define the portentous times. Notably, the Animals, a rough-edged, Newcastle working-class group led by the deep, bluesy-voiced Eric Burdon, opened. The rumble before the groundswell, they broke up soon after we saw them and rebranded as a psychedelic-rock, Fillmore West band: Eric Burdon and the Animals. That next year, the summer of 1967, at the Monterey Pop Festival, they joined a bevy of '60s musical icons: Buffalo Springfield, Simon and Garfunkel, the Grateful Dead, Jefferson Airplane, the Who, Otis Redding, Ravi Shankar, Janis Joplin, and Jimi

Hendrix. The first of its kind, a diversity of music, a Pop Festival. It was the Summer of Love, and Monterey provided its soundtrack.

On this night in Little Rock, a country mile in space and time from Jimi torching his guitar at Monterey, Burdon was attired in a tee-shirt, Cuban heels and aviator shades, a worthy unregenerate role model. The band played like demons, with a short set featuring hit singles like the folk-rock favorite "House of the Rising Sun" and an excellent cover of Nina Simone's "Don't Let Me Be Misunderstood." "It's My Life" (and I'll do what I want) was next and had my crew standing and shouting the lyrics above the young gals encircling us. Burdon and company closed with what would become anthemic for myself (slightly more wised-up) and other Vietnam vets, "We've Gotta Get Out of This Place."

We came to Little Rock for the Animals and Eric Burdon. The Hermits, the main act, were pure fluff—sweet, sappy, and sentimental teen-idol rock 'n' roll, Brando's version of cornball. Pubescent baby boomer girls were the biggest class of record buyers of the Hermits' saccharine odes to adolescent thrills.

Peter Noone, the lead singer and blond-haired, blue-eyed *As the World Turns* heartthrob of the Hermits, arrived pope-like, kitted out in tropical whites, a thin black tie, and a plaid Greek sailor's hat, perched high in the back seat of a spanking new 1966 white Cadillac convertible. Crossing the sacred turf of the Arkansas Razorback football field, he was greeted, no less than the Beatles had been received, with a delirious chorus of teenage beauts and belles. Budding breasts. Curving keisters. Powdered and perfumed. Festooned in '50s-era sundresses, summer white flats and hair ribbons in their beehives and bobs. Fragile looking as Dresden dolls until the band played, then they came alive, catching the beat, busting some moves, bearing the collective face of a grand Aphrodite, pained and innocently ecstatic expressions. The Hermits were shooting stars, riding a wave of pop *Billboard* top-ten hits.

The sultry thickness of the Southern air rent with screaming, red-cheeked teenage girls is my clearest vision of that night. At times, I thought I was being joshed, having my leg pulled, as all the moshing, fainting, and frenzied spontaneous welling of emotions took hold. Like the bobby soxers at a '40s-era Sinatra show, it was more than a sideshow within a main act. Sex was a part of popular music. The screaming got more air time than Peter Noone's voice. Chomping at the bit, a belly flop into the bosom of all that hot mess of swooning flesh became an urgent fantasy. But it was more than girls just screaming and acting out. It was a way of howling out their frustration and finding their own identity, as I was doing. The garage band craze made perfect sense to them as well.

A close second as vivid memories go of that evening was bumping into a friend from Pine Bluff. "Karber, why don't you relieve me of two of these?" he said, flashing four tickets to the Beatles in Memphis coming up in a few weeks. When I asked how much, he threw back some ridiculous nose-bleed price like ten bucks each. Unless I robbed a liquor store or pawned Dad's guns, no chance I could raise the scratch from my paper route for the ticket cost, a road trip to Memphis, and a motel room. What we would have given, though. The promise of the unseen. It all made my head go kablooey!

It wasn't until a year later in Tulsa, though, when I really got hooked on the stadium circuit shows the Beatles had set in motion. My friends with cars all had eight-track tape decks, a coin of the realm for coolness. Most had rock 'n' roll progenitor James Brown's *Live at the Apollo* queued up, much different music than the sock-hop fare.

In Arkansas and eastern Oklahoma, as an early adolescent, many a late night I had stumbled into all-black juke joints in the middle of "the projects" to drink, listen to music, and dance with swagger. Never, though, had I seen funk and soul tunes (or any other) shake the walls down like those performed by James Brown and the

Famous Flames at the Tulsa Convention Center. And never had I acted out so passionately, freely, and unpretentiously to what amounted to black music and shameless dancing. It was berserk!

Conked hair, dressed in all white, tunic to patent leather–tipped toes, Brown had a rapport with the screaming audience that was on full display when he performed his rhythm and blues hit "Please Please Please." He shouted the words as if emotionally injured by a crowd of lovers before him. With theatrical timing, toward the song's end he kneeled, appearing to be on the verge of falling over in the fetal position, only to be rescued and phoenix-like brought to his feet by the "cape man" to finish the set: *Honey please don't go / Ha, I love you so, please, please / Please, please don't go.* Five thousand fans, more black than white, all entering through the same door, danced together, pumping the pelvis with sweaty abandon, up and down the aisles and bleacher seats—until the Godfather of Soul sang, shouted, spun, shuffled, moon-walked, and knee-dropped to his final curtain call. A true shaman, Papa and his big band sound gave us all a brand-new bag that evening.

Sharing the joys and emotions of music and song with others is as old as time. It stays with you. Emma Goldman, a kindred spirit, once said, "If there is no dancing at the revolution, I ain't coming."

Rebellion and Disillusion

Part Two

Hell Raisin'

Chapter Five

BY MY FIRST YEAR OF HIGH SCHOOL, bad hooch, budding rap sheets, late night poker games, hot checks, hockshops, blowing off school, mindless cruising, brawling, and a handful of other dunderhead diversions had become my calling cards. My face and head had been stitched in three places, my nose and jaw broken…all before I had hair on my chest. Drinking protein-shake meals through a straw with a wired jaw ain't all it's cracked up to be.

Greg wasn't acting much better. One of his more celebrated exploits occurred at age fourteen when he appropriated our only surefire weekend ticket out on the town—a beat-up 1959 Volkswagen Bug left by my mother. (She had skedaddled in a new Swedish-made Saab that Doc bought her as a signing bonus.) Greg's early Sunday morning joy ride in her hand-me-down lasted a mere ten minutes before he managed to roll and total our shared wheels on one of Fort Smith's dead man's curves. No coincidence it was across the street from his girlfriend, Janie Bryant. He staggered away, dodging the cops, bourbon drunk—compliments of Dad's back-of-the-pots-and-pans cabinet stash.

Stan and I found Greg slinking in through his bedroom window at daybreak, feigning sleep, wrapping his head under the covers. His face looked all beat to rags. He stood up, mistook the closet for the can, then bounced his way down the halls and out to the garage and puked in the washing machine. It was hard to be mad at Greg.

Stan, on the surface, played it straight. He had a steady gal most of the time, made good grades, and was active in school academic clubs. But all wasn't cricket with him. Never was. Fits of rage and flip outs targeting Greg or me occurred too often. But we were all young and forgiving, willing to move on. The next day after a blowup we would push aside what had happened and be brothers again, connecting until the next collision. From early on, Stan was also our Judas goat: He had a nose for mischief, and Greg and I would follow him off the side of a cliff to make sure we were in on it too.

Running from the cops, versus not running, became a no brainer for me and my rebellious friends. Cops wore blacks boots and were generally slow. Alternatively, we were all blessed with rabbit blood and good getaway gams. My zero hour was the night J. Thomas ordered me out of Andy Core's car and told me I was "under arrest for minor possession of beer." Before he finished that sentence, faster than you could say Peter Rabbit, I told him to fuck off and fled. He didn't take it well. In a show of what I thought of as bad sportsmanship, he furiously hurled some sharp pointed adjectives, nouns, and flat-out threats: "You pissant pussy, I'll whip your mongrel renegade motherfucking ass." When words failed him, the twitchy-trigger-finger son of a bitch continued chasing me down Towson Avenue, past the Little Buckhorn Bar and Peno Robinson's motel, firing warning shots into the night air.

Gamely as the lead-footed bozo tried, he soon lost my trail and wasted no time calling in two siren-blaring backups, with spotlights raking through the darkness, to smoke me out while I curled up like a trapped snake in the damp crawlspace of a careworn house behind Peno's. After a few hours, I made my way through the alleyways and backstreets to Trucker's Paradise at the Towson Avenue and Zero Street curve, rewarding my successful escape with the truck stop's *pièce de résistance*, a two-for-one chicken-fried steak with mashed potatoes and gravy.

Well-timed friends Johnny Berry and Steve Tyler showed up for the same late-night feedbag and took me out of the danger zone. The hounds of justice caught up with me two days later at my dad's house on Pendell Lane. It's reasonable to surmise that Andy's uncle, lawyer Ben Core, had dropped a dime on me for a lighter sentence for his nephew. I'd run out of rabbit's blood. Near the giant magnolia tree in the front yard, as four cops buzzed around me like hornets, I was cuffed and taken to jail for resisting arrest and minor possession of alcohol. The city was safe again.

Growing up, I was told there were a few nondrinkers in Fort Smith, but I never personally met any of them. They had to be an army, though. It certainly took more than a few Sabbatarian crusaders to get blue laws passed prohibiting the sale of alcohol on Sunday, and more ambitiously, to completely vote out alcohol sales in Fort Smith's surrounding counties. A snarl of Billy Sunday types in the whereabouts of Grand Avenue Baptist Church in cahoots with the monopolist-minded liquor store owners were the likely culprits. Even so, Prohibition was long gone and balls-to-the-wall boozing on weekend nights in Fort Smith was considered high art, if not a grassroots form of patriotism and spiritualism, the *genii locorum*. Going to one's reward by bingeing or suicide drinking is still considered by most Fort Smithians to be as natural as dying of heart disease or cancer. To be sure, many friends and some family members were offended and thought of it as breaking ranks if you weren't drunk by noon on weekends.

On Thanksgiving eve of 1967, Johnny Berry throttled his blue-green, black vinyl–topped spanking new GTO out of Nation's Drive-In onto Rogers Avenue. It was after 11:00 o'clock, past closing time. Judy, the sailor-tongued carhop and part-time squeeze of the owner Bill Lovett, had chased us and Drew Warner off the payoff pinball machines and locked up. We had started on the machines earlier in the day at Steve's APCO, moved over to Pagliaccis in the early evening, taken a social break at the Dairy Grand, and finished up banging away at Nation's. Drew, who carried a good fake ID, took off in his car toward downtown, headed to the Band Box to see a shoeless Bobby Don Selby sing "Cherry Pie." I was riding shotgun with Johnny, unbuckled. We had just polished three Thunder Beers, a concoction with kick: two parts Busch tall boy, one part Thunder Bird wine. Four of those and you'll talk to God. We had had three. Johnny was pie-eyed on the first one. As we turned by the Bird Sanctuary on South 31st Street, where I tasted forbidden fruit for the first time with another fourteen-year old, Johnny raised the RPMs. While I was recounting with relish that romp in the bushes—*she slipped her panties aside, took my Johnson in hand, and delicately slid it pearl-deep inside of her moister oyster...*—bam, screech, holy fuck!

Out of the darkness, a 1964 Delta 98 had made a quick left turn into the rear side of Johnny's new ride. No time to react. We careened off the road at full throttle, smashing head-on into a giant oak tree, narrowly missing Fred Buford's bedroom at the corner of Reeder and 31st Street. My face planted straight ahead into the windshield, leaving a gaping hole shaped perfectly to my noggin. A cloudburst of blood splattered the windshield, pooling in my lap and the bucket seat.

Hearing the crash, Fred Buford turned up on the double in his back yard. According to Johnny, Fred fessed up to having a snoot full and said he couldn't drive me to the hospital. Returning to the house, he phoned the police and my dad. In the interval, Ms. Lucie Yantis Waddy, who was Drew's sixty-something spinster aunt and director of the local Red Cross chapter, bailed out of her car, staggering into the street, dazed and confused. She had a few scrapes on her head, but nothing more serious than being drunker than a boiled owl. Thirty minutes on, she registered .18 on the breathalyzer—which earned her a four-hour stretch in the drunk tank.

At the same time, a carload of Dairy Grand chicks came upon the wreck scene. They quickly recognized Johnny's car and (rashly) piled out to help. We'd all been drinking Thunder Beers earlier. Fred had already assisted in getting me, slightly in shock, to lie down in his back yard. My nose was badly broken, face lacerated in several places and pocked with shattered glass. The girls, half-crocked, decided to eat lipstick before the cops arrived. They said it would mask the alcohol breath, so Johnny ate a tube of ruby red, too. It worked, lucky boy: No cops up his ass and not a scratch on his baby face. At some point, I wondered if Johnny hadn't been wearing crosses and garlic around his neck. This was the second occasion he had gone uninjured and I took the hit: The first incident was a fight he started at the Dairy Grand. I came away with a broken jaw then, and now a smashed-up face in a car he was driving.

Dad arrived from Pendell Lane, a few blocks south, through the alleyway. He was sticking to the shadows, having taken house-drunk that night. Once out of the car, he asked Fred, a church-going friend of the family, to call an ambulance. He was worried the cops would get a whiff of him.

By now, it was midnight. The ambulance driver whisked me into the Sparks emergency room on a stretcher. Smelling of whiskey, Dr. Harold Richards arrived moments later from a cocktail party in a seersucker suit and a pair of two-tone doctor shoes. With dispatch, he removed the shards from my face, stitched up my eye and nose, and, for all I know, after making a sudden exit, returned to the cocktail party. He never set the broken nose. His hooched up handiwork left me with a scar across the bridge of that broken nose the size and shape of a well-fed caterpillar.

In the ensuing weeks, my nose bone began to jut port-wise. It migrated a little more each year, swelling and reddening the twelve-legged-pest stitch marks. Wise guy friends like Mark Stouffer would greet me by saying, "Phil, get that damn caterpillar off your nose."

Cheap shots by a spinster do-gooder and a drunk surgeon had left me with a wonky nose, scarred like a prize fighter.

After several months, and a couple more direct hits, I underwent reconstructive surgery, performed in the cold light of morning, by Dr. William Forrest, a sober cosmetic surgeon in Oklahoma City. The mundane upshot of that nothing-burger, holiday Wednesday night way back in the 1960s was that the whole goddamn city was higher than a Georgia pine. Liquor-ridden, marinated in gin, rum, whiskey, moonshine, Milwaukee's Best and Anheuser Busch's finest, that's the way my hometown rolled, recorded again and again in the tablets of time. Generation unto generation.

"There is no Sunday west of St. Louis," goes the saying, "and there is no God west of Fort Smith." Founded as a garrison in 1817 on the banks of the Arkansas River, Fort Smith's original mission was to make peace between the westward-migrating Cherokees, pushed out of their tribal lands in Georgia, Tennessee, and the Carolinas by white settlers, and the Osage Nation, whose wise and warlike chiefs feared the fate and religious force of Jefferson's westward ho. Their fears were not misplaced. In 1830, Congress passed the Indian Removal Act. Before long, the U.S. government drove the footbound, Five Civilized Tribes—Choctaw, Chickasaw, Seminole, Creek, and Cherokee—out of their ancestral homelands and herded 60,000 people like a colony of feral dogs on a deadly journey known as the "Trail of Tears." One in five did not survive. Crossing from the south and east into what was designated as Indian Territory (present-day Oklahoma), emigrating tribes encountered Fort Smith as the pivotal last supply depot, civilization's last stand as it were.

At the time, from a few miles west of Fort Smith all the way across the southern plains, the power of horsebound and hostile bands of Comanches was inviolate. The interior of Africa, it has been said, would not have been less known or understood.

In the same way nature abhors a vacuum, the torch-bearers of Manifest Destiny disdained chaos and criminality. After the Civil War, the South faced fiscal ruin and a sorry state of disorder and discontent, ideal circumstances for lawless gangs to flourish as the face of frontier justice. Former slaves had also flocked to Indian Territory in hopes of forming a state for blacks, settling in more than fifty towns in the Cherokee and Choctaw Nations. One of those freedmen penned a blues song: "Going to the Nation/Going to the Territory." Soon enough, Indian Territory provided a safe haven for marauding non-Indian outlaws to escape and hide out, beyond the reach of tribal law and the resources of the U.S. Marshals Service. Newspapers began referring to these badlands as "Robbers Roost" and "Land of the Six Gun." These were desperate times in which many of these renegades would split you like a chicken if there was a dollar in it. The almost unchecked lawlessness persisted until President Ulysses S. Grant garrisoned more troops in the region and appointed a new federal judge, Isaac C. Parker, to the Western District of Arkansas in Fort Smith.

His first courtroom was located above the Hole in the Wall saloon. In due course, Parker, a respected and feared jurist and politician who sported a brown billy goat beard, earned a reputation as the "Hanging Judge." This in a town that had long been known as "Hell on the Border" for the wretched, overcrowded conditions of its jailhouse. As if a high holy day, he swung six at once in September of 1875 while curious ticket-holding spectators sang "Amazing Grace," vendors hawked hot tamales, and hucksters sold sections of the hanging rope as souvenirs. Bad hombres of the highest order met their maker on Parker's gallows, often with names as colorful as their crimes were cruel—Jack Spaniard, Lucky Davis, Sinker Wilson, Colorado Bill Wiley, Cherokee Bill, Abler and Amos Manley.

Fort Smith has enshrined the judge's whitewashed gallows as its main historical attraction. There is no such memorial a few blocks from those gallows where a white mob hanged a black man. At the risk of dwelling on the contrasts with our frontier neighbor and counterpart, if St. Louis was the Gateway to the West, Fort Smith was its side door.

Fort Smith saw progress, but vestiges remained that transformed old frontier customs into contemporary laws of conduct. For the foreseeable future, past and present were often one in the same.

What is now called Fort Chaffee, used as a German prisoner-of-war camp during World War II and as a training base for the 6th Armored Division and later the 100th Infantry, is a couple of miles east of Fort Smith. Alas, in 1962, Secretary of Defense Robert McNamara closed Fort Chaffee as an active-duty infantry training center. Left behind was a skeleton crew of regular army to manage and maintain the base. Fort Smith businesses, particularly those located on Garrison, once chock-a-block with bars, restaurants, retailers, and cathouses, shuttered left and right with the mass exodus of so many good-paying customers.

Still, it took more than a decade for Fort Smith's finest brothels—Como, Ozark, St. Charles, Palace, and Rex Rooms—to call it a wrap and shut their doors. The Como, in 1975, was the last to do so. *Hustler* magazine, owned by Larry Flynt, who had recently published nude beach shots of former first lady Jackie Kennedy, ran a story on the fabled house of ill repute with a photo of a sign on the shuttered front door: *Closed. Beat it.*

Well into the '60s, Moffett, Oklahoma, a short hop across the Arkansas River from Fort Smith, was the only town completely off limits to active duty military in the U.S. Located in Sequoyah County, where Pretty Boy Floyd's brother E. W. Floyd had been a nine-term sheriff, it was a Klondike town with all the sin but without the gold. Once forbidden-fruit magnets for hundreds of hormone-soused GIs, Moffett's gambling houses, pole dancing joints, whorehouses, and liquor stores in my high school years were wriggling in their last throes of peddling anything-goes decadence. Nothing was on the square. Regular rules did not apply. If Moffett had had a town motto it would have read: Fuck You, Our Way or the Highway.

These fleshpots, blind pigs, and gaming dens, the innards of a frontier town's soul, were my crowd's own small-town Sodom and Gomorrah. My dad, as county agent, organized several local 4-H Clubs (Head, Heart, Hands, and Health) in the '50s and '60s. Quite the opposite, my rebellious crowd boastfully took up the knightly code of the 4-F Club: Fight, Fuck, Fast Cars, Fifth of Whiskey. We all had a nose for nonsense, ears that were deaf to the squish of bullshit, eyes blinded to destiny, mouths battened to bigotry, and cocks aimed north to any cradle of friendly thighs. Between desire and actions fell no shadow.

It was not uncommon during my years of juvenile dementia to drop off our pretty-faced debutante darlings early and class up for a late-night walk on the wild side in the sinks of Moffett. It was the norm on most weekends to run into my Dad's Rotary Club friends, Elmer Smith, Bill Eads, and Bobby Cutting, at these haunts. Elmer and Bobby were also dads, respectively, of two of my best running buddies, Greg and Randy. After twenty years of patronage, the trio were well known for possessing double the drinking indefatigability of most men. They were treated like local royalty, always escorted to a favorite booth by the grifter types acting as doormen. Though Bobby was more of a barroom hail-fellow-well-met than a brawler, Elmer and Bill were big guys and tough as nails. They had both been defensive tackles for the celebrated Coach John Barnhill at the University of Arkansas. If called upon, they could bang some heads in a bar but were more likely to buy a round to keep the peace.

My crowd would often kick off at Eddie Mondier's Private Club, a puke-twice-and-show-your-razor-to-get-in kind of joint. Closing time was whenever. Eddie's co-owner, Buddy Walker, a jowly, cigar-smoking man in a secondhand suit with no tie, was Moffett's equivalent of a mob boss. Gambling, if you could call it that, went on till customers tired of losing to gaffed wheels, marked decks, loaded dice, juiced tables, and crooked croupiers. The house shill, Charlie Hatfield, lanky and stylish in his pleated Gant shirts, was often dealt a pat hand, while routinely doubling down on his winning ways by taking home the waitress of his choice. Walker's main tough, boxman Duck Lackey, a Vegas type with the instincts of a gut fighter and a lattice of scars across his face to show for it, wore a visor, red bowtie, black vest, and white shirt. Duck's stick man, Pat Barker, who also refereed the cockfights on Sunday morning next door to the Shady Grove juke joint, kept up a pitched vibrato at the craps table: *One down, look around. Craps six, ace he lost the race. Snake eyes, take the line, pay the Don't and Field.*

If by chance lady luck filled your pockets, with indignation you were accused of cheating. Late one Saturday night, Elmer Smith was sitting next to me at the poker table. The dealer was shorting the pot and I'd seen him palm a card in five-card stud that I should have won but instead lost the whole ball of wax. In the enveloping din and glare, I leaned over to Elmer and whispered, "The game is crooked." He bent over my way and said under his breath, "Crooked as a dog's hind leg, but it's the only game in town." Like carnies at the two-headed cow and hermaphrodite tent, the dealer's job had less to do with holding all the aces and palming cards from the bottom of the deck and more about lying with a straight face.

From Eddie's it was a short stagger over to the Top Hat for more watered-down whiskey and talking it up with the G-string and pasties-covered pole dancers. Those Top Hat girls, whose cheap perfume lay heavy in the air, all tended to claim Louisiana or Texas roots. But why wouldn't an easy make from Sallisaw—twenty miles west—prefer that migratory plumage? Drawing too much attention, acting out rambunctiously among the heaving breasts and lunging haunches, dancing with brio, trying to get something for nothing, I could be my own worst enemy in the hurly-burly of clip joints like the Top Hat. If "Bull" Stouffer, chief protector of my primate group, who was stronger and tougher than Hercules and Mike Fink put together and feared nothing on two legs, weren't with me, my practice was to always palm a buck or two to the bouncer, Gary Isaacs. If things got hairy he would have my back.

Driving out of this province of anarchy was yet another menacing affair. We were never sure till we got to the crossroads if we'd turn right toward the bridge and home or left and go a short piece to piss on or pay homage to Pretty Boy Floyd's grave at Akins Cemetery near Sallisaw, ground on which thousands had gathered for the Robin Hood outlaw's funeral. Some say the largest in the history of Oklahoma. "He was one of us," admirers of Pretty Boy would say. "Never got above his raising." Many fans have paid tribute at the well-trodden gravesite by leaving casings from .45 automatics, Pretty Boy's chosen handgun. Jim Beatty, the cemetery's caretaker, who was raised up near Akins like Pretty Boy, told me on one of those forays out of Moffett that on the day of the funeral, Highway 101, a dirt road at the time, looked like a cattle stampede for all the dust clouds raised. As far as the eye could see, he said, horses, carts, bicycles, tin lizzies, tractors, and foot traffic proceeded to the cemetery to pay their respects.

Beneath a shady elm tree by Pretty Boy's grave, one evening Beatty also imparted that, back in the day, when Pretty Boy robbed a bank, he would often ask for the mortgage documents and then destroy them. Hard to tell everything that was certified true, but the cemetery keeper passed along many more fine tales of the fugitive rock star, all of a piece with local lore. Woody Guthrie codified the Robin Hood legend when he wrote the tribute song, "Pretty Boy Floyd": If you'll gather 'round me children / A story I will tell / 'Bout Pretty Boy Floyd, an outlaw / Oklahoma knew him well.

From the cemetery, depending on Bull Stouffer's whim if he was driving, we might continue on west to Tulsa and Greenwood and Archer streets for some "brown sugar." Or, more times than not, just circle back to Fort Smith.

Sonny Gillam, a bear of a man who fit the stereotype of a Southern sheriff, ruled Moffett with an iron fist and an open hand. The across-the-bridge lawlessness of Gillam was arguably equal to the infamous Judge Roy Bean's west-of-the-Pecos venality. Gillam was not shy about letting his siren wail and putting those blue lights of bad luck on my crowd's fresh-polished fast cars. Rather than making a formal arrest for underage drinking or any number of other charges, real or imagined, he'd shake us down. We didn't take it personal: Sonny was democratic in his venality. The trick was to make your getaway while he was hosing another Fort Smith–bound car of revelers.

Once over the bridge and beyond Sonny's tollgate, we would honk and screech like a murder of crows coming to roost. On the Fort Smith side of the river bottoms, once a red-light district inhabited by the likes of brothel owner Pearl Starr, winos usually jungled up around fires, a hobo camp—a tin can circle full of "canned heat"–drinking drifters. The spines and boxcars were fifty yards away.

Funds permitting, we horndogs might make one last pit stop at the Como or Palace or Ozark or one of the other classy Garrison Avenue brothels. If we did, with the urgency of sailors, the "love-making" usually played out in thirty glorious seconds at sunrise on Sunday morning with yet another thirty-year-old Louisiana town trollop or blowsy Arkansas pulp mill casualty. Judging by their twangs, they were all raw-boned country girls, raised on a playground of roosters chasing hens, bulls mounting cows, boars after sows, partiers of the cornfields, rougher than corn cobs. Eyes often hollowed from a vale of tears, skin sallow as a cave salamander from long days of working and living in sunless rooms that smelled year around of stale sex. After a while it saddened me that they all seemed to fit a certain profile of rural Southern poverty.

My suspicion was that as early adolescents any given one of them could shoe a plow horse, milk a cow, wring a chicken's neck, or spit in the face of a coiled cottonmouth before putting on some blue eye liner and ratting their hair to look like ripe wheat prior to catching the school bus. There was certainly no shortage of barnyard spunk as the chemise and panty parade came down in the brothel's gloom-filled reception area. They presented themselves with cloaking names like Dallas, Angel, Dixie, Cherry, or Candy. And, there was no denying I amounted to no more than a dressed-up, two-legged farm animal capable of coughing up, at tops, a five-spot for the business at hand. "Nothing free here but the grace of God," Big John, a black dude working the desk at the Ozark, told me more than once.

The cheap-perfumed chippie of my choosing would, as a rule, command me over to the confessional lighting of the basin for a VD inspection. Passing the 'ol tallywhacker over the sink to her like a baton, it was the seductive interlude in which confidences, boasts, fears, and backstories poured forth, accompanied by a soapy washing, bringing me to near climax before "lady love" indifferently parted her loins to finish off my passion in lightning time. It was all very nice and at the same time really dreadful. If her earth moved as mine had, there was no trembling body or guttural fireworks or other faked satisfaction to show for it. Douche, douche, down the drain, next, one after another. Special sex was hard to come by.

More often than not, the circle was unbroken when five hours later I picked up my choir-girl date and arrived at First United Methodist right about eleven, as church bells pealed out across town. With decorous solemnity, we would take a back-pew balcony perch among the do-right crowd, the genteel kind of townspeople with social heft who wouldn't look out of place in a Dutch Masters painting. There were always a few familiar faces from the night before who, like me, might have had a nip before brushing their teeth that morning. Known as the most segregated hour in America, showing up for church, imbibing a dose or two of religion, the thinking went, made better men out of us.

Truth was, as it turns out, Hell on the Border, Moffett Mores, and Primates Unplugged gushed through my veins like ditchwater in a dark, sulfurous-clouded alleyway. Penitence and self-loathing during those Sunday morning time sucks was customary in those days, but it was about all I could muster. The rest of the week, or for that matter the rest of the day, cleaning up, slowing down, or reversing course were lofty aspirations for some but not necessarily me. Fort Smith had imprinted on me a feral lifestyle no different from a mama baboon teaching her young to mate, forage, and fight.

A Moveable Feast

Chapter Six

YEARS BEFORE I READ *A Moveable Feast* in the early '70s I was already acquainted with certain male rituals from Ernest Hemingway's bohemian days. The experiences had been adding up. By age fifteen, I knew by heart *Hoyle's Rules of Poker,* had a bookie, played untrained bridge, read the *Daily Racing Form* with my dad, shot craps, could rattle off the special lingo of the devil's bones (eighter from Decatur), and readily quoted lines and recalled shots of the self-assured Minnesota Fats against hotshot "Fast Eddie" Felson in the high-stakes pool shooting drama *The Hustler.* As a cheap imitation, my passions emerged in full form with more envy than the actual success or skills of Fats and Fast Eddie. There were, however, a few fine days when we all fed at the same trough.

Early on, betting on the come was my idea of strategic financial planning. I never made it to the parimutuel booths at Paris's Longchamp Racecourse as Hemingway often did, and certainly didn't have the amateur handicapper's luck of his first wife Hadley, as he described in a letter to Gertrude Stein and Alice B. Toklas: "I get up at dawn and study the dope-sheet, and then after my brain has cracked under the strain, Mrs. Hemingway, with about three cocktails and an indelible pen to aid her, picks winners as easy as cracking peanut shucks. With the aid of her alcoholic clairvoyance and an old friend of mine that I think sleeps with horses, we've had 17 winners out of 21 starts."

105

Such a streak on my turf at Oaklawn Park in Hot Springs, Arkansas, was unheard of. But I, along with friends Leo "Speedy" Byrum and Steve Tyler, didn't rule it out. It was no secret that, with the right shake of moxie and gut feeling, luck could be raised to an art form.

More than a few of our touts hung out on the apron near the sixteenth pole, always a revolving gate of railbirds, many of whom occupied the late-night benches at the downtown Greyhound bus station: pickpockets, pimps, dope fiends, hippies, bikers, country jakes, shiftless sportifs, hucksters on the skids, and suspicious out-of-staters. Inclined to half-baked schemes, this motley bunch of misfits bet between races, literally, on which direction a bird on a wire might fly.

Taking in all the not-born-yesterday patois around me, there I was, in demimonde Hot Springs, at age sixteen, on March 11, 1968, in the sixth race, with a third share on a two-dollar T. Town Tony win ticket. At the time, the tote board at Oaklawn Park only registered two digits. T. Town Tony, a chestnut three-year old stallion, went off at around 102-1, a sucker bet.

Thing was, that day Speedy had picked up at the "corned beef" condiments stand of the Daily Double Deli what he called "solid intel" from a twenty-something-year-old woman named Christie, whom he nicknamed Shortcakes, which was to say she was petite and cute. Shortcakes supposedly clocked horses in the morning and worked the parimutuel window nearest the paddock in the afternoon. Yet when pressed, Speedy came half-clean: She hadn't actually clocked T. Town Tony that morning or any other morning. Decked out in high, black leather boots, matching hot pants, heavy on the makeup, and hair high—creating the illusion of being taller than five feet—Shortcakes had merely laid a sly wink on Speedy from behind her fake-jewel-rimmed harlequins, while confiding that she knew people who knew people who had clocked T. Town Tony. To the rest of us, it sounded more like flirting, or a tomcat catching the scent, than three-times-removed "late mail" intended to bolster confidence in Speedy's otherwise solid early hunch. I'll give it to Speedy, though. Something about Shortcakes and her cat glasses conveyed a tarot card reader's air of authority and intuition, the gift of always having the answers.

Certainly, our bet didn't look good on paper. Reality was that T. Town Tony was Eastern Oklahoma bred, had been trained on the cheap, and had never won a race. On this day, he had an outside post position against a full field.

Trainer Glenn Gorbet, who had worked the thoroughbred circuit since the late 1920s, from Hot Springs to Havana, once told me: "Buy the best and hire the best or go broke chasing dreams." With our wager on T. Town Tony, we were chasing the dream with a ghost of a chance. The odds said as much. Apart from Shortcakes's shady intel and some back-of-the-envelope math, all we had favoring us, according to the racing form, was the butter-mud slick and sloshy track. Even that advantage faded as the pelting rainfall turned into a lazy mist, and then a weightless spritz.

In anticipation of losing, with our finances running on fumes, we plotted how to scare up beer and gas money to get home. Working options included liberating a case of empty Coke bottles, finding a fence for the stolen wire wheels in Speedy's trunk, or whipping out the "Arkansas credit card"—a siphon hose and gas can.

Our plans had showed more foresight on our previous foray to the track. We paid up front for a bungalow at the Cottage Courts on Park Avenue when we hit town. Problem was, at five the next morning, we woke up to a mattress fire with white smoke engulfing the room. The bottom of the only trash can in the room was rusted out, leaving us with no vessel that held water to extinguish the fire. We pooled our marbles and did the only thing our young booze-addled minds could think of at the moment: drag the smoldering mattress out into the courtyard and sound the alarm by gunning Speedy's souped-up Fairlane out of there, shooting arcs of decorative white pea gravel everywhere, pinging cars and rooftops like hail as we headed for the hills.

Speedy had checked in to the Cottage Courts under a fake name, Barry Bragg, a well-known gambler and racetrack regular from Fort Smith. Small chance the pension-age motel managers would catch up with us, demanding an inflated ransom for the lumpy, cum-and-piss-stained mattress that was surely a full-on bonfire by the time we turned up Ouachita Avenue and cleared town that Sunday morning.

Paying for our shenanigans was always a catch-as-catch-can affair, a dissonance between adolescent entitlement and available means. None of our dads made as much as ten thousand bucks a year, and no one's mom worked a paying job. My family of seven lived on the equivalent of a teacher's salary. Steve was the prodigal preacher's son. Speedy's dad managed a small public golf course, on which gambling skills and the game of patience married up perfectly.

Depending on the day of the week, what Steve, Speedy, and I thought of as cash flow added up to what was given, earned, won, or taken. An empty gas tank and lint-bare pockets gave the voice of the devil's advocate an extra octave or two. Of course, we all knew a win by T. Town Tony would change that sorry, down-and-out thinking.

We watched in agony from the crack of the starter's pistol to the final turn of the race. It was neck-and-neck, down-to-the-wire horse racing. At the top of the homestretch T. Town Tony broke from the pack and swung wide. Chic Anderson's inimitable voice from the announcer's booth boomed above the cry of the crowd. Stretching his call with pitch-perfect synchronicity to the horse's homestretch stride, Anderson let rip, "Teee-Toowwn-Toonee has taaaken the leeed." It was life at its fullest, lungs filled, living on a prayer, as T. Town Tony thundered past the woebegones-on-the-rail with a three-length lead. The railbird crowd roared above the pack of pounding hoofs as the long-shot chestnut with the heart of the great Seabiscuit all but leapt across the finish line. The three of us whooped and yelled and charged through the crowd to the closest betting window. We collected $205.80, the highest two-dollar win ticket payoff in Oaklawn's history.

Like Hemingway, we became hooked on the celebration. Easy come, easy go. Money is everything when you don't have it. When you do, it burns a hole in your pocket. Penury to plenty; winner, winner, chicken dinner!

Speedy, two years my senior, played school boy golf, sported a hounds-tooth Gatsby cap, had traveled to many a country club tournament, and had seen the inside of more than a few fancy dining joints. The high life of Hot Springs for this country club charm guy was his home course, and the historic Arlington Hotel lobby bar was the 19th hole. By coincidence, Steve, who attended the Roman Catholic Cascia Hall Preparatory School in Tulsa, had arranged to meet up with a former classmate from Chicago at the Arlington.

Behind Rocky's Corner, where Speedy's Fairlane was parked, we stumbled upon Shortcakes. She was snuggled up to a pony-tailed geezer in a tie-dye tee-shirt, bib overalls, and red-white-and-blue leather boots. It took Shortcakes a minute to register who we were, then she smiled, waved a wadded handful of bills in our direction, and declared, "It's easy to make money in America." She then turned her back to us, switching gears to pitch a would-be customer.

Working from the tailgate of a '50s-vintage Ford pickup, Shortcakes and the proto-hippie were selling black velvet paintings of Marilyn Monroe and Jesus Christ steering a boat with a backdrop that bore a striking resemblance to the Beacon Manor high-rise apartments and the Highway 70 bridge on Lake Hamilton. Speedy, shrugging off the dissing, grumbled aloud, "Jesus meets Marilyn Monroe behind Rocky's. What's that all about?"

Ten minutes later, Joe Fusco Jr. awaited us on the Central Avenue sidewalk below the twin towers of the century-old, Spanish Revivalist–style Arlington. He and Steve yee-hawed upon seeing each other. Joe came across as what he was, an exuberant big guy with a soft heart and a deft personal manner. Six foot three, wide-shouldered, with short-cropped black hair, he was smartly dressed in a starched Oxford shirt, pleated pants, and shiny, pointed black shoes. Of southern Italian heritage, he spoke with precision in a thick Chicago accent, full of nasal timbre.

The manager had watched us from the mezzanine, scurrying down the curved marble stairway to be at the front desk, as we hooted and grab-assed our way in. He saw us as an unruly party of prepped-up, low-bred philistines, fresh out of the hills and hollers, as he conveyed with his watchful eyes and gung-ho body language. Had to know at first glance that we were not of age to drink—and should certainly not to be allowed to do so openly in the airy, grand elegance of the famous lobby bar.

Joe thought differently. He directed us to a gold-leafed four-top. Two Fancy Dans in white shoes and Brooks Brothers blue blazers sat an arm's length away. Never glancing our way, the old sports drank French brandy from crystal decanters, fussily sniffing and shaking their goldfish-bowl glasses from side-to-side between sips.

We faced the bar and a whimsical Edenic mural of tropical pastels, shaded in Granny Smith–apple green. Below the mural, two "colored" waiters, liveried in floppy single-breasted black dinner jackets, pressed white shirts, and black bowties, polished fresh glasses. An air of gentle decay fell over the bar's tall arched windows, high curved ceilings, and corn-colored walls, all traced in flourishes of ornate plaster. Hurrying over to our table, in a froggy voice, the manager commanded one of the liveried waiters not to serve us alcohol. In this starchy residuum of yore, it wasn't a surprise move on his part given that I was, and very much looked, sixteen years old.

Joe Fusco came to his feet as if resolving conflict was his calling. He extended his hand and eased the manager around between a Christmas-tree-sized candelabra and a table of four manor-born, middle-aged women in festive hats, sipping novel umbrella drinks. In the bar side corner, the piano player spiritedly sang Al Jolson's cover of George Gershwin's first and biggest-selling hit, "Swanee." Joe's confab with the manager was drowned out. We could, however, see that he was doing most of the talking and that he was gesturing the way a mime artist does. The Fancy Dans suddenly dropped the self-regarding brandy ritual and came to their feet, arranging the two spare chairs with a cotillion-trained precision. Angling their way were two Southern belles accoutered like sisters in matching white sleeveless pant suits, bleach-blond hair in a French twist updo, dripping in Cartier gold and crisscrossed with tangerine clutches. They each flirtatiously cut their eyes our way before sliding gracefully into their chairs and turning on their good-girl etiquette for their beaux. Minutes later the manager appeared to enjoy a crystal moment, breaking into a smile and returning to our table. Letting bygones be bygones, he invited us to go downstairs to the English pub in which a bucket of cold beer awaited us. A victory of sorts, so Joe led the way.

The pub was perfect, more our style anyway: A smoke-filled, wood-paneled bar, with padded leather chairs, a level pool table, and the hubbub of salty small talk. Didn't even have to flash our Lowry-Alley-produced fake IDs—Selective Service cards all with the same name, Bernard Oscar Sherman, Birthdate: September 20, 1945. (Definitely tricky when we had to show them all at once.) Money-as-a-measuring-device had rescued us, though. On the turn of a dime that dark-clouded March day, we were big shots squared, like the Chicago fat cats who had long given cachet to hanging out at Oaklawn.

It soon came to light that Joe's dad owned Van Merritt Brewery Co. and several liquor distributorships in Chicago. Turns out he was a former close associate of Al Capone, and in 1931, had been indicted with Capone on 5,000 violations of federal prohibition laws. The Chicago Crime Commission tagged him Public Enemy No. 29. Arrested on several occasions, he was never convicted or served time for his underworld crimes. For the last eleven years, his official residence was a suite in the Chicago Conrad Hilton.

During racing season at Oaklawn Park, beginning in the 1930s, Joe Fusco Sr. snowbirded it south to the "Spa City." He stayed at the Arlington, bet the ponies, fraternized with fellow big fish mobsters, and strolled beneath the southern magnolias on Central Avenue to "take the waters" on Bathhouse Row. Creed, color, or criminal past mattered not. Hot Springs tradition was to throw down the welcome mat to all comers, especially high rollers.

For centuries, the Valley of the Vapors, the sacred mineral-rich thermal waters of the Caddo Indians, had been drawing those in need of healing rheumatism, cerebral palsy, piles, gout, constipation, diabetes, dropsy, skin woes, stress and whatever else. Following the money of the post–Civil War bathing craze, known as ablutomania, gambling houses and brothels opened. City officials spread their hands. Gun-toting sharpers and shit-kickers arrived from the defeated Confederate army and the lawless underworlds of East Texas, Chicago, Memphis and New Orleans. It was a prosperous time to be in the outlaw trade. In January of 1874, former Confederate "bushwhackers" Jesse and Frank James and the Younger brothers held up a stagecoach outside of Hot Springs. When the outlaws found out passenger G. R. Crump had fought for the Confederacy, they returned his possessions. A harbinger of the new brand of frontier justice taking hold in these parts.

Stephen Crane, noted American novelist and short story writer, who arrived in Hot Springs via the Diamond Joe Express in 1895, described the resinous air of Arkansas' pine belt and the stream that now runs under Central Avenue as "[looking] like a million glasses of lemon phosphate [brawling] over the rocks." As Crane's word spread about the Spa City and horse racing took off in the 1920s, "all men and moods" descended on Hot Springs, including America's most famous gangster, Al Capone, who once frequented Oaklawn Park, Bath

House Row, the Southern Club (casino), hootchy-kootchy joints, auction houses flogging real and fake diamonds, and the Arlington Hotel, a sybarite's dream of luxury and repose, all situated on Central Avenue. The Arlington and the Majestic, located at the intersection of Park and Central avenues, were also favorite spring training landing places for the Boston Red Sox and New York Yankees.

In those days, the city's open embrace of vice had the feel of nineteenth-century Dawson City on the down low in the Ouachita Mountains, smack dab in the buckle of America's Bible Belt. G-Man Melvin Purvis was nowhere to be found. Boss Gambler Mayor Leo Patrick McLaughlin controlled freewheeling politicians, police, and police fixers. "The mob was making much more in gambling than it ever had in the bootlegging trade," wrote David Hill in his book *The Vapors*. "For one thing there was no supply to smuggle. There was only probability, odds, chance. They were selling dreams to suckers. And the demand for dreams was insatiable."

The big shot mobsters arrived with their own bankrolls and bombast. As a rule, they all put up a law-abiding front while in town to avoid making headlines and drawing attention to themselves and the city's endemic palm-greasing and gangsterism.

Damon Runyon, the famous New York Prohibition-era newspaperman, known for assigning colorful nicknames to gangsters, dubbed Owney Madden, a notorious mob boss, the "Duke of the West Side." Before taking up residence in the Spa City, Madden killed half a dozen people in New York, served nine years in Sing Sing for manslaughter, promoted heavyweight boxing champions, dated Mae West, and ran the famous Cotton Club in Harlem. Ducking the limelight that followed his storied life, he married the local postmaster's daughter, Agnes Demby, played golf regularly at the Hot Springs Country Club, tended his flower garden at his modest home on West Grand Avenue, became a pigeon fancier, contributed handsomely to the local Boys Club and high school band, and backed off from assassinating his enemies.

With all that cover, when Owney's mobster friends, such as Lucky Luciano, the most wanted man in America, felt comfortable openly strolling the streets of Hot Springs, things started to get sticky. The press, FBI, rival factions, and Baptist do-gooders gradually threw the lid open on Owney's not so well-kept secrets: his stake in local gaming clubs and control of a national wire service. From the early '40s on, the affable, short-statured former Duke of the West Side, was aptly re-christened the "Arkansas Godfather."

After World War II, during the city's sordid heyday, my father and mother were married in Hot Springs on Central Avenue at the First Methodist Church. They honeymooned at the Arlington, drank Manhattans and danced at the Belvedere Country Club, picnicked in the infield at the races, took the waters at Quapaw Baths, and years later landed a table at the Vapors the night Tony Bennett first sang "I Left My Heart in San Francisco."

During that honeymoon weekend, downtown streets teemed with veterans, freshly rehabbed from the city's castle-like Army-Navy Hospital. One afternoon, my mom and dad were walking back to the Arlington from Bathhouse Row and watched in disbelief as brassy brothel owner Maxine Gregory drove her new girls like queens perched on the back of her pink convertible Cadillac in a rodeo parade down Central Avenue. Mom was embarrassed that Dad waved, as did several uniformed veterans. All the girls waved back.

The romantic version of snappily dressed mobsters, catch-me-if-you-can wise guys, not the respectable guests of the same era—FDR, Harry Truman, Lefty Grove, Smoky Joe Wood, or Babe Ruth, who in 1919 hit his first 500-foot home run, in Whittington Park—cemented the reputation of Hot Springs and the Arlington as the stuff of legend.

Into the late '60s, for big Joe Fusco and his mob associates—and for me and my new pal, Joe Fusco Jr.—the Valley of the Vapors remained a favorite sin-city getaway. Only months before our big win with T-Town Tony, newly elected governor Winthrop Rockefeller, who initially came to Arkansas on a lark, made good on his campaign promise to clean up Hot Springs once and for all, dispatching state troopers to destroy slot machines and poker, roulette, blackjack, and craps tables.

A villainous attitude, though, isn't so easy to scrub away. Hot Springs' fondness for vice, after a fashion, retreated to the shadows but didn't disappear. Pole dancing joints, back room brothels, and gambling parlors, horse bookies, and con artists continued to thrive down every alley of the white side of town and Malvern Avenue's Black Broadway. The Spa City absolutely had spots that couldn't be changed.

In the smoky basement bar of the Arlington hotel that afternoon, Speedy and I lured two butch-cut Phillips County planters into a nine-ball game for ten bucks apiece. Speedy, a dark-skinned bird who had the paunchy body type of Minnesota Fats, had adopted the pool shark's bantering style of play. For him, psychology went hand in hand with proper English and good shape in shooting pool. When he caught our challengers concentrating too much, he'd let go a bark of laughter and deadpan for all to hear, something like, "Well, Katy, bar the goddamn door. They're too good for us, Phil."

The chatter worked; he'd played them like a bow fiddle. On two occasions the chumps flat out choked, a miscue and a missed straight in, giving me a short run and Speedy an easy out to clear the table. Had their wives not arrived and the bar filled with a more genteel crowd, those burly farm boys might have broken some thumbs. They paid up alright, each throwing a sawbuck on the table as if flinging Cassius Clay jabs in our direction. Speedy shot back, "We're even-Stephen, boys. Let's do it again sometime." The older of the two got really sore, confronting Speedy, "This wasn't your first hustle, was it Jelly-Roll boy?" The taunt was backed up by an under-the-breath threat to go berserk.

Guzzling our ice-cold Buds, we rounded up Steve and Joe and warmly thanked the manager and bartender, both of whom we felt to be like family now. Drinks were on the house! As we toodle-ooed our way up the stairs and out the stately brass front door onto the veranda, we laid plans to see Joe the next weekend. Mood and money in motion, rolling like the rich swells, was a new kick in my bag of tricks.

Swept up in the moment, on Speedy's timetable and tour, we made our way to Coy's Steak House, situated on a side street off Bathhouse Row. Best in Arkansas, he assured us, as he dropped us like fat cats beneath the restaurant's porte-cocheres that, aesthetically speaking, could have been a gas station roof. A parking attendant greeted us and opened the car doors. As we entered, the maître de and two waitresses welcomed Speedy, asking about his golfing partners, Steve, Rick, and Jerry. "They couldn't make it," Speedy replied, pooching his belly out and rubbing his Gatsby cap on it like a pregnant lady trying to soothe a kicking baby. "But we'll eat their share."

It was early, so getting a table was no problem. Escorted to a corner booth, no sooner than we sat down, our waitress delivered a tin of saltine crackers with a house-made Thousand Island dipping sauce. After divining what a salad fork was and which bread plate belonged to me, the rest was easy. Speedy showed us the way, somewhat versed in the art of Arkansas fine dining, his mind brimming with the energy of a runaway horse, galloping through spending options and opportunities to make more at a T. Town Tony clip. We shared crab-stuffed mushrooms, which I picked at tentatively, and then ordered a bacon-wrapped filet mignon topped with a dollop of garlic butter and served with all the fixins', salad, baked potato, and biscuits with honey. The wine list was beyond Speedy's gourmand skill set, or anyone else's, so we stuck with what we knew, cold Bud.

Our usual dine-out splurge was truck stop food: a plate of chicken-fried steak and mashed potatoes smothered in a heavily peppered white gravy. But on this late afternoon at Coy's our taste buds were ignited like never before. As Steve remarked, it all "made your tongue slap your brains out." We ate like pigs, scarfing it all up. Only a smear of blood remained on any of our plates. The whole fancy pants feedbag, six bucks as I recall, struck me as a one-off. It was like a prison riot and we were sated to the gills on the warden's food.

After less than an hour at Coy's, we lit out for Little Rock, the opposite direction of home. Flush as sailors and with Speedy smelling more "action," as if life itself depended on it, our never-say-die Judas leader had hatched a new plan. We swung right off of Central onto Park Avenue, passing beneath the hulking Velda Rose Hotel and by the infamous Vapors nightclub (née casino), where comedian Brother Dave Gardner, known for his drawling schtick on stupid Southerners in Hot Springs sellin' healin' water to them brilliant Yankees, was headlining.

We paused briefly at the last stoplight on Park Avenue, before Speedy goosed it through a red, never looking back, bound for the 1968 State Basketball Championship Game at Barton Coliseum in Little Rock. Fort Smith's crosstown rivals, the Northside Grizzly Bears, were going up against the Southside Rebels (some things die hard). Speedy couldn't stand to miss out on a lead-pipe cinch. He hoped to make a killing.

On arrival in Little Rock, we sprung for a white-washed cottage at the Magnolia Inn on Roosevelt Avenue, near the coliseum and state fairgrounds. After filling the bathtub with iced-down Pabst Blue Ribbon and apple-flavored Boone's Farm, we were soon in the cottage's jonquil-filled garden hosting a pregame party of mostly familiar faces in town for the showdown. Giving up six points, Speedy was taking all bets against Northside.

As the pre-game alma maters were wrapping up, we double-timed it into Barton Coliseum, having promised to reconvene the party with three Little Rock chicks after the game. The atmosphere was charged with dueling performances of bands and spirit teams, not unlike a decade before, my only other evening at Barton, when the Ringling Brothers and Barnum & Bailey Circus was in town and the entire coliseum floor was taken up with monkeys, elephants, lions, clowns, acrobats, jugglers, fire breathers, and trapeze artists. Shards of that experience and memory and the attendant feelings of exhilaration came together as Speedy, Steve, and I settled into our ring-side seats for the next best thing to the Greatest Show on Earth.

Seconds before tipoff, Speedy booked two more bets with Rebel fans, Randy Cutting and Wimpy Tays, who sat near us behind the Northside bench. It was not easy for me to pick a side that evening given that I had played with almost everyone on both teams at one time or another and knew most of the cheerleaders. Between expulsions, I'd attended Northside. School spirit, however, had disappeared for me faster than spit on a hot skillet a year or so before when I checked out of sports. Run off, some said, but I was juking the rules, gravitating more towards *rebel* than role model.

The championship game was nip and tuck. The Bears, who had defeated the Rebels twice in regular season, and held a superior record, trailed the Rebels most of the night. Bears guard and childhood friend, Philip "Droop" Willcoxon, who typically played the role of facilitator, kept the game close by penetrating the Rebel defense, scoring several key baskets from around the elbow. By the fourth quarter, teammate Almer Lee, one of two African American phenoms who had recently transferred from Lincoln High School to the newly integrated Northside High School, helped even the contest.

In a late-game time-out, as the Southside band struck up "Dixie," the school's fight song, Darrell Cluck, costumed as Johnny-

Reb in blue and gray, joined the high-kicking, dancing Dixie Belles to rouse the crowd. Moments later, Northside's band, cheerleaders, pep squad, bear mascot, and fans responded: *Fighting for victory / Never give in / Fight till the end, boys / Fight and might will win…* The coliseum was on high heat. A real nail-biter, judging from Speedy who was chewing his down to the quick.

With four seconds to go, Jerry Jennings, the other half of the talented duo to transfer to Northside from Lincoln High School, sank a jumper from deep in the corner. The shot cleared my neighbor and good friend Robert Stephens's six-foot-five, fingertip reach by a hair's breadth. The win for the Bears was clinched, bedlam broke out, fans stormed the floor. Minutes later, the refs cleared the court and the clock ran down. Amid the celebratory cries and sobbing, Speedy ducked out. He had gone all in and booked over $200 in bets, laying off nothing. Odds were high that he would welsh. Final score, Northside 46, Southside 44.

A band of thunderstorms rolled in around midnight. When the chicks split in the wee hours, the lightning and thunderclaps had moved on and the rain was singing in soothing pitter-pats on the shingled rooftop. I woke up on a jonquil-littered floor around noon on Sunday cradling a bottle of apple-flavored Boone's Farm, whiffing scents of garlic and oregano from a half-eaten plate of Bruno's Little Italy meatballs on a chair next to me. The leftover meatballs were candled in lipstick-stained, stubbed out cigarettes. Foggy-headed and grainy-eyed, my mouth was so dry I was spitting cotton. Through a crack in the curtains, a slash of sunlight fell warm on my face. Speedy was snoring like a chainsaw, spread across the bed in his Pepto-Bismol-pink golf shirt and bleeding Indian madras pants. Steve was missing in action. My wheat jeans and white tee-shirt were mottled in mud, the effect suggesting a spotted mutt.

Checked my pockets first thing to dope out the damage. Still had fifty-five bucks of my one-third split of the T. Town Tony win ticket and the sawbuck share of the pool game. An ample stake, if the urge struck me, to light out for California. Outside, the sky was a wash of azure…without limit.

All this remains with you, moving through time. Feasts of memory echoing the way it was. The lament of youthful lust, the smile of lady luck, the glorious salad days, an empty-belly portal to life turning into a roman-candled, sky-is-the-limit evening. That's a moveable feast.

The Judge's Grudge

Chapter Seven

SOON AFTER THAT MOVEABLE FEAST epiphany, I did light out for California with three friends, passing VW vans of flower children breast feeding, cheeching, and waving the peace sign the entire 1,500-mile drive on Route 66. A procession of sorts leading to some mind-blowing Promised Land of boomer rebellion. We hung out the windows of our Ford sedan and flashed it back, digging the bohemian spirit of the moment. This being our first trip to the ocean, we beelined it to Santa Monica Beach, plopped down with an ice chest full of beer and soon passed out from the sleepless, 24-hour drive. Several hours later the rising tide slapped us awake. We were cooked like lobsters. That evening we prowled Sunset Boulevard, the world of the perfectly coifed Kookie Burns and *77 Sunset Strip*, or so we thought. Passersby jeeringly referred to us as the Bobbsey Twins for our conventional dress. We checked out the head shops, scored a matchbox, and dropped into *Whiskey a Go Go* where a local psychedelic rock band played like wizards, melting the paint off the walls. The ganja wafting in the air, the neon lights and cacophony of music, beeping horns with cars loaded with hippie chicks, and street crowds of shaggy-headed free spirits costumed in Day-Glo bell bottoms and harem pants, beaded necklaces and leather headbands, were simply surreal. It was a visage not likely to be forgotten, a dress rehearsal for things to come. Meanwhile, another very different procession of boomers awaited me.

Change happens, by design or not. I wish I could say I was a person of vision and chose the stars that I followed out of my ancestral home. That wasn't the case, though. The authority figures in my life reckoned that this failed-to-launch, morally bankrupt bad boy's only future was the Green Machine, the U.S. Army.

After my sixth or seventh arrest, I served four days in the county jail. The first day of that stretch, two trusties, Freaky Fink and Whitey Williams, both in for six months for probation violations, sized me up for assets with the hungry eyes of stray dogs before deciding I should join their ranks. The two-person, six-by-eight-foot trusty cell with a semi-private toilet and a creaky ceiling fan circulating the dank air was a step up from the sardine-tight, eight-person lockup. Three packs of Winston Reds, an Arnold Palmer windbreaker, an alligator belt, and a not-well-kept-secret sawbuck squirreled away in my Bass Weejuns were assets I thought of as negotiable. Small price of admission, for sure. Ladling out pannikins of greasy soup and a sop of brown gravy on white bread and holding a chair each evening in a less than genteel marked-deck poker game were markers of high jailhouse status. The first night I won handily. But surprise, surprise, Freaky's toothy grin conveyed. The goddamn fix was on. My fortunes turned abruptly on day three and four. The togged-up look vanished altogether. When the desk sergeant released me to my father, I was penniless, shoeless, beltless, and down to my tee shirt, shellacked from head to toe. Dad surely thought of me as looking the fool—wearing a snarl as I stepped away from the halcyon days of youth.

Mark Twain perhaps had me in his sights when he said, "There is nothing to be learned from the second kick of a mule." The gimlet-eyed Judge Cloninger, a molder of young men, had stared down at me witheringly and threatened to slap me with "serious jail time"—or the army—if seen again in his courtroom. Unchastened, if not spoiling for more run-ins, two weeks after that stint in jail and the judge's gaveled warning I was sitting with my dad on the long wooden benches in front of him again, charged with minor possession of alcohol and resisting arrest. Four nights before I had run like a sprinter while officer J. Thomas chased me and fired warning shots in the air as I so easily left him behind. A James Dean–worthy licking I gave J. Thomas, but thin gruel on this day in court. Bob Dylan knew the drill:

> *The judge, he holds a grudge*
> *He's going to call on you...*

When the judge called on me that day in Municipal Courtroom 201, with J. Thomas watching, still hotter than a pistol at having had to chase me, I chose the army before he had time to spell out the alternative. As readily as switching from football season to basketball, sports that once ruled my ambitions, I was eager to jump yet again from one environment of foundational male power into another. The bald facts suggested I was not going to change anytime soon, so there was no other way out. My high school years had become a kaleidoscope of broken images. Home was no longer an inner sanctum of happiness. Most of my friends were in college or the army. My age mates were seniors in high school and there I was a second semester sophomore, stuck somewhere near reverse. In a relatively telescoped period of time, I'd been through a Rolodex of counselors, coaches, deans, straw bosses, preachers, probation officers, principals, and, not the least, the social whiplash of three high schools in three different towns. The green baize of pool halls and shadowy back rooms with poker tables and pinball machines colored my escapes from school. Away from blackboards, textbooks, and teachers it was safe to be ignorant as long you were street savvy and periodically ran the table in nine ball, hit a five in a line on the pins, drew into a straight flush at the tables, or merely lagged quarters for beer money and won more often than not.

My school attendance record took on the rhythm of a barn cat, coming and going as I pleased. I'd have rather drunk castor oil every morning than get up and go to school. Classrooms gave me the shivers, a fingernails-on-the-chalkboard reaction. In fact, I hadn't attended classes regularly since Dean Grace at Northside gave me the boot for publicly bucking him. Puffed up like a blowfish at the main entrance when the morning bell rang, he watched me and Ernie Clark walk off campus the day of Martin Luther King's funeral. The Fort Smith School Board had voted to allow black students only to leave school to watch the funeral on television. Ernie and I were not social activists, or the good kind of "troublemakers" like the Freedom Riders; ours was not meant to serve as a catalyst for others, it just seemed like a good idea at the time. If anything, we wanted a day off from school and took it, come hell or high water.

The time to get unsnarled was upon me. As a parting shot in Municipal Courtroom 201, Judge Cloninger, with his usual judicial stoicism, gave me an out-of-left-field lecture, analogizing the patience and good deeds of cops to mallard hunters who restrain themselves from shooting a circling spoonbill till they have no other choice. The judge had never been so poetic as that day when he all but called me a shit bird.

Judge Cloninger wrote a cordial, Panglossian piece of half-fiction to the local recruiter, letting him know that I was most certainly not a danger to society and would fit in like a champ among men in uniform. My Dad and my probation officer, Jim Hanna, sent similar recommendations, all too kind by half. The letter campaign was successful. All arrests were "waived." A month after turning seventeen, as a promising wannabe Cool Hand Luke, too young to be taken seriously, I left my former frontier hometown of Fort Smith, Arkansas, under the care, custody, and control of the United States Army.

At this turning point, circled by neatly curated iterations of myself, my zip code was about as racially and culturally isolated as the North Pole. What little knowledge I had of the world beyond came second hand (or from the scratchy broadcasts we listened to when Dad was probing the ionosphere on his army surplus AN/ARC-5 ham radio). Through my neighbor and pal Leon Marks, I did know about the Jewish high holidays, latkes, and lighting the menorah, and my high school running buddies included a few blacks, but I knew nothing of Buddhists, Hindus, Muslims, Poles, Puerto Ricans, or "paddy-crawling" Asians. Rowdy and experienced with life's underbelly before my time, I had otherwise been shaped in the android mold of a classic, white middle-class baby boomer, the next generation variant of Jack Armstrong All-American boys. Daily exposure to other cultures in the absence of "round" blue eyes and silky blond hair was nada. In due time, carted off in a Greyhound from my good-old-boy cocoon of splendid isolation, I was whisked like egg yolks into the military mash-up to spend two years in Southeast Asia, mostly in northern Thailand, as part of the Vietnam War. As the exotic ether of parts unknown tardily percolated into my homegrown ethos, I inhaled it all, shape shifting my way down binding new pathways. It was a heck of a round-the-world path of soul-searching and shameless sin the judge had pushed me down for all my bad-boy behavior.

Less than a year after my sayonara court appearance, as an SPC Four (E-4), I was home on leave, with orders for 13th Finance in Qui Nhon, Vietnam, Americal Division. I had been arrested two nights before for minor in possession of alcohol and a curfew violation (under eighteen years old and on the streets of Fort Smith after 10:30 p.m. on a weeknight). As I stood alone before a duty-bound Judge Cloninger, spruced up in my U.S. Army dress uniform, he gave me the maximum fine of $125, which was a month's pay, then smiled benevolently and wished me luck as he gaveled for the next case.

My basic training platoon at Fort Polk, Louisiana, included a small squad of pro football players—Jim Beirne, Roy Hopkins, and Larry Carwell—Houston Oilers all. They were celebrity stud ducks, signing autographs when out of sight of the drill sergeants. It seemed unfair at the time that those prime physical specimens—seemingly possessed with tough-guy courage—had found their way into the Texas National Guard, in the off-season no less, and would be taking a pass on the war in Indochina. They were accompanied by an elite group of educated white guys, the "fortunate sons" they were called, who had found their own connections with the local draft boards and National Guard units.

At the same time, no one called anyone yeller for taking a pass on the unpopular war. Throw into the mix that boomer chicks weren't by any stretch flocking to the butch-cut men in uniform over their closer-to-home, shaggy-headed civilian counterparts. Students at both Fort Smith high schools, awash with the sons and daughters of World War II heroes, voted overwhelmingly in polls against the Vietnam War. Given the backdrop of an absence of a strong community commitment and the constant grim news from Vietnam, you didn't have to be a fortune teller to figure out the early warnings to keep the head down, no flying leaps. The vast majority of my tough-guy, late teenage friends were jumping through hoops with student deferments, bad backs, bone spurs, flat feet, near sight, and babies of convenience to stay out of Vietnam. The draft board was always following behind, marking time for a false move. Wait lists for the National Guard and military reserve units, with little or no chance of being activated, were at an all-time high.

Ninety percent of my platoon in basic training were middle or working class, without connections, or, like me, on the precipice of serious jail time and in need of army discipline. Notably, there was also a disproportionate number of black recruits from the abandoned plantation towns of the South and the rundown urban centers of the North. On day one, though, we all suddenly developed a lot in common. In our identical uniforms, shiny boots and buckles, and shaved heads, we were designated cots, quarantined for spinal meningitis, given gamma globulin shots that felt like they were being dumped from a five-gallon bucket, and faced with bat-eared drill sergeants up our ass with a torrent of insults all hours of the day and night as we all jonesed for some booze and cooze.

In those first days of basic training, if you had asked me what it was like to be black I would have replied that I didn't have a clue: I was still trying to figure out what it was like to be me. In short order, though, I learned that many blacks surrounding me were a platoon of in-your-face rage, uniformly down with stand-up brothers such as Bobby Seale and Huey P. Newton, founders of the Black Panther Party and disciples of Malcom X. We white guys of course felt threatened by the audacity of these beret-clad "negroes with guns," fully oblivious, as I was, to the Panther successes in community service projects in healthcare, food security, and education. From the parade grounds and barracks of Company C, 2nd Battalion, 1st Brigade at Fort Polk, across the fruited plains and purple majesties, my newfound black friends were cosmically connected to damn near everything that went down at the Panther headquarters in West Oakland. They were outspokenly angry to the bone at whites—and not at the Red Hordes of Vietnam. Muhammad Ali (née Cassius Clay), the heavyweight champion of the world and a conscientious objector, spoke for them while galling white folks when he (allegedly) declared, "Ain't no Viet Cong ever called me nigger."

Near the end of basic training and after a long day at the rifle range, I was mustered into formation together with several black draftees, many from inner Detroit who had been part of the '67 riots that left the city smoldering. Like a work gang, amid a dictionary-sized onslaught of drill sergeant slights, we unwashed high school dropouts boarded a deuce and a half that took us to North Fort and "Tiger Camp," the dreaded infantry-training center, where we were offloaded and ordered into an empty World War II–era barracks. Bleary eyed and bone tired, we spent the next two hours taking the

GED exam. That was my high school graduating class. My "yearbook" pictures from basic training featured me half-showing a peace sign. My travel boots were just getting some traction; Indochina was echoing in the distance.

That same month, Rick Wynne and Warren Stark, both friends from Fort Smith who I had entered the army with, cleared out of Fort McClellan and Fort Polk in the night, deserting. They had plenty of company, as several hundred thousand American servicemen and draft evaders flew the coop, mostly fading into the landscape, keeping a low profile until war's end and an amnesty deal could be struck. Rick made his way to San Francisco and Warren to Canada on a well-worn path that over 30,000 others had taken. Can't be certain to this day if they were just saving their hides or if it was a true act of conscience, but I do know I never laid eyes on either one of them again, not a word, only crickets.

The Lord's Prayer, Pledge of Allegiance, and grits for breakfast were not to sustain me. A fresh and often fierce world of eyes-open empiricism had contaminated my cherished beliefs in God, country, and middle-class Southern sensibilities. "Shoot the ones from the North," Drill Sergeant Skillern instructed me in basic training at Fort Polk, Louisiana. "How will I know who they are?" I asked the highly decorated sergeant, his valor envied by all. "You'll know," he assured me, sparing me his volcanic rage of verbal vomit.

As it turned out, I wasn't designated a combatant, killer of communists, so shooting the ones from the North never came up again. But dehumanizing the enemy (pseudospeciation, psychologists call it), the Vietnamese in this case—as yellow-to-pink-to-red by color; as blood-thirsty, life-is-cheap commies by emotion; and as rice-eating, slant-eyed, godless gooks, dinks, chinks, and zips by nature—was mother's milk for many trainees. They became imprinted with a religious fervor of hate no less than a Hindu's imagined reality of someone born an Untouchable. It was infinitely more complex for those destined to be "ass in the grass" in Vietnam and wading across the River Styx (rice paddies fertilized in human excrement) into a realm of wanton violence and self-preservation.

John Musgrave, a straight-talking kid from Independence, Missouri, inspired by the Cold War tensions of the day, volunteered for a U.S. Marine combat role in Vietnam. In a documentary film on Vietnam, Musgrave explained that after his first kill, as a matter of survival, he had to cut a deal with the devil:

> *I will never kill another human being as long as I'm in Vietnam. However, I will waste as many gooks as I can. I'll wax as many dinks as I can find...but I ain't going to kill anybody. Turn the subject into an object. It's Racism 101. And it turns out to be a very necessary tool when you have children fighting your wars, for them to stay sane doing their work.*

In late '67, after almost a year in intense combat, Musgrave was critically wounded near the DMZ and medivaced out. (Vietnam hangs spectrally over his life. He still has to sleep with a night light.)

After basic training and finance school, the army sent me to Fort Knox, Kentucky, for a six-month holding pattern until I turned eighteen years old and was eligible for service in Vietnam. The five-month arc of my rise from juvenile delinquent to Spec-4 finance clerk at Fort Knox, home to the United States Bullion Depository, made my hometown crowd proud. Every dog gets his day. Word had leaked out that I was charged with guarding the gold—the entire wealth of the country that sat behind blast-proof doors and granite walls, at the intersection of Bullion Boulevard and Gold Bar Road. I was happy to shine at something besides the glare of negative news.

The James Bond movie *Goldfinger*, released a few years earlier but still popular, fueled and fanned my story. In the film, the nefarious characters, Odd Job and his boss Auric Goldfinger, hatched Operation Grand Slam to irradiate the Fort Knox gold with an atomic device and in turn enhance Goldfinger's own wealth in gold by tenfold. Of course, the story was preposterous. I had been to the perimeter of the depository, but no one ever went inside the vault and actually picked up gold bars.

What was true, and what seemed a bit rushed, was that the army trusted me inside a vault to handle and control the disbursement of millions of dollars. My charge in the finance office was to process a new cadre into Patton's 1st Armored Division. We wore the familiar triangular red, blue, and yellow patch with a black tank in the middle. The insignia and uniform were so fetching, I wanted even more regalia.

One summer night when I was higher than a Georgia pine at the NCO club, on a dare with a couple of buck sergeants, I passed an empty table of four olive drab drill sergeant campaign hats, each centered with the golden Great Seal of the United States, and stopped and fitted myself out. My buddies watched from the bar, breaking into fits of laughter as I exited the club. Swaggering and spewing and singing like one of Patton's bad asses: "Forward march. Yo left. Yo left. Yo left, right, left. A little bird / with a yellow bill / flew upon my windowsill. I lured him in / with crumbs of bread / and…then smashed his MOTHERFUCKING head (hard left stomp). Sound off, one, two…" The success of my audacious hat trick was due largely to my being far from the drunkest in the Fort Knox NCO club that night. The four drill sergeants, I was told, shit their collective colons when they returned. That booty remains the only artifact of dress from the '60s in my closet, like a cap without a gown to memorialize a proper high school graduation.

By May of 1969, with Nixon's drawdowns having just begun, the new cadre were mostly Vietnam combat returnees. That desk-bound job is how I learned the geography of Vietnam and the backstory on who carried the heavy loads—the ragged ones, those with the middle-view stares, the world weary, those still standing. Few and far between were those that Hemingway liked to apotheosize in his *pièce de résistance* about war, *For Whom the Bell Tolls*—those who were taking part in a crusade-like adventure and feeling a consecration of duty toward all of the oppressed of the world. If it ever existed, that vision had been shattered. Employing a few self-taught algorithms, I learned to size up returnees while they sat in a line of gun-metal folding chairs, gleaning certain details about their lives, or as they walked toward the chair in front of my desk before they ever handed me their pay records.

The two-year-hitch draftees returning from Vietnam ranged in rank from E-3 (Private First Class) to E-5 (Sergeant or Specialist Fifth Class), but mostly E-4 (Corporals or Specialist Fourth Class). The rare E-6 (Staff Sergeant) draftee was always the recipient of a jump-step battlefield promotion, his platoon obliterated and in need of a leader—Horatio at the Bridge, among the piles of the slain. Rectangular ribbons of various colors, often with gold clusters, above the right pocket typically indicated an award for a combat unit's outstanding performance. Individual service and combat meritorious ribbons—Bronze Stars with Vs for valor, the rare Silver Star and not so rare Purple Heart for the wounded, or as I had seen on corpses, killed in action—sat above the left pocket. I checked atop the ribbons for the CIB (Combat Infantryman Badge)—a Springfield rifle on a blue field—awarded to those who had come under enemy fire at least once, the goal of any foot soldier in a war. All these patches, ribbons, and other accoutrements I scoped out, partly for the records, but also because they held status with me and my peers within the army cult of masculinity. It was only natural to be curious about who had done what, to glean from the ground pounder his stories of the monsoon deluge, suffocating humidity, jungle rot, blood-sucking leeches, bamboo vipers, the ghost of Charlie Cong and of the quick and the dead, while also picking up on a returnee's attitude. They ran the gamut from gung ho to fuck the army to Vietnam is a shameful quagmire to you-wouldn't-understand silence from the honest-to-god heroes. But for all that, by my reckoning, Napoleon wasn't whistling Dixie when he said, "A soldier will fight long and hard for a bit of colored ribbon." These combat-tested returnees, irrespective of attitude and experience, weren't without pride. They were present and accounted for.

Tap, tap, tap, ding, ding, I typed in the bones of the soldier's tour in Vietnam. The "Tropic Lightning" right shoulder insignia told me they were in the 25th Infantry Division, base camped at Cu Chi. Departed Vietnam from Bien Hoa Airbase on Pan Am flight so and so. Crossed the International Date Line and landed at Travis Airbase, California, the same day they departed Bien Hoa. About the time I had typed all that out, they would sit down and hand me their records. In a flash, I'd see their hometown was Kilgore, Texas (or somewhere), and I'd say, "You flew from Travis to Love Field in Dallas and caught a ride with family or on a bus to Kilgore, right?" They'd say yes, and I'd hand them their complete itinerary since leaving Cu Chi or the Americal in Chu Lai or 1st Air Cav in An Khe or wherever. Many would look up and ask me how I knew all that. "It's what I do all day long," I'd respond.

My map of Vietnam included no contextual narratives of the Vietnamese, only American army base camps with Vietnamese names. The stouthearted anecdotes I randomly collected overlaid my map. After interviewing (talking to) well over 1,000 returnees my first couple of months, I could quickly sort out the ones who were little more than rear echelon chest beaters. "The louder the boast, the bigger the pretender" was a serviceable rule of thumb. I expedited the travel and leave pay for anyone who asked, but the grave-faced boys with the most ribbons, the tip-of-the-spear transcendent ones, didn't have to say anything. They could pick it up as soon as they left my desk.

❂ ❂ ❂

While hitchhiking on a three-day pass from Fort Knox to Nashville, I decided to turn right and go west to Arkansas to my brother John's wedding. My hitchhiking buddy, Ralph Richert from Cincinnati, turned left and went east for a long weekend at the Atlanta Pop Festival.

When we returned to Fort Knox the next week, Ralph, still buzzed on LSD, shared with me a new bag of marijuana and his stories from the mosh pit of performances by Joe Cocker, Janis Joplin, Canned Heat, and the Butterfield Blues Band (all destined for Woodstock). In turn, I told him about my brother John's wedding and the unexpected arrival home of Carl Bates, a soldier's soldier. That was a story that stuck. The morticians at Edward's Funeral Home in Fort Smith, Arkansas, bandaged and puttied with makeup the top of Carl's head. Traveling at 2,500 feet per second, a single 7.62 x 39 mm round from a Russian-made AK-47 had blown through Carl's brain. Dead before he hit the deck.

At his funeral, Carl wore the Combat Infantry Badge and a Purple Heart. The backstory was that he'd received a "Dear John" letter while working a cush gig in Cam Ranh Bay as a company clerk, went all macho and volunteered to be a door gunner with the 57th Assault Helicopter Company. No one doubted his heroism. But it just felt like a Pavlovian response, not of purpose or patriotism but of wounded pride and machismo.

The evening before his fateful mission, Carl and fellow crewman Steve Hayduk shared C-rations, rapped about home, and listened to music, "Crimson and Clover" played over and over:

> *Yeah, my, my such a sweet thing*
> *I wanna do everything*
> *What a beautiful feeling*
> *Crimson and clover over and over*

When Steve was grounded with a fever the next day, Carl volunteered to take his place. The crippled chopper he had protected on a mission into Laos to retrieve an LRRP team returned with his corpse to its base near Kontum, leaking fuel and riddled with over thirty bullet holes. An open casket funeral, with a twenty-one-gun salute and an American flag for his mother, was a wedding day kind of special thing. I puked at both events that day—John's wedding and Carl's funeral—for different reasons. "Vietnam is what we had instead of happy childhoods," wrote U.S. war correspondent Michael Herr.

By June of 1969 I'd wrapped up six months in the army as my childhood friends and peers attended high school graduation and prom. In my smallish viewfinder, the '60s, the Age of Aquarius, and the topsy-turvy legacy of the times could easily be telescoped into the months of that summer of '69. Racial tensions in the army spiked, gay rights activists confronted police outside the Stonewall Inn in Greenwich Village, two of my friends returned from Vietnam in body bags, the Beatles song "Get Back," a commentary on immigrants, topped the charts, the counterculture film *Easy Rider* was released, Neil Armstrong walked on the moon, Mary Jo Kopechne drowned at Chappaquiddick in a car driven by Ted Kennedy, the Manson murders sent shock waves through L.A., the freak circus of the Woodstock music festival blew all our minds, the once-pathetic Mets were on a roll, and, on September 2, 1969, the endless summer ended with the death of Ho Chi Minh, Vietnam's beloved revolutionary leader.

It was hard to know whether to shit or go blind that summer given the firehose of bad news and the changing political and cultural landscape. Although I still held a high level of respect for the draftees, combatants, and the uniform, over the course of those summer months (and forever after), my psychic tectonics began a marked shift from cultural bad boy to political dissenter. Increasingly, I was informed by an unjust war, one in which humankind's deadliest deeds became the daily bread for a region of peasants (and for many young

American men). Similarly, my Southern antecedents' way of thinking had been molded a century before by a war that ended—in their perspective—unjustly. But the lessons drawn were more often as far apart, in place and time, as the lost causes of the wars themselves.

At Fort Knox, a month before I turned eighteen, a few weeks after Ho Chi Minh died, orders came down for 13th Finance, at the Americal Division headquarters in Qui Nhon, Vietnam. It was my turn and I was ready. Whisked off to RVN (Republic of Vietnam) training, mostly at the rifle range, for a week, I then said goodbye to Fort Knox and a barracks full of buddies never to be heard from again, taking a thirty-day leave.

Sticking my snout too far into all the hogwash the army served up was, at best, a leap of faith. By the time I arrived in the Vietnam theater, Nixon had begun withdrawing troops. The veneer of rectitude had been torn off. Lieutenant William Calley and twenty-six others had just been charged with the My Lai mass killings of as many as 500 civilians: men, women, children, toddlers, and infants. But for the heroic actions of helicopter pilot Hugh Thompson, the death count would have been much higher and the massacre might have gone unreported. For the most part, the human jackals responsible for the massacre and the subsequent coverup never got their just deserts. The military protected their own as they would when the lids came off on many more American-inflicted atrocities in Vietnam and elsewhere.

After My Lai, with the war winding down, morale hit all-time lows, drug addiction reached new highs, discipline was often optional, and traditional bonds of trust between officers, NCOs, and their men waned. In some cases, the inmates—the enlisted ranks—were running the asylum.

In parallel, body counts and casualties were no longer an evening news abstraction. In 1966, acquaintance and hometown football hero Charlie Belue came back a double amputee after taking one wrong step onto a landmine in Quang Tri province. In July of '68 my brother John's Kappa Sigma fraternity brother John Halsell was killed when he tripped a booby trap in Quang Nam Province. While I was in basic training in early '69, neighborhood track star and Navy pilot Phil Neisler crashed off an aircraft carrier in the Gulf of Tonkin. His remains, never recovered, eternally dwell in the fathomless sea. The same summer of '69, in addition to Carl Bates, a close childhood friend, Jackie Gilker, returned from Vietnam in a body bag; both gone head-long into the night, like meteors, forever. Far away in time and space as they might be, they will always be missed, because missing is a way of remembering. Embedded in my active memory, I can visualize their winning smiles, their names rise often from my lips, and, in the Irish tradition, their spirits have assumed powers and an immanence like the red color of Mars that mere mortals are denied.

My brother Stan was already in Vietnam, stationed 130 miles down the coast from Qui Nhon in Nha Trang. When I arrived at Travis Air Base to ship out, word had followed me that I had a brother in Vietnam. After the five Sullivan brothers were killed in World War II, the army laid down restrictions on brothers serving in combat zones. Like me, most brothers tried to ignore those regulations. My dodge was to hang tight in the finance corps and out of combat, not to avoid service in Vietnam proper.

Several events may have conspired to inform the army that I had a brother in Vietnam. At the behest of the Red Cross, the army had granted me a few extra days leave to visit my grandmother, Myrtle Karber (or Maw), who was on her deathbed in Alpine, Arkansas. Ms. Waddie, the drunk socialite who caused the car crash that broke my nose and scarred my face in high school, had become an Alcoholics Anonymous 12-Stepper in a matter of months. Now, head of the local Red Cross, she was jumping through hoops on my behalf (guilt-ridden maybe), sending regular updates by Western Union from Travis to Vietnam. Whose desks those messages landed on and what they said, I have no idea. Other than the Red Cross, the only other possibility was my mother. Against my protests, she had threatened to call Senator Fulbright to discuss having two sons in Vietnam at once. Years later, she claimed to have not made that call.

By the time I landed at Saigon's Tan Son Nhut Air Base, thirty-six hours after departing Travis, orders had come down to re-assign me to the leeward side of the Vietnam theater. A few days later, I was in Bangkok, catching a C-130 north, grateful for the work-around and not to have been sent back to Fort Knox.

For over a year, I managed the computation section of 35th Finance at Camp Friendship, Korat, Thailand, APO (Army Post Office) 96288. Once intended to be a Cold War forward operating base for the 25th Infantry Division, Camp Friendship and the air force tactical fighter squadrons next door at the Royal Thai Air Base occupied land and facilities used by the Japanese army in World War II. Crosshatched with street names like Gettysburg, Argonne, and Normandy, not a tree or bush sprouted anywhere. All had been chopped down and defoliated with Agent Orange. Security, the thinking went, necessitated an open view like a firing range of Camp Friendship's perimeters.

The finance office had a payroll of 5,000, mostly advisory and logistics forces, as well as the Thai army of over 1,000-foot soldiers. Four draftees worked for me, two of whom were already certified public accountants (Arnie-Add-Em-Up and Clean Gene). The other two, Stu "the Fargo Kid" Naden and John "Slow Talking" Hepburn, had completed one-year combat tours as door gunners in Vietnam. They were wrapping up their service time in the Vietnam theater on Finance Easy Street so they could take advantage of a five-month early out.

By late 1970, the Nixon withdrawals had cut troop strength in Vietnam (and Thailand) from a high of almost 600,000 to 350,000. Camp Friendship was reduced to a skeleton crew, and I was reassigned. Like the Fargo Kid and Slow Talking Hepburn, this Hillbilly, as I was re-christened early on for my thick accent and Ozarks roots (the old slow-train-through-Arkansas cliché), was also hanging around on a second tour so as to secure a five-month early out.

Omega Gene Hibbert was our first sergeant. A three-war combat veteran, World War II, Korea, and Vietnam, he had more chest fruit salad than Audie Murphy. He had enlisted at sixteen in World War II, lying about his age. His last tour in Vietnam proper had been with the 101st Airborne Rangers, where he fought near Dak To and across the Laotian border.

Omega Gene was old school, defining the intergenerational fault lines. Sporting sharply creased fatigue pants and spit-shined jungle boots, polished brass and a gold crucifix around his bull neck, white sidewalls and a high-and-tight flattop that always appeared freshly trimmed, he proudly showed off his sleeves of blood-and-soil tattoos acquired long before his white nationalist brethren took up the guise. A worthy mascot for radical reactionaries of the day, he might have coined the nativist taunt, *America, love it or leave it.*

Omega Gene liked the army before Truman's race policy of desegregation in the military twenty years before. "Nigger," "spear chucker," and "jungle bunny" were part of his everyday vocabulary, marching out of his mouth in a cadence of certainty that defined him. He refrained only when a stranger of superior rank showed up and he was unsure of the man's racial attitudes, which was not often.

Omega Gene also might have been the most well-read NCO I met in almost three years in the army. If you believed his Stanford-Binet IQ score at 134, he may have attained genius status. But we all knew a "first sergeant genius" was like a "giant pygmy," a walking contradiction. On his first tour in Vietnam in '67, he married a village girl from the Central Highlands and took her back to the States. Or the Land of the Big PX, as he liked to say, mocking his wife. She lived in base housing at Fort Hood, Texas, while he was wrapping up his army career with one last overseas tour of duty.

By day Omega Gene, always on the verge of bubbling over with anger, attempted to impose discipline on our less than *strac* company of mostly educated white guys. In our minds formations and barracks inspections were something you did stateside, and a PT-test had come to mean a Sick Call visit to the infirmary after too much Poon-Tang down on Bar Row or up Sweetheart Alley. As a unit, we responded swiftly to Omega Gene's focus on discipline with a takeoff on the film *M*A*S*H*, which came out with an unambiguous anti–Vietnam War theme the same month he arrived at Camp Friendship. It was April 13: the region was celebrating the lunar-solar New Year's holiday of Songkran, a Sanskrit astrological word meaning shift or transformation. A time for merit making, washing Buddhist statues, and cleansing sins by splashing water on other celebrants. We flooded the barracks cleansing sins and turned up the music.

Led by Bob Walter, aka Waltauvos, playing guitar and singing "Onward Christian Soldiers," I kept rhythm by beating a trash can with a baseball bat. As many as twenty more joined us in marching around the MP barracks, knocking back pints of Mekhong, a 35-proof rum infused with local herbs, like water. After several warnings, and most others having gone to bed, Arnie-Add-Em-Up and I were still roistering at two in the morning. For a hot minute we ruled the roost. Then we were arrested amid a debris field of empty pints and given Article 15s for drunk and disorderly, and destruction of government property. Fresh paint on the side of the MP barracks read "FTA" (Fuck the Army). As in *M*A*S*H*, we had very publicly satirized those in command who put God on our side in this sorry ass war, from Omega Gene on up to General Vessey, commander of army troops in Thailand and later head of the Joint Chiefs. The MPs reported every detail of our silly mischief. In time, perhaps for reasons of social isolation, our antics had the effect of taking some of the starch out of Omega Gene. He was less underfoot and never really jacked with us again about military discipline.

Omega Gene had his own problems shining up to authority as well as burning it at both ends. Only attaining the rank of E-7 in twenty-six years of service spoke for itself. With his war record, command sergeant major should have been a given. After a few months at Camp Friendship, he relaxed his martial stride, got soaking drunk every night at the NCO Club, and took a *tealock* (a prostitute girlfriend) out of the Americana Bar up Sweetheart Alley in Korat. From that point on, he spent a couple of evenings a week with her priming his pump at the Happy Home Bar and overnighting at the Army Hotel. One thing he never slacked off on, though, was trying to thin our ranks of blacks. "Flies in the buttermilk," he liked to say when the subject of integration came up.

Jeremiah Washington, who wore Black Power wristbands and an Afro, joined our unit two months after Omega Gene arrived in early 1970. He immediately took up with a group of like-minded friends in the 538th Engineer Battalion. Rarely did we see him after work or in the barracks other than to change fatigues in the morning. Following an altercation with two Carolina boys who called him a "nigger" after seeing him thrust an insistent fist in the air at a USO show in which the all-black band played "Say it Loud, I'm Black and I'm Proud," Omega Gene engineered a lateral transfer for Jeremiah to South Korea. He was gone in two days.

In Harper Lee's bestseller, *To Kill a Mockingbird*, Atticus Finch enjoins Scout: "You never understand a person until you consider things from his point of view...until you climb in his skin and walk around in it." Climbing in anyone's skin was a bridge too far, but empathy was not, and standing up for friends when the situation called for it came easy for most of us. But not all. Waltauvos and I whaled the living tar out of those two Carolina boys for spewing racial epithets at Jeremiah before he shipped out. Once he was gone, Omega Gene wore the cocksure smirk of a bully boy until Jeremiah's replacement arrived a few days later.

Marvin Fluker hailed from Hattiesburg, Mississippi, the buckle of the Black Belt of Alabama and Mississippi. Before being drafted, Marvin had graduated from Dillard, an esteemed all-black college in New Orleans. Following basic training and finance school, Marvin reported to 47th Finance in Bangkok. When the first sergeant saw that he was black and not the fair-haired German that his family's slave name implied, he had Marvin shipped up country the next day, to my unit. Omega Gene also attempted to transfer Marvin when he first clapped eyes on his pigmentation. Second Lieutenant Dennis McNamara, deputy commanding officer of 35th Finance and former schoolboy sports star, thwarted him when he learned that Marvin was an exceptional athlete. He was saved yet another humiliating reassignment. Drafted and dispatched by the U.S. Army to the Vietnam War as part of an overall mission to guarantee democratic freedoms that he didn't enjoy at home in Mississippi, Marvin was nevertheless proud to serve, knowing full well all soldiers were not created equal.

As I got to know Marvin, I came to admire his enormous capacity for resilience. He told me about his father, a hardworking truck driver, who, unlike Marvin, was short in stature, tight-lipped, and no aficionado of jazz trumpeter Miles Davis. Marvin was only eight years old when he lost his mother. In the late '40s and early '50s, every two years his family visited an aunt and uncle in Connecticut. As part of the second wave of the Great Migration, known by some as "the window out of the asylum," his relatives had fled the Southern caste system during the labor crisis of World War II. *The Negro Traveler's Green Book*, published annually from 1936 to 1966 during the era of Jim Crow laws, listed hotels, restaurants, and gas stations welcoming to black travelers and advised readers to drive under the cover of darkness. Few accommodations were open to blacks in any case. On his family's return trip in 1955 they broke the rule, drove during the day, and a truck full of rednecks intentionally ran them off the road in broad daylight in Virginia. Two aunts were killed and his mother died a year later from her injuries. The culprits were never prosecuted.

Omega Gene may have been a genius, but he was easy to read. Although Marvin was reluctantly cast into the edgy, self-conscious role of being the raisin in the rice pudding, he knew how to work above Omega Gene. At his core, Marvin was more a we-shall-overcome, Jackie Robinson, let-bygones-be-bygones guy than a Black-Power-payback person such as H. Rap Brown or Stokely Carmichael. He caught a raft of Uncle Tom crap from the militant brothers, but he floated over it with his own style of Black Belt freedom, kept his head down at work, and never gave anyone a reason to reassign him.

When I was reassigned, Omega Gene, as he had done with my good friend Waltauvos, rolled up my Article 15s (misdemeanor offenses), tied them in a bow, attached a farewell card that simply said, "Valedictorian," handed it to me, and flounced off. It was the last time I laid eyes on him.

By some quirk of fate, I served my final eight months in the army at Ramasun Station, a listening post and home to the 7th Radio Research Field Station, a cover for the Army Security Agency, or ASA. Using Morse telepathy for the whiz kids running the war, the ASA tracked various targets in the two Vietnams, traffic along the Ho Chi Minh Trail, Chinese military movements, the secret war in Laos, the insurgency in Cambodia, the Thai army for coups, and the larger Cold War. Splendidly isolated 300 klicks north of Korat, near the village of Ban Nong Soong, the original tented base camp was given the call name Cobra 7 after construction engineers found nests of cobras at the first groundbreaking. By the time I arrived, the Pentagon had spent $50 million and turned the former cobra nest into a state-of-the-art installation with its own power plant, water supply, twenty-four-hour lighting on primly landscaped concrete streets and sidewalks, and air-conditioned barracks. Once repurposed, Cobra 7 was aptly renamed for the local "thunder god," Ramasun—simply because what went on there on any given day provided the trigger for the earth and skies to rumble, shake, and explode with American firepower.

The ASA at Ramasun, 500-strong after Tet of '68, was composed of Foreign Service Institute–trained lingies (linguists), ditty-boppers (Morse intercept operators), techies, and civilian National Security Agency (NSA) analysts. We all dwelled in the shadow of gun-metal gray Thai army guard towers and possibly the world's largest high-frequency, direction-finder circularly disposed Wullenweber antenna array. Or the "Elephant Cage," as the array was often called. With a range of 5,000 miles, looming over an area of at least one football field filled with trip flares, the two-story band of antennae plucked fresh waves of North Vietnamese, Soviet, Red Chinese, Laotian, Thai, and Cambodian war talk from the sky. To me it had all the sci-fi makings of a flying saucer casting its beam to some alien receptor.

Ditty boppers (05Hs) worked twelve-hour shifts, twenty-four hours a day, seven days a week in an air-conditioned, windowless concrete operations (OPS) building filled with radio receivers and tape-recording equipment. Known as the Box, it was off limits to me and everyone else without a need to be there. Tables turned, it was the kind of super-villain, over-guarded control center author Ian Fleming would have dispatched James Bond to infiltrate, off the grid, not found in an atlas.

According to M. H. Burton in *Tales of Ramasun*, from the Watch Office entrance manned by a lieutenant and the house mouse (gofer for a day, dump the trash, clean the shitters), down the middle of the Box was a tunneled hallway with the air force supervising one end and the army the other. Headsets on, ditty boppers monotonously translated and transcribed encrypted Morse code messages, often from the "bad guys." Awaiting a beep to react to, dit-dah-dah, dah-dit-dit, they worked side by side with army, air force, marine, and navy lingies who variously spoke Lao, Thai, Vietnamese, Chinese, Khmer, and Russian. Known collectively as HAWGs, an acronym for Hazard Analysis Working Group, the upshot of their work was to monitor traffic of, let's say, the Pathet Lao, NVA, or Lao Neutralist, to pinpoint bearings and communicate strike zones for B-52s, Phantoms, artillery units—you name it. "Death by Morse code," such dot-dash connecting was christened. Following strict time protocols, if a code was not broken in maybe twenty minutes, a Z-Gram, or high-priority message, was sent to the crypto-analysts at the "Puzzle Palace," the National Security Agency in Fort Meade, Maryland. Enemy troop movements, a downed American pilot, a friendly position under fire—all required a Z-Gram.

The laws of unintended consequences—collateral damage, primarily—were known but certainly not visible from the Box. No one was allowed to talk about what they did. Burnout was high. After the biblical rains of the monsoon season, during the dry winter months, the heavy fighting cranked up in Laos as the Pathet Lao and North Vietnamese forces advanced westerly. Monitoring those movements, the Box crackled round the clock. On a few occasions, I witnessed complete breakdowns in the cold light of day, sobbing, screaming, the message being: get me the fuck out of here. It reminded me of the torture Lucas Jackson (Paul Newman) endured after a long stint in the "box" in the movie *Cool Hand Luke*. No such stress found its way into the cage from which I was disbursing money.

Given my police record, I'll leave it to the sphinx to decide why the army gave me a top-secret security clearance when I arrived at Camp Ramasun. Beneath the MARS (Military Auxiliary Radio System) tower, our single-story, concrete building was identified as a Class B Agent Finance Office. As a Class B Agent, which like a B movie suggests some taint, I was charged with paying the lingies, ditty-boppers, the evil octopus of NSA supervisors, the CIA's paramilitary operatives, Bill Lair's Thai Paru supporting the 30,000 Hmong guerilla fighters in Laos, and other less notable coverts in the region. Needless to say, with all the espionage and eavesdropping going down at the ASA camp, security was high, often approaching Keystone-Kops-silly. In certain circles, nothing was as it seemed, always a cipher. Soldiers worked in civvies, and NSA civilians wore army uniforms. Talking in whispers was the norm.

To feed this machine, which required cash transactions, Captain Buster and I made money runs to 47th finance in Bangkok, driving an open-air Willy through the busy, klong-hatched streets of the city, protected only by our sidearms, hauling a wooden footlocker in the back seat with up to a million and a half dollars. Before we boarded the spotter plane for our return to the Udorn Royal Thai Air Force Base, the pilot always handed me a parachute, but it was never obvious where the rip cord was. Once at the air base, we hopped on a Huey (UH-1) for a mere eight-mile ride to Ramasun, emerging on the landing pad of our well-guarded base with M-16s at the ready. Take it to the bank: Had I ever encountered Thai Cong or civilian armed robbers on the streets of Bangkok while transporting a foot locker full of money, they would have been shooting at my back side as this Class B Agent booked it away. No Custer-riding-into-battle glory in dying for someone else's money.

We were at the edge of the war, attempting to plug the holes of insurgency started in the time of Father Chin, better known as Ho Chi Minh, who lived in Isaan (Northeast Thailand) disguised as a Catholic priest long before my arrival. The unassimilated descendants of the anti-colonialist Vietnamese he lived among now accounted for as much as 25 percent of the local population. Never could identify them visually, but their bird-like tonal speech patterns betrayed their presence. On several occasions, I stayed overnight on

Soi Jintakarm near the Friendship Highway intersection with a Vietnamese bar girl named Phuong, which means Phoenix. We met at the Tip Top Club but, over the course of a couple of months, spent most early evenings at the Junpen or Golden Horse, listening to music, drinking Singha beer, and dancing.

In her shared bungalow on Soi Jintakarm she kept a radio receiver and homemade antennae above her bed next to the ancestral altar, traditionally arranged with incense in a brass bowl of uncooked rice in the center, lotus flowers in a porcelain vessel to one side, and offerings of mango and banana on the other. Squeaking geckos fanned out on the walls and ceiling, keeping the mosquitoes at bay. On my visits, she always tuned the receiver to Hanoi Hannah and practiced her English ("How are you, GI Joe?" she chirped). Though I was a know-nothing as far as active "intel," we giggled out loud at the psychotropic effects of the "Laotian Tops" and the Mata Hari–like effusions. She may have been a Viet or Thai Cong, who knows. Like the many Viet Cong I would later meet, our commonality far outweighed our differences. It's hard not to think of those nights with Phuong as visitations to what psychologists call the Third Space, that place in which sworn enemies, two people full of hate for one another, come together and sing from the same page.

When I was not enjoying time with a bar girl, sitting in a vault or iron cage camouflaged by cash, I was hanging out with a handful of fellow REMFS (Rear Echelon Motherfuckers) on the Mekong. We often caught a sampan below the cliffs at Nong Khai (near the present-day Friendship Bridge to Laos) to a random island in the middle of the river. Only an occasional shrub or willow sprouted on those abandoned islands, leaving us scant shade to while away a day at the beach drinking hot wine and smoking Laotian Tops, harvested by monks under the holy *Wesak* moon—or so the seductive sales pitch went. When we tired of drinking wine, we ran hot beer sorties to the eastern shores of Vientiane, an illegal destination for GIs at the time.

That is, unless one was working at the embassy or USAID or among the Special Forces types out of Company C at Lopburi who had "jumped the fence" in a tactical reconnaissance or combat role. In any case, they were probably "sheep dipped," soldiers-turned-spooks. Otherwise, an American crossing the Mekong to Vientiane was likely a deserter headed to the Swedish embassy. We were the exception.

With the sun hotter than a match head, after a beer run we often took a splash in the margins of the big muddy Mekong with one of the Isaan country girls, all the time watching and listening to the steady migration of metallic birds crossing overhead—C-130s, AC-47s, T-28s, H-34s, AC-119s, O-1s, C-123s, C-124s, F-105s, A-1s, U-17s, CH3s (Jolly Green Giants), OH-6s (Scouts), CH-47s (Chinooks), and UH-1s (Hueys) whop, whop, whopping, F-4s swooped in low and B-52s floated high as our Mississippi-flyway mallards back home. We out-of-uniform voyeurs had a front-row seat to the secret war, a Pentagon's Parade Day set on a provincial Potomac. Only a few miles away, and divided by a river, life was quite different.

Fighters and bombers dropped their payloads over the Plain of Jars, the Ho Chi Minh Trail, and North Vietnam, all widely known by the press and public at the time. Indeed, enabled by the geographic proximity, 80 percent of all U.S. airstrikes over North Vietnam originated from seven airbases in Thailand. In Laos alone, we dropped 260 million bombs, making it, per capita, the all-time most-bombed country on earth. Working beneath the radar of common knowledge, the transports, helicopters, spotters, and vintage bombers, piloted by a gang of CIA cowboys and air force mavericks known as Ravens, were all destined for Long Tieng, "Spook Heaven," the CIA-built base northeast of Vientiane. Secretly known as the Peppergrinder missions, flights hauled refugees, transported the wounded, or dropped rice supplies on war-torn Hmong villages. Mostly though, they ferried "hard rice"—weapons and ammo—as well as heavy equipment to Long Tieng and General Vang Po, leader of the Hmong hill tribe army. Until the press discovered the clandestine operation in 1970, Long Tieng was the second-largest city in Laos and arguably the most secret spot on planet Earth.

The real folly of those languid, transforming days on the Mekong, at least for us little guys looking up, was that truth *is* the first casualty of war, calling to task many of the iconic influences in my life. All cloaked with God and Country, inflicting mass carnage was airily termed pacification; the military invasion and occupation of another country was called liberation; and search-and-destroy really meant destroy-and-search. The Pentagon then and today refers to such organic deceit as "incestuous amplification." Outsiders define this as "a condition in warfare where one only listens to those who are already in lock-step agreement, reinforcing set beliefs and creating a situation ripe for miscalculation." During the Johnson and Nixon years, almost all those who disagreed with the president on war tactics or strategy were either not invited back to discuss the topic or else simply fired. Chancellor of the German Empire, Otto von Bismarck, nailed it long before, "People never lie so much as after a hunt, during a war or before an election."

One man who certainly did disagree with the lizard-eyed logic of Johnson and Nixon was Daniel Ellsberg, the defense strategy analyst who made history by leaking the Pentagon Papers. "He had drunk from the secret cup and then betrayed the priest," wrote Jann Wenner in *Like a Rolling Stone*. The resulting court case ended with a landmark legal precedent favoring a free press. In November of 1968, long before Ellsberg went public with his views, Henry Kissinger acknowledged Ellsberg's expertise before a think tank audience, "I have learned more from Dan Ellsberg than from any other person in Vietnam."

Despite this, Kissinger failed to heed Ellsberg's advice. For the next three years, as Kissinger and Nixon secretly bombed the bejesus out of Indochina, they started to resemble caricatures in a *Saturday*

Night Live sketch rather than levelheaded public servants. Nixon's White House tapes tell the story better than I can:

> President: *How many did we kill in Laos?*
> Kissinger: *In the Laotian thing, we killed about ten, fifteen [thousand]...*
> President: *See, the attack in the North [Vietnam] that we have in mind...power plants, whatever's left—POL [petroleum], the docks...And, I still think we ought to take the dikes out now. Will that drown people?*
> Kissinger: *About two hundred thousand people.*
> President: *No, no, no...I'd rather use the nuclear bomb. Have you got that, Henry?*
> Kissinger: *That, I think, would just be too much.*
> President: *The nuclear bomb, does that bother you?...I just want you to think big, Henry, for Christsakes.*

They did think big: talking about casualty numbers as dispassionately as a stockbroker recounting last year's trades. Billy Graham, America's own firebrand evangelist and presidential spiritual advisor, thought big too when he counseled Nixon to destroy North Vietnam's dikes with nuclear weapons in what could have been called a Carthaginian Peace. No flies on Billy's ass, only ambition, trying to out-crazy Goldwater, Body Count Bob (McNamara), and the mad leader. The Nixon White House was capable of much grander deeds, even with Kissinger's mild objections. In a year and a half, it authorized seventy-five times the explosive equivalent dropped on Nagasaki to be showered over Indochina. Which makes me ponder aloud: Were the "rules of engagement" that limiting, as many bomb-them-into-the-Stone-Age-minded American pilots would have us believe?

In early July of 1971, Lennon (Randy with owlish wire-rimmed glasses), Shecky (as in Green), Egg (short for Egleston), and I walked to the motor pool at the backside of the base. Word had filtered over to Ramasun that the Michael Wadleigh's documentary *Woodstock*, released seven months after the concert, would play for one night at a small outdoor theater smack in the middle of the Royal Thai Air Force Base near Udon Thani. Base Commander Colonel Ricky Lee Ragsdale wouldn't allow it shown at the Ramasun theater.

With me at the wheel of our company Willy, the three of us started off on the eight-mile drive up Friendship Highway, a road financed by the Pentagon and partly constructed by American army engineers. Across the road from Ramasun, near the village temple of Ban Nong Soong, I pulled up to Papasan's roadside *khao phat* (fried rice) shack and bought a bottle of *lao khao*, a punchy rice whiskey steeped in herbs, and, if you're lucky, dead scorpions for added kick. Papasan, his wrist wrapped in rubber bands with plastic bags full of ice and straws handy, wanted a dollar extra for the scorpions. Shecky waved him off and poured the *lao khao* into the plastic bag with a straw. Isaan's Molam music, traditional working-class sounds featuring a singer and a bamboo mouth-organ player (*khaen*), blared from waiting *songthaews* (passenger trucks) surrounding the bamboo shack. It wasn't rock 'n' roll, but Thai (and Lao) country folks embraced its simple messages of hardship and unrequited love. We didn't know better; to us it was just the whanging background noise the locals called music.

Beyond the shack, near the village entrance, saffron-robed monks chanted sutras at the foot of a flaming funeral bier. From an open pavilion, family and villagers watched stoically the ritual of death and the transformative power of the fire that was spitting smoke and burning embers into the early evening sky. In light of the crowd size, the village headman may have died.

Farther along, stooped peasant women shadowed by young boys atop water buffalo tended paddy green fields tinted phosphorescent by fog, transplanting germinated shoots. At the sound of the village temple bells, the communal toil in the fields came to a halt for a moment of reflection. The repetitive scene recalled a Chinese scroll painting for dozens of miles in any direction, ordinary people in what to my wide-open eyes evinced an extraordinary way of life. Exotic, yet reassuringly familiar; in the moment, yet timeless.

It was hothouse muggy that early evening as we wheeled up to the front gate of the airbase with IDs flashing at one American MP and two Thai guards. Security was always by the book. The airbase was home to the U.S. 7/13 Air Force and Air America, a private airline the CIA owned and operated for covert operations in Southeast Asia.

It had upgraded perimeter defenses, trip flares, bunkers, and towers since VC (or Thai Cong) sappers hit the base back in '68. They cut and blasted their way through the fences, attempting to destroy the F-4s that skirted the runway. In the attack, tech sergeant Paul Yonkie and a Thai guard were killed, and four air force security police were wounded. Yonkie was at the base to escort two recently released POWs back to the States. Three of the guerilla attackers were dispatched, while half a dozen or so hightailed it into the night, leaving behind AK-47 rifles, incendiary ammunition, six satchel charges, and three Soviet-made hand grenades. High alerts for more of the same became the new normal.

Recognizing Shecky, security waved us on without examining the IDs. Curling around the three-story Air America/CIA headquarters, ten minutes later we were front and center as Crosby, Stills, Nash, and Young teed off the documentary with a "Long Time Gone." Way more "heads" than "juicers" filled the outdoor seats. Air America birds whop-whopped overhead and F-4 Phantom-IIs loaded with racks of bombs blasted off screeching like banshees into the half-darkness to sow Freedom and Democracy. High from the ride up on *lao khao* and Laotian tops, we chanted and sang along with Country Joe McDonald, letting rip "I-Feel-Like-I'm-Fixin'-to-Die-Rag": "Give me an F, give me a U… What's that spell? One, two, three, what are we fighting for?" In no particular order, a medley of iconic performances, psychedelic antics, mud-caked peaceniks, and memorable stage announcements kept coming, rat-a-tat-tat. "The brown acid that is circulating around us is not specifically too good… of course it's your own trip, so be my guest"; Richie Havens robed in saffron like a monk, in his inimitable gravel-road voice (guitar mic please), improvising "Freedom" based on the old spiritual "Motherless Child"; "Think really hard, maybe we can stop the rain"; Joe Cocker clad in a rainbow tie-dyed shirt, writhing spasmodically, channeling "With a Little Help from My Friends" like a man possessed; "What we have in mind here is breakfast in bed for 400,000"; the Who's Pete Townshend's windmill and Roger Daltry's tour de force "See Me, Feel Me/Listening to You," delivered at sunrise in a buckskin suede suit; and the meticulous craftmanship of Jimi Hendrix rocking it the last morning of the Aquarian Exposition, as the festival was billed, with his evocative Vietnam-version of "The Star-Spangled Banner." The visual accents on screen, the thrumming props overhead, the roar of afterburners low in the sky—a panoptic competition of '60s images—conjured a Dr. Strangelove-moves-to-the-Haight aura of psychic confrontation.

The war had reached its "sell-by" date. Everything around me screamed to be heard and was more proof that things can and will fall apart. Refugees were already crossing the Mekong into Thailand in droves. American "exceptionalism" was bankrupt. Like a phantom army, blowing holes in Cambodia's night skies was our end game.

I had taken a pass on combat, did not "fight long and hard for a piece of colored ribbon." Indeed, most of us in the Indochina arena were never blooded to the metallic sounds and effects of war: 80 percent of the 2.5 million Americans who served in the Vietnam War (a tooth-to-tail-ratio of 5 to 1) did not have the envied combat infantry badge. Still I am very much aware that my presence alone in the U.S. Army in Indochina meant that I took part in something obscene and evil, laughably considered patriotic. Mostly though I think of myself as the converse of the frustrated infantryman described by the eighteenth-century English writer Samuel Johnson: "Every man thinks meanly of himself for not having been a soldier [combatant]." "Ass in the grass," falling on swords was thankfully not my fate. I showed up, but I never fully bought into the bold commitment, sung from the mountaintop by President Kennedy, that so many valued friends took with them onto the battlefields of Vietnam: "Ask not what your country can do for you, ask what you can do for your country."

Chapter Eight
The Age of Aquarius Rocks On

COMING-HOME STORIES cross all cultures and time, from *The Odyssey* to Oz. Rarely are those journeys linear, or the arrival home as fluid and unchallenging as imagined. As my tour wound down, I couldn't just pass through the revolving door without a good rumpus with the brass. Bearding the lion in his den was all but a new norm in my army. It took a formal letter of inquiry from U.S. Representative John Paul Hammerschmidt, a pilot friend of my father's, to back off Major Ricky Lee Ragsdale, a bullying base commander whose authority I had challenged in writing for harassing a couple of married friends with petty fines they could not afford. On any given day, he thought he was General Patton, walking around with a riding crop and slapping it down on desks to intimidate people. He embodied the old saying: "The higher a monkey climbs, the more it shows its ass."

Also gumming up the works was an ongoing investigation by CID (Army Criminal Investigation Department) of our finance office, aptly known as the 47th Follies. Long-deceased Major General Butler Smedley, the most decorated marine of his time, was on to something when he declared "war is a racket." The investigators alleged the all-too-common crimes of graft and corruption, endemic throughout the Vietnam theater. It didn't help that Congress was also holding hearings and asking lots of unfriendly questions. Billions of dollars had disappeared out the back door into the Asian ether. Padding the payroll with "ghost soldiers" and "flower soldiers," troops who either didn't exist or stayed at home, was a common practice among Thai army generals and Vietnamese commanders. As J. C. Watts, a friend who worked in army intelligence gathering in Saigon, wrote about the latter, "You don't survive a thousand years of Chinese suzerainty without knowing how to deceive your allies."

The local saying was that the fish rotted from the head down. Even in the rear we knew as much. War was no time for ordinary morality; grifters at the public trough were as old as time. Shortly after the American withdrawal, Anong Vejjabul, a glorified clerk in our Korat office responsible for paying 1,000 or more Thai infantrymen fighting in Vietnam and providing security along the Mekong and Cambodia borders, bought a hotel off of Sukhumvit Road in Bangkok with her cut of paying the good general's "ghost soldiers."

"Such a system demoralizes and 'selects out' the able and dedicated who do not play the game," wrote former Vietnam war correspondent Arnold Isaacs. That the trickle-down effects of corruption sapped the morale of the rank-and-file South Vietnamese army, Isaacs contends, set the stage for the South's walk-in-the-park defeat by the more lean-and-mean NVA and NLF (Viet Cong).

As I was the NCO at Ramasun Station in charge of disbursements to American troops, all money, at one time or another, had to pass through my hands. Unstrapping bundles of cash, counting it out lightning quick like a Macau card dealer, and posting the decimal point details of the day into a dull crisscross of columns and rows was my domain. Balanced to the penny every day, clean as a whistle. On the other hand, I would have really been up Shit Creek had the good Major Fujimori, who was leading the local investigation (assisted by my friend Edward K. Dwyer III), shone a light on my financial dealings while on R&R in Bangkok: Selling stereo systems out the back door of the PX on the black market. Or punching out the Class Six card to supply local bars with American-made booze and cigarettes. Half the soldiers I encountered were already knee-deep up that Shit Creek. It added up to nothing more than Econ 101: The Circular Flow of Money. Fujimori, however, wasn't after those U.S. bucks that bubbled up like seed stock out of Bangkok (and Saigon, and Danang, and you name it).

Captain John Buster, who sat five feet from me in the "cage" next to the reinforced concrete vault, was from Guymon, Oklahoma, almost a homeboy. As CO of finance operations, he signed off on every voucher I paid. He was one of the few officers I trusted. We often drank together across the road in the village of Ban Nong Soong, in a dirt floor bungalow bar among a huddle of stilted teakwood houses. He assured me that I was not the focus, only a cog in the wheel of a methodical process. Major Fujimori's investigation carried on through the summer of 1971.

When the dust settled on the CID investigation, I was cleared, mustered out on time, and shipped out from Bangkok's Don Muaeng Airport on August 7, 1971. Thirty-six hours later, at midnight, my face was plastered to the window as the engines droned and the freedom bird banked east for Travis Air Base. The lights of San Francisco and the Bay Area flickered radiantly like the jeweled mists of an inverted aurora borealis.

My thoughts had been of Noi, an Isaan country girl whom I had shared a bungalow with off Soi Samphan for two months. She had been at the Udorn train station, along with my buddies Shecky, Lennon, Boz, and Egg, to bid me farewell. It seemed likely to me that one of those buddies might pick up where I left off with Noi. For no particular reason, I had turned down the C-130 flight to Don Muaeng that all other returnees took. Standing on the platform waiting on the slow train coming from Nong Khai, no one shed a tear as it heaved and hissed to a stop next to us. We all knew there was a good chance it was the last time we would ever see each other, but there was no need to dwell. Ritually, we gave each other the Brother shake, and then I briskly followed the conductor to a second-class cabin.

In a few minutes, the vendors crowded the hallway. I grabbed a Singha beer and a banana leaf of *khao pat kai* (fried rice with chicken). As the train left the station, listening to the lonesome whistle, the pumping pistons, and the iterative clanking of the wheels against the rails, I stretched out on the bottom bunk and let my mind race in a circle from past to future, running all the red lights of the present. Finally, I slipped into a deep slumber, my body and mind relaxed, suffused with upbeat reveries of ecstatic colors and exotic smells, tastes and imagery: royal red rubies, green curries, Golden Buddhas, Emerald Buddhas, burning joss sticks, heavenly devas, celestial nymphs, nagas, Chanthaburi sapphires, fresh dragon fruit, frangipani blossoms, lotus flowers, blindingly beautiful temples. Next thing I knew, the conductor was banging on the door. Evidently, I had been undisturbed by the arrival whistle and grinding brake-blocks, when moments earlier the train had chug-chugged into Hua Lamphong (Bangkok train station).

As I stumbled down the short set of steps and onto the platform, anonymous under the weight of my duffel bag, I fell into a chaotic scramble of saffron-robed monks, debarking Isaan pilgrims taking their first steps to a fresh start in the fast life of the city, the odd Western hippie or Peace Corps volunteer, and awaiting well-wishers waving to high heaven. The grandiose, half-dome depot was a world unto itself, a neo-Renaissance portal straddling past and present like some Asian Pearly Gate, tricked out with stained-glass windows, marbled floors, and ornate vaulted roofing designed by Italian architects during the kingships of Chulalongkorn and his son Vajiravudh. Straight ahead, positioned high above the come-and-go hubbub, the giant marble clock on the dome's front gable struck 9:00 a.m. It was Friday morning; my last day in country was ticking away.

Minutes later, I pushed through the crowd at the front entrance, stealing a glance up at the omnipresent portraits of the fairy-tale royals, King Bhumibol and Queen Sirikit, and out into a bright early sun. Catcalling prostitutes orbited around. Still peeling the grout from my eyes, standing street side, away from the station's porte cochere of Ionic columns, I heard a familiar voice call my name. Feeling a sudden shock, I turned, and saw it was Noi, beautiful (*swy*) as ever, tallish and slender, shapely in her snug-fitting denim bell-bottoms, her midnight hair tousled across her bare, golden shoulders. She had taken the same train, traveling on the hard seats in third class. She wasn't wacky, moonstruck over me, but she did think of me as a one-way ticket to the States and a more promising life removed from the seamy world in which she lived. She deserved better, but doubling down on work and worries just as a footloose life beckoned wasn't happening. Limping through my best "Tarzan" English and Thai, we talked and I looked into her big, beautiful almond eyes and told her for the second time in twelve hours, good luck and goodbye. Without tarrying for a response, I turned away, ran for a beat-up Mercedes taxi parked near the klong boats, and soon disappeared into the crush of Bangkok traffic and the calm of giant Buddhist statues, pointed in the direction of the Prince Hotel. I was nineteen years old. She was probably seventeen.

Listening to the wheels touch down at Travis Air Base, my thoughts of Noi's disappointed face and dulcet voice faded against the deafening roar of the engine's reverse thrust. Jesus was a corporal last time I stepped on U.S. soil, or, as we called it, the "World," a term more freighted for the combatant whose life had been almost extraplanetary in which time is shrunken and age is accelerated. For me, it had been long enough to have all but forgotten who I was the day I puked on the way to the bus station, leaving for the army.

In an off-runway World War II–era hangar, drugs were on the minds of the army customs officials. In anticipation, I'd spent the last two weeks at Ramusan drug free. Heroin use was rife among troops across the Vietnam theater. The crisis had received a lot of attention back home and now all returnees were required to submit to a drug test. On my arrival in Vietnam and Thailand in late '69, the crude form of heroin known as Red Rock was on every corner along with China White. I'd tasted heroin more than once but never got the habit. Failing the shakedowns or drug tests (known as Operation Golden Flow) before returning to the U.S.—as buddies Augie and Vanickus had—meant the army packed you off to Okinawa for two weeks of rehab. This night at Travis, they dumped my duffel bag across a long wooden table and pawed through everything in forensic detail. No drugs, a couple of sets of civvies, uniforms and boots, the army-issue Gideon bible, heat-worn photos of six girls from back home, my Webster's Dictionary and word lists—mostly the things I had carried with me almost two years before. But for one! "What are you doing with this marine sleeping bag?" an eager second lieutenant named Bumps, whose boots shone like a nickel up a goat's ass, asked as he displayed for me the black stenciling on the bag: Issue Date 1960 and Property of U.S. Marine Corps.

"My company commander, Captain Buster, said it was mine to take," I told Lieutenant Bumps.

"Sorry, soldier, this is U.S. government property, not yours. He had no business telling you that. Now, repack your bag," Bumps commanded me, motioning toward the rumpled and bestrewn chaos of my worldly belongings.

When the conflict of the warring princes of Laos heated up in 1961, President Kennedy dispatched troops to Udorn Thani. Eisenhower warned Kennedy that Laos—not Vietnam—was the wobbly "domino" to watch. The Kremlin responded to the deployment by shipping arms to the Pathet Lao. Still, the superpowers' "open" confrontation over Laos soon fizzled after Kennedy and Khrushchev signed the Geneva Accords of 1962, forbidding the presence of U.S. or Vietnamese troops in Laos. The sleeping bag, left behind by the marine battalion dispatched by Kennedy, was a souvenir, a reminder of where I'd been: The beginning of something that had no clear ending. No one had given me permission to take it.

Mamasan, Dao, a forty-something Thai-Laotian who cleaned my cube, had offered me two dollars for it and I'd turned her down. She used to squat on the rolled-up bag, as if it were hers by some right of a decade of adverse possession. On her cushioned perch, she would crush *mangdas*, roach-size insects found in rice paddies and under the barracks, into a spicy chili paste known as *namprik* in Isaan. I'd slept in the bag dozens of times—in my cube, on the sandy spits of the Mekong, beneath the serpentine arches of the Sai Ngam banyan tree, and romancing the stones in the tumbled wake of moldering *apsaras*, mossy lintels and brooding Buddha statues at the ancient Khmer temple of Phimai. The bag smelled of an Asian spice rack of curry, chilies, basil, coconut, soy, coriander, garlic, ginger, and fish sauce, and earthy like *mangdas* and monkey scat, along with my skin and glands and sweat and sweet tropical blossoms. All that, I thought, calling dibs on it made it mine. But I was wrong…as I watched Bumps toss it into a Goodwill-type bin, I thought that it should have been Dao's sleeping bag. She had been there from the beginning.

What they could not confiscate from me was the thunderous truth that the Vietnam War, known logically by locals as the American War, had been wrong from the beginning. Only weeks before my return, Daniel Ellsberg and the *Pentagon Papers* had exposed in high relief the layers of deceit, confirming what I suspected anyway: that the war was unwinnable. Post-army, I wore that certainty of cumulative knowledge about America's fool's errand into Indochina on my sleeve like a combat patch insignia. Not dogmatically anti-U.S. government or stoked with righteous certitude, but the static voice that gradually broke through the ionosphere of conformity and received wisdom. Those two years framed my identity and inspired a catechism of sacred beliefs, a timeless template crosshatched by a few hard-red lines: War is immoral, corrupt, and illegal. Truth is the first casualty of war. Proxy wars have human hosts. Protest is patriotism. Fuck the war wizards. Fuck the bloodsucking profiteers. Naming a war is important!

Americans, including me, were spoon fed a deceitful narrative. Body counts, battles won, breeding capitalists out of peasants like rabbits, all in care of the Five O'clock Follies. Shot through with a final departing helicopter image that the so-called *Vietnam War* ended on April 30, 1975, with the fall of Saigon. 58,220 Americans had given their lives, along with 8,000 Australians, Thais, and South Koreans who fought side by side with us. Hard to know how many Vietnamese perished in the war, but most agree that three million, north and south, would be a good starting point. The civil war in Laos, the American "Secret War," which was square on my radar screen, took a minimum of 350,000 Laotian lives (including 50,000 civilians). In Cambodia, the Khmer Rouge genocide was a direct result of Nixon's 1970 invasion, and the destabilizing power vacuum it created. The American bombings drove over a million peasants into Phnom Penh like lambs to the slaughter. At least 1.8 million Cambodians perished of hunger, overwork, torture, and execution in the '70s alone.

A tidy history it is not. More like the infamies Dante would describe. A chastening reminder to all of the wicked web we and Henry Kissinger and Body Count Bob wove and left behind in *Indochina* and Main Street America.

Two old friends from Arkansas, Randy Cutting and Dennis Bearden, awaited me at the back door of the arrival hangar on Travis Air Base. A sight for sore eyes if ever there was one, each in pitch-perfect 1960s attire: A fresh tie-dye and favorite beach-bum tee, braided bracelets and neck beads, leather sandals and hair longer than Jesus or Joe Cocker. Words of welcome followed a round of the druggy-in-cahoots, hippie handshakes, a coded variant they offered up two or three times removed from the more familiar "Brother" shake. As if cosmic ferrymen or greeters from another planet, Randy and Dennis carried with them first-hand stories and free-spirited attitudes of the "World." I gulped it all in like nectar from the gods, delighting in the spirit of things, restarting the clock. It was Saturday night, August 7, 1971. The Apollo 15 mission, an extended lunar landing, joined me that evening in its return to planet Earth, the "World."

We crashed in a flop-house railroad apartment near the Haight, the counterculture navel of the universe. It was tight quarters, barely space to swing a cat. We flipped for the bed, and Randy won. Dennis and I slept on the floor. Rap sessions ran long into the night until I had heard the stories twice or more of Led Zeppelin concerts, hitchhiking to folk festivals with the Nitty Gritty Dirt Band and B. B. King, old girlfriends tuning in, dropping out, and discovering mysticism, the whole freak scene in Arkansas. In the early morning, deferring to Dennis and Randy's cultural checklist for San Francisco, we breakfasted at Fisherman's Wharf, scored a matchbox in Golden Gate Park, and walked the steep streets of Chinatown, more illusory than real—the implacable Groundhog Day. Shortly after noon we traversed south on the coast road, Route 1, along the diamond-blue waters of Carmel-by-the-Sea and Big Sur. Down that scenic coast road, I was intent on missing nothing, inclusive of checking out all the gorgeous California girls, many of whom were climbing rocks, hitchhiking, or sprawled in bronze splendor on the beaches.

Those Rip-Van-Winkle-like first impressions of lost time gave me the feeling that I was flipping the sun-kissed pages of a spanking new *Playboy* magazine. And sure enough, in Carmel, off of those pages (or some stone-carved frieze of *apsaras*), a gorgeous, long-legged girl sashayed up to me in a pink two piece and gushed, "Oh my god, I love your tie-dye. Where did you get it?"

"Bought it in Bangkok two days ago, a real Thai-dye," I said, as I impulsively yanked it off and gave it to her. "It's for you. Got out of the army yesterday and today is the best day of my life."

The accent, or perhaps the mention of the army, gave her pause. Then, almost matching my six-foot height, she lunged forward and bear-hugged me, misty eyed with thanks and welcoming me home. As she pulled away, a fragrant citrus scent wafted in the air and on my chest. "What a fine sunny day," I told my homeboys. "That was better than a parade. Made my heart sing."

We spent that second night catching up, soused as sailors, singing a sea shanty ("What will we do with a drunken sailor..."), stargazing on Goleta Beach in Santa Barbara, and passing out like sated driftwood at long last tossed ashore. Yet for me, as it turned out, the drifting had only just begun.

A few days later, back in Arkansas, I stuck my dress khakis, adorned with a handful of colorful ribbons, in the closet like an old football jersey never to be worn again. The experience, however, of cultural dislocation and the louche memories that I wore every day as a Rear Echelon Motherfucker (REMF) were not so easy to put away.

Were those underwhelming military kudos worn across my chest badges of honor or scarlet ribbons? The inside joke was that I only fought two battles and lost both: drug abuse and VD! Still had the clap when I got off that bird home. The army had been my pimp, trafficking my teenage libido through the better brothels of Thailand. Donkey shows in beer-can built bars in the bowels of Tijuana were barely a worthy warm-up act to the choose-your-own-pleasure menu of tawdry tricks (and tropical rot) found by American GIs on R&R in the backrooms of Bangkok's Patpong Road and Soi Cowboy. The dirty deeds added up. A doctoral dissertation couldn't cover the depth of my education on the sociology of lowlife. The thrill of being thrown out of a brothel was only equaled by the irony of being held hostage by a pimp in one.

The judge had partly misread me, through no fault of his. The very "society" he had deemed unthreatened by me was now in the bull's-eye of my justified alienation and restlessness. Within weeks of returning home and taking my place in the work-a-day world and college classroom, my new siloed life of more authority figures began to feel like a watered-down version of army discipline and spoon-fed news and information through the Command mouthpiece of the army *Stars and Stripes* newspaper and the house organ of Armed Forces Radio Services.

Nostalgia, a word of Greek origin, meaning in its deepest sense "pain for return home," had certainly gripped me while abroad, at times like a tropical fever. But once back, I couldn't commit to a serious relationship with a single one of the five or six co-ed pen pals I had shared stories and sweet nothings with for two years. Had my sense of alienation spiked when the pain of separation ceased to exist? Were working girls and one-offs my new norm? Loved the chase and bored with the conquest? In any case, the bloom was off the rose. Nostalgia felt more like an unwanted emotion. I now harbored an irreverence for the past that had been fermented by distance and time.

We all had had a lot in common until we didn't. It didn't help that one co-ed's dad was the doc who'd treated me for the clap at the local public health clinic with a monster shot of penicillin that felt like he took a baseball bat to my ass cheek. And the leading contender for my affections, by no coincidence, was proposed to by a steadier suitor two months before my return. The short of the matter was that no one else was to blame but me: I was unreconciled to life as it had been. It had taken on an abstract, distant fairy tale quality like wishing upon the star that you can never touch. While deployed an ocean away, the pangs of nostalgia I felt had probably been more about a romance with my own oversized fantasies of a remade future than the restoration of some made up past. Like growing out of old clothes, my energies and illusions were now too dissipated to be suspendered.

The world had brimmed over, and I felt completely out of joint, in need of a good laundering of the soul and a footprint bigger than my past. Paraphrasing Robert Penn Warren in *All the King's Men*, I'd left the house and gone into the convulsion of the world, out of history and into history and the awful responsibility of Time.

When Dad signed my enlistment papers in November of 1968, less than a month after I turned seventeen, his best hopes were that I would take the GED and pass, beat the dragon and return from service with my marbles and mobility, go to college and stay out of jail forevermore. It wasn't pretty, but (fleetingly) even I thought I had rounded the corner of something. The Old Phil, the providential thinking went, had effloresced into a broad-shouldered man who held up responsibility and ambition as laudable virtues. But the truth was that keeping an acceptable level of discipline and military mindset had been no guarantee. I stayed overseas as long as I did to avoid the more spit-shined duty in the States and the temptation to tag out and go over the hill and join some traveling circus of stray cats and Commie fire-eaters. Winding up in the brig had been an existential fear. Dad was sure happier with me upon my return than he was when I left. He was a career army officer, active for four years and a reservist for twenty-four more. I hadn't kicked over the traces and embarrassed him, which was cockle-warming and for a moment filled us both with pardonable pride.

Three weeks after my discharge, on the sound advice of my oldest brother John, a doctoral candidate in economics, whose approval was always important to me, I enrolled as a freshman accounting student at the University of Arkansas. My brother Stan and I paid cash for a new Toyota Corolla and rented a duplex on Mt. Sequoyah in Fayetteville. We were both rolling in the clover with allotment savings. Stan had been a supply clerk in Nha Trang, Vietnam, with 5th Special Forces for two years, overlapping with my tours almost precisely. We had spent two R&Rs together in Bangkok. Often employing the military phonetic alphabet to sound more official, we talked weekly on a theater-wide, secure army phone line. Both with healthy savings accounts and a monthly GI Bill check, it was our cookie-cutter world to fuck up.

The army had taught me the simple algebra of accounting: assets minus liabilities equal net worth (cash). The humdrum of balancing to the penny the cash and daily Summary and Certification Sheet (Army form S&CS) defined my military occupational status (MOS), 73-Charlie, a country mile from the trenches of 11-Bravo.

Equations with variables, cold potato mathematics, I had a knack for all that. A glorified abacus, a double entry dandy, a mind like a spreadsheet, that was the new me. Digits did not dominate my dreams, but I talked and felt them in every waking hour. They emboldened me like a congenital disease of the spirit with the power of doubt: Trust but verify, goes the adage. Whether memorizing and sorting out the meaning of the longitudinal and latitudinal coordinate lines on a map or contextualizing natural history's timetable, finely brushstroked numbers became my inherent medium for comprehending complexity and appraising the world. It so happened that analyzing numbers, processing data, and regurgitating results was a profession as old as civilization. The first Sumerian clay tablets were not of poetry, philosophy, or prophecy, but a bean counter's tabulation of mundane crop yields. Palm to the forehead, Whiskey Tango Foxtrot, I had stumbled onto a commodified skill to be brandished like a "get out of jail free" card when the chips were down and I was otherwise preoccupied by a bohemian life of the mind.

Southeast Asians and the war had taught me that no river is too wide, that no point of view is permanent, that *everything* is negotiable...*everything*, inclusive of one's self-determination. It wasn't exactly Buddhism, but I had more than an appreciation of the Noble Truths, the concept of Duhkha, or the painfulness of a mundane life. The big ideas of mindfulness, an awareness of the here and now, and everything changes, had been planted. Easier said than done, but the connection had been made, good enough for a first step. Above all from those earliest footsteps across cultures, I had picked up the travel bug—a cultural contamination condition that I discovered over time alchemizes the fattier, more paleo and philistine walls of the brain.

When I returned to Arkansas the fall semester of '71 (Rod Stewart's "Maggie May" played twice an hour on the local radio), the case could be made that three families ran the entire state, and four fraternities ruled the University of Arkansas. The sought-after shiny penny for the proud sons, often bearing Southern Gothic names (Jr.'s, IIIs, and so on), was to join a fraternity, rally as brothers for panty raids, and marry a sorority girl with a county named after her who would never have a job that came close to paying her dry-cleaning bill. Okay, slightly hyperbolic: There was also a back-to-lander food co-op and thriving counterculture community to go with the mint julep crowd and Tara-imitation, antebellum architecture of the sorority houses and other bastions of sweety-pie segregated harmony.

Within weeks, reinventing myself as Joe College felt like Br'er Rabbit's return to the briar patch. From my first freshman wake-up call, it was clear that the stale rituals of college classrooms had made not a path forward. In my economic theory course, Adam Smith's *capitalist creed* that the shoemaker's reinvested profits create collective wealth took on the animal scent of an old fox's cunning trickery. Ricardo's theory of *comparative advantage*, the clubbiness of First World countries trading together (British textiles for Portuguese wine was the classic example), wasn't settling in much better. What's more, I could only compare my soul-sucking, deskbound and bored state, which I was forced to digest daily, to the botulism and amoebic dysentery I contracted several times while soldiering. It was not complicated. You become what you consume. Stepping out of one impersonal Tar Baby hell into another meant taking a rain check on the Moon in the Seventh House and Jupiter aligning with Mars, the final precession of the Age of Aquarius.

The Road was tugging at me, no two ways about it. Something better would turn up if only I got moving. No royal roads, dead ends, or anything too time sensitive or terrain specific, but the whole wide universe of the utterly unpredictable, unexpected, out of context, random, and ricocheting. A shapeless place without bureaucratic lines and military angles; out of range of the trumpets for reveille and the sound of drums to which I had marched. If nothing else, wonder, wanderlust, the vagabond story, letting the jostle of the road dictate the script, would have to do. Like Gulliver or Ferdinand Fucking Magellan, go there, to ports unknown, beyond the earth's curve, see what's shaking and gulp down all that makes you better.

For all that and more, my well-combed life got scuffed up at a gallop: I grabbed as many vices as available and dropped out after a semester, an old habit that was proving hard to kick. It bothered me to disappoint brother John, whose diabetes was starting to take its toll, but he'd seen my personal anarchy before. Someday, as I came of age, I would have to come to grips with my disdain for authority figures and deskbound hierarchies, and my phobia of self-revelation, of hearing my own voice in a crowded setting, an intractable kind of stage fright. Not just now, though. Kicking that demon on down the road hurt no one. The coming-of-age dynamic of staying on track, of rising in the east like the sun every day, had lost all purchase in the turbulent axis of my state of mind. Mailing it in, flipping off the nattering professors and bumbling conformists, getting my freak on, I leaned into all this with pent-up passion.

A war, pandemic, or natural catastrophe has a way of shining a bright light on fractures in society and government. In that glow, stereotypes surface and often reveal a lot of truth, as much as I had tried to avoid such things. Shortly after I dropped out, my father and I were having a drink on a Sunday afternoon at the Fort Chaffee Officer's Club. A brouhaha erupted from across the barroom. My beard and promising ponytail had apparently offended the manhood of a very drunk colonel, better known as Doc Stewart, a retired army veterinarian. (Admittedly, hirsute pursuits had been fully absent among neighborhood men or Dad's friends and age cohorts when coming of age in Fort Smith.)

Unsteadied by the numbness of diabetic feet from a life at the bottom of the bottle, Doc Stewart had worked his way sheriff-like around the bar and tables, recruiting several of his fellow red-faced warhorses to get the sergeant-at-arms jacked up enough to give me the ol' heave-ho. All the to-do about nothing left me not knowing whether to smile, spit, or swallow. These men, mostly World War II vets, had saved our bacon from the Germans and Japanese. And, even as civilians, their patriotism hewed to some ancient Spartan code of never breaking ranks. Their collective bitterness was as assaultive as the outrage emerging from the burgeoning anti-war movement. A decade before, as a ten-year-old, my summer had been partly consumed by brushing, rubbing, and spit-shining officer's boots for 50 cents a pop and cleaning the leftover quarters and bone-dry bottles of bourbon from their poker tables. From shoeshine boy to soldier in my own right, these were the shoulders of giants I had stood upon, only to discover now their sizable feet of clay.

My father leapt to my defense, hammer and tongs. "What the fuck is going on here?" he asked, as he pushed his barstool back and stood and addressed the room, looking everyone in the eye, one at a time. He told them that I had served the better part of two years in the Vietnam theater. At the time, I carried a copy of my discharge papers for student loan and GI Bill purposes. Rather than cuffing an old coot or two, which did cross my mind, as Dad talked I reluctantly held up the papers as Exhibit A, revealing that I had received the perfunctory Vietnam Campaign and Service Medals. He had shamed them. Sheepishly, they deliberated as a jury in private, and then, one by one, the sad-sack drunk Colonel Stewart first, they bought me a drink. Acquitted of wearing an unpatriotic hairstyle, I guessed.

After draining the free whiskey, we left. I never returned to the boorish exclusivity of their last beachhead, a drinking club, defined more by what the mossback members didn't like, their fears, their astigmatism in perception of the changing times, than the hopeful world the Greatest Generation had once held up to me. Showing those papers shamed me as well. Why did I need a veteran hole card or clutch commentary by my father to grow my hair? That day at the Officer's Club signaled my departure from a life-long association with the military. King Canute no longer controlled the tides. Living passively like a particle in the ocean while someone else made decisions for me was old school. In the same moment, I stepped up my solidarity with the anti-war movement, singing the songs of peace. A formal sundering with God Almighty himself was not far behind.

If not for the war, the '60s would have turned out much differently. It had become a point of pride that my peers had galvanized the movements that continued to convulse the country. The world as I had understood it, once again, was vastly changed. With a rucksack on my back, from a California commune and a hideout in Big Sky Country to Kurdistan and the Cradle of Civilization, for four years I chased the fading gnosis of the '60s right into the mid-'70s. There was no direction home.

The Road to Perdition

Chapter Nine

ROAD TRIPS ARE EXPERIENCES freighted with meaning, full of forks, bumps, twists, turns, and routes to ruin, recovery, and better places of the soul. James Baldwin once wrote: "If the concept of God has any validity or any use, it can only be to make us larger, freer, and more loving. If God cannot do this, it's time to get rid of him." And, that's what I did. Six months before moving to Santa Barbara I abandoned fully my already flagging faith in Christianity. The denouement came about on a rollicking road trip with what felt like a chancy focus group of Doubting Thomases: A carload of old friends cut from the same convention-breaking cloth, who had fed at the same trough of cultural comfort food.

In late December of 1971, Dennis Bearden, Randy Cutting (RC), and I gave Greg Smith a lift back to D.C. and Georgetown University in my spanking new Corolla. What seemed like only days before, sports and the Boys Club, not church or school, had connected me with this pack of hell-raisers, now clumped together like unwhisked grits.

Over the course of our red-eye jaunt to D.C., Dennis, Greg, and RC hammered away at whatever itsy-bitsy shred of blind faith to which I still clung. Having all recently completed their university Western Civ courses, they fancied themselves worldly and world weary. Adopting a kind of rabid reductionism, they held no fancy illusions about matters of religion, human origins, or civilization. The narrative was old hat, almost linear. Kicked off in the Fertile Crescent and spread inexorably to cave-dwelling hominids of Europe. Then came Athens, Rome, Albion, Norse land. From that European clay, the civilized world was molded. Simple as that, tie it in a bow and live with it.

The sky was pink and purpling behind us as we crossed the Big Muddy to Memphis and rolled on across Tennessee in total darkness. My educated boon mates made no mention that early evening of little frosty Eskimos, pyramid-building Nubian kings, Mansa Musa's riches, dreamy Shakya princes, the Vedic Sanskrit hymns, the Analects of Confucius, the Yellow River, rice domestication, and the Four Great Inventions: papermaking, the compass, gunpowder, and printing. Never mind that Western Civilization was enabled by the absorption of Eastern ideas and technologies. As upper-classmen pulling rank, the College-Joe seniority system played out like cardinals instructing a choir boy. Their rolling anti-religion blitz on me and my sophomoric intuitions came down something like this: "Hitler was a Christian. Every civilization, the Romans, Greeks, Assyrians, has had their gods. They are all the same, killing in the name of religion," Dennis, who suffers no fools, asserted. "You think America's favorite snake oil salesman Billy Graham ain't promoting Nixon, Kissinger, and killing godless gooks in Vietnam? Right. Think again, read the paper."

Greg was taciturn, but when he spoke he let out a casual boom and the muscular wisdom of his words came down with the gravitas and thunder of higher authority. Earlier than most, Greg was quick to grasp complexity. In high school, he was a page for Senator William Fulbright, head of the Senate Armed Services Committee. He still worked for the senator's office, part time, while he pursued his International Relations degree at Georgetown. "LBJ's war council of commie-hating Christians upped the ante in Vietnam with the Gulf of Tonkin Resolution," he discoursed, followed by a bark of laughter. "Fulbright broke ranks with LBJ over that bald-faced lie.

What did Vietnamese babies do to these Christians to deserve to be napalmed? It's a big bear hug of money, politics, and the Pentagon."

And, so it went, a colloquy of gamely exchanges that intellectually challenged the mere truth of Christianity and morally objected to the cruel, petrified precepts laid down by men of another era. After two years of a noncombatant role in the Vietnam War, an object lesson in Eastern Civ, I knew their words to be true. To their point, my personal god of mercies had become a stranger during my two consecutive tours, thanks in part to the Christian war wizards whoring up the narrative. This had always been so. In World War II, Nazi, American, and Soviet Christians relied on the same god to answer their prayers. The omnipotent Saint George on the horse with his Zeus-like powers was so fungible that he could answer the prayers of opposing armies who hated each other with a vengeance. On and on, more questions and paradoxes than answers and meanings about the Lord's Mysterious Ways.

Deep in the night, with me at the wheel, winding through the Great Appalachian Valley near Knoxville, RC, a young man with the polite manners of an Old World grandee, guffawed wickedly like the devil incarnate. "No one believes a pair of penguins hiked up through the Sahara to secure passage on Noah's Ark. That's a sucker bet." RC, who could tell a spicy story, was just getting warmed up. He challenged me to walk everyone in the car through the Christmas Eve donkey ride in the desert, the virgin birth, Joseph cuckolding God, and the Easter ghost story (the resurrection). "Tell them about the prostitute finding him and everything else that came down at Calvary," he goaded me. It was his Lenny Bruce riff, putting a clown nose on everyone. Worked like a charm, tag-teaming a punch drunk.

The entire 1,150 miles, we never quit jabbering, regurgitating our coming-of-age lessons. We smoked cheap dope and Winston regulars with abandon, and popped steady doses of tiny white pills. Talking a leopard out of his spots was fair game.

Conversations that night kept looping back to a certain rapturous anatomy, drug-taking heroics, Hogball, Vietnam, Western Civ, Christian hope, matters of eschatology. The radio crackled in and out, as did Don McClean's chart-topping hit, "American Pie": *Drove my Chevy to the levee but the levee was dry…good ole boys drinking whiskey and rye…singing this'll be the day that I die.* Drunks in a midnight choir doesn't fairly describe four tone deaf Arkies on a cross country brain-bender in a palsy-walsy sing-a-long.

We made booze stops, but nary a one for nosh. By the time we arrived in striking distance of D.C., I was beaten down like a tongue-tied troglodyte. Together, Dennis, Greg, and Randy were incontestably a few chapters and verses ahead of me when it came to the ideas and innovations of Socrates, the Magna Carta, Galileo, Rousseau, Darwin, and the Declaration of the Rights of Man.

And, I suppose Dennis nailed it to the barn when he deadpanned: "People should watch what they make up. You never know what folks are going to believe 2,000 years from now."

More last straw than blinded by the light, on the eastern banks of the Shenandoah River, on a piss stop beyond some listless tank town, I impulsively threw my arms up to a crisp and churning Virginia firmament. In the gesture of a referee signaling a touchdown, I screamed a Grand Canyon Fuck You to the O Bearded Wonder and the Goddamn Stud Horse he rode in on! My boys kept on yammering, fertilizing, and ho-humming my apostatizing milestone as just another piss stop on the road to D.C.

Had a headache when I came to. But no guilt, sweats of mortal fear, earthquakes, tidal waves, or sulfuric odors of hell. The sun rose, the birds sang, and the bacon was salty. It was the first day of undertaking a process of unhitching and reshaping, which was far from hurried or mechanistic, not an overnight thing. Fair to say, embracing the Temple of Reason, as a way of being, called for a lot of dismantling. A pillar at a time, years upon years. There was no logical path forward; anything was plausible and everything was inchoate.

A tricky wasteland of doubts and reconsidered gospel truths grew in my mind and conspired to gather all the fresh sunshine. Mindful of the cognitive constraints, my goal was to retune the hierarchical Judeo-Christian credo into a nonreligious key, more truth seeker than Christian sheeple. Elevating the reasoning mind above the babel of tribalism, dogma, religion, and self-interest was a challenge to inertia, an act of "cognitive debiasing." My sea legs were on, though. The flat earth had begun to recede. It was precisely a coming-of age-moment, not to be too confused with growing up.

On December 24, 1969, I had attended Bob Hope's Christmas USO Tour at Camp Friendship, on the outskirts of Korat, Thailand. It was my first of two Christmases in the region. Hope's wise guy jokes delivered between golf swings were certainly entertaining. For a field full of lovelorn soldiers and airmen, however, it's safe to say we were more enthralled by Connie Stevens, Teresa Graves of *Laugh In*, and Dean Martin's Golddiggers. A distant runner-up was astronaut Neil Armstrong, who had walked on the moon five months before. As the Soviets sneered (and the Vatican scowled), I wanted to believe that Copernicus smiled broadly as Armstrong witnessed the sun's reflection on planet Earth just as we view the moon at night. On this Christmas Eve, he launched into a rousing speech, full of "can-do" exhortations that championed the spirit of exploration. It took a few seconds to adapt to the moonwalker's haze-free, earthbound, three-dimensionality, a sight packed with poetry surpassing the mythic imaginations of the ancient Greeks.

At the time, across the Mekong in Laos, your average villager didn't know about Armstrong's walk on the moon. When a lunar eclipse occurred, Laotians were known to freak out in a violent expression of primal awe and shout and shoot at the moon, scaring away the "cosmic frog" that was trying to gulp it down.

The juxtaposition struck me as the classic mind-matter dilemma. On which side of the Mekong would St. Augustine find his truth were he to witness such parallel universes? Stone Age superstition or Space Age science? Or might he have welcomed the paradox and straddled the river? Nobel Prize–winning physicist Niels Bohr made that case: "The fact that religions through the ages have spoken through images, parables, and paradoxes means simply that there are no other ways of grasping the reality to which they refer. But that does not mean that it is not a genuine reality. And splitting this reality into an objective and subjective side won't get us very far."

In *Zen and the Art of Motorcycle Maintenance*, Robert Pirsig captured humankind's soft spot for doubt, fallacy, and mystery:

> *You are never dedicated to something you have complete confidence in. No one is fanatically shouting that the sun is going to rise tomorrow. They know it's going to rise tomorrow. When people are fanatically dedicated to political or religious faiths or any other kinds of dogmas or goals, it's always because these dogmas or goals are in doubt.*

Subjective spirituality was made for you and me, goes the thinking. If I'd done two combat tours in Vietnam as a machine gunner on the DMZ with the 3rd Marine Division from 1967 to 1969, I might have become a fundamentalist Baptist preacher just as high school acquaintance Tommy Jordan did. But I didn't share his foxhole or the burdens he carried home.

The switching of spiritual gears carried many challenges. Some things were not possible to just "will away," to kick off like a pair of old sandals. Guilt and penance come to mind first. Nested into my everyday temporal essence, those psychic responses, as one, hovered like buzzards ready to swoop down on the third rail of my joy.

My instinct was to throw the baby out with the bathwater. I had been nursed on the milk of three mothers: the biological one, the Boys Club, and the Methodist Church. All that abided of that three-legged stool was the Methodist Church, which I related to in the same way as the late, great Brooklyn Dodgers president Branch Rickey. Asked why he handpicked Jackie Robinson to be the first black baseball player in MLB, Rickey responded. "He's a Methodist. I'm a Methodist. God is a Methodist."

The Methodist church was the cornerstone of my organic whole: culture, country, spiritualism. My decision to vamoose this foundation so freighted with memories left me conjuring the unimaginable future.

As the modern *Homo sapiens* brain achieved its present size, a cognitive revolution took place. Fear, respect, cooperation, language, a smelly corpse, superstition, grieving, whatever the reasons, the act of burying the dead became a signal departure from the purely secular lives of hunters and gatherers. Similarly, to my myth-making ancestors, death as the ultimate democracy weighed on me (and still does). Grieving surely took on an added kick in the ass without some faith in eternity beyond this side. It's the unending absence we all fret about. As family and friends would pass, as a nonbeliever, I would come to accept that the hereafter—the Good Lord taking us home—came down to no more than an exhaled nothingness of pain-free oxygen molecules. Dead as Custer's fucking nuts, in other words. That I was no longer living life waiting on something that didn't exist in turn put the kibosh on fictive notions of a treacly Karber family sequel yonder in the New Jerusalem where wolves lay with lambs and leopards with kids and time is all topsy-turvy: one day is like a thousand years and vice versa. A favorite photo resurrecting me on the wall would have to do in my new atomized material world, a continuum of animate stardust, in which everything disintegrates.

Too much reality is hard for anyone to bear. The awareness of an "ending," I worked out, gives a life its meaning and passion, similar to the Japanese acceptance of the paradox of taking pleasure in the cherry blossom season while being painfully conscious of the blossom's cycle of life. The pink landscape will disappear, so try not to die before you die, is the brass ring.

Impermanence can be beautiful. Living day by day—my new way of thinking instructed me—was as long range and close to eternity and infinite wisdom as it got. None of this was self-explanatory, much less written down as settled criteria like some godawful 12-step program. One day at a time, by the seat of my pants.

What's more, the false hope of a lottery ticket never improved my finances and praying to a personal god never got me out of a tight spot. My will-o'-the-wisp bedtime ritual of prayer was soon replaced with an alter-ego-like voice that still chatters in the back of my head, not unlike the wise and wisecracking dummy Charlie McCarthy. Someone once told me that 98 percent of thought was unconscious. If true, it explains why my Charlie McCarthy chatters like a magpie, without break. As it worked out, prayers and dummies' voices are perfectly interchangeable soul soothers.

If a Jew becomes nonobservant it's still likely that he or she will continue to participate in Passover Seders as a celebration of freedom and liberation. Or, as a pragmatist might do, now and again, attend a service. Not a mutinous Gentile. Our reinvention usually signals sayonara to Sunday put-ons. Even the illusion of the sanctuary as some kind of stained-glass mystical cave all splattered with shards of sunlight begins to crack from the middle out like a busted windshield. It felt like a zero-sum exodus, a full gainer from the Ark of Safety. Without too much forethought, this became the painful calculus of my new bargain.

On Sunday morning, chimes had always rung in my head. The peal of those bells summoned a panoply of moods. It's the time of the week to scrub up, shut my pie hole, writhe with chimp-like distress into those new hand-me-down Sunday best with a clip-on tie and white socks, and, most of all, be reverent. More far reaching, the sound of church bells brought to mind that ineffable spiritual (god-inspired) sense of connectivity to a broader group and all the foundational customs and rites that gave rise to its flourish: Miss Edna Earle Massey blasting out a medley of sounds on the pipe organ, the choir's chorus of nasal sopranos soaring with Charles Wesley's "Hark, the Herald Angels Sing," proud young parents offering up their white lace-wrapped babies for the sacramental plunge, Dr. Roebuck's grace-filled exegesis of Beatitudes, the backbench Sunday morning camaraderie among friends, church league baseball games and fellowship picnics beneath the Big Slide at Creekmore Park, John Guthrie's slideshows of his mission trips to the war-torn Congo, licking the envelope to send another $10 donation. The abrupt absence in my weekly rhythms of those customs and more left me jonesing for a backup, another fulcrum, or place of solidarity, in the local cosmology.

The existential conundrum of how to recreate that comfort zone of communal reflection about life's deeper matters was double-edged. In Fort Smith gossip is an art supreme, if not the second-oldest profession. The stain from the small-town tattoo of troubled-kid-from-a-broken home would never go away. One too many times I had been broadsided by my fellow church-goers, clutching their pearls in tongue-wagging frenzies, flavored with hearsay about a certain dissolute homewrecker. The faithless wife, as old as Eve and the serpent, was a juicy story, made more lurid by the prominence of the characters. The busybodies didn't know the half of it. Even so, it had become an adult Sunday school game of Chinese whispers conducted mostly by the respectable hat-and-glove biddies whose obsession with the topic almost bordered on envy. Faced with going somewhere else, fact is, I ain't the "joining type." Never would be. Enough. Gone. Good riddance.

So rather than puzzling out a happy medium, I spent Sunday mornings defiantly smoking plump, sticky buds of Toad Suck Thunder Fuck and Eureka Springs Sensimilla. Couch locked, I read voraciously, flipped channels, and decried the Christianity-rooted evils of Irish and British terrorism; the cross-bearing KKK; abortion clinic bombers; freelance salvation-selling ("Once the coin into the coffer clings, a soul from purgatory heavenward springs"); wrath-spewing impresarios like Garner Ted Armstrong, Jimmy Swaggart, Jim and Tammy Faye Bakker (Praise the Lord); and faith-healing Pentecostal fantasists such as Oral Roberts. All sententious, white-bread devils with Juicy Fruit smiles and, but for Tammy Faye, costumed in black Sunday suits. Slow inhale, slow exhale, toke, toke, rip: Fuck the Westboro Baptist Church.

Hanging on to the logic and moral consistency of the Gentle Jesus was another matter and not so much a conscious decision. After fifteen years of listening to mindful sermons by the venerable Fred G. Roebuck, who was wise as old Solomon and never invoked the devil or God as a cruel master in his sanctuary, there was already a "patterning" of my soul. Fred G.'s sermons had sunk down deep like bedrock, vestigially steeping me in the radical walk and talk that Jesus laid down. More political than religious, the core gospel message taught me that he was an anti-establishment champion of the poor, the sick, the homeless, and the stranger; a faithful friend to sinners; and an arch-foe to greed and parasitic power.

It's all relative, they say. The lessons of the historic and very human Jesus held fast with no fear of the hounds of hell lurking beyond my Sunday wake-'n'-bake. In fairy tales, they say, the "power of three" has always made for a more satisfying story. Based on no need for further myths, I chucked the inventions of immaculate conception, the Father, the Son, and the Holy Ghost out of the rabbit's hat they arrived through and stayed with something akin to what Thomas Jefferson called the Life and Morals of Jesus of Nazareth, in which he scissored out all the references to miracles in the New Testament.

Mark Twain, river boat captain, humor-lit medium of Tom Sawyer and Huck Finn, and keen observer of foreign cultures, once said that he "never let his schooling interfere with his education." My fondness for spinning globes, thumbing atlases, reading books and creating a more accessible world, gave me a respectable reality as an autodidact, a recovering reprobate with high aspirations for a rich life of the mind. That early yen for travel, and for the longer sweep of human history and literature, lit up my neurons and began to open new doors of profound mystery and beauty. Chapter by chapter, missing links to living organisms took on a seriousness akin to holy writ: Leakey's *homo habilis* to the aboriginal's migration, Gilgamesh's epic to Homer's odyssey, Hammurabi's code to Herodotus's histories, Rome's fall to Constantinople's rise, Mohammed's journey to Magellan's discovery. Nuanced rhythms of time and place, of peace and destruction, liberated my thoughts, which began to twirl in different directions like the rooster atop the farmhouse roof—red flagging the cycles of elemental humanity, birth, growth, death, rebirth.

As I freed myself of conceptual bias, the Old Testament allegories like Jonah and the Whale, David and Goliath, and the Books of Ecclesiastes and Exodus became eminently readable literary touchstones. American novelist Thomas Wolfe described Ecclesiastes as "the greatest single piece of writing I have ever known, and the wisdom expressed in it the most lasting and profound." Ernest Hemingway's first novel, *The Sun Also Rises*, which depicts the eating-the-apple aimlessness of the Lost Generation, took its title from chapter one of Ecclesiastes: *"One generation passeth away, and another generation cometh: but earth abideth forever. The sun also ariseth, and the sun goeth down, and hasteth to his place where he arose..."* Pete Seeger, folk singer and social activist, put to music and slightly modified verses of the third chapter of Ecclesiastes to create a chart-topping hit and generational earworm, "Turn! Turn! Turn! (To Everything There is a Season)." Six chapters beyond the inspiration for Seeger's anthem, God seems to give a ringing endorsement to me and my newly chosen here-and-now lifestyle: "a living dog is better than a dead lion." Amen, Ecclesiastes. (Pardon my picking and choosing of another verse, but one of my army nicknames was Dog, so it's personal.)

The story of Exodus equally resonated. The Hebrew narrative of slavery, revolt, flight, infighting, and the binding and arrival of diverse peoples in the Promised Land speaks volumes to our common ancestral journey. America is no exception, populated by a majority of immigrant diaspora families such as my own.

The Founding Fathers had to have been profoundly aware from their reading of the Bible that a free people must be bound by laws and not think of themselves as Chosen People as Paul Kruger imagined Afrikaners to be in apartheid South Africa. The Exodus narrative of fleeing for refuge depends on themes of resilience, freedom, and equality. Freedom, especially, is why America's Founding Fathers chose religious neutrality by not once mentioning God in the Constitution. Jefferson, as usual, provided in his only book, *Notes on the State of Virginia*, this commonsense statement: "It does me no injury for my neighbor to say there are twenty gods, or no god. It neither picks my pocket nor breaks my leg."

The sixty-six books and 773,692 words of the Bible, the dualism of God and the devil serpent, the polytheism of saints, the ghosts of the dead, I understood, were like Grandma's nightshirt, an attempt to cover everything. Among the dark alleyways of cherry-picked prejudice, hatred and hell-fire theology, the Bible is packed with countless pearls of universal truth and a rich folk history of people.

In its own time, my dewy set of beliefs in the secular, humanistic realm took its daily bread from the brain-racking awareness of my own fiends and faults, and the task of transcending my "self-incurred immaturity." For all that, sinning, as Hemingway expressed in *The Nick Adams Stories*, remained my favorite part of repentance.

> "You're going to have things to repent, boy," Mr. John had told Nick. "That's one of the best things there is. You can always decide whether to repent them or not. But the thing is to have them."

We celebrated that first night in D.C.—the rape and murder capital of the U.S.A. at the time—by getting even more gassed than on the drive up. Like good urban anthropologists, we probed the Georgetown bar scene, beginning with the Crazy Horse and Silver Dollar, where Greg had worked as a bouncer on weekends. By the wee hours we found ourselves across town on DC's 14th Street, a neon jungle of porno film houses, chasing a few enterprising Mary Magdalenes. Turned out we had stumbled into a bevy of black transvestites (as they were commonly termed at that time) and we were in no condition down that dark alley to tell a "he" from a "she" in a dress. Once the light came on and the pants got zipped up, you've never seen four Arkies make tracks like we did back to Greg's house in white-bread Arlington. Some divine intervention was needed to raise this depraved hound dog's head up the next morning at Union Station, awaiting the Amtrak to New York.

We eternal amigos returned to college that spring. As usual, I was lured with the force of a magnetic cue to migrate on…and I did. By April, I had dropped out, with a celestial heading drawing me to coastal California. It was another new page with no fixed formula, murky, unshaped, sponge-like, full of life, a no-man's-land of faith, mystery, and doubt. Years on, when I read Keats's thoughts on looking into Chapman's translation of Homer, I recalled all the possibilities of that spring moment:

> …Then I felt like some watcher of the skies
> When a new planet swims into his ken;
> Or like stout Cortez when with eagle eyes
> He star'd at the Pacific—and all his men
> Look'd at each other with wild surmise—
> Silent upon a peak in Darien.

Sojourns and Wanderings

Part Three

California Dreaming

Chapter Ten

WELL NOW, HELLO FREEDOM. Don't mind if I do. Turning on, tuning in, and dropping out was my new spoken word. Life had only just begun for this newly freed spiritual bum. It was my *Easy Rider* moment to toss the watch in the sand, kick it into gear, and vroom off into the unformed and unrevealed wilderness.

California communal living was the perfect post-army counterculture warm-up. Mark Stouffer, a fellow Arkansan who was attending Brooks Institute of Photography, found me and Sad Eyed Sadie, a temporary companion, an upstairs room in a shabby two-story corner house at 336 Cota Street in Santa Barbara. Four nudists—Ralph and Vern, naval-academy-turned-antiwar-activists, and their girlfriends—shared the upstairs space, a revolving door at times.

Palm trees on the southwest end of the postage-stamp yard blocked the view of the California Motor Vehicle office and blunted the background hum of U.S. 101. Tibetan prayer flags representing the five elements, a blooming jacaranda, and a lemon tree from which Ralph picked fresh lemons the size of oranges every morning flanked the front stoop and sidewalk leading into the street. A right turn on the palm-lined sidewalk led to the cliffside perch of Santa Barbara City College and beyond to the harbor and city fish market. In the opposite direction, four blocks east and north, was historic State

Street, chock-a-block in Spanish Colonial and Mission architecture, climbing up and into the Santa Ynez Mountains.

Tropically lush California bungalow yards made up the neighborhood grid in between 336 Cota and State Street: orange, avocado, lemon, and African flame trees; Canary Island date palms; Mexican fan and blue palms; and Caribbean royal palms and jacarandas. Wind chimes, peace signs, psychedelic art, Che-in-the-Beret portrayals, and macramé mandalas adorned the porches, and most yards displayed a McGovern-for-President sign. Sun-splashed days, a gentle ocean breeze at nights, always smelling of the sea… I had been transplanted like everything else in Santa Barbara on a magical urban patch of ground that felt more Mediterranean-let-your-freak-flag-fly than Main Street America.

The South that fed my youth was larded in myth and twisted logic, leaving my cultural and political gestation far from developing root and branch. Still in fetal form, striving, not fully fleshed out, I remained a Bildungsroman without a table of contents. Mind and soul, I was a free-floating grab bag of alienation, anxiety, and despair. Unwittingly, it was those tendencies that nudged me further and further out of that comfort zone of ordinariness to become a manic seeker of experiential truth. And often as not, my newly discovered truth had an illegal, stick-it-to-the-man, iconoclastic warp to it, a fine truth nonetheless.

The whole hipster canvas had been painted, but better late than never to pitch in with the Woodstock Nation. Only recently, I had sat saucer-eyed through a stem-winder delivered by Abbie Hoffman, inveterate political prankster and founder of the Youth International Party, on the merits of his storm-the-barricades-style revolution. That early September night on a makeshift stage on the dirt floors of the University of Arkansas's Barnhill Arena, where so many years ago I had provided half-time entertainment as a Boys Club basketballer, Abbie, often with a clenched revolutionary fist in the air and without notes, rattled the pillars of power with incendiary grenades for an hour and twenty minutes. He was a walking, talking flamethrower, a one-off in a world full of beige. "Vietnam is the cutting edge of American Imperialism," he declaimed like Eugene Debs on the stump during World War I before giving the packed arena a call to action. "We must reorganize our whole thinking about crime and theft. We must steal from them [the government]." He wrapped it up with a bitter assault on corporate cupidity and how to beat the draft and the telephone system.

Fortified with Abbie's holy words and having liberated his book, *Steal This Book*, from the Book Den, an exquisitely curated bookstore off of State Street, out I went into this brave new ideological foment. Whenever short on cash, which was often, I thumbed the pages of *Steal This Book*. For starters, it instructed that most grocery chains (no cameras at the time) received soda bottle returns on the honor system at some designated spot near the store entrance. In the day, a case of empties fetched between a $1.50 and $2.00. A couple of times a week I made a run to Vons (Safeway), or its local competition, and picked up bread, bouillon, Ramen, Vienna sausages, canned sardines, TV dinners, Falstaff or Blatz. A swell menu, staples all. The scam began and ended at the register, requiring a minimum of tactical guile, a few words to the checker, and a nonchalant gesture: "four cases" followed by a finger wag toward the front door. Affecting that body language of lying-to-the teacher indifference—with a smile—was a well-honed talent of mine. The checker would reflexively glance over at a wall of fifty or more cases, and ring me up. It was too easy. They never questioned my count, fish-eyed me, or even walked over to look at which cases might be mine. Often, I got change.

Ralph and Vern, both electrical engineers, showed me one of the more sophisticated anti-corporate scams going down in California (and an incipient Silicon Valley), "phone phreaking," created by Stuart Brand's *Whole Earth Catalog* crowd of acid-taking, music-loving, anti-war hippies and hardware hobbyists. They preached sharing of resources, control of your own tools, opposition to central authority and held a special distaste for the military-industrial-complex and the monopolistic IBM mainframes, symbols of government creep and corporate dominion. "Power to the people" was the catalog's driving ethos, and LSD was the creative catalyst the Bay Area community of engineering minds used to think outside the box.

Using a bosun whistle found in a Cap'n Crunch cereal box, "phreaks" could build a Blue Box capable of reproducing tones that would match AT&T frequencies on a telephone operator's dialing console. This allowed the Blue Box hacker to simulate an operator and enjoy free long-distance telephone calls.

Founders of Apple computer, Steve Wozniak and Steve Jobs, were early Blue Box pranksters (and LSD takers). Rich with irony, scamming AT&T, the world's largest corporation, paid off. The Promethean narrative that started in California's Bay Area as anti-bureaucracy corporate theft gave rise to personal computers and smart phones that have done more than politics ever did to empower individuals and change society.

No wage slaves resided at 336 Cota Street. We were all on the dole, diddling the man, catch-as-catch-can. Self-imposed poverty presented a precarious business model, though. Selling drugs, collecting food stamps and unemployment, hornswoggling AT&T's phone card system, financing by pawn shop, panhandling on State Street along with the robed and powder-faced Hare Krishna in front of Charlie Chaplin's 1920s-era Arlington Theater. Hypnotically, those sweet guys chanted "Hare Krishna Hare Krishna / Krishna Krishna Hare Hare…" so many hours a day I was sure they fell asleep with lockjaw.

Never made any money panhandling, mostly because I was just tagging along. My heart wasn't in it. I was too embarrassed to look people in the eye and hassle them for money that way. While Ralph and Debbie worked the crowd, actually picking up a few bones a piece, I liked shooting the breeze with a Texas transplant, Sam-the-Sham the Preacher Man. His jiveass patter was always amusing. Tall and skinny as a snake with beady eyes like a possum, Sam occupied a corner spot every day and greeted all comers with jazz hands and a "praise the Lord, the Rapture is here," delivered in a booming Texas twang that resonated like thunder across the theater plaza. But for his "Jesus Saves" tee-shirt and aviator sunglasses, the fashion of many a good actor, he dressed like a cowboy fresh off the family goat and cotton farm near the community of Stampede, Texas. His handwoven laundry basket, half-full of dirty clothes, half-empty short pints, and packs of nonfiltered Camels, was covered in quarters and dollar bills by the end of each day. Sam was a talker, with a vivid imagination, devoted to the marketing maxim that says if you have a good theme, flog it. When closing in on his next sucker, he'd squint his beady eyes, rub his hands together to husband the holy power, and reel off born-again Bible verses with the rapid-fire cadence of a barnyard auctioneer selling spring lambs: John 3:16 (For God so loved the world…), Acts 2:38 (Repent and be baptized…), Revelation 1:8 (I am the Alpha and Omega…), and his go-to spawn-of-the-devil invocation, 1 Corinthians 6:18 (Flee from sexual immorality…). When not praising the Lord and warning of the rapture, Sam was nipping on some red-eye and telling tall tales about fighting and fucking.

The first time we met, he told me he had been kicked out of the Alamo Christian Foundation down the road in Agua Dulce for giving several followers the clap. "Tony [Alamo] was fucking them too. Could have been him," Sam said.

"Why didn't you roll over on that phony piece-of-shit of a prophet?" I asked.

"I did, but his wife Susan [Alamo] was the judge, jury, and executioner in that marriage. She decided to make me the fall guy. That's okay. They'd bought some land near her hometown of Alma, Arkansas, and were talking about moving the foundation there. I'd go home to Stampede before I'd follow Missus Edith Opal Horn [Susan] to Podunk, Arkansas. Nothing against your darling Razorbacks, friend, you understand."

My favorite Sam whopper was about when a mountain lion leapt at him while he was camping with two lesbians in Yosemite. He said he knocked that big cat cold with a Palooka punch and rejoined the campfire orgy. "Keeping my powder dry. Didn't want to waste any bullets," he assured me, letting go a foot stomping howl.

"Sam, did you leave the mountain lion just lyin' there?" I deadpanned. He didn't miss a beat, the quicksilver mind of an inspired fabulist wheeling in a thousand directions at once.

"Hell no, skinned that fucker and made feral love on the pelt till the cows came home. They purr'd off to sleep after sunrise."

Cling, cling, cling, I threw a couple of nickels and a dime in his basket, afraid to ask him if those lesbians had whupped him up some mountain lion backstrap for breakfast.

Abbie, of course, passed along many more useful subterfuges that the more seasoned souls at 336 Cota Street ritually relished. Most memorable was diving into the dumpsters on Wednesday afternoon when our patron saint, Safeway, tossed out the bruised fruit and vegetables.

Vern was our de facto point man. For some reason, he always seemed to be the one who leapt first into the fetid-reek in his tattered jean shorts and bare feet. The number-one son of an academy-trained admiral from Norfolk, Virginia, Vern had a peace sign tattooed on his shoulder and a red macramé Nepali wish bracelet on his wrist. At first glance, he reminded me of Art Garfunkel with his curly receding hairline and side-whiskers. But Vern was much more. At twenty-four, he had already achieved a Zenlike inner-calm, self-possessed, not at war with his past. He spent days at a time studying, meditating, and practicing Kundalini yoga at the Bodhi Path Buddhist Center. Vern devoured every arcane text he could find on right living, homeopathic remedies, and macrobiotics, and the dietary yin and yang of mung beans, sunchokes, and chaparral tea.

Ralph, stocky, deeply tanned with a ship tattoo on his left arm and a chestnut ponytail, was high energy—an alpha dog, a balls-to-the-walls adrenaline freak. I learned this well on several rides with him at high speed on the back of his 750 Suzuki. Like Vern, Ralph was also in search of a cosmic breakthrough. He took up meditation in a converted ice cream factory off State Street with the Brotherhood of the Sun, led by a disciple of Paramahansa Yogananda, who authored the popular book *Autobiography of a Yogi*.

The Brotherhood had recently bought 150 acres out Gibraltar Road and started the Sunburst commune. Weeks before my arrival, Ralph had started volunteering on the commune's vegetable farm and in the juice factory. Other than meditating and helping out on the farm, like me, he had nothing but time on his hands.

Vern and Ralph came to UC Santa Barbara, a radical hotbed, to finish their engineering degrees—after a two-year stint in the enlisted navy as payback for the free ride they received at the U.S. Naval Academy. They were not part of the bomb-thrower militancy that thrived along a radical rhumb line from UC Santa Barbara to UC Berkeley, but they sure as hell didn't mind being in the neighborhood.

Ralph, in his Rajasthani pants, always followed Vern into the Safeway dumpster as if still paired in a buddy system venture back at Annapolis, competing on the obstacle course. The rest of us joined in with a greenhorn's gusto.

It was an easy vault into a loafer's plucking glory, a freeloader's bonanza. We came up looking like rats fresh out of a drainpipe, clutching an embarrassment of riches. Pooling our resources, we threw a monster party with a loose clique of neighbors and friends. Like kitchen magicians, back on Cota Street with the spoils of our sinus-searing forage, we cleaned and cut and plopped and placed the adzuki beans, rice, and a rainbow of veggies into boiling kettles and casserole dishes and smothered it all in Sunburst commune's goat cheese. Voila, salad bowls soon dripped in a chill mix of homemade Hidden Valley Ranch dressing and the piping-hot honey-based Tassajara bread came out of the oven.

Ralph and Vern knew their way around a recipe or two, but the driving force in the Cota Street kitchen was Ralph's girlfriend, Debbie, a nineteen-year old runaway from Ventura County who had left home at fifteen. Debbie's dad was an off-and-on roughneck in the Rincon oil fields, and Debbie and her mom were seasonal pickers in Oxnard's strawberry fields and lemon and avocado orchards. Debbie had dreams of getting off the farm and away from an abusive, drunk father, so, one morning, she left home for the fields with a packed bag and lunchbox. While waiting roadside for fellow workers in a pickup, she hitched a ride in a VW van up Pacific Coast Highway 1 right past the farm gate and that night alighted on State Street, homeless and busted, a lost waif. After a few palmy days of panhandling, she found work at Joe's Café on the lower end of State Street and honed her cooking skills.

Ralph met her a couple of years later, full grown, with a cascading mane of naturally curly hair, ethereal eyes, a monastic bearing, and a body for business. She ran the register and read tarot cards on the side at the bakery on the Sunburst commune. Two days after their meeting, she moved her meager basket of belongings and an armload of seedy vegan bread and fresh honey from the hive into his corner bedroom, which, along the baseboard, was ritualistically lined like books on a shelf with empty bottles of Bali-Hai wine, uncorked and full of stories. Then and there she took off the "pain free" cotton clothes she had on—wearing nothing that was dead—and for the next three months, she and Ralph paraded around the house in the altogether, their bohemian version of Nero's pleasure palace. Sexually, they were taboo free.

In their telling, the arc of their lovemaking took on new mysteries every day. As if an open invitation, their bedroom door was always ajar even as they contorted themselves on Ralph's Maasai red and blue plaid blanket in mind-body embraces of controlled breathing, slo-moing their way to some monster Tantric orgasm.

Our gatherings after the Safeway pillaging were more Dionysian revel than dinner party, with a touch of Hesse's Magic Theater: Mad Men Only. Walleyed speed freak surfers dressed like Tarzan (Jimbo and Arlo), tree-hugging Buddhists kitted out in Om necklaces and dhoti pants (Buzz and Mia), one snooty red diaper baby in a black beret with Fuck It tattooed down his left forearm who claimed rabbinical ancestry back to King Solomon (Mel), two literary odd ducks wearing dashikis (downstairs neighbors Walter and Lizzy), and another runaway girl named Golden Eagle, a walking, talking, dancing-in-sweet-joy psychedelic art poster with flame red hair, dyed chicken-feather headdress, and twinkly kohl-lined eyes. On impulse, Golden Eagle would often take off swirling like a dervish in a trance, confident that if she willed it, at any moment she could take off and fly. Bohemian theater, no costume, no character. All the while at those lavish feasts we yelped ecstatically our praise to friends and to Abbie for showing us the way and to Safeway's dumpster for the health-giving, larruping good grub. No one struck up the old hobo song "Hallelujah I'm a Bum," but there was a tribal sacredness to it all that begged a choral response.

Even for those of us more routinely tuned in to sub-astral mental frequencies, we respected each other's madness, vulnerability, and disdain for authority. Given that everyone was having an existential crisis, we all clung with religious fidelity to the glorifying idea that freedom and equality are as freedom and equality do. Golden Eagle's fantasies, fabulations, and especially her moral casualness and notions of individual freedom guaranteed mine and vice versa. "Each singing what belongs to him or her and to none else," Walt Whitman penned in his poem *I Hear America Singing*. The conceit of our full-flavored hub of celebrations, ideas, and conversations was that *Peter Pan and Joe Hill were alive as you and me.*

In travel, the fluky, unexpected milestone always awaits one's awakening. Three months passed while I safe harbored on Santa Barbara's Cota Street. On weekends, I went to the Cave Bar at Isla Vista (UC Santa Barbara) with my up-and-coming cinematographer buddy, Mark, who lived around the corner in a garret at 716 De La Vina.

In the previous three years, Mark's older brother Marty had taken up wildlife photography and had recently won an award for a documentary film on bighorn sheep (Bighorn!). Now Marty, with Mark's help, was working madly to finish a film entitled *At the Crossroads— The Story of America's Endangered Species*. He desperately needed footage of the California condor—and Marty was always persuasive. In hindsight, filming America's endangered species seems like an obvious path for a young and adventurous wildlife filmmaker. In the moment, at least in the USA, it was Richard Attenborough-cutting-edge.

Growing up, no one I knew was what I would call "in the know" on endangered species. There was ample reason for that: We were sheltered in the slipstream of status quo, judging the natural world to be not only full of wonder but bountiful and boundless. At the time, my relationship with the environment was not exactly about photographing and petting coons or green heads. But I also wasn't putting any serious stress on the flora or fauna. Well, maybe a dash of that.

For shits and grins, on Friday nights, we loaded up in GTOs, Fairlanes, and '57 Chevies with drunken shooters, armed with .22s, and brought the wrath of hell down on the rat infestation at the riverside abattoir and city dump. The girls even took a shine to those *Sweet and Lowdown* nights and would caravan out to that cesspool with us.

Our conditioning, if not the gestalt of the time, insisted on a certain tension with all things of the wild. As kids, on our path to manhood, we conquered the trees, rock formations, and waterholes and randomly shot at anything that moved just as we might take down an opponent on the basketball court. A competition above all, fur and feathers a-flying and trees a-falling.

That foundational feeling of boyish wonder in the outdoors was lost over the years. In my late teens, however, that incautious tension with nature took a turn. Brother John introduced me to canoeing, camping, and fishing the upper and middle stretches of the Caddo and Buffalo Rivers, especially at the right moment of the season: October after the harvest when vibrant fall leaves dapple the water; ducks and geese are migrating, cackling, honking, and quacking; and the Hunter's Moon is full. Or in March and April when the waterfalls flow, spring creeks surge and sow rebirth, dogwoods and redbuds bloom, the passerines' chorus fills the air, sunfish and smallmouth are jumping, and waterfowl begin their hejira north. John instructed us in Emersonian tones about cultivating solitude: making do with less, alone on the river, barred owls hooting and bullfrogs throbbing in the crisp night air, sharpens the focus until everything within and without starts to speak to you. Put another way by landscape painter and Buffalo River enthusiast Thomas Hart Benton: "There is something about flowing water that makes for easy views. Down the river is freedom from consequence. All one has to do is jump in a skiff at night and by the morrow be beyond the reach of trouble…"

On my first trip to the Rockies en route to Santa Barbara, I loped with Benton's "freedom of consequence" and the confidence of a mule deer down the craggy slopes of the Elk Mountains near Aspen and two days later pitched a camp near Jackson Hole beneath the Grand Teton after watching elk, bison, pronghorns, grizzly bears, and diving osprey in Yellowstone National Park. Among those heroic mountains and abundant wildlife, the artifice of everyday life receded from view and I realized that as a twenty-year-old, I had not been fully inhaling nature's vapors (or apprehending the parlous nature of flora and fauna). The primal need to wander in wild places began to haunt and tug at me as if my old dog Jip had been resurrected and was trying to show me the scent of his off-grid path.

Mark rang one Friday night and asked me to accompany him early Saturday morning on a photo shoot of the California condor at Mt. Pinos in the Los Padres National Forest. Like most days on Cota Street—call me easy—I was along for the ride, Mark's aide-de-camp. The next morning, two hours down the road, we were corkscrewing up and into the park's montane chaparral and evergreen forests of firs and towering Ponderosas. Chirping tires, pipes rumbling, pulling some hard g's on the curves, and raising those RPMs on the short straightaways, Mark was schooling me on the plight of the California condor.

In the early 1970s, the condor's numbers were obscenely low: maybe twenty in the wild, tops. The reasons varied. The condor only gives birth to a single egg per nesting attempt, which is usually once a year. Their plight was magnified, he continued, by several recent deaths from illegal hunting and lead poisoning picked up from the carrion that is the condor's staff of life. Survival expectations for these giant birds who had been soaring the skies of North America since the days of the saber-toothed cats and woolly mammoths were especially grim. He then pitched out a relatively new coinage adopted by conservationists to describe the natural extinction of a creature in its hereditary habitat (not in zoos): extirpated.

Up to this point, Mark appended, the way most people got "close to wildlife" was by gunning them down, mounting them, and putting them in their homes as proof they loved animals. "Without laws," he said, "wildlife would only be viewed in zoos, which receive more visitors each year than all spectator sports combined." In the

'50s, when French author Albert Camus visited America, he noted this uniquely American custom: "the love of animals—this last extending from the gorillas in the Bronx Zoo to the protozoa of the American Museum of Natural History..."

In the '60s, the terms "environmentalist" and "charismatic species" had yet to make the Oxford English Dictionary. Although hunting wild animals to extinction is an old story, the word "extinct" as it relates to wiping out a species was hardly on your Average Joe's tongue until the turn of the twentieth century. At that time, the passenger pigeon and dodo had just been hunted out of existence. The American bison and a Noah's Ark of others were on the brink. In walked John Muir, fresh off the trail of twenty years of Western wilderness adventures. In 1892, he founded the Sierra Club and became the patron saint of the conservation movement. But very little was ginning on the political front until Teddy Roosevelt, known as the "conservationist president," heard the warning cries of the wild.

Respond Teddy did. During his presidency, TR set about creating 230 million acres of public lands, 150 national forests, fifty-one federal bird reserves, four national game preserves, five national parks, and eighteen national monuments. Truth be told, my pencil is not sharp enough to sum up the almost infinite blessings of TR's visionary acts.

The specter of not acting was stark: post-apocalyptic forests, deserts, waterways, and mountain fastnesses come to mind. Think of an America if you take away Yellowstone, our first of fifty-eight national parks. Its rich diversity of wildlife is no less unspoiled today than it was in 1872. America is beautiful and bountiful, and Teddy's path was the only way forward. His vision gave us the groundwork for habitat conservation. In due time, however, it became obvious that the red and blue lines on nature (or humans) are not always neat fits for migratory fauna. As with most visions, there were blind spots.

In the post–World War I era, market hunting was still widespread. The wood duck and several other wild game birds were on the verge of extinction. The National Audubon Society called for an urgent response. The U.S. and Canada came together to forge the Migratory Bird Treaty Act. Ratified by Congress in 1918, it was the first legal document in the world dedicated to the protection of migratory birds.

The Migratory Act was toothless, though: No endowment enforced it. A politically savvy someone was called for to push TR's vision onward and raise real money to fund it. With almost Churchillian timing—Americans will always do the right thing after exhausting all the alternatives—the stars found near perfect alignment in the editorial backroom of the *Des Moines Register*. J. N. "Ding" Darling, a Pulitzer Prize–winning syndicated newspaper artist/cartoonist in the '20s and early '30s, had a passion for waterfowl, hunting, and conservation. "Ducks took center stage in his cartoons—portrayed with anthropomorphic features and often depicted as being mistreated by humankind," reported a Cornell ornithologist. "Ding's provocative cartoons prompted a deeper societal discussion about our relationship with nature, hastening a U.S. revolution in environmental ethics." Conservation was rapidly becoming known as a discipline with a deadline.

There were a couple of small hitches to anointing Ding into the affairs of state. He was a Republican and a special kind of gadfly on President Franklin D. Roosevelt's New Deal policies. Ironically, politically right-wing duck hunters wanting to protect the duck habitats were among America's first environmentalists, and, by no surprise, FDR was no stranger to juggling complex politics. He saw an opportunity to silence Ding's editorial vitriol by appointing him chief of the U.S. Biological Survey, forerunner to the U.S. Game and Fish Commission. And Ding was certainly the personified answer… at precisely the right time.

Ding adroitly brought together hunters, artists, conservationists, and a divided Congress to pass the Duck Stamp Act, no mean feat. Proceeds from the stamp, sold to every hunter of migratory birds, were earmarked for securing and managing federal wildlife refuges. The results were profound. In 1934, the year the Duck Stamp Act was passed, migratory waterfowl populations were at an all-time low of 27 million versus today's count which is well north of 60 million. Ding came to be known as "the best friend a duck ever had."

The snowy egret, wood duck, whooping crane, and sandhill crane were but a few that narrowly escaped extinction. More than 1,000 migratory birds, mostly native to the United States, including the California condor, found protection under the Migratory Bird Treaty Act.

By 1970, Congress had outlawed the pesticide DDT and President Richard Nixon had proposed and established the Environmental Protection Agency. We celebrated the first Earth Day on April 22 of the same year. Mark and Marty Stouffer caught these early gusts of the shifting winds of conservationism.

Mark backed his California muscle car, a mellow yellow, '67 Super Sport, into an open area so he could work out of the trunk. He was a model of time and motion efficiency, with the fast and nimble hands of a pit crewman, something he had been in another life. Straightaway, he unpacked and put together his German-made Arriflex 16mm camera, the workhorse at the time for outdoor documentary shooting. He handed me a 35mm Nikon F still camera with 600mm Nikkor lens and gave me a quick tutorial. Mark was in the zone, though the odds were thin on even seeing a condor.

Clustering near Mt. Pinos's most commanding vista were four or five no-nonsense ornithologists, binoculars aloft all. We angled our way into their savored space. I chatted it up as Mark made room for his tripod. Standing to our right was a slight-figured man in his fifties, wearing Jungle Jim khakis and sporting a long gray ponytail. He told us he had driven up from Ventura every day for three months to get the money shot, a condor flyover. "Spotted one way out two weeks ago with these," he told Mark, holding up a pair of eight-power binoculars and pointing to the misty ranks of the Sierra Nevada, where condors nest, often in pairs, in the cliffside caves and sequoia groves of the vast mountain range.

At roughly 8,000 feet, the air was limpid and intoxicating. A slight wind hissed from the southwest. The view was vast, Olympian and ruggedly patchworked. In one direction, the southern Central Valley. In another, the Santa Barbara County Mountains. Beyond, the Sierra Nevada.

In no more than an hour, one of the ornithologists spotted a condor four to five miles away, soaring high in the southwest thermals. At 30 to 40 miles per hour, it had likely been flying for hours, carrion hunting. Mark and I expected it to come our way—and that happened faster than we thought. Everyone was in the moment, raptly panning, scoping, and adjusting with long-range lenses. No chance to change out. Then, suddenly, cobra-quick, the great soaring raptor was upon us, checking us out, sharp eyes and fierce bill vectored our way like a 20mm Vulcan, meeting the onslaught of our pointed cameras with a gaze of mutual curiosity and intensity. And as if we needed any convincing of its grandeur, as it passed overhead, it flapped its humongous black wings twice, seamlessly tacking like slowed-down film and thrusting away into the oncoming air of a splendidly clear sky. At four feet long and with a nine-foot wingspan, flashing a blur of white underneath, it gave the impression that a dark bushy cloud shadow had brushed by and then scudded off, riding a timely gust into the blue.

I do believe Jungle Jim had a minor orgasm. We all exchanged holy moly glances. "Great hand of god," someone declared. Mark and I joined the chorus of cheering, adrenal glands gushing in overdrive.

The footage of that flyover was included in the *Endangered Species of North America* film Marty and Mark presented at the 1974 World

Expo. A couple of years later, on an NBC special, Robert Redford narrated *The Predators*, another Mark and Marty film, which included Mark's condor footage. PBS later bought *The Predators*, opening the door for Marty's popular series *Wild America*. In the same moment, triggered by the plight of the whooping crane (and not the California condor), Congress amended the Endangered Species Act to provide federal protections for the first time to threatened and endangered species. "To my way of thinking," Marty wrote in his book *Wild America*, "there are no creatures freer, and therefore wilder, than birds."

My ethical family framework, though in flux, had never fully pondered pitiless nature and the fact that wildlife needed to be protected from humans. Turned out that the California condor did go extinct in the wild. In response, the San Diego and Los Angeles zoos set up a controversial but ultimately successful captive breeding program for the twenty-seven surviving condors. Though they are still critically endangered, the numbers have rebounded to over 200 wild and free-flying California condors. (Recently, I've pored over photos that included thirteen condors perched on rocks in northern Arizona.)

"The word ecstasy is always related to some sort of discovery," wrote English traveler Freya Stark, "a novelty to sense or spirit, and it is in search of this word that in love, in religion, in art or travel, the adventurous are ready to face the unknown."

Mark's knowledge about the California condor, which is legendarily sacred to Native Americans, and the experience of filming such a majestic, Pleistocene creature on its way to extinction hung bright in my mind, triggering in me a lifelong, larva-to-butterfly appreciation of our biosphere. On Mt. Pinos that day, the margins of the ordinary and supernatural felt murky. We're talking goosebumps and a head full of dopamine and serotonin. Neurologically magical but not magic. A classic case of being thunderstruck by something that should be ho-hum while also undergoing a psycho-physiological response: mini-synapses firing, blood flowing, white matter growing, emotionally feeling more than what is seen. It was like a happy day in childhood, a rekindling of the wonder years in which the experience is greater than the sum of the events: Why is the sky blue? How does Bernoulli's principle explain wing lift?

I am no mystic, but unlocking your soul to somatic episodes with nature made perfect sense, for all I knew a hungering that has existed for all of time, something innate, tapping into objective truth without the noetic quality of mystical experience. Many of my newfound California friends, however, were almost scornful of my near-rationalist reality: Nature is all there is. I was "playing with the margins of the mystical," Ralph told me in one of many stoned rap sessions about consciousness raising. "Your whole trip is to hear the music but you are not dancing."

California was a marshy landscape rife with numinous possibilities. Spiritual frisson for Ralph and many others, I learned, came through a host of self-conscious philosophical and alternative reality movements, including primal scream, crystals, New Age this and that, Jesus-freakism, and transcendentalism.

The well-publicized pilgrimages to India and Japan of the Beats and the Beatles had done their part to influence the Western fascination with Asian mystics and metaphysics. Zen acolytes believed in the power of nothing, I was told, and the ancient practitioners of Taoism (the Way) sought to perfect the virtues we share with animals (bats and longevity, bees and industry). Similarly, I learned while soldiering that Thai Buddhists are steeped in the Pali Canon concept of "metta," loving kindness and moral concern to all (including geckos).

Time passed. The deeper I scratched, the palette of faiths increasingly turned to more earthy and natural shades. The Great Spirit of Native Americans, the Medicine Wheel and Old Man Coyote, the animist cultural beliefs of Africans and ancient foragers, the shamanism practiced by the Mongols and other Asians. Then there was the existentialist credo of American author, anarchist, and environmental advocate Edward Abbey: "Belief? What do I believe in? I believe in sun. In rock. In the dogma of the sun and the doctrine of the rock. I believe in blood, fire, woman, rivers, eagles, storm, drums, flutes, banjos, and broom-tailed horses."

"If it feels good do it" and "do your own thing" weren't just idle boomer sayings in Santa Barbara. On any given day, Hare Krishna chanters, chakra healers, Bahá'ís, Buddhists, Freewill Baptists, Adventists, Christian Scientists, Scientologists, and at least one Sufi dancing for international peace constellated on downtown State Street. Sandwich boards pointed The Way for pedestrians. Dooley Thomas, an aspiring journalist who lived in the Cota Street neighborhood, sent me to the dictionary one afternoon when he proclaimed to be a deistic, druidic animist. Everybody was looking for something. Groovy people spiritually awakening, giving the finger to old realities.

Add it all up, the collusion of species and spiritual archetypes is more universal than not, while reality itself, by most measures, approaches infinity. Self-evident also is that reality's many discrete echoes are reachable by any ol' hungry and thirsty mind and soul with a cocked ear to the ground. Once sounded out and given dimensionality, it can be evoked with the spiritual magic of an Om necklace, the Seal of Solomon, the old rugged cross, a crescent moon, a stout oak tree, a tattoo, or any other object of the human imagination.

Think about it. There I was, infinitesimally small me, the cosmic evolution of 13 billion years of hydrogen atoms, occupying a clump of Nowheresville dirt, a trivial waypoint on the condor's search for food. Spinning on the blue planet's axis at 1,000 miles an hour, while circling a sphere of gas and fire, a single star, at 67,000 miles an hour. "Millions" of Milky Way stars and "trillions" more beyond in the Spiral Galaxy, silently sharing my gravitationally balanced universe, and spanning more than 500 million light years.

Then Big Endangered Raptor, one of fewer than twenty in the universe, pays my clump of Nowheresville dirt a flyby look-see. Bang, pop, boom, shiver, and bingo. Unity, an antidote to ego, was in the air. Harmonious as the ancient Greeks thought when they coined the term cosmos, meaning both order and world.

Such primal wow moments of direct perception have kindled my imagination many times since. Most often, they come in breathtaking solitudes of natural beauty, a whiff of primordial soup, landscape as muse: A foggy forest in the Virungas, a fire-orange sunrise atop Kilimanjaro, a phosphorescent sea or a star-littered Southern sky around Pemba Island. Or observing in the wild the balancing rhythms of natural selection: a bee's nest connecting the whole forest, the hemispheric migration of breeding birds, a million and a half wildebeests annually crossing the crocodile-filled Mara River for greener pastures, or me scuba diving in the plankton-rich Galapagos with Darwin's penguins, sea lions, interminable schools of barracuda and big-eye jacks, the finely tuned Pyramid of Life, plants to herbivores to predators.

It all works like a Swiss clock until our "otherness" and shared red-in-tooth-and-claw tendencies get out of sync. The uroboros (the snake symbol of infinity) no longer swallows its tail. Emerson taught us that all life is an exercise in cause and effect. The plight of the California condor was karmic.

Whether soldiering-from-the-rear in Indochina, having an eye-opener on a piss stop on the eastern banks of the Shenandoah with RC, Dennis, and Greg, or filming condors atop Mt. Pinos, countless yet identifiable such passages have vitalized an inner energy in me that has, one by one, purged, purified and plumbed new depths. Like everyone, I am the synthesis of those transgressive 'miracles of enthusiasm,' the power of which is internal. That upending of old verities, youthful flirtations and 'sifting of reality' through the head and heart until it becomes your soul is a fluid adventure. At its prettiest, it's a messy and mysterious cauldron of tripe, gristle, headcheese, pig's eyes sloshing and a rare dash of flavorful fat to chew on. From that rare dash comes my silly sense of reality, my philosopher's stone, my Walden, my Peach Blossom Spring, my harmony with infinity, my world as exposited by me.

When Mark picked me up that Saturday morning, I knew next to nothing of the California condor or of conservation and threatened wilderness. Going forward, for every new bird, fish, forest, mammal or other non-human life I have taken in, the world's complexity has become incrementally more awe-inspiring.

Kissing the Joy on the Fly
Chapter Eleven

MY POST-ARMY CALIFORNIA SOJOURN resembled being a child inside a giant Whitman's sampler. Most days back at 336 Cota played out differently than filming condors—empty by design. Though the choices were many, on those days, I was often drawn by the siren of the sea. Hangin' at Hope Ranch's nude beach topping off my body tan and turning on had a certain groove. Voyaging on atomic-grade tabs of Sunshine and saffron skies, arcs of rainbows that spoke to me and the occasional unicorn and water sprite who listened. The invisible turning visible, the streaked wakes of western gulls, pelagic cormorants, and squadrons of brown pelicans as clear to see as a jet's vapor trail. The interplay and perpetual motion of sea and sky, everywhere, breakers, riptides and undertows, rolling deep and disappearing, ferrying my mind-bending reveries far beyond the white lines of the breakers and the cool, blue curvature of the earth. Good vibes were around, intoned by some invisible piper.

Nights were less nuanced and languorous, with true blue Kentucky whiskey and a bong that was rarely without bubbles. We motored up on white crosses and black beauties from a Buddha bowl on the community coffee table, scattered with a cornucopia of manifesto-like reading material: *Whole Earth Catalogs*, the *Berkeley Barb*, *The Autobiography of a Yogi*, Mao's *Red Book*, and Baba Ram Dass's *Be Here Now*. Vern always kept the latter opened to page two, which read, *Consciousness = energy = love = awareness = light = wisdom = beauty = truth = purity. It's all the SAME. Any trip you want to take leads to the SAME place.*

The voice of LA's favorite DJ, Charlie Tuna, spinning Top 40 hits could be heard on a Zenith AM/FM tube radio atop an old milk crate in the corner, provided by the landlord. Individual (and group) assets were scarce as hen's teeth, as were new clothes. A rotary dial black telephone in the kitchen was the closest thing to a clock or a watch in the house. If someone needed to know the time of day, they dialed POPCORN and a recorded voice spit it out.

One early morning in August of '72, the voter registration folks dropped by Cota Street. After several rings, Sad-eyed Sadie and I caught a wave overboard from the waterbed, found some clothes to put on, and invited those worthy imitators of Mormon missionaries into our lurid lime-green living room. Debbie and Ralph were in the kitchen frying bananas for breakfast but had ignored the doorbell because Ralph was delivering a "morning discourse" on "human potential." Creativity, happiness, and actualization peppered his pre breakfast sat sang. In various stages of undress and mussed hair, they joined us along with Vern and a new lady friend. Sadie had the wits to stash the chalice but left the bong openly displayed along with a few loose sopers.

The registration folks, two primly dressed City College grad students, presented us with a handful of three-by-five cards to fill out. It had the whiff of some kind of Big Brother overreach, a fessing up statement destined for a secret dossier. We knew shit was happening. How could it not be? The political pendulum had swung hard right with the election of Tricky Dick Nixon in '68, a tumultuous year that saw the assassinations of Martin Luther King and Bobby Kennedy, riots and rampaging cops from sea to shining sea, and the degeneration of Chicago's Democratic convention into a Gestapo-like show of brutal police clubbing and gassing protestors. This election cycle, the political buzz had it that the "youth vote," an untapped

25 million new baby boomer voters, including myself, if mobilized would throw the bum out. But the whole '72 Democratic primary had been a hot mess of wigged out hacks.

Rolling Stone magazine's gonzo political journalist Dr. Hunter S. Thompson was on top of it, thankfully, reporting that perennial contender "The Hube" Humphrey was strung out on some exotic uppers known as Wallot and Senator "Boohoo" Muskie had summoned a Brazilian medicine man to treat him with Ibogaine, a strange mind-altering drug known to cause rage, which seemed to explain Muskie's erratic behavior in the Wisconsin primary. Thompson never revealed his sources, but the storyline that drugs were in play was easy for my pill-popping comrades to swallow.

Meantime, the day before the registration boys arrived on Cota Street, the big news dropped that Democratic presidential nominee George McGovern's pick for vice president, Senator Thomas Eagleton of Missouri, failed to come clean about multiple treatments for depression with electroshock therapy and the anti-psychotic Thorazine—a drug that hammered me fast to the couch for two days the only time I tried it. The thought of someone shocked-up and on Thorazine near the nuclear football didn't play well. McGovern's poll numbers nosedived even as Eagleton was forced out. The June 17 Watergate burglary was in the news, but Nixon hunkered down, kept quiet, and let his henchmen pooh-pooh any connection to the White House. *Washington Post* reporters Woodward and Bernstein were still in foreplay mode with Deep Throat, a secret source code-named for Linda Lovelace's popular porn movie. On November 7, 1972, Nixon beat McGovern and his new running mate, Sarge Shriver, like a gong, winning forty-nine states. For the not-so-silent minority, the election spelled four more years of deceit and bellicosity directed at protesting students, the National Guard killings at Kent State still fresh on the minds of the hell-no-we-won't-go folks.

Of course, California was no stranger to King Daley's or Nixon's heavy-handed tactics against dissenters. Governor Ronald Reagan's crackdowns on students across the state had raised the level of political violence. In Santa Barbara, notably, the coals were still smoldering from the February 25, 1970, riots and burning of UC Santa Barbara's Bank of America on Embarcadero del Norte.

On that day, angry students reacted with violence to a spirited speech given at a campus event by leftist lawyer William Kunstler. A tried-and-true radical litigator, he had represented Abbie Hoffman and the Chicago Seven following the 1968 Democratic National Convention. Kunstler's speech made a point of connecting the dots between national issues and protests at the university, bringing in the draft and Vietnam War, the Union Oil spill in Santa Barbara channel, police beatings on campus, and Governor Reagan's and the conservative establishment's opposition to the hiring of liberal sociology Professor Richard Flacks (who my wife-to-be had studied under). All that mattered. Things reached a boiling point.

Students chanted, "Bring the war home!," and then burned down the Bank of America building, long considered a symbol of government. Susan Lutz, an acquaintance, was among a group of students who brought along football helmets filled with rocks and weaponized the chin straps to sling-shot the police. Governor Reagan declared a state of emergency. Protestors backed up, but not for long. Two months later, Santa Barbara police gunned down twenty-two-year old student Kevin Moran on the steps of the trailer that had become the new Bank of America.

By the time I rolled into Santa Barbara, the Bank of America trailer on Embarcadero del Norte was no less than a Kent State–like symbol of provocation. (In 1981, the university built a lecture hall on the site with a plaque remembering Kevin Moran.) The state had cleaned the Santa Barbara beaches of the sticky tar from the Union Oil spill, but the GOO (Get Oil Out) movement stuck in every politician's craw.

So, in the party affiliation box of the card the voter registration folks presented to me, I wrote Communist. Not because I was, but for pure fun. No one ever gave The Man straight answers on Cota Street, irrespective of the obvious fact that the registration folks were anti-Nixon too and only trying to get the vote out. Temperamentally, our Cota cohort was freebasing attitude, self-consciously bohemian. Distinctive, we imagined ourselves, not cursed by the sameness of our buttoned-down forebears. We had no shame in being held up as communists, anarchists, libertarians, socialists, existentialists, scoundrels, scavengers, debauchees, feminists, Beats, hippies, vegans, pagans, gays, lesbians, back-to-the-landers, unrepentant thieves, smashers of phallic imperialism. Anything but reactionary and Average Joe and Plain Jane. It was the Age of the Individual and Renewal.

After three years in the army and a year of rambling, I turned twenty-one in the fall of '72. I could vote and buy beer in all states. When I did vote that November, my broadside to the political system was to write my own name in for president. The predicted youth vote never materialized. The graffiti down on Mission Street zoned in on my apathy and cynicism: "If elections were about change, they wouldn't allow it."

The '60s liberation struggles of women, blacks, gays, farm workers, and the anti-war movement instructed us that the personal was political. But the army had taken me out of sync with the '60s timetable. During those first months and years as a civilian, my rebellious angst was more personal and social, tapping into a bohemian sensibility rather than that of an inflamed fighting-in-the-streets proletariat. Evolution more so than revolution. If pushed to die defending the hilltop or to prostrate myself in protest on the 101 at rush hour—if I had had a serious vision of the future—I would have burned Washington down, salted the earth, and reconstituted the whole sorry lot with values of equality, diversity, and justice for all. My reborn nation-state would have been a socialist utopia, one in which everyone was fed their human due like in some bounteous Israeli-style kibbutzim of chubby li'l Gerber babies. I believed wholeheartedly that from the "redwood forest to the Gulf Stream water," Woody Guthrie's upbeat song of promise, "This Land Is Your Land," should be our national anthem (and mood), with a celebratory crowd singing it, not a solemn soloist, and all land-of-liberty lovers capering in a conga line, not frozen in fun-deprived rapture with hand over heart. Our cultural DNA would then be roused by feelings of "this land is made for you and me"—and not by bombs bursting in air and the brand of flag-waving patriotism that oppresses others.

In late August, Debbie did a tarot reading for me. My card was The Fool, the picture of a ragged wanderer standing at the rim of the world, shouldering hobo-style a stick with a bindle sack on its end. She interpreted the card as a traveler embarking on a character-shaping new adventure, of an unknown nature, but also as one who needs to think before he leaps. Nifty analysis and advice, I told her, coming from a random cut of a deck of cards.

It is definitely possible to stay too long inside a Whitman's sampler. That endless summer of going naked into the world and becoming one with the tides ended with its ritual, seasonal timing, as did the cheap rent on Cota Street. The debris of downfall were everywhere. Food stamps and unemployment had run dry, the army savings kaput, the spanking new '71 Toyota long gone. UC Santa Barbara had denied me resident status.

As my jackpot of lotus-eater leisure was circling the drain, *in extremis* was also a rent-sharing, open relationship with the woebegone Sad-Eyed Sadie, a lissome long-chestnut-haired lady who carried a white lace parasol putatively to block the California sun. The rare smile she gave was elusive, a hard-to-read twist of the lips, like the Florentine clothmaker's wife Mona Lisa. To my thinking, the parasol and enigmatic smile evoked a walled-off quality, an impenetrable dark side. A modern-day Salome, the seductress dancing with the head of John the Baptist maybe. Like me, Sadie was of suspect means and reliability: barkeep, drama student, pole dancer, and, in the same sandals, a newly minted free love California hippie chick.

Sadie, whom I had met when she was working in San Francisco at Coke's go-go bar down on Broadway, started out the old-fashioned way back in Boise, Idaho, as a frumpy and self-conscious fifteen-year-old sophomore in the high school drama club. Drama was her passion and she took leading roles in the theater's musicals, *Oklahoma!*, *South Pacific*, *Brigadoon*. By the time she graduated high school, she had overcome frumpy and taken up waitressing and pole dancing. We'd slept together a few times at my friend Tony Allen's flophouse on Russian Hill, not far from Coke's, where Tony was a barker. All to say our ties were romantically tenuous when Joey Schneider, who I had ridden with to California in his white Ford van, announced we were heading south the next day.

Right away Sadie began lobbying to jump on board. She could no longer afford the rent in San Francisco. We finally agreed to drop her off anywhere of her choosing on the road to Santa Barbara. She loaded up the back of the van with two cardboard boxes of her dishes, and a (honey) sack of denim short-shorts and skimpy halter tops for waiting tables. She was good company and latched on tighter to me the farther south we drove. She talked about the change of scenery as an opportunity to restart her studies in musical theater. She was still in the van when we arrived in Santa Barbara. So, we struck up a rent sharing arrangement that amounted to taking over an empty room with a water bed. Over the course of a few weeks it became obvious that free love was in her blood. She disappeared for nights at a time, thriving on the attentions of older men, and turning Rita Hayworth's promiscuous boast in the 1940s movie *Gilda* into a way of life, "If I had been a ranch, they would have called me the Bar Nothing."

After one of her nights out, she could usually be found around the corner from the Ala Mar at Sambo's (the flagship restaurant of the controversial national chain). On the few occasions that I showed up at Sambo's around noon for the Mama Mumbo Special and to check on her, she had flamed out, on her last sizzle, ready to crash at 336 Cota, libido tamed. I felt like the Buddhist pilgrim who releases a bird for merit only to see it immediately fly back to captivity. I suppose I was crazy like that, too. Her doing her thing was okay by me. Sad-Eyed-Sadie was last seen naked with her signature white lace parasol, walking along Hope Ranch beach with an acidhead flower-power plainclothes priest from San Diego. An older man.

Restless, broke, and game, I packed up my army duffel bag, cleaned the jewels of lavender and Sunkist orange pills from my nightstand, and dogged it back to Arkansas. Didn't even require a bluebird day to set out on a Greyhound bus across the country. Only the impulse. Mark advanced me the scratch for bus fare, and Ralph fronted me 10,000 white crosses for a business transaction I was brokering. California dreaming was a fresh pin on my psychic map. It had been the perfect asylum, a beautiful thing, doubling down on weird at times. Never made it up Highway 99 to the verdant Central Valley to those culturally conservative towns of Bakersfield or Fresno, but I sure fed (via the dumpster) from that cornucopia of carrots, cabbage, eggplant, tomatoes, artichokes, broccoli, squash, sunflowers, and all manner of fruits that originated from there.

Scratch beneath the surface, shake us up in a time capsule and out tumbles the kaleidoscopically diverse fragments of all the migrant tales of woe identified with California. Okies, Arkies, Asians, Mexicans, actors, gold diggers, drifters, fruit pickers, farmers, geeks, lumberjacks, lefties, surfers, roughnecks, flower folks, bohos, and hobos. Once rooted as a Californian, fertilized with Wampums and West Coast frontier ethos, the slate was clean, a vague or nonexistent past, only the present and future. Yes, California was a magnet for the restless soul, the apotheosis of a dreamer's paradise. It held the future, the Postmodern era.

But I never could shake that feeling of being a stranger in a strange land, the roll-your-own, sideways-looking drifter. Ralph was aware that I was not always on the same wavelength with Cota Street. He rarely missed a chance to point out my separateness. For starters, the deep Arkansas accent, recognizable by any good linguistic ear as from *Lum and Abner* land. My hair and dress weren't sufficiently unkempt. I had been squeamish at first with the dumpster diving and scavenging like alley cats in the shadows. Failed to connect with the Trappist monk who often crashed at Walter and Lizzy's and who couldn't talk but could be overheard squealing like a banshee during sex and chanting *om shanti om* until Kingdom come. Lacked the rock-ribbed radicalism of most. Didn't need a Weatherman (or group think). Castro was a shuck. Uninterested in three- and four-ways with Sadie and other guys. Ralph was sort of right. I was wading in the shallows of this West Coast laboratory. The relational dynamics of H. G. Wells's backward, underground-dwelling Morlocks and the long-haired, life-of-ease Eloi often danced through my mind.

Ralph's reinvention as a Californian was foursquare. Mine was not. It was okay to keep one foot in Arkansas and the backwoods. Being a credentialed freelance cultural outlaw was a lofty enough goal. My way was to go on playfully pushing sand against the tide while hopscotching the planet on red-blooded adventures: way-out, wayward, and far and away. Reinvention was a dynamic state of mind, not a State.

It made no difference if I were coming or going. My mental energy needled between happy and sad, never too far in either direction: the hedonic treadmill, bouncing back, adjusting to ambient conditions, in the analytical language of psychologists.

A wonderful thing happened on that bus ride of otherwise down-and-out passengers. Peachy magic for those of us addicted to the ideals of romance and awash in unguarded emotion. A fresh start with a fresh woman always raised the hair on my neck. Made me walk with an extra spring in my step and wake up with a noble purpose. The needle had struck happy. My *deus ex machina* had arrived like an out-of-season cardinal. Yet again, from parched to full-of-mush, I had traveled.

At Union Station in Los Angeles, a German student named Katya Moller boarded the Greyhound. Amid the hustle and bustle, she bore her shining blue eyes on me and beelined my way like a beautiful apparition. Passing several empty seats, she unshouldered her backpack, and, bingo, bango, bongo, plopped down in the seat next to me. Her shoulder-length blond hair diffused a scent redolent of the sea—airy, fresh, elemental, and tropical. Braless, wearing a loose-fitting, narrow red halter-top to match her hot red lipstick, and tanned like a Riviera goddess, she breathed the possibility of another femme fatale. Serendipity had delivered me a long cool drink of water on a blazing hot day of travel.

Soon, LA's traffic-choked freeways and smog-covered mountains faded as the Santa Ana winds blew sparingly. Like a hound dog on a hot biscuit, for the next twenty-four hours, I sweet-talked, jelly scratched, and gave my best shot at wooing Katya into my nomadic dreamscape. Crying out in the desert, the bus wailed across the biblical terrain of the Mojave.

Katya was on her way to Virginia and the family home of a general's son she had met in Germany. She had recently finished university in Hamburg and was taking a year off before graduate school in anthropology. She had written her undergraduate thesis on the pioneering ethnographer Bronislaw Malinowski and the Trobriand Islanders of Melanesia. She effused that he had famously taken anthropology "off the veranda" by immersing himself in the everyday lives of the islanders.

Katya had only recently traveled in Malinowski's footsteps to the Solomon Sea and Papua New Guinea's Trobriand Islands. She made much of chewing betel nut, eating yams, and sleeping rough in stilted huts made of thatch, encircled by coconut trees, clan totems, and highly stylized yam houses on the coral atoll of Kiriwina, in the sacred village of Omarkana. There, Malinowski's plaited hut was preserved like a holy place, only a stone's throw away. All history was present on the Trobriands, she said, referring to the matrilineal culture she witnessed among this polygamous, pre-literate tribe of islanders. Known for their magic spells and non-linear linguistics, they chewed and spit betel most days, leaving their mouths blood-red like a clown's.

Harvest season was cause for daily celebration, she told me, continuing the thread. Bare-chested girls in flower necklaces and grass skirts would fill a flower-adorned ground cover beneath a hibiscus tree with roasted pig and wooden bowls of yams, taro, pumpkin, rice, coconut juice, and bananas. Yet custom had it that everyone ate alone, avoiding observation by others by going off into a hut or the forest. After the feast, branches of betel and slaked lime to tone down the taste of the betel would arrive like a mirror full of cocaine, compliments of an important clan member. Relationships unfolded. Only when a branch was picked over and bare would the euphoric spluttering and spoiling for romance wind down to a prolonged spell of the mopes, coming down.

"Wantokism," a traditional welfare system that says you literally empty your pockets to the less able, is the crazy glue that binds each tribe of the Trobriands, she explained. Under this system, as a politician representing the Trobriands, it's incumbent to divert government funds to your people; as a businessman you must raid the till until all the bride prices, funerals, beers, tobacco, and betel are paid for. "They wait for the food to fall from the tree, or swoop up the fish in a net," she added. "The rest of the time they chew betel."

She described the matrilineal system, from the social position of her host contact, whose English name was Brian (I think). Due to his clan lineage, he couldn't be chief; his aunt's son would have that title. Once Brian's father died, he would have to leave his father's village and live in his mother's. He supplied his two sisters with food just as his brother-in-law provided him with food. Spouses were shuffled and re-dealt, while topless girls in the flower of youth were encouraged to fool around. Having a dry run or two at marriage was the norm. A cornerstone of their traditional belief system is that magic spells cause pregnancy. Brian, who had five wives and eleven children, said wife selection often focused more on work ethic than beauty. But it was always the woman's choice to marry. Courting, from what Katya could tell, amounted to no more than a suitor's presentation of a bouquet of areca nut wrapped in betel leaf. She went on explaining the island's premodern traditions in fascinating detail and depth, all tonic for a mind that on a good day runs a mile wide and an inch thick.

We stopped at roadside beaneries or for short doses of bus stop slop, and, in Flagstaff, bought a jug of Hearty Burgundy. Talking, talking, talking, in a delicious rhythm like two jazzbos trading stretched-out riffs and syncopating the moment. Third World travel was the heartbeat of those rhythms. In one of the front seats, a dark-skinned Mayan boy wearing *huaraches*, a *serape*, and a straw hat blew clear and crisp high notes on a *chirimia* flute. Barreling along Steinbeck's Mother Road, Route 66, stations-of-the-cross towns like Flagstaff, Tucumcari, Albuquerque, and Amarillo dissolve around us. Wrapped as one in our combined sleeping bags, she had my imagination churning overtime: exotic tribes, tripping off the grid, getting laid.

Around noon, screeching airbrakes jolted us awake. As we trundled on to North Walnut Street in downtown Oklahoma City, breathing each other's stale breath, we unraveled from our backseat cocoon. We both had bus changes at the nearby Greyhound terminal. As we gathered our packs and debarked, the Mayan boy played his last note. We made our way inside the terminal and waited side by side, in tender closeness, in the rackety ferment of gate calls, wheezing engines, hissing doors, the faceless swivel of footfalls, and the muddle of accents. After a few minutes, we each stoked a square while I tepidly encouraged Katya to blow off the general's son in Virginia. Uphill, blowing dandelions, for sure, but it seemed like there was so much more to say. He was privileged and had paid for her cross-country bus ticket. In Teutonic tones, she spelled out that she would never be forgiven. Their families were friends. She did briefly consider my offer. But by the time that happened, the page was turning. There were a few minutes of gloomy silence.

Like an angel on the shoulder, I got a brief verbal prompting from an imaginary chatty friend, a free associative inner roommate who told me I was playing a fool's game losing my head over a beautiful woman. Meeting and making it with Katya was like something written in wet sand, soon to be washed away. We had taken each other by storm, both turned on by fresh encounters of the flesh, loving the one you're with. Down deep, I didn't want to be a native or a loyal lover, my inner spectator jabbered on. My whole proposition of more time with Katya had the fishy whiff of Stage 1 of life as a toadstool. Besides, I was not sure that I had the psychic wherewithal needed to have love or complete loyalty last a long time. Burning hot and burning out were my twin trademarks. Way before Erica Jong's book *Fear of Flying*, I had mastered the zipless fuck.

Before making her final retreat on the north-bound bus, Katya asked for my address and for the 14" x 20" portrait I had been schlepping of me costumed as a bearded, Renaissance artist (a project of Mark's at Brooks Institute). That twenty-four hours of requited romance with Katya—almost a record with my history of hookers and one-night stands—left me with the monopolizing illusion, not unlike a lucid dream, that I had scratched open a thin layer of the portrait's theme of a rebirth of the human experience as the center of existence, of a rediscovery of learning and love, the crown jewels of any life well lived. Don't cue the trumpets, yet. In those days, for me anyway, it was hard to tell rebirth from rock bottom. I had become conditioned to lust fulfilled, with the promise of love foregone. Before she vanished onto the St. Louis-bound bus, she whispered in my ear, "May you be the most of you forever." After a double take, I got a catch in my throat.

Weeks passed, and I never got that letter Katya promised. Things must have worked out with the general's son. Or she figured rightly that I was full of risky business, not a bonding type. No matter, it was a bus ride for the books. Got laid on a Greyhound, learned about the Trobriands and Malinowski and soon read his book *Argonauts of the Western Pacific*, the foundational document for modern-day anthropology. And for days, her artful farewell spun in my mind until I was almost dizzy.

My mooning phase over Katya, whom I came to think of as more like a bewitching shadow than the real thing, was soon loosed to the four winds. But not those of Malinowski, and it was Blake who reminded me to keep stoking the wonder and to answer the call to life wherever you find it:

> *He who binds to himself a joy*
> *Does the winged life destroy*
> *But he who kisses the joy as it flies*
> *Lives in Eternity's sunrise.*

Hemingway's Key West

Chapter Twelve

FOR THE NEXT YEAR, Arkansas was my favored way station, my true north. It was not easy to escape its gravitational field. Like a sailor in port passing through in moments of emptiness and struggle, I never stayed long, only the time it took to get my ducks in a row to light out again for the next moon on the water. On this occasion, after a mere three weeks, as if facing a bad meal I couldn't start much less finish, I checked myself out of the University of Arkansas. I had drawn a chunk on my student loan account and received my first GI Bill checks for the semester. I didn't even buy the books. It was road money, my ticket to ride.

Friends Tommy and Susan Horton were mulling a move to somewhere. In their new marriage, they were bumping up against the mind-numbing rhythms of being in the same place with the same people doing the same things their entire lives. He was also ready to give the old heave-ho to pre-med, a choice he had made to appease his father-in-law more than himself. As both were boon companions, I recommended they change scenery to a more beneficent climate. Rootless as I had become, my mind was always awash with daydreams of different ports of call. Soon, I insinuated myself into their aspirations and doubled as a fifth wheel for a move they decided on to Tampa, Florida.

Tommy and I had met in late junior high. Both styling ourselves as juvenile delinquents, we smoked cigarettes behind the Mirador

Apartments before the bell sounded at Ramsey Junior High and soon went to the barricades with coaches, especially Bill Malone, over hirsute fashion: Butch wax, flat tops, ducktails gave way to Beatles bangs and Freewheelin' Bob's frizz. Coach Malone's idea of negative reinforcement—getting your ass bloodied with paddles fashioned like weapons and running twice the red lines of every other jock—did not sit well with us.

Otherwise, Tommy was a first-rate student and could scorch a fastball. I was fresh off tip-top football and basketball seasons but had never been an eager front-rower in the classroom. Together, like Mark Twain's characters, we drifted from the civilized confines of adolescence to the anarchy of smoky pool halls and back alleyways. About that time, Tommy and Susan coupled up. She was artsy, attractive, cool, caring, and easygoing. They married a few years later (and have now been together fifty years).

Following a short search in Tampa, we loaded up a U-Haul box truck in Fayetteville for Tommy to drive, and Susan and I drove their two cars. They leased a one-bedroom apartment near Busch Gardens, on Channing Circle, seven to eight miles northeast of downtown. Orange groves bracketed two sides of the complex. For three months, I lived on their tawny-colored velour rollaway couch with a matching tapestry of a majestic, grave-eyed Simba peering down on me. To earn room, board, and walking around money, I took jobs as a casual laborer in construction, at times a hod carrier, and working like a rented donkey, loading cases of booze onto box trucks on the warehouse night shift for ABC Liquor. On days off, we beat a hasty path to the flour-white Madeira and Clearwater beaches. A couple of weekends, we scuba-dived without certification in the Crystal River. After a month, I discovered four co-eds from Arkansas living in a shared house out on Madeira. They started to host me on weekends. When Tommy and Susan needed some alone time, I borrowed the "Blue Beast," their '67 Ford Fairlane, and across the harbor bridge I blew—sniffing all the way the jasmine and lavender fragrance of the fair sex slathered in Coppertone.

My brother Greg and his girlfriend, Beverly, soon arrived in our slipstream. Beverly was a talented artist I had dated in high school. As for Greg, he had hatched a plan with the University of Arkansas, and got it approved, to take twenty-one transferable hours in political science, in one semester, at the University of South Florida. Beverly lived the artist's life, waiting tables in a cocktail-waitress-costume at what was surely Tampa's early '70s version of Hooters, the Pink Cricket. There was no cover charge at the Cricket for girls in hot pants.

Word of the Arkansas migration to Tampa began to spread among our wellspring of friends. Leon Marks, likely my oldest of friends, showed up at his sister Janet's house in central Tampa. He had just graduated from Tulane, playing number two seed on the tennis team for four years. He joined me on my weekend runs to Madeira, and by coincidence, he became the manager of an ABC Liquor retail store near his sister's house. We began to talk up the idea of the Fort Smith Mafia taking over ABC Liquor.

Weeks later, Dudley Flanders showed up, taking a semester off from Dartmouth. He moved in on Jo Mar Drive with Greg and Beverly, all age mates from Fort Smith. First day there, Dudley bought a tool belt. Tommy also had a tool belt and had become a rising star straw boss on a nearby apartment building construction site. Dudley became Tommy's eager, upwardly mobile assistant. When they both strapped on those tool belts, their lazy sauntering way of walking turned to a strut, filled with puffed up pride and the confidence of a hired gun. Upward mobility, kissing the boss's ring, material aspirations—all this remained a bridge too far for this budding sidewalk socialist.

We all drank together at the Cat's Eye, a neon forebear of the sports bar for neighborhood nighthawks. One uneventful Friday evening, shortly after the semester had ended, Greg left the bar early to be at home when Beverly arrived from the Pink Cricket. She had been homesick for Arkansas for some time, so they packed it up and left in the night. Dudley got a call two days later telling him they wouldn't be back.

I checked out of Hotel Horton and became Dudley's new roommate on Jo Mar Drive, sleeping on a pestilential Goodwill couch. I had done it before, and all else was working out just hunky-dory. A day or two before Beverly made tracks, I sat in a kitchen chair in the apartment house parking lot and she cut my ponytail. It was a half-hearted shot at counterpunching my alienated, angry young man leitmotif. Dancing to the music of my mercenary side, or more commonly known as "selling out", the next day I interviewed for a manager trainee position at Pan American Bank. Finance had been my gig in the army. Bank work in Florida in the early '70s would be a walk in the park by comparison. In fact, I had come around to thinking that working around a bevy of young women would be a step up from the testosterone-sated casual labor pool I had been shoulder to shoulder with for too long. Keeping a lid on my past—high school dropout, police record, drugs—was no easy feat. Telling a white lie was one thing, but weaving a web of untruths was never my strong suit. Somehow, I pulled it off.

Dudley's parents were always sending him care packages—hams, turkeys, and cheeses—which he shared. My pressing problems were clothes and transportation. I had no wheels and was still living out of my army duffel bag. Since Dudley was riding to work with Tommy, he soon came to the rescue, volunteering the use of his car along with his Ivy League wardrobe—blazers, crisp blue and white Oxfords, and khakis.

In the first few days at Pan American, beclowned in Dudley's duds, I tallied receipts and deposits while unconsciously and obsessively swiping my free hand (left) across the back of my neck. Two of the tellers, Tammy and Debbie, picked up on this odd tic along with the ragged, unprofessional clip job. As a duo, both pert and flirty, they confronted me, arms akimbo, asking if I had had a ponytail before coming to work at Pan American. Busted, yet denying it to Kingdom Come, I listened to their whispered tones telling me that what went down in our cubicle dwellings stayed away from the padded offices and mahogany paneled corridors of the bank officer claque beyond.

Debbie Woods was statuesque and black, sported an Afro, more in the style of the early '70s than as a black militant. We dated off and on for a couple of months. There was certainly chemistry overlaid with a whole bunch of curiosity, but mostly we were a study in contrasts. I met her parents while we sat in the preacher's room (living room) of her humble Southern Baptist home, with framed scriptures, a wall of bold crosses, and a well-polished lectern for the Bible. Her parents liked that I had served in the army, so that's what we talked about. On that first date, we went to see Robert Redford in *Jeremiah Johnson*. As if a test had been passed, a few days later I indulged her by spending a week's paycheck at Tampa's historic and upscale Columbia Restaurant, gustily downing mojitos and a pitcher of sangria and delighting in the house special, pompano in a bag. Didn't have five dollars in my pocket to pay down on rent when we snorted a ten-dollar chaser of cocaine and staggered out in each other's arms with a first mortgage on the starry dome of a night.

Johnny Berry, who had recently mustered out of the army, and his girlfriend, Becky Abbot, showed up unexpectedly in Tampa on an unscheduled break from the University of Arkansas for a road trip to Key West. I was easily persuaded to join them. With Johnny, Becky, and Debbie in Johnny's beige hand-me-down '67 Delta 88, we barreled down U.S. 1, south of Key Largo, shooting past abandoned trestles of Flagler's Overseas Railroad, fishing piers, and long stretches of iron-spans-to-nowhere over turquoise seas and coral reefs.

At Fleming Street in Key West, we had arrived at the southern tip of U.S. 1. Cuba was ninety miles on across the water, but in the early '70s, it felt culturally much closer. "Conchs," the century-old name given to locals due to their shellfish diet, jumbled together in Key West with Cubans, Bahamians, retirees, tourists, hippies, yachtsmen, fishermen, and gays sowing the seeds of another Old Town comeback. Once considered America's wealthiest city per capita, Key West greeted us with a rakish spirit and decadent air of a faded heyday.

The six-story La Concha Hotel and the nineteenth-century St. Paul's Episcopal Church dominated the Main Street skyline. The movie *Deep Throat* played at the Strand Theater on Duval Street, and Jimmy Buffett crafted his carefree, sailor-singer-songwriter character for drinks down at Captain Tony's on Greene Street. The 1930s-era gingerbread trim homes, washed in fresh pastels with shiny tin-peaked roofs, and the street corner *bolita* hawkers and cigar shops had been thinned out. Roosters still wandered freely on sidewalks rimmed in coconut palms, but the cockfights had turned tail into backyard oblivion. Roistering rum bars spilled out on every corner. The outlaw spirit of the Prohibition era had moved on to scoring nickel and dime bags of marijuana down secret alleys. The louvered shutters of the Truman White House at the foot of Whitehead Street had been boarded up; Give 'Em Hell Harry was laid to rest only months before. Old Zach Taylor's Fort down by the Truman Annex had kept the pirates of the Caribbean and the Confederate blockade runners at bay but had long ago gone to seed and given away to archaeological crews digging for nineteenth-century artifacts. An Australian pine forest stretched beyond the fort's overgrown moat and a long floury-sand beach faced south along a line of breakers and cool blue sea all the way to Cuba.

Key West was my first brush with the touristy force fields of Ernest Hemingway. Although I was familiar with his books and the contours of his machismo reputation, nothing about the real-life characters or distant backdrops he'd novelized had percolated impactfully into my consciousness at that point. It didn't take long, however, to discover that Key West was a treasure trove of all that lore, a living history as well as a myth-building circus led by the Conch Train. The more I discovered and dusted off, the more he became bigger than life, the deeper I wanted to go. His literary and geographical reach was vast, and his aura, at least around Key West, was like air, everywhere, ruling the roost. Buried beneath the Hemingway lore, it took research to learn that literary titans Tennessee Williams, Robert Frost, Ralph Ellison, and others had also thrived artistically for long stretches on the end-of-the-road island.

Though it would take decades, this seminal trip to Key West would set in motion a lifetime of reading Hemingway's books, traveling to his homes and haunts around the world, and over time, meetings two of his friends, a Kenyan great white hunter and a Cuban fisherman. I came to see Hemingway as a colorful and highly accessible 20th century link in that historic chain of men of action and limitless ambition. The more profound effect he would have on me was not so much his famous novels or his inimitable pared-down writing style, it was the crazy quilt details of his life: his travels, his hunting and fishing destinations, the wars, bars and women and everything he had seen and known. At that point, I would understand the characters and terrain of his fiction.

In 1935, at the height of the Great Depression, the Guidebook for Tourists included the 907 Whitehead Street Hemingway house on its sequentially numbered "must sees" map. Key West saw tourism as the newest, best answer to the town's boom and bust history. The city's glory days soon became Hemingway's time, to be circled over and over again, until his legend grew wildly and was grafted onto the Key West landscape no less so than now—with age, the Indian banyan's "prop roots" he had planted in his yard took over the tree's own hulking trunk. All the attention and intrusion rankled Hemingway. So, the story goes, he had friend Toby Bruce, a classmate of Pauline Pfeiffer, Hemingway's second wife, from Piggott, Arkansas, build a head-high wall of Baltimore cobblestones to keep "gawkers" out. After the privacy wall went up, the undeterred gawkers arrived in bigger numbers, entertained by black kids from the Bahama Village who tap danced with bottle caps between their toes. Street painters and more performance artists followed, selling an illusion of reflected good-old-days glory.

An older Bahamian black woman, Ariana, who introduced herself as a former domestic worker for the Hemingways, gave us an early afternoon rehash-of-the-legend tour of the estate. The blazing hot August temperatures kept the hordes at bay that day. We were the only tourists in sight.

As a wedding present, Ariana told us, Pauline's rich Uncle Gus purchased the Spanish Colonial house for $8,000 in cash. While Hemingway was away covering the Spanish Civil War, Pauline added an in-ground saltwater pool (at a cost of $20,000) in the backyard space he once used for a personal boxing ring. The ninety-foot-high Key West Lighthouse stood across the street, commanding a bird's-eye view of the property. The inside joke among friends was that Hemingway needed a navigational aid to totter home every night from Sloppy Joe's bar.

Famously, the property hosted a score of six-toed cats, all descendants of Hemingway's Snow White. Taken from a litter of Sea Captain Harold Dexter's polydactyl cat Snowball, Snow White was a gift to Hemingway's children, Patrick and Gregory. "One cat just leads to another," the author once deadpanned, as if to signal that one day they would have the run of the place. To be sure, Snowball's descendants drank from Sloppy Joe's urinal, lazed in the gardens and around the pool, plopped on the shiny Honduran pine floors and the Italian marble fireplaces, slept atop the seventeenth-century Spanish walnut dining table and the Chenille bedspreads, ate ground filet mignon, and, when they finished, licked the tastefulness from the French chandeliers and Miro's *The Farm* if they damn well pleased. The coddled cats remained beloved residents, not guests, as their names suggested: Bugsy Siegel, Fred Astaire, Ginger Rogers. The famous felines whimsically curled up around Hemingway's Royal typewriter on his writing desk, from which he banged out *Death in the Afternoon*, "The Snows of Kilimanjaro," *To Have and Have Not*, the stories collected in *Winner Take Nothing*, and more.

By the time of my visit, Charles Thompson, who owned and ran a hardware store while his brother Norberg employed a third of Key West in the fish, sponge, and turtle business, was the last one standing of the Hemingway Mob, an inner-circle of hard drinking, high machismo Conch friends and fishermen who shoaled around the author soon after his arrival in Key West. Wherever Hemingway lived or traveled, he drew people into his circle and became the irreverent ringmaster, the alpha social chairman. As was his habit, he teasingly rechristened each member of the Mob, a name earned among peers not a birthright. He even bestowed a nickname on Key West, "the St. Tropez of the poor." It was a far cry from the café culture of Paris in his early years.

It was the spring of 1928. Hemingway had arrived a few days earlier from Havana by steamship. Late one afternoon he was bridge fishing near George "Bee Lips" Brooks, a Key West attorney, when Hemingway ran out of bait. Bee Lips, named for the peculiar way he curled his lips around the Chesterfields he smoked, struck up a conversation, and offered to share his bait. They instantly connected.

A day or two later, Bee-Lips introduced Hemingway to Charles "Old Karl" Thompson (a year older than the author). Both were competitive sportsmen. Old Karl wasted no time in teaching Hemingway how to saltwater fish in the Marquesas on Captain Eddie "Bra" Saunders charter boat. Days passed and Joe "Josie" Russell (aka Sloppy Joe), who "bottle fished" (ran rum) in his boat the *Anita* from Cuba during prohibition and owned the Blind Pig speakeasy on Greene Street, fell in with the Mob. J.B. "Sully" Sullivan, Hamilton "Old Sack of Ham" Adams, Earl "Jewfish" Adams, and seasonal Key West arrivals, artist Waldo "Don Pico" Pearce and Lost Generation novelist John "the Dos" Passos, rounded out the posse of boozers and fishermen. As the group took shape, Hemingway christened himself the Great Master. And when he wrapped a towel around his head, which he often did to keep the sun off, the Mob called him the Mahatma.

For over a decade, members of the Mob inspired and featured prominently in Hemingway's short stories and books. Charles "Old Karl" Thompson is the professional hunter in *Green Hills of Africa*, which Hemingway dedicated to Old Karl, J. B. "Sully" Sullivan, and Kenyan great white hunter Philip Percival. Old Karl's friendship with Hemingway, the story goes, was tested on the African savannas when Hemingway discovered that the bull kudu Old Karl had shot was bigger than his.

Sloppy Joe is the model for Freddy Wallace of Freddy's Bar in the novel *To Have and Have Not*, set in Cuba and Key West, a playground for the idle rich in the maw of the Great Depression. Harry Morgan, the book's protagonist, (a composite of Old Karl and Sloppy Joe), is a boat captain, who, to make ends meet with a crumbling financial situation and a family to support, resorts to running rum and Chinese illegals across the Florida Straits. Captain "Bra" Saunders, the old timer of the Mob, is the fictional model for Captain Willie Adams. Shady lawyer, "Bee-Lips" Simmons, brokers Harry Morgan's last desperate contraband run that goes amuck with Cuban Revolutionaries. Humphrey Bogart and Lauren Bacall would star in the first of many film versions of *To Have and Have Not*.

Hemingway was said to have lived a dissolute life in Key West. Mining material from his travels and everyday life, however, I came to understand that Hemingway was sober, focused, and alone with his muse a hell of lot more than legend and his larger-than-life-persona would have us believe. He was a committed stone mason. His was a life of full contact, enjoying complete freedom, eschewing all people and systems that attempted to constrain him. He not only sought to craft a story with the somber details of the noble and notorious, but also to make it come alive, to be right and true and believable. Drawing us in to scratch deeper for the backstory into the real-life characters of those he romanticized on the page was his rare and impartible talent.

Charles "Old Karl" Thompson and his wife Lorine, both old and frail, lived in the middle of a rickety row of turn-of-the-century Conch-style houses on Seminary Street. Their two-story on wooden piers with a covered porch had seen better days, but visitors reported a rich collection of books, a Waldo Pierce painting, and, not least, the corkscrew horns of that bull kudu that bested Hemingway's.

A few blocks south of the Thompsons, Old Bishop Kee, a preacher in the Bahamian community, peddled pink conch shells at the head of Whitehead Street, the Southernmost point in America (they say). He tooted his fluted conch horn and waved to us when we swung around the corner as he did for every other tourist and boat person casting about for America's Land's End. At the foot of Whitehead Street, near the harbor, the Customs House and Cuban tobacco warehouse stood empty.

That first evening, the four of us plopped down on the edge of the wooden dock formerly owned by Mallory Steamship Company, a U.S.-to-Cuba ferry service that had gone belly up during the depression. Two forty-foot sailboats tacked off of Sunset Key. They sailed amiably into the white-hot sphere of sun as it dimmed and dropped. Seabirds had awakened, their silhouettes, like Miro's painting, blotted against a bruised red-and-blue-on-orange sky. Across a purplish sea, the golden disc laid a rippled trail of glitter right up to the tips of our dangling bare feet. Johnny passed around a joint. Debbie shared the bota bag, and I unwrapped the newspaper of conch fritters and spread it between us.

The Conch Train, a tourist bureau brainchild of the '50s, delivered a dozen or so other-side-of-forty tourists, all done up in Panama hats, white pants, shell-pink shorts, Hawaiian shirts, deck shoes, Hemingway-on-safari duds, cameras slung around necks. Holding shopping bags of Key West kitsch in one hand and fanning slightly sunburned faces with the other. Angling our way, they came to a bewildered halt in front of a dreadlocked busker belting out a Buffalo Springfield tune: "Young people speaking their minds / Getting so much resistance from behind." Wearing expressions of resigned irritation, the Conch Train tribe turned to the next curiosity, a white-faced juggler with rouged cheeks standing atop a stool on one leg.

A stormy crowd of sparsely dressed hippies, hardboiled nomads, raw-assed bikers, brothers in boonie hats, and cosmic cowboys (and girls), pitched up at intervals near us, holding all the youth culture trappings of a party on the fly. If he had been looking in our direction, Castro could have mistaken the cigarette and pot vapors mushrooming from our ship of fools as a smoke signal from a troop of stranded, asylum-seeking *brigadistas*. The two assemblies of sunset watchers were perfectly antipodal and kept it that way.

That evening we wandered Old Town. Sloppy Joe's, Hemingway's favorite Key West watering hole, sat a few doors down from Captain Tony's, on the corner of Duval and Greene Streets. Hemingway claimed to be a silent partner with Sloppy Joe, his friend and fishing buddy. Sloppy Joe also owned and ran the Blind Pig speakeasy at the Captain Tony location until the repeal of the Volstead Act and the Eighteenth Amendment—the end to Prohibition and his bottle-fishing venture. At that time, the Blind Pig, the Mob's hangout, was renamed after Hemingway's favorite dive in Havana, Sloppy Joe's. When the landlord raised the rent, Sloppy Joe and his council-of-customers moved the bar's furnishings during late-night business hours a half a block away to its present location, a former Cuban restaurant. They never missed a beat, carrying on unfettered with the same bar stools, booze, and Mob cohorts. In the move, Hemingway insisted on taking the urinal, an old Spanish olive urn, to his Whitehead Street home as a water trough for his cats, and, "a reminder of how much money he had pissed away" at Sloppy Joe's.

We took four stools on the Duval side of Sloppy Joe's horseshoe bar and began glugging our way through Johnnie Walker Black scotch and sodas, Rum Runners, and Papa Dobles (daiquiris), all favorites of Hemingway. They were a buck a piece. Ceiling fans creaked overhead. The louvered doors swung open to the perpendicular Duval and Greene streets and let in a cross breeze. We dined on red-loaded spicy conch soup and drank in the fumes of the past. Walls of yellow-stained photos, *Life* magazine covers, newspaper clippings, pirouetting fish mounts, and watercolor paintings of dark-skinned islanders. Sloppy Joe's 300-pound black bartender, Skinner, was memorialized for his sawed-off pool cue the size of a baseball bat that he called the "peacemaker." Featured in *To Have and Have Not*, Skinner's peacemaker hung near Hemingway's stool at the end of the bar.

After Hemingway's death in '61, his footlockers, filled with two decades of slightly mildewed photos, letters, manuscripts, notes, and other ephemera, were discovered in Sloppy Joe's backroom bookie business. In 1940, when Hemingway and his new mate, journalist Martha Gellhorn, hightailed it out of Key West for good, bound for Cuba, he had left the footlockers behind in the care and custody of his old drinking buddy, bookie, and fishing mate, Sloppy Joe Russell, who died of a heart attack the next year.

Becky and Debbie were acting as switched on bankers, holding without interest our collective funds. Based on touts by two drunk Conchs, they judged it was time to hit the dive bars. Off we stumbled for 15-cent beers at the Green Parrot on Southard and Whitehead, near the abandoned naval base. Once an open-air sailor bar, the Green Parrot was now a down-and-out hippie hangout smelling of patchouli oil to mask the marijuana odor. We rhapsodized about making a life of jolly poverty in Key West, communing with ghosts' past, capturing the Cubano vibe, landing the big fish, contemplating fiery sunsets, and swilling cheap beer every evening. Martha Gellhorn echoed our hobo-on-ham-sandwich reverie when she wrote to First Lady Eleanor Roosevelt with her first impressions of Key West:

> *It's the best thing I have found in America. It's hot and falling to pieces and people seem happy. Nothing much goes on, languidly a sponge or a turtle gets fished, people live on relief cozily, steal coconuts off the municipal street, amble out and catch a foul local fish called the grunt, gossip, maunder, sunburn and wait for the lazy easy years to pass. Me, I think all that is very fine indeed and if all the world were sunny I daresay there'd be much less trouble as well as much less of that deplorable thing called officially progress.*

From the Parrot, we circled around to the Midget Bar, on Greene and Simonton Streets near the shrimp docks, and drank Havana rum out of the bottle. Thirsty shrimpers fresh off the boat at midnight joined us at the cramped hole-in-the-wall bar. Johnny and Becky, who were holding each other up, decided to follow the shrimpers' lead and ordered grits and grunts. Thirty minutes later, a single plate made it out. The barkeep, new on the job, apologized, saying they had run out but please come back at seven in the morning when they reopened. We converged on a low table in the back room and downed the fried fish slathered in grits in four bites. About that time, we heard the wail of a ship's bell, as if signaling last call and reminding us we had blown our wad and should move on.

Johnny's car was parked nearby, around the corner from Captain Tony's. First, we picked up a Pirate Punch roadie at Tony's, and, from the trunk, grabbed a small ice chest and sleeping bags and tottered a pathless route around the archaeological dig and Old Zach's moat. Soon we were into the cover of Australian pines, verging the empty white sand beaches. We spread out beneath the trees on a sandy bed of pine needles where Sex on the Beach was not a bar drink. A trade wind breeze blew cool through the whispering pines. Nothing but the distant glow of skiffs checking crab and crawfish pots, and shrimpers, and, beyond, empty ocean of tossing waves all the way to Cuba.

Above the rhythmic crash of breaking waves spreading over the nearby shore, roosters crowed, and the roar of a seaplane banking in low, woke us before daylight. As the sun poured down through the sweet-scented pines, I went for a swim. The aquamarine sea surged over me, warm diamond-tipped wave upon warm diamond-tipped wave, drowning me in my own daydreaming indolence. A mating pair of anhingas perched on the rocky spit, and before me the odd pelican plunged into a rhapsody of coral. Old Bishop Kee once again blew his conch shell on Whitehead Street. The gas tank was empty. We breakfasted on our stash of bologna and white onion sandwiches. Another grab bag day had dawned.

A Big Easy Social Call

Chapter Thirteen

A LONG-TERM RELATIONSHIP with Debbie was a bridge too far, and at $600 a month, the bank job was a hollow charade of fake-it-till-you-make-it that I found hard to keep up. I trusted money for its transactional worth but regarded the moneylenders and kings of capitalism with contempt. The art of sycophancy—shakin' the tree, boss—was lost on me. While working at Pan American, I felt like a commodified couch potato, straitjacketed by the color of green to a daily rhythm that unspooled frame by frame. A mind-numbing hell on earth not unlike *As the World Turns* meets *The Edge of Night*. The zing and zest of life in Tampa had fallen short of my inquisitive needs, which signaled that the time had come to clear out, to make tracks. Careerism remained beyond my ambition, so I pulled yet another end around the work-a-day-world. Once again, vagabonding felt more like the life I wanted to live than just a lifestyle. Jim Harrison described this nomadic conviction in *The Road Home*, "Hoboes had begun by moving on to look for work but after a while they just moved on for the sake of moving on."

After six weeks and several beers at the Cat's Eye, I pink-slipped Pan American by dropping my bank keys, insurance card, and unused checkbook off in the night depository. I did leave a note to my lickspittle unit manager, saying, thank you, I had a nice time, and so long (to be my epitaph someday). Before splitting, I, the banker manqué, squared up with Dudley, using my last paycheck for a pile of bills we owed on the Jo Mar crib.

The army had prepared me for life's separations, the ol' *hasta la vista* moment. Often invoked impulsively, moving on came as naturally and necessarily as a bird or butterfly's migratory rhythms: survival, psychic fodder, and freedom all come to mind. Rat holes and rainy days were memes for the sedentary. And now my fortunes were right side up, if not for long.

The next morning, Tommy gave me a lift to the northbound ramp on I-75 in the flux of rush hour. There, on the side of the road, I did some guerilla marketing and held up a sign with "Arkansas or Bust" sprayed in red across it. Soon, I was hopping in an 18-wheeler and explaining my wandering ways through a fog of Pall Mall smoke. Never caught his name but his CB handle was Walrus Moustache. Sporting a buzz cut, a bulbous gin nose, a nicotine-stained, bush-covered mouth, and a black mesh–backed VFW cap, he was over twice my age and a bred-in-the-bone, flag-waving, CB radio-yapping road warrior who happened to be driving for Arkansas Best Freight and headed for a terminal in T-Town (Tulsa). I surmised that due to my trimmed hair and army duffel bag, he thought he was contributing to a worthy cause and kindred spirit by giving me a ride. Our alliance was suspect from the get-go.

He'd been a marine in Korea, he told me, while hard smoking unfiltered Pall Malls till his face turned purple. So hard it occurred to me that he might be more satisfied if he ate them. At the time, I didn't smoke during the day, certainly not in the morning. But in an act of self-defense, I blew smoke-ring clouds of Winston regulars back at him. Take that, bam, bam, bam. Whatever I'd done or tale I told, he'd trump me. My best efforts at tuning him out didn't work. It would have taken a loaded gun to get him to shut the fuck up. Surely, he was jacked up on a handful of Black Beauties. He thundered, cursed, and honked at every flower power, hitchhiking hippie we passed: love it or leave it, motherfucker, toot, toot. His buzz cut, talk of killing slant-eyes and kicking hippies' asses, and valorization of the white trash America he loved started getting under my skin. Somewhere in the panhandle before Tallahassee, in a lapse of caution, I went on a rant about that lying son of a bitch Richard Nixon and the Vietnam War. Mr. Walrus Moustache piped down and in the same instance decided it was time for me to catch another ride. His "99," or final destination, had suddenly changed, he said, with unconvincing lameness. I hightailed it without so much as a fare-thee-well handshake and threw away the Arkansas sign. Two rides later my "99" had changed: I was in New Orleans drinking with an old army buddy, Edward K. Dwyer III.

Nothing says New Orleans like the tumult of Bourbon Street. An hour after Ed retrieved me from the zip-code-less world of highways, we were quaffing Hurricanes as if they were Dixie beers by the flaming fountain at Pat O'Brien's courtyard bar. The house photographer was having a banner evening with all the young couples making their debuts at Pat O's, clenching their souvenir Hurricane glasses in smiling embraces for the camera. "Ching, ching," Ed said. "I wish I owned this racket. It's like a tollgate for first-time tourists. Once they've passed through and paid the fare, they can get on with seeing New Orleans."

Ed and his deeply rooted Louisiana family had supported John F. Kennedy in the 1960 election, as did most of heavily Catholic New Orleans. "Kennedy was a hero in life and a martyr in death," Ed said. "My reverence for the vibrancy he exuded will always remain."

In the decade that had passed since he and his classmates at De La Salle lined St. Charles Avenue to catch a glimpse of the first Catholic president and his motorcade, Ed had become a rising star on the tax staff at Peat, Marwick, Mitchell & Co., one of the Big Eight, as the elite international CPA firms were then known in the world of business. His politics had changed accordingly. He now identified as a rock rib Republican and had supported Nixon. He was also a dues-paying Chamber of Commerce member who thought New Orleans had become a caricature of itself. "Abandoned to tourism," he said.

We never really talked politics in the army. We were both against the war and that was as far as most of us got. Didn't matter if back home you were Republican or Democrat—in the army we were all the same. But on this evening Ed wanted me to know a few things about the business side of politics in New Orleans. I was all ears.

"A culture of corruption and anything-goes decadence has shaped and continues to shape New Orleans," he began. "Not much has changed other than the players and the times. Indeed, that is the genesis of its 'Big Easy' appellation. Think prostitutes, dope, alcohol, tourism, to the exclusion of legitimate business. The name alone invokes an attitude that we can go there and do things that we wouldn't do at home. The largely cash economy fosters a pervasive laissez-faire attitude on all things political, social, and business. That's the reason I'm quitting the Chamber of Commerce. They promote and perpetuate this image because they say it is good for New Orleans, good for the underworld, and maybe good for a few merchants. But legitimate businesses and big corporations are fleeing in droves. There are virtually no public companies left here."

Although I was only passing through and had no skin in the game, I told him, "New Orleans without jazz, pirates, prostitutes, Cajun cooking, and voodoo queens sounds a lot like Houston."

"That's the point," he said. "Houston is drinking water from a fire hose with all the big corporations relocating there. They come here only to party, to do things they wouldn't do at home. Keep the jazz and 'jambalaya, crawfish pie, and filly gumbo' and send the prostitutes and pirates somewhere else. The tourists will still come."

"Easy on the pirates, Ed. I've always liked rum and I'm a sucker for staying up all night drinking the stuff. Sort of makes me one of 'em."

"Okay, we'll keep the pirates."

We paid our tab in the courtyard. Ed wanted to show me the rest of Pat O's. First, we stuck our heads in the piano bar, which was permeated by the smell of spilled drinks and stale ashtrays. Dueling pianos played college football fight songs for a room full of frat boys from LSU and Arkansas out on a roaring rip snorter. "On your toes / Razorbacks to the finish / Carry on with all your might /…Fight, fight, fight," sang the Arkansas crowd, taunting the LSU students. Then the Tiger fans had their turn to kick out the jams and Ed squished in closer to sing along: "Like knights of old, let's fight to hold / The glory of the purple gold / Let's carry through, let's die or do / To win the game for dear old LSU…" All repeated with religious regularity.

As we passed through Pat O's standup (no stools or chairs) locals bar, Ed spotted Hot Rod Hundley. He was leaning on a high-top table. A West Virginia basketball legend who had had a six-year NBA career, Hot Rod was now the announcer for the New Orleans Jazz.

As all Jazz fans did upon seeing Hot Rod, Ed waved and shouted, "You gotta love it, baby," one of Hot Rod's trademark sayings. Ed had all the New Orleans patois down, including Hot Rodisms. I stood aside as they greeted each other and jawboned about the game that night, which the Jazz had lost to the Houston Rockets, 113-100. It was the Jazz's inaugural season, and Pistol Pete Maravich, who embodied the highest of the franchise's hopes, had scored 22 points. The loss that night was the Jazz's seventh in a row. Before their parting, Ed stepped back and performed his best rendition of Hot Rod's rapid staccato delivery, ending in a roar: "Pete inbounds the ball from Barnett, hippity-hops it across mid-court, fakes left, drives right, leaping leaner, good if it goes…PISTOL PETE."

"You missed your calling," Hot Rod said, as he gave Ed a farewell shake.

We made our way up and down Bourbon Street, taking our time, slinging back shots of rum and tequila. It was easy to be astounded at the roiling mass of partying slapdicks and dunces, nothing genteel about it. Strip club pitchmen outfitted like Central Park South doormen, complete with ringmaster hats, offered up cold beer, pretty mamas with tits like soft-boiled eggs, and hot poontang. Beckoning girls in string bikinis flanked the swinging mannequin legs at Big Daddy's (née Lafitte's Boudoir). "This is all new," Ed said. "Bourbon Street in the early '60s housed jazz clubs, bars, and a few burlesque shows. Now this circus of neon-flashing strip clubs is openly selling sex."

We paused to watch two black boys tap dance for tips as we entered Jean Lafitte's Bar, at the corner of Bourbon and St. Philip. Sketchy as the historic details are, the original two-story, brick-between-post structure dates from 1722, making it a contender for the oldest bar in the United States. It never closed during Prohibition. In the 1940s, it was a gay café, a comfortable distance from the center of the French Quarter. Noel Coward and Tennessee Williams were regulars. If only walls could talk, Lafitte's plaster-washed bricks, which are rumored to be haunted, also bore witness to New Orleans's past of privateers and pirates: Cut Nose Chigizola, Dominique You, Rene Beluche, and the Lafitte brothers, Pierre and Jean. Between 1772 and 1791, legend has it that the Lafitte brothers ran a blacksmith shop on the premises that served as a front for their smuggling operations in Barataria Bay, an important sea approach to the city.

It was almost midnight. Lafitte's house pianist Johnny Gordon was tearing it up on the ivories, barricaded by a boisterous wall of revelers, singing along to the Louis Armstrong tune "Just a Gigolo": *I'm just a gigolo and everywhere I go/ People know the part I'm playing/ Paid for every dance, selling each romance/ Ooh, what they're sayin'.*

We wedged into a space at the bar. Bob Smith, known as Horrendi (plural for Horrendous), who had been a Kappa Sig fraternity brother at LSU with my childhood friend Cactus Clyde Lockwood, bartended at our end. Sliding us two Sazeracs, he asked about Cactus.

"Don't shed any tears for Cactus. He's been in Montana for a month filming big-horn sheep with Marty Stouffer," I answered him.

"He hasn't been my way in a while," Horrendi said. "He'll pop in before long."

Ed and Horrendi Bob talked about the Jazz's bad start, while I watched the after-work flow of pole dancers, prostitutes, beer-jerkers, bookies, bikers, frat boys, gays, confidence men, country jakes, and cotton traders—black, white, Creole, the whole bouillabaisse that feeds Bourbon Street. Ed turned my way and said he had seen a few of those faces on post office walls. "Probably so," I said, while thinking that some of these stray cats living on the margins enjoyed more freedom than most. After getting whisked together with so many other folks in the army, things didn't feel right when I spent too much time in a mainstream white boy world, away from the eddies of what I'd call "otherness." Made me claustrophobic, deficient in spirit, hopelessly snagged like a foul-hooked fish. I had come to think I wasn't just watching these stray cats, that I had over time psychically sidled up beside them, licked 'em on the ears, lapped up the lifestyle, and become one of them. No ontological mystery to it, we were all God's critters, with our beating hearts.

When Horrendi returned to the bar from a joint break, he pointed out his friend and favorite bookie, T. J. Jackson, perched in the corner on the St. Philip Street side of Lafitte's. Horrendi invited Ed and me to join their *bourre* game in another hour when his shift ended. "T. J.'s backer, Mike Ratliff, is over there," Horrendi said, pointing to the tall and tanned blond man at the bar wearing sharply creased, starched jeans, a long-sleeve white shirt, caiman cowboy boots, and a college class ring with a diamond-encrusted five-karat blue sapphire. "He's a cotton broker from Metairie. If he plays tonight, the stakes will double." The game was at T. J.'s garret in an old Creole mansion off Esplanade, near Frenchman's Street in the Marigny. I'd played *bourre* a few times with Cactus Clyde, but my skills were not up to scratch, especially in Cajun country where the game was invented and is played daily by local gamblers. Meantime, Horrendi passed along a few tips for Saturday's races at the Fairgrounds: Rio Bravo in the 5th and Combat Ready in the 6th.

The quiet guys in the corner are always interesting. In a Walter Mitty kind of way, they hide some human flaw in the shadows by making a virtue of being mysterious. Crossing the cement-flat floors, I introduced myself to T. J., who was dressed like a riverboat gambler and drinking Jim Beam and Coke at a candlelit wooden table, up against the double louvered doors. When I asked him where he was from, he told me Evanston, a suburb of Chicago.

"You came downstream," I said. "Salmon head upstream like all the good jazz men…Memphis, St. Louis, and Chicago. What brings you here?"

"Black chicks. I dig black chicks," he said as blasé as an orange picker would tell you why he went to Florida. "I followed a girl down here named Rosa Lee whom I met in Chicago. She was raised up the road in Bogalusa. We lived together in a cottage on Gallier in the Bywater for four months. Then, out of the blue, she ripped me off for everything I had, stereo, television, even my pots and pans. Hocked it all for some horse. God's honest truth, I felt dumb as a sack full of doorknobs for not seeing it coming. Her cousin Mary told me she had kicked her out of her house because she didn't want to wake up with a corpse on the couch. Mary thinks Rosa Lee left town, went back to Bogalusa, maybe. That's okay. I'm not chasing her. She was born a nickel and had a chance to be a dime. Plenty more black chicks here for me. They're my jam."

"Looks like you could start in this room," I said, glancing at two sisters with dyed blond jerry curls, sporting red high heels, sitting beneath the amber glow of a gas lamp next to the smithy's old stone fireplace. T. J. glanced their way, grinning like a possum on a sweet potato.

"By the way," I said, "any chance you could get a bet down for me on the 5th and 6th tomorrow at the Fairgrounds?"

"You're in the right place, friend."

I slipped him a Jackson and a piece of paper with Horrendi's picks. I was going big.

Mid-morning now, Old Hickory was riding high in Jackson Square. The square's modern Parisian parklike beauty concedes no visible traces of the many incarnations of cruelty that took place in the former military parade ground—slave auctions, hangings, beheadings, lashings with cat-o'-nine-tails. In 1828, a teenaged Abraham Lincoln guided a flatboat to New Orleans, the first big city he ever visited. The slave auctions he witnessed in Jackson Square flew in the face of his moral sensibilities. He never forgot. When citizens lynched eleven dark-skinned Sicilians in the square on hoked-up murder charges, the Italian government protested so loudly that President Benjamin Harrison sought to appease them by calling for a national observance day of Columbus, a Genoese explorer, who never touched the shores of the continent of North America. The proclamation worked: Italian immigrants became more acceptable...and white.

Beyond the famous statue of Old Hickory, the sun splashed across the stained-glass windows beneath the three towers of the St. Louis Cathedral. Reputed to have been the inspiration for Walt Disney's castle, the cathedral ranks as the oldest of its kind in the United States. Palm readers and portrait artists, buskers and contortionists, jugglers and jewelry makers arrived for work along with black-robed priests. An Arkansas friend, Leroy Gorrell, and his nineteen-year-old partner, Lucinda Williams, had lived out of their truck camper parked on the Esplanade and posted up seven days a week in front of the cathedral, busking and (between songs) making jewelry. Tussling over turf was a daily affair along the square's iron fence, red brick row houses, and shops and on up the old Pirate's Alley, a stretch of cobblestone with a colorful past.

Ed and I stepped between a line of horse-drawn carriages and crossed Decatur to the river side in front of the Jax (Jackson) Brewery. A line already awaited a tasting tour. The blast of tugboats whistling their way down the Mississippi sounded as we walked on to the Canal Street trolley stop near Liberty Place, the scene of a mass riot in 1874 against the Reconstruction government.

A few minutes later, the streetcar, a Perley Thomas 900-series built in the 1920s, arrived half empty. After Ed paid the driver, we each took one of the hard seats of mahogany near the back. Once moving, Ed leaned my way and said that inflation was killing him. "They've doubled the rates from 7 to 15 cents," he lamented. "On me next time," I promised, steel wheels clanking in the background. We were circling around to the burial site of New Orleans' most famous Voodoo queen.

While coming of age, Voodoo to me was nothing more than a word used to frighten children. Only in literature was I remotely familiar with anyone who actually held Voodoo beliefs (or a suspension of disbelief). But come to find out since the early 1800s people of New Orleans and Southern Louisiana had widely practiced Voodoo. It had first migrated with the slaves through the doors-of-no-return dungeons on the Gold Coast of West Africa, from Quidah, Benin, the southern tip of the former Kingdom of Dahomey, and the cradle of African Voodoo.

Voodoo in New Orleans reached its heyday when boatloads of refugees, slaves and free blacks, arrived from the French colony of Santo Domingo (Haiti). In 1804, following a Voodoo-inspired rebellion 13-years before, Santo Domingo had won a hard-fought war of independence with France. The expense of funding an expeditionary force to fight in Santo Domingo depleted France's coffers and the shortfall forced Napoleon to agree to the Louisiana Purchase, thus opening the city gates of New Orleans to a robust river and sea trade and to successive waves of immigrants. Steamers stacked sky high with bales of cotton bound for Europe were a common sight at the Canal Street docks. By 1840, over 100,000 people lived in New Orleans, including several thousand Haitian emigrants.

As with all else in New Orleans, Voodoo is a mixed bag, over time seasoned to fit local tastes no less than the roux and 'holy trinity' of a finely cooked creole gumbo. Every household observes it differently, but most followers put their faith in the hands of a single God, Bondye. Taken from the French term *Bon Dieu*, meaning "Good God," Bondye, Voodoo's unknowable Supreme Creator, steers clear of human affairs. His will is expressed through intermediaries, the cosmic and natural spirits known as *loas*, of which there are thousands. In practice, emphasis is given to animal fetishes and gris-gris amulets. Often packed with a pastiche of herbs, roots, goofer dust, stones, coins, crystals, seals or personal effects, the amulets invoke a chosen spirit (*loa*) for anyone in need of a cure, a charm, a spouse, a baby, a bank loan, protection or a partridge in a pear tree. If there is a rub to this peaceful and positive religion, it might be the time and energy expended each day making transactional offerings to, and interacting with, the countless *loas*.

In the interest of recruitment, French priests and the Catholic church long ago solved the camel through the needle's eye of Voodoo deities and Christianity's dualism of god and the devil coexisting in the same household. It wasn't tricky. They simply rationalized that the intercession of *loas* in the daily lives of slaves and colonial subjects was no different than the powers held by Roman Catholic saints, takeoffs on the ancient polytheistic gods, to involve themselves in human affairs. One became identified (or syncretized) with the other. St. Patrick, for instance, who legend has it drove the snakes from

Ireland, is coupled with the Voodoo serpent *loa*, Damballah. The venerable Papa Legba, some say the most powerful *loa* in the Voodoo pantheon, is associated with St. Peter, the gatekeeper to heaven, St. Lazarus, the lame beggar at the gates of the rich man, and St. Anthony, the patron saint of all things lost. Over time, the Archangel Michael and John the Baptist and other Christian icons have become *loas* because of their own special qualities.

Dr. John, the Voodoo inspired white jazz man and boogie-woogie rocker, whom Ed had known since junior high on the streets of Carrollton, once wrote: "In New Orleans, in religion, as in food or race or music, you can't separate nothing from nothing. Everything mingles each into the other—Catholic saint worship with gris-gris spirits, evangelical tent meetings with spiritual-church ceremonies—until nothing is purely itself but becomes part of one funky gumbo."

Yet Voodoo practices, unlike the Catholic sacraments, often bring to the non-African's mind descriptors like juju and black magic. They stoke fears of people of African descent and of their tribal traditions: drumming and dancing the bamboula, worship of ancestors and gris-gris amulets, possession of spirits and fetish priests. Because Voodoo has been gratuitously distorted to be seen as purely a dark art of hostile hexes and dolls-as-pin-cushions, New Orleans born and bred Voodoo Queen Marie Laveau captured the fears and vivid imaginations of all, believers and not.

Laveau's stock soared among whites, blacks, and all shades in between when she came to the rescue of a wealthy merchant's son. The story has it that the son had been arrested for a crime he didn't commit but was being framed by a political enemy. On the day of the trial, Laveau put three guinea peppers in her mouth like a chaw of Red Man and prayed long and hard at St. Louis Cathedral. She then dashed to the courthouse and goofered the judge's bench with the guinea pepper chaw only moments before he entered the room.

By all accounts, the prosecution presented overwhelming evidence that day for a guilty verdict. Yet the judge acquitted the merchant's son. The pleased-as-punch father rewarded Marie Laveau handsomely in cash and with a deed to a shotgun cottage on St. Anne's Street, where she lived until her death.

Ed and I entered the St. Louis Cemetery No. 1 off Basin Street, entombment site of Marie Laveau and location of one of the most memorable scenes in the counterculture classic *Easy Rider*. Opened in 1789, the above-ground cemetery is smack dab in Treme, the oldest African American community in the United States. Developed by Claude Treme and located out of the Vieux Carre, this community of immigrants and free people of color, including Haitians, became known as Faubourg Treme, or Treme's Suburb. Through time, the neighborhood gained fame for the spectacle of slave dancing on Sundays in Congo Square, the fabled Storyville brothels ("The House of the Rising Sun"), the grand Creole mansions on Esplanade Avenue, the Creole and African American jazz clubs, and jazz greats like Louis Armstrong, Sidney Bechet, and Buddy Bolden. Since 1819, the Northside Skull and Bone Gang have awakened the African spirits of Treme before sunrise on Fat Tuesday, kicking off Mardi Gras, by donning skeleton costumes and papier-mâché skulls, beating drums and dancing and chanting warnings such as: "Wake up, live right, or the bone man is coming to put you in the ground."

Before Ed picked me up on the highway, my idea of the Big Easy stemmed from his rites-of-passage stories told in the army and those of friends like Cactus and from books and films. It was exhilarating to connect the dots of those associations with eyes-on travel experience. As in most things, you never forget your first time.

The summer of '69 while stationed at Fort Knox, Kentucky, I had watched on the silver screen the haunted grounds of the St. Louis Cemetery No. 1 in the movie *Easy Rider*. Those cinematic images began to come together as we hooked a left to the Italian Benevolent Society Tomb, which towered above all other crypts. On the lower reaches of the tomb, Wyatt (Peter Fonda) and Billy (Dennis Hopper) had dropped Orange Sunshine with two prostitutes, Karen (Karen Black) and Mary (Toni Basil). A guerilla production, Hopper-the-director and Fonda-the-producer had no permits to film anywhere in New Orleans.

Garbed in hippy threads, Hopper, who took a page from David Crosby with his bushy moustache and wild tangle of chestnut hair, along with Fonda and film crew, easily blended into the taboo-busting bacchanal of second-line merrymakers, Mardi Gras Indians in riotous plumage, trinket-throwing krewes and marching brass bands playing the city's adopted anthem, "When the Saints Come Marching In" (February '68). Like most acid trips (and Mardi Gras parades), nothing was scripted, they made it up in the streets and cemetery as they went. Everything was disconnected, jump cutting from Wyatt to Billy and the girls shucking their clothes to swirling skies and blasts of blinding sunbursts. It's a safe bet that the New Orleans Archdiocese would not have sanctioned the tripping-on-acid theme of the shooting or the girl's nude scenes capering among the sun-bleached crypts.

In one unsettling scene Hopper directs Fonda to call up the memories of his mother committing suicide. A Canadian born socialite, Fonda's mother Francis Ford Seymour, cut her throat with a razor while a patient in a New York sanitorium. In the movie, wearing a tie-dye t-shirt, Wyatt (Fonda) crawls up into the Italian tomb niche. On the lap of, and face to face, he hugs a carved female statue, unleashing a torrent of tears and emotion: "Oh mother why didn't you tell me? ...Shut up! ...How could you make me hate you so? ...Oh God I hate you so much."

As Wyatt melds into the statue, a tribal drum beat pounds in a rhythm not unlike the West African bamboulas so long ago heard in Congo Square. The innocent voice of a young girl is heard solemnly reciting a declaration of faith: "I believe in God, the Father Almighty, Creator of Heaven and Earth. ...And in Jesus Christ his only son. ...Born of the Virgin Mary. ...Blessed art Thou amongst women, and blessed is the fruit of Thy womb, Jesus. ...Holy Mary, Mother of God, pray for us now..."

Turned out to be a 'bad trip.' At the end of the scene, Mary and Karen have fallen down a rabbit hole of horrors, crying out: "I'm going to die. I'm dead..."

Mardi Gras, or Fat Tuesday, a variation of Carnival, translated from its Latin origin means "a farewell to flesh." It's the day before Lent, marked by festivals of debauchery throughout Hispanic cultures. *Easy Rider* eulogized the freedom and rebellion of the '60s. Shot on the fly, showing St. Louis Cemetery No. 1 during Mardi Gras may be the movie's crowning stroke of artistry. The Cannes Film Festival jury judged it a whiz-bang feature, honored it with a first prize, and France subsequently banned it for the depiction of illegal drug use.

"We were ready to bring back the pillory stocks in Jackson Square for Hopper and Fonda," Ed said, his Jesuit upbringings preceding my Johnny-come-lately way of talking about the movie. "I never saw their acid trip, disturbing the decency of the dead."

Standing in front of the marble statue that Fonda had mounted, Ed explained that when someone couldn't afford a personal or family tomb he or she was buried in these "society" tombs. Italian, French, Irish, Portuguese, Creole societies, he said, "all had tombs in the cemetery."

"There are only twenty-four vaults in the Italian Benevolent Society Tomb, but over 1,000 people are buried there," Ed told me. "If it was a Volkswagen and not a tomb it would be in *The Guinness Book of World Records*." Pausing to pull some tall bristle grass from the tomb's edge, he continued, "Most people were poor, afraid of disease. They worried about the high-water table and how it affected their burial space. The Spanish passed along the custom of vaults. But city ordinances didn't allow cramming corpse on top of corpse. If a family corpse was recently reposed in the vault, the next body in had to be placed in a 'receiving vault' along the cemetery wall for a year and a day."

"For a year and a day," I said. "What's up with that? It sounds like they are aging race horses. They all turn one the first day of the year regardless of when they were born."

"Same kind of logic. The ordinance says two years, which has been interpreted as one year and a day. The reality is that it's 250° inside there," he said, pointing at a vault in the Italian Society tomb. "It's like an oven. Takes no time for the flesh to melt down to bare bones and fully decompose. After a year and a day, the morticians shove those bare bones to the back of the vault and make room for more."

The cemetery's windowless and whitewashed tombs often resemble houses with gabled roofs, complete with decorative iron fences. The tombs face onto a miniature grid of streets, dead ends, and blighted alleys of crumbling bricks and graffiti. Mark Twain dubbed it the City of the Dead.

Ed seemed to divine a few right-angle turns on the cemetery's weed-strewn walkways. We circled around the crypt of Dominique You, Jean Lafitte's partner in piracy, and the guest-cottage-size tomb of civil rights icon Homer Plessy, overgrown with weeds and begging the care of a sexton, and made a slow pass by the family vault of Alicia Villa Ayala, Pancho Villa's daughter. A couple of steps on and we were standing in front of Voodoo Queen Marie Laveau's Greek Revival–style tomb. Votive offerings of Mardi Gras beads, burned candles, and half-empty cups of booze littered the ground. Ed translated the French inscription on the tomb's marble face: "Family of the Widow Paris, born Laveau."

We holed up that evening in Harry's Corner bar, a quiet retreat, removed from the goth and lace of Bourbon Street. A diminutive older woman in tweeds with a bird's nest for a wig that was turned sideways perched at the Dumaine Street end of Harry's bar. The high-ceilinged room was blue with smoke. Blackie, the barkeep, a quiet type, let it out that the older woman had been ordering Sazeracs since noon. Her husband, turned out, had died two days before. She was not doing well with speaking in sentences, staying awake, or synchronizing her cigarette lighter to her Salem 100s. Every so often we heard her avian-like voice chirrup, "One more for the widow Beauregard."

The only other customers in Harry's that Sunday evening were a forty-something couple from Port Arthur, Texas. They had arrived mid-afternoon in the custard-yellow Karmann Ghia out front with its white-walled left front wheel proudly lopped over the curb. "A Bug in a party frock," Ed said of the car, echoing the gearhead opinion of its low performance but sporty look. Celebrating an even-year anniversary (or something), the Port Arthur couple slow danced in the same spot, as if in a pose, staring fixedly, trancelike at the pattern of their feet moving in a tight left-right metronome. Over and over, they punched the Select-O-Matic jukebox with the same belly rubbin' music, Al Green, Marvin Gaye, Ray Charles. They paused their private slow dance between songs only to swill more Jax beer and fire up another straight.

Ed and I leaned on a high-top table by the door. Our nattering jumped around from the army to his boss Major Fujimori's investigation of me to speculating on how soon Saigon would fall. At some point, a black street magician from Belize who lit up the room with his megawatt smile and neon green sweatshirt, agreeably busted in on us. He launched into a medley of tricks, turning a dollar bill into a ten, putting a cigarette out on my shirt without leaving a mark, moving pencils with his mind, and making coins vanish into

Voodoo ether. We each decorated his palm with a Georgie Boy while waving him away from entertaining the waxen-faced widow Beauregard with his magic.

Later in the evening, after Ed and I had hashed out the urgencies of our time, with a green light from Blackie, I circled behind the bar and rang T. J.'s night-time office at Lafitte's to check on how my ponies had fared. They said he had gone uptown on Napoleon Avenue for some Cajun music and dancing, a *fais-do-do* or something. An hour later, T. J. rang back. Blackie waved me over and handed me the phone. "Out of the money, friend, 5th and 6th on a fast track," T. J. promptly informed me, shouting over the din of accordion-led music and stomping feet. "See anything you like tomorrow?"

"No chance man, my wad is shot," I shouted back, stirring the widow Beauregard to blink her eyes open. "Catch you next time. Good luck with the sisters." Returning to the table, the news fell on me like a ton of bricks.

"Let's go have some oysters at Felix's," Ed said. "They're on me. Then we'll call it an early night. No need to raise a ruckus on a Sunday."

Ed's tour of New Orleans left me weighing up the dues-paying nature of the newcomer's struggle to adapt and meld with the unlikely ideas of a country that, as its guiding principle, has yoked together all these seekers, sinners, and ship jumpers who've washed ashore from far-flung places, seasoning the melting pot one piquant flavor at a time. That a one-time snake-and-alligator-infested indigenous swampland, rife with malaria, could be sliced, diked, thrice colonized, and colorfully transformed into Caribbean-like Carnival with cathouses on top of French Catholic cathedrals and Creole and Cajun cooking on every corner, left me gobsmacked. As Ed and I said our goodbyes that morning, I thought, ain't New Orleans made for you and me?

Embarrassed to ask Ed for a grubstake for my self-immiserating enterprise of no return, I daydreamed that morning about how I might game the system like the street magicians, turning dollar bills into ten spots. As Ed U-turned his '69 turquoise Galaxy with a black top to the opposite side of the road, keeping it real, he shouted over to me: "Come back in a year when the Superdome opens. We'll go to a Jazz game…PISTOL PETE."

Furry Sang the Blues

Chapter Fourteen

A MISSISSIPPI KITE with its dark liquid eyes watched me from a live oak across the road, periodically whistling a mellow call. Catching rides was slow that morning. Sitting on my duffel bag in the full blaze of the sun, swatting flies and mosquitos, marooned for six hours on State Highway 190 near Opelousas, between Lafayette and Alexandria, the boredom was crushing. Beneath the kite's tree, white blooms of swamp hibiscus encircled the roadside stand of a redbone lady wearing a blazing yellow and orange tignon. After watching her do a brisk business all morning, thinking one of her customers might offer me a ride, I had worked up an appetite. I left my bag on the side of the road to mark my space, approached her, and asked what everyone had been stopping for. She recommended the crawfish boudin made with rice, peppers, and cracklins' for $1.50. From her apron, she fished out a bottle of hot sauce, a sleeve of saltines, and napkins. "No charge," she said.

A short distance down the road, I found a bench at a service station to perch on and eat. No sooner than I had sat down, a skuzzy attendant who went by his last name, Thibodeaux, tried to shoo me along by showing me Polaroids of five cottonmouths hanging on a barbed-wire fence. Said he had shot them in the tea-colored slough from which I was trying to get a ride. Things being as they were, after finishing the boudin, it struck me as time to move on anyway.

Before doing so, I used Thibodeaux's pay phone to give Dad a collect call and hit him up for twenty-five bucks. A bus ticket and some pocket money, was my thought. He answered the call but quickly hung up—almost as if he anticipated me putting the touch on him. Didn't give me time to invoke my favorite vagabond defense: Jesus went rogue between ages twelve and thirty. In Dad's defense, it was, after all, a collect call, a mode of conversation with which he had experience not just with me but with three of my brothers as well.

Dad was old school, a firm believer in the therapeutic "no." It bothered me more than it did him that I had become a big disappointment. Not being able to occasionally call on Dad for bus money or to bail me out was an emotional Rubicon I needed to get over. He had been my ballast and gentleman teacher, and, in most ways, that had not changed. The call turned out to be a good lesson, one of life's speechless sermons. If I were chasing knowledge and truth, a higher morality and a richer, more creative way to express myself, it was time to practice some dignity (even though Jesus the Son of God left a blank slate until he was thirty years old...). After that call, I never asked Dad for another dime, which he deeply respected. And I liked myself better for it even though owning my choices and pushing back against forced maturity, for the moment, remained at odds in my life. In biological terms, I was still pupating, a chrysalis. In spite of the army making men out of boys, I was resistant to adulthood, confident that the best part of a man is the boy that lingers within.

The footloose pace synched perfectly with my metabolism. Mudsill jobs here and there as a means to an end, madly pinballing the planet, postponing the future, following my bliss down any road—all these remained comfortable compass points. Maybe everything wasn't admirable, but I was fairly certain that I had it better than most working stiffs and had been "around" more than my College Joe bros and boon mates. Most were on board with all the conformist, procrustean nonsense that included a haircut, a change of threads, giving up the jive talk, and walking-the-new-walk of a righteous, consumer-driven, debt-encumbered, middle-class life. That hivemind of worshiping the cold-eyed lords of the dollar and acquisitive success, I found, from deep down in my big, bruised and tender bosom, to be equal parts terrifying, censorious, and a cop out. The thought of sanctifying the American Dream by shimmying up the greasy pole just made my soul (and adrenal gland) want to shrivel up and die.

In his book *Dharma Bums*, Jack Kerouac described my good-hearted compulsions and spiritual angst: "Like the ants that have nothing to do but dig all day, I have nothing to do but do what I want and be kind and remain nevertheless uninfluenced by imaginary judgments and pray for the light." Jack was talking about living, not making a living, about presence of mind and spiritual growth as a higher reward than money and mindless productivity.

That being so, rovers like me had no problem calling on a friend for an advance. Tommy Horton wired $25 to a Western Union a mile down the road, which also served as the Greyhound station. I spent the night on an outside bench, homeless, sleeping deeply, flushing some, but not all, of those snakes from my head. At first light, on the bones of my ass, I felt about as valuable as the latex memento beneath the bench. My imaginary friend, who could furrow my brow and make me talk aloud, let me know that better days were aloft and that I should stop fretting about becoming someone's hamster on a wheel. The world was full of bummers. Soon the talking stopped and the jukebox in my head switched on, and I whistled along: *I picked up my bag, I went lookin' for a place to hide / When I saw Carmen and the Devil walking side by side…*

Rarely did the delicious taste of nostalgia linger for long in the place conferred upon me as home. It's that Ithaca region of the mind, anchored by all things past. In my estimation, having a conflicted relationship with your hometown is as American as apple pie. Upon returning to Fort Smith, which I often thought of as a social quicksand, I would revert to character, seeking out my old hell-raising buddies, soon swallowed like a blind coyote in the mucky swirl. All bad habits got worse. It was a short leap from willpower to willful folly and occurred as naturally and logically as when in Rome... If Cota Street in Santa Barbara was my summer of love, Fort Smith in early '73 was my winter of mad substance abuse. The bus from northern Louisiana arrived around nine in the evening at the Sixth Street station in Fort Smith. Shouldering my army duffel bag, first round on my dance card was Core's Grain and Feed.

At age sixteen, I had been Andy Core's best man at a civil ceremony in the courthouse in Stilwell, Oklahoma, a popular destination for eloping teenagers in the '60s. Andy had dropped out of high school and was working the boneyard shift at the smelter on Zero Street. Jacquie, his bride, had just started nursing school at Sparks Hospital. Andy was seventeen years old, and Jacquie, who was pregnant, was eighteen. Their impeccable good looks, winsome smiles, exultation of life attitudes, and youthful animal spirit made us all feel flawed. Beautiful, perfectly paired, was their lustrous opening act.

In a backroom of the courthouse, some downhome grandma justice of the peace gave a lecture about lust and teenage sex, performed the ceremony, collected the fee, and issued the license. It all seemed natural because historically it had been, and eastern Oklahoma never had given a flying goddamn how they made their money anyway—teenage weddings, late-term abortions, juke joints, cockfights, pole dancers, you name it.

Five years on, Andy and his brother Kit kicked off their bar business in faded-glory-central of downtown Fort Smith, USA. Their chosen location was an 1890s-era, refurbished brick building that was once the blue-collar Brass Rail bar. It was next door to the St. Charles Hotel and across the street from the Palace Rooms, both recently shuttered brothels. Kit, who as a seaman had learned his way around the world's bar scene, had just cashiered from the navy after a four-year hitch. Given that experience, pouring all his savings into a bar seemed a good idea. The business plan had Kit tallying the books in the morning and managing the lunch shift. He came up with a food menu that featured a hoagie-style sandwich laden with a horse bite pile of roast beef or ham (from Portas on Grand) with a pickle, chips, and a pint of Michelob for two bucks. It was a bargain as well as a vitalizing base to cycle on, one day taking care of the next. Pint jars cost only 50 cents, so it wasn't unusual for the not-too-employed patrons to stick around all afternoon.

Andy ran things at night. He loved roots music and promoted local and, on occasion, national musical talent. He played acoustic guitar, couldn't sing a lick, but fancied himself a rock star and had that lifestyle down pat, alpha to omega.

Ernie Cromwell, a critically failed-to-launch acquaintance from my Boys Club days, who left slime behind him like a snail with everything he touched, and Jon Holden, an old friend and highly decorated former 101st Screaming Eagle in Vietnam, worked the bar at night, made sandwiches, and took the door.

After Vietnam, Jon was stationed with the 82nd Airborne at Fort Bragg, North Carolina, a major arrival point for heroin from Southeast Asia, the ravages of war coming home to haunt. On the occasional retreat to a base camp in Vietnam, John had chased the dragon. But once at Fort Bragg, he and his fellow combatants upped the ante. Busted out for possession of heroin and paraphernalia (like needles), rather than court-martialing everyone, the army discharged these combat veterans, and in Jon's case, put him in the custody and care of Gene Wells, a poet and an English professor at the University of Arkansas living in the outback of rural Crawford County.

When Jon and I reconnected at Core's, it was hard not to think of him as a warrior poet and musician. He often jammed on drums between sets of visiting bands or spelled someone on guitar or drums while they ducked out back to get high. Jon rocked, a guy's guy, a cat's cat. He, along with Clyde Randall, a Summer of Love Haight-Ashbury resident and regular solo act at George's Lounge in Fayetteville, introduced me to the great outlaw troubadours who were making their marks at the time in Nashville and Austin's Armadillo World Headquarters: Willie Nelson ("Whiskey River"), Townes Van Zandt ("Pancho and Lefty"), Kris Kristofferson ("Sunday Morning Coming Down"), Waylon Jennings ("Ladies Love Outlaws"), Jerry Jeff Walker and the Lost Gonzo Band ("Up Against the Wall Redneck Mother"), and the gold standard of new songwriters, John Prine ("Sam Stone"). They were all keenly observant, sometimes deep and dark, always breaking down walls (bringing hippies and rednecks together), with a knack for storytelling and capturing raw human emotion.

Jon Holden's poetry also had the depth and darkness of many a heart-worn highway. A piece of VC shrapnel in his head may have helped stir his haunting dreams and creative drive. If looking for a model, and there were many, he was John Prine's drug-addicted Vietnam vet, Sam Stone.

Apart, and especially together, Andy, Ernie, Jon, and I were, as the saying goes, mad, bad and dangerous to know. We preferred the deep water in the pool of poor choices.

I bowled through the back door, hopped up a short set of stairs, and slid my duffel bag in behind the bar on the duckboards. The draughts of Budweiser flowed freely. Trout Fishing in America, an eclectic folk/rock two-man band out of Austin, Texas, was giving it hell that weeknight to a rowdy and crowded house, smelling thick and musty of spilled hops and cigarette smoke. So much smoke it was unbreathable unless you were exhaling your own.

Good vibes had welcomed me back on home turf, in the bosom of old friends. Before the evening was over, I was Core's Grain and Feed's newest bartender, waiter, and doorman rolled into one. Andy decided to go big and offered a generous pay package: all you could drink, ten bucks a night plus tips, a place to crash on Andy's and Jon's couches, a ride to work every day, and plenty of hookup opportunities in the bar. When all else failed, brothels around the corner. Living the dream, we shook on it.

We were at the zenith of the golden age of free love. The birth control pill had hit the market a decade before in '62, and it would be about ten years before the first cases of HIV-AIDS were made public. It was also the heyday of hard drugs, the '60s cascading into the '70s. Nonstop "fear and loathing" were not my thing, though. I watched up close and personal many a friend turned junkie and more than a few got to the big house, or worse, cashed out.

At the time, I thought of myself as a seeker of kicks, a recreational and experimental user, never a tortured fiend or full-time slave to drugs. Equal spells of clarity, not least the Sunday sabbatical to control the burn and collect my thoughts, were vital to staying onboard the gyre of madness—as I thought of it. Shapeless days and nights in hidden rooms—drawing my own blood, smelling my own death—were not my idea of kicks. My compulsions were glandular: Give me a pop and show me the people and the party. And if I took too large a dose of anything—heroin, coke, Dilaudid, LSD, Desoxyn—I'd move on while I was ahead. Never romanticized the acts of a monster, or its doppelganger, a corpse.

In those drug-infused days, on two occasions I know damn well I went too far and found myself peering into the abyss. And as Nietzsche pointed out, the abyss gazed back at me. While working at Core's Grain and Feed, we smoked, popped, shot, snorted, sniffed, drank, dabbed, bit off, baked, chewed, cracked, cooked, absorbed rectally, inhaled, huffed, and ate anything that altered the mind, body, and soul and was fairly priced, cut rate even. The works.

We Core folks all convened early one weekday afternoon at Jon's house on North 36th, next door to Pretty Boy Floyd's former hideout, across from Tilles Park. Shooting up was a brazen act, a plummet to the bottom of the barrel of human progress, a far remove from the ordinary quiet desperation of most of my cronies. It also had its thrills. The first and only time I shot heroin, after the familiar sting and before fully depressing the plunger, a strange metallic taste surged up my eustachian tube and washed over the back of my throat. Though it amounted to no more than a corn nubbin cooked down to a molasses color, I knew a narcotic freight train was throttling around the bend and also that my bags weren't quite packed. It was an adult dose. Blood felt like it had circled the body in one mighty pump of the heart and then surged out, leaving nothing to circulate but a warm wave of glory from a hot spoon. My tongue tied and eyes rolled so far back in my head I'm fairly certain I saw my ass and Kingdom Come all in one. Somewhere in that moment of glory, I dropped to my knees, tingling up and down my spine and from my nose all the way to my toes. It surely crossed my mind that I might fall over and bang my head, but the "I-give-a-shit-impulse" never happened.

Andy, Ernie, and Jon watched, marveling, almost cheering, at the superb rush that had swooned me, that freight train banging all 'round my brain. Without delay, they cooked up more, borrowed my jabber, fired away, and tossed the empty balloon and bloodstained needle in the trash and the burnt spoon in the sink.

"That's it, folks," Ernie said. "Let's go play basketball." With me turtling up the rear, tongue lolling, out we went for a pickup game of hoops. Just like the old days at the Boys Club. As they shuffled about throwing up air balls and errant passes, I spent the afternoon crawling around the court trying to come to, afraid to relax and shut my eyes.

No chance of a fast break or a jump shot by me on that day, a worthy role model for Leonardo DiCaprio in the *The Basketball Diaries*.

As the experts say, there is nothing like your first time. Soon, I moved on to Desoxyn, a top-shelf member of the amphetamine family and preferred upper of the day.

Dr. Lambert was a general practitioner and former army colonel. After retiring, he opened a small primary care practice on Main Street in Lavaca, Arkansas, thirty minutes from Fort Smith. For a $10 visitation fee, and a short spiel on energy levels and lethargy, he would prescribe thirty tabs of Desoxyn. As he wrote out the "script," he instructed us to fill it next door at his pharmacy, Lambert's Drugs. It would have been sacrilege to not honor the good Doc's wishes.

Once the scripts were filled, we'd duck into the pharmacy restroom and get those pellets marinating. Thirty minutes later, back in Fort Smith, that jar of pills looked like leeched out bones in a pool of golden mercury. In a jiffy (and a jab), my brooding nature was infused with a sense of well-being; my mind turned to something that felt like warm dripping honey. And this bitch had legs. It was time to go to work, vampire hours, play all night.

Aldous Huxley described *doors of perception* as always open, but for me, lysergic acid diethylamide, better known as LSD, was rarely an inward journey of controlled meditations. Wearing white robes and love beads, sitting in the lotus position, staring into lava lamps, and divining universal truths from a Tibetan mandala, or whatever staged setting and mindset, was for the professional acid makers, takers, and Pied Pipers.

From a creative thinking standpoint, I did, however, intersect with those psychedelic pioneers who understood that LSD allowed us to mentally venture outside of systems of authority—church, military, school, government, and, foremost, the hierarchies of the mind, the superego, ego, and subconscious. Strictly speaking, though, the attainment of the supreme was collateral to copping the supreme buzz, which gonzo writer Hunter Thompson described as "Walking with the King." That's not to say Carlos Castaneda and his shamanic peyote ceremonies were never invoked around a campfire in the Ozarks. Matus, Castaneda's Man of Knowledge, may well have been one of those flying pigs we caught a glimpse of at Shore's Lake one wintry night after taking some of the original Sunshine, a small, soft barrel-shaped pill that rubbed off on your fingers. Some of the last clean acid made in those days.

I found LSD, peyote, and psilocybin, like all drugs and alcohol, to be more tests of will and stamina to "function in a socially interactive milieu" while ripped out of my gourd. In fact, endurance and high-volume intake mixed generously with headlong velocity were the basic calculus for legend status in the burgs of Arkansas. Put it this way: The mere mortal who could drink a fifth of whiskey and still talk and drive 90 miles an hour was accorded respect. The larger-than-life man who could drink a fifth of whiskey, shoot Desoxyn, take a hit of LSD, and still drive 90 with the lights off was Mt. Olympus bound. The logic went something like the more brain cells you killed, the more you must have, ergo the respect, the beau ideal, the tin pot hometown hero.

On one particular Saturday evening, I had dropped a dainty lavender pill known as Purple Haze and was drinking straight shots of bourbon at the Electric Flag bar on 10th Street in Fort Smith. I'd spent yet another fruitful day in the great chronicles of aimless living. Bobby Don Selby's band was blowing the roof sky high with Rolling Stones covers to a standing-room-only crowd. Richard Wilson, a tough hombre and a late-night carousing buddy, was working the door. He wore a gray Stetson, hung low over the forehead. It wasn't even 10 o'clock and the LSD had me, as the term of art goes, by the ass. Reality was changing faster than the score of a basketball game, slipping away, with sparks of clarity and long spasms of disorientation. The booming throb of music, the bristling crush of longhair rednecks, the pulsing lights—all conspired to make me want to run for shelter. Hard to know where, though. Radiant tracers shot across the bandstand of harlequin banners. Sounds weren't just amplified; I could "see" them like mutinous starbursts. Boing, boing, boing, rang my smoke rings across the bar while a backbeat of pool balls cracked like thunder over my shoulder. Brother Greg, my acid guru, at one point scuttled up to me, cast a wry grin, and bleated something token like, "What's up, Phil?" Together we lost it, weak-kneed, falling over and paralyzed by our own hysterical goofiness.

Into this clownishness and trip of trips walked our beloved former probation officer, Jim Hanna. I hadn't seen him since I had left for the army four years earlier. As a volunteer citizen probation officer, he had stood up on my behalf and pled with the judge for lenience on several occasions. He had done the same for Greg. Now, here Greg and I were, all but on the floor cracking up at our predicament, each incapable of crossing the room and shaking hands.

Problem was, Jim recognized us immediately. It also appeared that Richard, the bouncer, and Jim were not getting along. They exchanged words, muffled from my remove like in a silent movie. Then, Richard poked Jim in the chest. Jim, several years older but a former Golden Gloves boxer, poked back. Richard loved a good brawl and had only recently had his gut slashed six ways to Sunday in a knife fight in which he showed up without a tickler. Bad move, but his fresh scars, worn like chevrons on a war hero, only emboldened him.

Greg nudged me toward the front door, screeching madly, "You gotta do something…something…something." The moment constrained me to act. Gathering strength in my cottony legs and blood in my brain, in a literal flash, my do-the-right-thing autopilot switched on and there I was the peacemaker, stepping between beast and prey and not being sure which one was which. At best it was a muddled effort at holding Richard and Jim at bay. You could have knocked me over with a feather.

My brain felt like it was both bleeding and had an aurora borealis blazing inside of it. It didn't help that I was sure that my face was melting as words sputtered out of my mouth in delayed cadences like in an old kung fu movie while I tried to look Jim in the eye. My only touchstone was to hold my face in the cup of my hand as if concealing bad teeth or it would surely spontaneously disintegrate into rubbery chunks, eyes here, nose there, and teeth everywhere. Stammering through my cupped hand, holding those voluntary muscles and proprioceptors together, I told Richard who Jim was and then we all stepped outside, with me still between the two, playing it through. Jim was happy to see me but had not quit fuming over that chest poke.

Mercifully, the band broke and crowds of people hit the door to get high between sets. Without a word, Richard fell into the slipstream of the crowd while Jim and I paused and greeted each other warmly. Jim stepped around me and peeked inside the Electric Flag to an empty house, and decided to say goodbye, scuttling off in a rush "to meet someone," he said. It was over like that. My facial spasms gone. I didn't see Jim again for four years, but when I did he threw up a trial balloon for an upper tier job at his rapidly expanding company. He had a probation officer's optimism.

For about a week, Andy fussed over how to get legendary bluesman Walter E. "Furry" Lewis to Core's Grain and Feed for a weekend. Like most bluesmen of Furry's vintage—born in 1893 in Greenwood, Mississippi—he came by his music through the rural abject poverty and racism he was bred into, lived with daily, and sang about nightly. The waypoints of his life—playing for chump change at fish fries, rent parties, busking on Beale Street, train hopping the Mississippi Valley gin joints from New Orleans to Chicago, and traveling the medicine show/old-plantation-town Chitlin' Circuit of the 1920s South—disappeared for Furry and many of his professional tribe with the Great Depression and World War II.

Then, out of the bohemian blue, came Harry Smith, a musicologist who in 1952 published the *Anthology of American Folk Music* (which made its mark on the social-political affairs of the '60s). Smith, who plowed through the boneyards and old neighborhoods of the South, prophetically bridged the divide left between the 1920s "golden years" of roots music and the Great Depression and following war.

Smith included Furry's 1927 recording of *Kassie Jones, Parts 1&2*, for instance, in his popularly received anthology. By early 1959, jazz and blues historian Sam Charters "found" Lewis, who no longer owned a guitar, and produced an album of his country blues for Folkways Records. The door jarred open once again for Furry, a second career, this time to be studied and mimicked as part of the '50s and '60s folk revival and to earn a modest living picking and singing on top of his meager wages for street sweeping, an occupation he retired from in 1966 after forty years.

Andy would fly with an idea, a new brass ring. He not only envisioned becoming a regional impresario and putting the imprimatur of the "best blues house" in the Arkansas River Valley on his namesake tavern, he was fairly certain there was a fortune to be made. The chance of a windfall—a thousand bucks a night, based on no more than Andy's olfactory receptors; he could "smell it"—was so tempting that I aspired for some action. The Rolling Stones, Leon Russell, Johnny Carson, Joni Mitchell, and a Burt Reynolds movie had yet to lay their fame and claim on Furry. At a C-note every evening, the shuffling bluesman was a bargain—and for him it was a far cry better than his dollar-a-night medicine show days.

Andy, who had made a few calls, sharpened his pencil and booked Furry for a July weekend. His hatched-together-while-high plan included the two of us leaving at daylight in his low-riding '64 blue Impala and driving the 570-mile roundtrip to Memphis on Thursday. The goal was to have Furry back in Fort Smith and on stage by 7:30 that evening. Then, after resting up on the Lord's day, with everyone rolling in the dough, we would take the slow road back to Furry's 4th Street rooming house near Beale Street.

The rest was easy. Gasoline cost $.40 a gallon, so it would take a full tank each way, or about $16 roundtrip. When Furry said he needed a place to stay—harking back a short few years to the Jim Crow days—Andy was quick to offer up the kids' bedroom. Overhead was everything, Furry knew the drill.

Furry's apartment was tidy, almost Trappist in its sparseness. A single bed, a few clothes, his well-worn guitar and case, a nightstand lamp, and a sign on the wall that spoke to an old dog's wisdom: "Please Lord help me keep my damn nose out of other people's business."

Treading gingerly, once in Andy's ride, Furry wasted no time directing us to his off-Beale Street liquor store for a pack of Pall Malls and his preferred brand of blended bourbon, Hiram Walker Ten High, a mean bastard that smelled worse than it tasted. Suited Furry fine, straight out of the short-pint bottle, one after another. In his gravelly, made-for-blues smoker's-voice, he told us that Jack Daniels was "bourgeois" whiskey. We had no truck with that thinking. The price was right. Turned out, Furry was more a sipper than his reputation let on anyway.

Within minutes, the car swung over the old iron trestle bridge on the Mississippi, T. S. Eliot's slow brown god, Huck and Jim's playground, and the Cotton Trader's Cotton Trail. In the 1680s, it was also here on the Chickasaw Bluffs of the Mississippi that Jesuit missionaries Marquette and Joliet first ministered to Native Americans while sharing hominy and dog on a spit.

Once in Arkansas, roadside fruit stands peddled bushels of peaches—Lorings, Jersey Queens, Elbertas. A commanding billboard rising out of the bottomlands blared a short and sweet message in blood red: Matthew 3:16, "Jesus is Lord." Furry muttered an "amen" as we passed. But for the forested sliver of rolling hills known as

Crowley's Ridge, the 130-mile former Military Road and Trail of Tears from Memphis to Little Rock scrolled by in a patchwork of cotton, rice, and soybean plantations, sprinkled with watering gantries and going-to-seed sharecropper shacks smacking of a Dorothea Lange photo collection. The same black families who, for generations, dawn to dusk, pulled and picked cotton—men, women, and children, strapped to long canvas sacks, dragging their harvest between rows—still lived in those shanties. On winter days, those fallow fields were often blanketed in snow geese while the skies were clouded with quacking mallards. As local turn row farmers were fond of saying, our soil is richer than Elvis.

From his medicine show days, Furry knew all the plantation towns and their juke joints—West Memphis, Helena, Forrest City, Marianna, Brinkley, Cotton Plant, Pine Bluff, and you name it. The combined effects of the mechanical picker and racism had crippled most towns (and the music venues). Main Street parades were of another time. To be sure, we were crossing Furry's backyard—fertile land and fecund breeding ground for poverty and beggary and the fatalism of its blessed music, the blues. All kinds of blues, too: ragtime/St. Louis blues, Delta blues, Chicago blues, jump blues, rock blues, gut-bucket blues. Only this black planter's soil, a vast sheet of alluvial sediment pancaked across the horizon all the way to Georgia, could have produced the likes of Robert Johnson, Muddy Waters, Ma Rainey, Little Walter, Sister Rosetta Tharpe, Sonny Boy Williamson, Howlin' Wolf, B. B. King, Bessie Smith, Big Bill Broonzy, Sleepy John Estes, Willie Mitchell, Pinetop Perkins, and Furry Lewis.

It's an odd mental note, I thought as we barreled across the Delta, but the cultivator and the cruelly oppressed were each necessary for the other's actuality. Those blues folks and their families and friends all witnessed the manifold stories told in the WPA Slave Narratives, taken down during the 1930s, of brutal whippings and other perverse means of torture in service to the unchecked market demands of King Cotton. The blues, they say, were a bond for people in bondage.

In discussing the subject of his play *Ma Rainey's Black Bottom*, August Wilson put it a more expansive way: "Blues is the best literature we have. If you look at the singers, they actually follow a long line all the way back to Africa and other parts of the world.... They are people who are carriers of the culture, carriers of the ideas.... I've always thought of them as sacred because of the sacred tasks they have taken upon themselves to disseminate this information and carry these cultural values of the people."

The West African rhythms, the antebellum-rooted spirituals of misery, the illiterate slave's shouts and hollers, the call-and-response form, gurgled out of the rich ground scrolling before us and mixed, mutated, percolated, and spread like an infectious organism into a musical attitude defined by feeling. A sorrowful feeling, summoning people and places past, and the pain and pleasure of moving remembrance. B. B. King described the melancholy tones of the blues as "an expression of anger against shame and humiliation."

Those same benighted delta towns in which slave-descendant blacks remain the majority also harvested a fertile crescent of down-and-out whites—Johnny Cash, Charlie Rich, Levon Helm, Elvis Presley, Jerry Lee Lewis, Carl Perkins, Sonny Burgess, and many more. Those white guys, to a person, were midwifed into rockabilly, rock 'n' roll, and country stardom by the black blues icons. In *Bound for Glory*, Woody Guthrie, who knew a thing or two about blues-talkin' root music, wrote that "songs [were] a music and a language of all tongues."

Furry told us he had known more than a few girlfriends and still had a Ginny who came by but they had never married. A few years later, on Johnny Carson's show, Carson asked if he had ever been married. Furry snapped back, "What I need with a wife long as the other man's got one." Carson fell over in laughter. Furry might have been holding out, and the real answer to that question could well be in the closing stanza of the first song Furry wrote and recorded for Vocallion in Chicago in 1927, "Big Chief Blues": "I said when I marry, gonna marry an Indian squaw / So the Big Chief can be my daddy-in-law."

Furry traveled light and dressed Depression-era dapper. He sported a shopworn fedora and a faded gray-black suit that hung from his slight body as from a hanger. The blue shirt with white polka dots made it all happen—clean as chitlins they would say in the day. He stored his dentures in his breast pocket. He was clinically blind but as long as he wore his thick glasses, he seemed to detect shapes and movement. Whatever toiletries or change of clothes Furry brought along came tightly packed in his aging Gibson guitar case. He spread out in the back seat with his prosthetic leg propped up, sipped the Ten High out of the bottle, smoked his Pall Malls when we smoked, and drowsed off at will. Funny thing, though, in my three days with Furry I never saw him slurring, rheumy-eyed drunk. He was a sipper, never too high or off balance, just a fine steady buzz. A man of anything, come what might.

Andy drove and kept his head half-cocked toward the back seat, flicking his Zippo open to light everyone's cigarettes while chatting up Furry. He whooped with laughter and grunted out incredulities as Furry riffed on life, women, the bulls, Jim Crow, and hard times. In 1917, he lost his leg in a nasty accident, he told us, hoppin' boxcars up in Illinois. Ouch motherfucker! I already knew the story but not from Furry's lips.

Starting at sunrise, on the front end of the Memphis loop, Andy and I jabbered furiously. We were both grinding the ivories on amphetamines. No matter, we didn't miss anything. It was sap-rising special to hear Furry tell of his tramping days. "Been hobbled ever since," he said, with a chuckle.

Lawdy mercy, I must have screamed, we weren't just road tripping with an eighty-year old bluesman, Furry was a hobo during the golden age of hoboes. I felt like Gulliver, occupying the same space but miraculously living in a different time.

The alchemy at Core's Grain and Feed was always highly charged, that critical mass of rumpus that more often than not leads to a police raid in Fort Smith. I was the doorman both nights for Furry's gigs. Fire code only permitted seventy-five people in the bar, but who was counting? We were doing a turn-away business. I'm sure at a five-spot per person, I took in over $500 each night plus sold (or gave away) six or seven kegs of Michelob and cases of everything from Stag to Heineken. Caught up in the beer-clinking bonhomie and smorgasbording on drugs, we were all bad about giving a friend a free pour every third or fourth pint. Our accounting and delivery systems were shambolic. Kit was the back-office guy, the numbers man with dough at risk; the rest of us were foaming-at-the-mouth first responders to the nightly blowout.

In many ways, that weekend with Furry as the marquee attraction felt like a high school reunion. I manned the back door and greeted and ID'ed the young and former gawky adolescents I hadn't seen in years and wouldn't ever see again who had now lurched into adult personas and body forms. Gone were the zits, braces, bouffants, or buzz cuts. Replacing them were ponytails, Afros, shags, denims, druggies, bar flies, good girls, bad asses, an aspiring transgender, and an awkwardly wrought few whippersnappers who still could have blended in at the junior prom.

Being doorman also meant sizing up the rowdy drunks, thugs, and eastern Oklahoma up-and-coming meth heads. Never knew who was carrying an Arkansas pig sticker (long blade) either. I had always been not exactly conflict-adverse, but not particularly inclined to physical aggression outside of sports. Also, having had one serious concussion from football, a broken jaw and nose, and my face and head stitched up on two occasions from fights and a car wreck, I had come around to thinking that honey was better than vinegar. A good street fighter is usually a poleaxer, hit first and ask questions later. That wasn't me.

Furry's warm face was lit up like the rising sun. He wasn't stewed; he was in the zone, under the lights, a showman and a storyteller. For three hours, he nimbly picked and blew and riffed. At times, he ran a length of steel pipe up and down the strings, enhancing his vocals with an expressive set of sliding notes. He had that Gibson slide guitar singing like a melodious backup voice, reeling off one tune after another: "John Henry," "Kassie Jones," "White Lightnin'," "St. Louis Blues," "Goin' to Kansas City," "Jelly Roll," "Rock Island Blues," "Everybody's Blues," "Big Chief Blues," and a dozen more. The air was dim with smoke, and spilled-beer-stench ripened the room's aroma for the mostly white audience who were like putty between Furry's calloused fingertips. They rhythmically swung and moaned and jived back at him, "Tell it, Furry"; "Make it greasy"; "Take it on down"; "Now you got it."

After closing on Friday night, we went to Andy and Jacquie's clapboard rent house two blocks from Northside High. Furry, who politely excused himself as he came and went from the bedroom, mostly sat on the couch and played those tunes again. Jon and Andy and Mike Boulden pulled out their guitars, tambourines, and mouth harps and accompanied Furry well into the jingle jangle of the morning. Damn near sixty years older than anyone else in Andy's living room, he was a machine, playing, sipping, cackling, and singing.

Furry packed Core's both nights. You could have put him on a stool anywhere, say in the middle of a soybean patch, and he'd be in seventh heaven just because he was playing the blues. His songs evoked moods of malice, unrequited love, spontaneity, soul bearing, and freedom. For Furry, the blues were a double helix, inseparable from his emotions. And more than anything, this self-effacing, humble old street-sweeping bluesman was authentic to the bone. Fame—and money—would never own him. Joni Mitchell, who Furry pegged as a little too glam, fairly draws the old bluesman's reactions to her in "Furry Sings the Blues":

> *But it's true*
> *We're only welcome for our drink and smoke…*
> *Fallen to hard luck*
> *And time and other thieves*
> *While our limo is shining on his shanty street*
> *Old Furry sings the blues*

A week after driving Furry back to Memphis, my time in Fort Smith drew to a fast close.

(My fellow bartenders at Core's, Jon, Andy, and Ernie Cromwell, who went to Cummins prison twice on bad paper charges, all eventually died of liver disease from hepatitis C, an asymptomatic virus pulsing like a time bomb through our bodies in the early '70s. Scientists would not even identify and name it until 1986.) In the day, I didn't need a doctor or shrink or Johnny Law to warn me to get out of Dodge. The writing on the wall was keening like a banshee. It was a coming to the senses moment not to be trifled with.

Ernie Cromwell called me one morning and told me to stop by his mother's house on the corner of Greenwood and I Streets. He had something for me. Andy was on his way, he said. Ernie's younger sister, Sarah, let me in. She then repaired to the kitchen with their mother, Mildred, a registered nurse, dressed professionally like Florence Nightingale in a starched white uniform, white cap, clinic brand shoes, and white stockings, on her way to work at Sparks Hospital. I hurried upstairs to Ernie's bedroom. It smelled like a doctor's office. He was standing in the middle of his sweeping master bedroom, looking remarkably fresh for someone who had been up all night. He dangled and shook a fresh-drawn syringe of Desoxyn at me, saying, "This one is for you. It's got your name on it, Philly Dog. Come on over here and I'll fix you up."

Liquid gold in the morning made my nose run, my skin crawl, and my feet all fidgety. I was a ghost of a person. The wolf was at the door. The lows were outpacing the highs; the down-and-out blues Furry sang about were running my game. I had nowhere to go but to highball it out of Hell On the Border yet again. To most friends it was an Irish goodbye. It had been a two-month stopover on my Ulysses.

Daddy and I got a jump on things early Monday morning. With our backs to the sun, turning in front of Immaculate Conception Church, which faces west and imposes its saintly tones on newcomers and the regulars traversing the Garrison Avenue Bridge from Injun Country. Along the avenue, banks and jewelry stores still thrived among the ten blocks of decaying buildings and depleted businesses. A snarl of homeless, lonely people fed the pigeons on Texas Corner. The sweet scent of Shipley's baking bread wafted in the air as we passed Marks' A&A Army Surplus, Core's Grain and Feed, Eads Brothers Furniture, Constantino's restaurant, Berry Dry Goods, and Miss Laura's old bordello before crossing the café con leche waters of the Arkansas River into Oklahoma and the Moffett bottoms. A few miles west, Daddy pulled to a stop at our usual drop-off point on the access ramp of I-40 near Roland. He was resigned to my newest caprice and knew that, for now, I wasn't going back to university. Enrolling in school, pocketing a couple of GI Bill checks as a grubstake, and then hightailing it without a hint of giving it the old college try, he grew to accept as a behavior of mine that would change only on my own clock. He couldn't help himself, though, as I jumped out of the car, saying, "Remember, son, if you lie down with dogs you get up with fleas. Be careful." "Yes, sir, I got it."

We finished saying our goodbyes and he pulled away as I leaned against my duffel bag with a strong west wind scything across the highway ramp, a place I had been many times with Dad. Leaving him and Arkansas behind left me with an empty feeling in my chest, but down deep he and I both knew that I was wild at heart and in desperate need of breaking loose.

In those side-of-the-road moments, post army, an idle Sunday fantasy I had conceived of put me on a donkey with Shan warlord Khun Sa's (meaning Prince Prosperous) caravans in the lawless lair of the Golden Triangle. The easy and edgy life in a lotus land of dancing apsaras, I imagined, smuggling and smoking opium for a living and fucking my way down the trail. More than once I had considered taking up the seasonal orbit of fruit pickers and gold miners and salmon gillnetters but decided it wasn't my beat: as with the professional class, too many peckerwoods in the pecking order. And besides seasons were inflexible; I operated on my own clock, chasing the moment, with no more rhythm than a bottle fly banging in your head. This made the easy and edgy life with dancing apsaras and Khun Sa a worthy fantasy to toggle in and out of.

The ground felt hard beneath my sandaled feet. I stuck my thumb up against the Oklahoma wind, glanced skyward at the swift-moving clouds, rolling and rippling and foreboding, an extension of my restive mood.

When you're on the move, the world teaches you to pay attention. Six hours and three rides further, my mental channel tuned to a different station, two Oklahoma state coppers had ordered me off the highway, at the junction of I-40 and I-35 North. For a moment, I thought they were going to search my bag. Turned out it was no more than petty harassment meant to discourage hitchhiking. In a phone booth at a nearby truck stop, I learned from my mother, who lived a few miles away in the upscale Quail Creek neighborhood of Oklahoma City, that my brother John, the "white sheep" of our family, a doctoral candidate in economics, and his wife Becky, also in grad school, had had a child, Julie, the first born of the next generation of Karbers (and their only child). The mental picture of John, the economist, the first one I ever knew, having a family, lifted my spirits. Made me think I could work out some of my foibles and frustrations and hitch it up a notch. Whatever that meant. I had no promises to keep, bound only to the promise of better days. On the road, time was not easy to understand, but one day I imagined with a Micawberish optimism that I would wake up older and, come what may, everything would be jake. Until then, my way of feeling alive was to stoke the peregrine spirit, to experience the world directly. Running from demons or chasing dreams, toss a coin; it was all the same to me.

Wild Country to Be Young In

Part Four

On the Lam

Chapter Fifteen

IN LATE SUMMER OF '73, David Huie, a credentialed outlaw friend from high school, had been charged with felony sale of marijuana in two states, Arkansas and Colorado. My brother Greg was working a summer job as a night dispatcher in the Sebastian County Sheriff's Office when the Arkansas warrant came down. He first called David, and then Mark Rankin, an acquaintance from high school, with a heads-up. David, who had recently been accepted in the pre-veterinarian program at Colorado State, packed up and fled Arkansas that night. Mark was arrested. When the Colorado warrant was issued, I was by chance crashing on the floor of two other Arkansas buddies' college digs in Fort Collins, Colorado, a couple of miles from David's farmhouse share.

I had hitchhiked in from Arkansas several days before. The revivifying powers of the road and its randomness had exceeded expectations. Although I had had a devil of a time patching together rides from the Oklahoma City metro area, I eventually caught a long lift, more like a joy ride, out of some flag stop burg in the Cherokee Strip with a fun-loving indigenous gal named Tallulah, from Durant, Oklahoma, the capital of the Choctaw Nation. No average Betty from the burgs, she was proudly Choctaw, telling me her name meant Leaping Water. Smallish, barefooted, and with waist-length dark hair, Tallulah wore dungarees and a tight white tee-shirt, unencumbered by a bra. At first, she was vague about her destination, mentioning only Salina, but then asked if I would chip in for gas. Fair enough, I said after a glance or two, trying to read something from her eyes-on-the-road, stoic expression. She then turned her head my way and spread her mouth wide into a luminous grin. Fishing out a neatly folded five-spot tucked away in my watch pocket, I licked it clean before giving it to her. She then licked it even cleaner. From that moment on, Tallulah and I were golden, cosmically thrust into a midwestern fast lane of my Khun Sa fantasy. Yapping like chihuahuas on amphetamines (and we were), after an hour or so driving north on I-35, she pulled over near Salina for a pit stop, and asked me to take over at the wheel. She topped off the tank, climbed in the shotgun seat, and casually slid over next to me, cozy and comfortable. Before long, Leaping Water's hand fell warm on my thigh and she offered me a ride all the way to Fort Collins. The proposition was hard to resist in that moment of rising goodwill, but it also meant throwing in together and blowing off her boyfriend she eventually told me about. He was working a road crew near Goodland, a cultural desert in the high plains dead zone of industrial feed lots and ripe rolling fields of sweet corn and Turkey Red wheat. The offer had appeal, and she did have a '63 Chevy. While we petted and partied our way across many a merry mile of those wind-lashed plains, we postponed the decision. Eight hours later, after a couple of spontaneous roadside stops, better judgment prevailed and we slipped out of that world unto ourselves as freely as we had arrived in it: I rolled my new friend, Leaping Water, another joint, and we parted in Goodland on the shoulder of I-70 West with big smiles of cannabis clarity, taking our love on the fly. That evening I caught a ride on into Fort Collins.

Mike Williams and Bill Pierce were my brother Greg's best friends, the inseparable kind. Mike and Bill had dropped out of college in Arkansas and gravitated to Fort Collins, living on Loomis Street in a four-bedroom crash pad with Bruce Phelps, a sleepy-eyed, cow-licked stock car racer and engineering student at Colorado State, and Dalton Dan, a sociology graduate and now a full-time ski bum. Straight out of central casting, they had taken up the Front Range fashion of ski-bums and lumberjacks: scruffy beards, washed-out flannels, faded blue jeans, and waterproof waffle-stomper hiking boots.

Mike was a big boy, 6'4, 220 pounds, with a jolly face and an infectious, booming laugh. He could clean your clock on a racquetball court, on a dirt bike track, or in the batter's box. A natural born southpaw, he delivered every pitch with extra mustard on it until his shoulder blew out in junior college. The first day or two I was on Loomis Street, Mike got a kick out of going out back and having me try to corral his heat from thirty or forty feet instead of the standard sixty. Bill watched as Mike let it rip, both laughing like hyenas when he almost took my head off. Funny fellows, like that. In his spare time, Mike coached girls' softball and taught his team how to chew and spit sunflower seeds. To get the saliva going, he passed out Dubble Bubble. As for paying bills, Mike and Bill were biding their time working for Old Man Dewey, a stone mason, sourcing rocks for him. Bill was Mike's able assistant.

My third or fourth night there, I had tucked into my sleeping bag on the living room floor next to the kitchen. Mike and Bill kept me up late that night banging the walls drunk with laughter while they target practiced in their bedroom with .22s on a tree trunk they had hauled in from the backyard. Sleep had already been spotty when David Huie began rapping on the screen door by the kitchen. I kept hoping whoever it was would go away. He then whispered my name as a cat burglar might do, "psst, Philly, psst, Philly." Barely awake, I climbed to my feet but before answering the door, I dumped ashtrays and cleared the tabletops of contraband. Mike and Bill sleepwalked in from their bedrooms, wearing their sleeping bags over their heads like burnooses, grousing and fingering the sleep from their eyes. Known for an abundance of self-assurance, David came in, pale as a biscuit, and told us, in the middle of blowing smoke rings from a chillum, that the cops had busted his two-story farmhouse outside of Fort Collins. In fact, it was a taped-off crime scene, he said.

Things were adding up. I had paid him a visit the day before. Dalton Dan had driven me out and waited in the car. But David's housemates weren't exactly welcoming as they shouted at me like anxious sentinels from the upstairs windows to stand back in the front yard while they found David, which took several minutes. Susie Seed, who owned the Seed, a health food store on College Avenue, in the Mellow Yellow complex, also lived in the rooming house, downstairs like David. She came out and introduced herself, and David followed. They had been in the kitchen baking an apple pie. They both knew Dalton Dan, who got out of the car, and we all talked for ten minutes or so before David and I agreed to get together in a few days. Then Dalton Dan and I split.

Better to skiddoo, David reasoned that night on Loomis Street, before the second warrant caught up with him. "We'll lay low till it all blows over," he said. We passed the chillum around a few times, and our wee-hours confederacy of three wooly-headed mammals, Bill and Mike and I, pooled our witlessness, coming up with no holes to poke in David's plan.

Other than hiding out for a weekend from Fort Smith police when they chased me on foot and fired above my head after I ran from certain arrest for underage drinking, I had never been on the lam. There was a kind of folkloric cachet to it, and David was a worthy recruiter. He had a plan, which was more than I had—and I was easily persuaded, having already spent a big chunk of my life wearing an illegal smile. Since mustering out of the army, I had been tossed in the cooler three times for possession of marijuana. Only once was I charged with a felony. After being drug through a public trial back in Arkansas, covered by local radio (KISR) and newspaper,

I skated clean as a hound's tooth by using a Fourth Amendment defense of illegal search and seizure. That said, the depth of news coverage stuck in my craw, feeling violated as if I'd been through a public, two-day-long colonoscopy.

Though his spirits never seemed to flag, David also hadn't exactly been turning up aces lately. He had lost his only two brothers in the last three years; his oldest, Charles, was killed in a light aircraft crash and Richard, the youngest, died of kidney disease while still in high school. In any case, there was no way I would have missed the trip once he told me about the cabin outside of Red Lodge, Montana, located fifty miles east of Yellowstone National Park.

Before packing up, I went outside to check out our getaway car. David's 1949, half-ton, black Chevy pickup, held together by spit and a prayer, was loaded to its gunnels—the hickory sideboards. A Honda 300 dirt bike was strapped between two vintage Klipsch Heresy speakers. Two sleeping bags and three or four gunnysacks loaded with Susie Seed's granola, all-purpose flour, and red potatoes were piled on top of a heavy-duty toolbox and cinched tight under a tarp. Squirreled away in the depths of the truck bed lay a Dutch oven and a box of spices, brown sugar, and coffee. The metal cave of a cab bristled with firepower, a .30-30 Winchester, a Remington 12-gauge side-by-side, and a .38 Smith & Wesson Special. A mason jar of 120-proof homemade bourbon was cached in the glove box. He had also jerry-rigged an eight-track tape deck below the dash, near the floorboard.

David, a regular *homo practicus*, was amply prepared to hide out in rural Montana. As he fled from one refuge in a storm to another, at twenty-three years old, he showed, more than most, a stamina for life. Never souring or allowing self-pity to curdle his insides, he was constitutionally as confident as a gambler doubling down on the come.

In short order I was cramming dirty clothes, a foil-wrapped packet of contraband, a frayed toothbrush, a used towel, the last gasp of my Right Guard, my well-thumbed Webster's dictionary, and my dog-eared copy of H. G. Wells's *Outline of History* into my army duffel bag. As the cobwebs cleared, a bolt from the blue and being at loose ends never felt better, the one-two punch of a fresh start. Providence had arrived through the back door in the shape of a wanted man. A couple of quick chillum hits, drawing down the tarp lashings, and it was Cheyenne by cock's crow. Making a wide turn off of Mulberry Street onto the I-25 North ramp, with a backbeat of grinding gears, David hummed and sang a few bars of that Jeremiah Johnson ballad: "The way that you wander is the way that you choose / The day that you tarry is the day that you lose…"

Once we cleared Casper, east of Shoshoni and Wind River Canyon, the transmission on that '49 Chevy began seizing up. The cab stunk with the fumes of burnt fluid. Almost rhythmically, gears grinding, engine whining, David would pull over, grab a wrench from the toolbox, crawl underneath and make a few adjustments, plug the leaking oil pan with "engineer's soap," hop back in, and jam it down in gear. Off we'd go, the afternoon a-wasting. As the grandeur of the Rockies opened up and the autumnal shadows widened, we found ourselves chugging alongside the white-capped welter of the Big Horn River, traced by the iron spans of the Burlington Northern Santa Fe line. Beyond the tunnels blasted from primeval rock, we pulled over among a tumble of wave-washed boulders that looked to be taller than Stonehenge. For an hour or so, we ate hungrily from tins of sardines and Vienna sausages and nipped on David's home-brewed bourbon.

Gray-to-rufous in color, the vividly stratified walls of Wind River Canyon soared above us like giant ramparts. If walls could talk, Trojan gods and kings would have been envious. This windswept country of wooly cliff dwellers, hemmed in between the Big Horn Mountains and the Absaroka Range, held a vibrant 2.9-billion-year-old record of heedless advance, accretion, successive sea beds, and volcanism, coming together no less than Hogarth's "lines of beauty." It spun my head to think about all the fury of heaving, rumbling and scarifying that had gone on hereabouts across species and the sweep of deep time, tilting the land across the high plains all the way to the Mississippi River. It struck me that the lost gestures of the living, undetectable as a melting snowflake, were entombed among the strata of shells, fossils, horsetail bogs, tracks, and traces. All of which made me yearn for a time machine. Plain as day, David and I were staring into the half-darkness at a geological ticking clock as big as all outdoors…at "time" itself.

The whitewater flumes of the Big Horn River droned on. A '58 Chevy Impala, brimming with three dark-skinned Hispanic men and one of a lighter tone, pulled alongside us in a rolling cloud of churned up dust and black smoke as thick as a Pittsburgh steel mill. Ranch hands we judged from their cowboy dress that included leather chaps and stampede straps on their rodeo hats. They spiritedly disgorged in a chorus of whoops and cries, and their exhaust smell soon gave way to the scent of tortillas, tamales and tequila. We circled around and sniffed out the situation like a pair of coyotes, then nodded our greetings and David returned to the glove box for the mason jar of small batch bourbon. He passed it around, toasting generously to Montezuma and woolly mammoths and all those who carry the heartbeat of the Motherland. Eagerly, each of them took a healthy pull, and shrieked like Comanches when it hit their throats. Their voices bounced from rimrock to rimrock, as they all but kissed David for his kindness. Hard to know what was understood beyond the raillery and ritual gesturing among young men.

Thirty-minutes on, darkness fell upon Wind River Canyon. As our cranky old metal hunks pulled away in opposite directions, a split screen of the evanescence of life (macro earth), dust to dust, and life's everyday gestures (micro man) glowed in the light of a rising half-moon. My oiled-up noggin had gone adrift with the traveling song of the fast-moving Big Horn River, the round-the-clock roar of its purling beat, its sharp, energetic sweep, never the same twice.

Our hobo hors d'oeuvres cut the stench of fumes as we pushed on. Signposts flashed up names like Thermopolis, Greybull, and Cody and trembled with the fury of a hard, northwest wind. David was more confident than me about the transmission holding up. Our quick-and-dirty maintenance stops were happening far too often. Jethro Tull's *Aqualung*, our only tape, was our mood music for the forlorn stretch of US 20-26. Well after midnight, beneath a star-filled sky, dark gray snow clouds rolled in like cottony tumbleweed. The truck was beginning to sway, moving along slightly cattywampus, the wind thumping the windows. We kept it at a clip of no more than forty miles an hour.

By the time we stopped at a single-pump Gulf station on Sheridan Avenue in Cody, we were running on fumes. Even more urgent, turns out, David said he had to shit like an old goat, and hotfooted it across Sheridan Avenue to the higher-end plaster thrones at the Irma, a hotel built by cowboy secular saint Buffalo Bill who named it for his daughter. Ten minutes later, as I pumped the gas and exhaled cumulus clouds of white vapor and Winston regulars, David returned. He glanced up, noticed the buffalo silhouette on the Wyoming state flag above the station door, and spit out some pithy post-shit-like-a-goat verities: "The Great White Father's strategy was if you eliminate the bison, you get rid of the Indian." Then he got on a high horse: "Buffalo Bill and his hide hunter friends took up the cause of history's oldest narrative, people grappling their way to better ground."

"Do believe it worked," I drawled, standing roadside, staring wishfully at the warm, amber lit windows of the hotel lobby. "He must be spinning with delight in his grave." Giving us the once over, two city cops passed by in a patrol car. After paying the attendant, we shoved on, bearing north.

An hour south of Belfry, a snowstorm blew in, big and fluffy flakes at first and then a slanting, wispy blur of white. Winter had arrived. Every few miles, small herds of pronghorn, which once outnumbered bison on America's great and grassy plains, appeared like phantoms. They stood stock still upon seeing our headlights, and then bound across the freshly powdered road, their white rumps fading into the wintry blur of snow.

David and I talked up the idea of pulling over and bagging a couple, but we thought better of it. We were both bleary eyed and blown away at the same time by the rich beauty of the rolling scenery. The storm picked up. The wind howled across the high plains like a pack of wolves. There wasn't a car or farmhouse for several miles. Seemed like a good empty stretch of road to take forty winks, although we weren't altogether sure where we were. That was okay, being without an actual road map.

David threw a tarp and sleeping bag under the truck, stripped off in the wicked cold, and crawled in for some long overdue shuteye. I heard him say something about his down bag trapping heat like a Dutch oven. I took him at his word as I curled up on the bench seat in the cab and wrapped my bag over my head, warmed by my own breath. The nexus of our getaway route, a boreal climatic corridor and a nocturnal passageway for pronghorn, kindled musings of solace and refuge and grandeur in the country ahead. Montana was announcing itself with a cosmic jolt.

We couldn't have slept more than a couple of hours before David was sticking a handful of his homemade granola in my face, saying, "Eat something, eat something, we gotta get." Tears splotched his face from the hard-blowing wind. He proclaimed his sleeping quarters to be colder than a well-digger's ass in Idaho. As I popped up out of a deep, dreamless sleep, I kicked the tape deck loose, silencing Jethro Tull and his songs of broken people. We tuned the crackling radio to Wolf Man Jack's high-wattage border-blaster station—XERF-AM—on the Rio Grande and turned up the jabber as I finished my healthy morning repast and then spelled David at the wheel.

He entertained me with the story he'd picked up back in Colorado of an Irish mountain man named Sully who lived alone in a cabin up in the high country near Glacier National Park. Sully had lost an eye back in the '20s in a coal mining blast in eastern Montana. After getting a divorce, he looked beyond the loss and became a big-game guide. His one eye, the story goes, was sharper than any two of most men's. He could spot a full curl ram from three miles and smell the musk of a bull elk two counties away. On his guided elk-hunting trips Sully always laid claim to the raw liver, salted with fresh bladder contents, a Shoshone practice for which he had acquired a taste. In all his solitude and time without a woman, he had developed an old Indian habit akin to a nervous tic: picking lice and cracking them in his teeth. As the years passed, Sully was plagued by the OLD diseases, especially the bibulous Irish one, 80 proof and higher. One late November, with days in darkness more than light, he wrote a letter to his family of leprechaun believers he hadn't seen in thirty years. After apologizing for not digging his own grave, he then stepped out into a blizzard and shot his two mules, a packhorse, and himself.

"Now that's a good son of a bitch," David concluded. "He didn't want his animals to suffer. He's dancing with leprechauns somewhere."

"Whoa, Nellie," David roared from the shotgun seat as if putting a stop on a horse. We were at a T-junction near Belfry. I backed it up a short distance and turned west on State Highway 308. From there we cautiously corkscrewed up the snow-dusted escarpment alongside Bear Creek. The snow clouds had cleared and the road leveled as we passed through the old mining town of Bear Creek. Tucked into the base of a gravelly cutbank, the town consisted of no more than a few unlit houses, buttoned up and sleeping. We turtled on up the steeper grade by Scotch Coolee and the deserted Smith Mine where the "great disaster" in 1943 killed seventy-three coal miners. Crucial to the boom story that put the Red Lodge area on the map, coal mining in these parts abruptly ended that day, gone kablooey.

As the night dissolved into first light, I tooted the horn at a herd of a dozen or more wild mustangs, bunched-up and grazing on the wheatgrass along a treeless bench upslope from the abandoned mine shaft. *Cayoosh*, as the locals call the Indian ponies, are a free-roaming 300-year-old leftover from the Spanish, known to historians as the Great Horse Dispersal. It was a revolutionary pivot for the footbound Plains Indians.

Soon we breasted Bear Creek Hill. Spreading below like Middle Earth land sighted by a castaway, Red Lodge and the Rock Creek Valley twinkled to life. It was from this same lofty perch that the white man's origin myth of Red Lodge came to be. Arriving by way of Bear Creek as we did, Jim Bridger—or some other pioneering worthy—looked down upon the Crow Indian council teepee painted in the local clay and named it "red lodge."

Windows down, along Rock Creek, we caught the whiff of trembling poplars in the frosty air. It was still predawn as we crept down Broadway Street. The neon lights had just flickered on in front of the Red Lodge Café—which we eyed lustfully. A couple of late '60s Ford pickups edged up to the sidewalk, exhausts puffing out white clouds. A Carbon County sheriff's car racked in blue cruised toward us, taking more than a passing look. David and I limbered up for the morning with a toke from the fat roach resting in the ashtray.

Like many of the turn-of-the-century red brick and sandstone buildings along Broadway, Red Lodge felt marooned in another time, a quaint Brigadoon. We counted seventeen bars, no obvious church steeples, a grain elevator, and a weathered water tower for replenishing steam engines next to the Craftsman-style train depot. *Walking Tall* flashed on the marquee at the Roman Theater. The Pollard Hotel, a few doors down from the diner, we would learn had played social anchor to the rough-and-tumble legend of the town's nineteenth-century coal-mining heyday. Buffalo Bill Cody, Calamity Jane, and Old West artist Frederic Remington were known to have bellied up at the hotel's hand-carved mahogany bar. The Sundance Kid (Harry Longabaugh) robbed the bank across from the Pollard while guests looked on. All sorts of folks, we would discover, had wheeled and dealt and wet their whistle in the witness structures hereabouts on Broadway: miners, cowboys, trappers, ranchers, riffraff, sheep shearers, hussies, bootleggers, and big-game hunters such as Ernest Hemingway. Amid the town's mythical aura, on this early fall but wintry morning, it was no stretch to call to mind a daguerreotype visage of legendary Indian scout Liver-Eating Johnston himself—who was reputed to have swallowed the livers of over 300 Crow Indians before he became Red Lodge's first marshal in 1888. Our arrival, given our circumstances, struck us as preordained.

My own family lore of Montana loomed large in that childish part of my memory. My great-uncles, Scott and Mark, had chased their dreams and desires to Big Sky Country, homesteading 1,600 acres in Beaverhead County. Skidding logs in Arkansas had provided the seed corn.

Once in Montana, they made their bones raising and trading horses and ranching cattle. But that wasn't enough for Uncle Scott. With the passage of the Eighteenth Amendment, opportunity knocked. During World War I, he invested in a used Cadillac Type 51, the first V8, and took up running Canada-made bonded whiskey to Montana's Native Americans—Crow, Shoshone, Blackfoot, and anyone else looking to wet their whistle. When the bonded hooch was in short supply, he traded in the aqua vitae of most nineteenth-century frontiersmen, an off brand of Taos Lightning, a bust-head rye mixed with cayenne peppers, gunpowder, and tobacco that fetched four dollars a gallon most days.

Not unlike the moonshining networks of the '30s and '40s and the car-chasing revenuers during Prohibition, the feds cornered Scott on a logging trail in Beaverhead County, loaded with a fresh haul of Canadian bonded whiskey. They were not amused. The feds gave him six months hard time in the "Old Prison" at Deer Lodge. The word that percolated down to Arkansas was that Mark sprung Scott early from a road gang by paying off the warden and they fled Montana, never to return. Scott landed in Prescott, Arizona, with a Shoshone wife, breaking and trading horses. Mark returned to Arkansas, reformed, a lifelong bachelor and community pillar in Conway.

Almost five decades on, Scott was a novelty, an entertaining sideshow, out of another time. In our living room, also known as the preacher's getaway for its lack of use, he would get comfortable on the antiseptic, all but plastic-wrapped plaid couch by the fireplace. Perfumed with alcohol and preceded by a nutcracker nose and chin from loss of teeth, at six-foot-two, Scott was broad-shouldered and still had the sinewy cast of a Montana-bound cowpuncher (of sorts), cussedly independent and tough as a barbed wire fence in the day. Pendell Lane was his last way stop from Arizona. After a few rounds of ricocheting storytelling, stout spirits and a tall glass of warm cornbread soaked in cold buttermilk, he would turn his decade-old Nash Rambler south to Alpine, Arkansas, my grandfather's home.

Untroubled by grammar, full of profanities, wrong turns and imperfect people, Scott's old wheezes were the authentic kind, drawn from a deep well of exemplary memory and double dipped in restless, pioneer history. Dad was also a good storyteller. He'd get Scott wound up on tales from his two years in Alaska during World War II. My favorite was about some Klondike "stampeder" nicknamed Nimrod who prospected near Eagle, Alaska. Ernie Pyle, the famous war correspondent, had written about him. Nimrod had lost all his teeth to scurvy, so he killed a grizzly, forged a set of dentures out of the teeth, and ate the bear with its own teeth. Scott would answer dad's well-told tale with a dueling version about a Montana Sasquatch character, a trapper (and customer) named Whiskey Earle but Whiskey Earles's molars came from a Big Horn sheep and the incisors from a grizzly. In either telling, the bear gets eaten by his own teeth, autophagia by proxy. Can't be certain but I believed both stories to be true.

Those memories of the rascally Uncle Scott floated down the piss-and-spit-stained sidewalks of Red Lodge on this morning, ripe and tangible as the day before yesterday.

We inched on to Third Street at the pace of a covered wagon and made a slow turn left up a slight rise onto MT 78, heading toward Luther. Red Lodge was not quite awake. David took the wheel. A few miles on, he handed me the scribbled directions to the cabin, compliments of Alvin Yates. More like a Conquistador sketch with all the blank spaces. We brooded over the squiggly arrows and smudged ink for a few minutes.

Al, as Alvin was known, was an ornamental-iron artist living in Fort Collins who first met David when he picked him up hitchhiking after David's pickup had broken down. They struck up a friendship. Al, along with his dad Big Al, and mirror twin brother Alan, a doctor in psychology at Princeton who was writing a book on multivariate factor analysis, assembled the cabin on the 500-acre family ranch, after purchasing it for fifty bucks from the 1920s-era Piney Dell Lodge, located at the mouth of Rock Creek Canyon. It hadn't gotten much use since being taken apart and moved and reassembled on the Yateses' property near Luther. We'd be the first to actually occupy it for an extended stay.

It was first light, which came on with a wallop, truly morning in America. Southwest of the Luther highway, Engelman spruce, lodgepole, and white bark pine forests advanced skyward up the rugged Beartooth Mountains, giving way to the primal solitudes of crystalline glaciers, sheer bleached-out headwalls, talus slopes, hanging valleys, mountain goats, and fresh-water tarns. According to Indian mythology, the Beartooth's rarefied reaches once embodied a nuanced, holy-as-Mt.-Sinai world tricked out with dragons and divinities. My heart rate slowed, my mind cleared, and my whole body sighed in marvel at the mood and texture of the soft light. David was mid-thought, in a different place, nose to the wind, gazing with a weather eye northeasterly across a sweep of honey-lit hills and a creek-filled ravine of cottonwoods and aspens.

"Got one, a mule deer at one o'clock," he exclaimed as he hit the brakes and reached with cat-like reflexes for the loaded Winchester, which he referred to as the old tick licker: It could shoot a tick off a dog's ass. Swift and springy, he cleared the truck, shoulder balanced, whip-panned right, drew a bead in one rapid motion—and blew to smithereens the morning stillness. He gave me a squint-eyed glance, a half-smile, and woofed: "Got that sucker." At 250 yards, exposed in the honeyed light, the eight-point mule deer had carelessly stepped out of the golden-to-crimson glow of cottonwoods, aspens, and sumac and into the native wheatgrass, nibbling away at breakfast. A perfect shot pinned the deer's shoulders together with 170 grains of copper-coated lead. It folded up like a sack of flour, dead before it hit the ground. The man had a predator's alertness with eyes like eight-power binoculars, was all I could think. The Viet Cong might have been lucky that this former paratrooper and rifleman with the 82nd Airborne never deployed.

David hopped the buck-and-pole fence and wasted no time field dressing the medium-size stag, its coat a shimmering silver brown in the light. Too small for the Boone and Crockett book, but good enough for our dinner table. Deft as a French butcher, he flayed the hide back and sliced through the white abdominal muscle with his bone-handled Bowie knife. Man, the toolmaker, he had crafted the handle days before from the antler of a mature bull elk he shot while astride a paint horse near Crested Butte, Colorado, tapping his mount on the head with his rifle before he fired.

Standing back from the splatter, I could still feel the buck's body heat as David cut from the bottom end of the sternum to the genitals. Disposing of the gut pile, he cut and whacked away a hindquarter. Ravens wheeled overhead, death nourishing life in more ways than one. Finishing up, in a post-kill communion ritual between hunter and hunted, David sawed off the head, turned it upright and faced it to the east and the rising sun. He grabbed a swatch of wheatgrass and stuck it in the buck's mouth. Silent and motionless as a statue for a few seconds, he raised up and said, "I do that with every animal I kill. Bid them fare well. Germans do it, too. They call it *letzebissen*, the last bite. Indians have their own sendoff traditions. It's a respect thing, a moment of transcendence."

While David washed the blood off his hands and from beneath his fingernails in the creek, I cleared a spot in back of the truck for the carved-up carcass. We loaded it pronto before anyone showed up asking about hunting licenses or calling around looking for out-of-state warrants.

We shoved on, the vultures flapping down on the gut pile. In low gear, the transmission was close to clanking and clattering its last gasp. The dominant tableau of "purple mountain majesties" had turned into a moody, leaden mantle of stratus clouds. Near the Upper Luther turnoff, a fattened-up black bear came out of a stripped and depleted thicket of chokecherries. He turned our way, puffs of vapor pouring from his nostrils. His small dark eyes glowered at us casually, the bear stare, known by Indians as the conversation of death. Then he turned north and bolted up the Beartooth foothills, disappearing into national forest stands of spiked spruce and lodgepoles.

A half hour later, working the smudgy instructions and looking for landmarks, we came to a mailbox with Volney Creek Road scrolled on its side. "That's it," I told David. "Back it up. We're here, sweet goddamn." A snow-dusted pasture with a small herd of black Angus spread away from a modest white prairie house and faded red barn. "That's Big Al's place," David said, his words filled with awe that we had actually arrived. We turned down the dirt road, scoping things out. The lodgepole pine cabin thrown up by the Yates men two summers before sat beyond the red barn and the yellow burn of cottonwoods, situated on a bend of the burbling Red Lodge Creek. As if the fulfillment of a Shoshone vision quest, we had arrived at the adventure I had been waiting for my whole life.

Moose antlers crowned the front gable. A native stone chimney rose squarely on the backside. A pyramid of chopped Douglas fir, three cords or more, coated in fresh snow, stood high as the cabin's eves. Way on the other side, an outhouse was tucked into a thicket of willows and junipers. And beyond the thicket, two flour-white ptarmigan pecked the ground for pods and buds beneath a thin pelt of snow. For good reason, those blend-into-the-crystalline-cover grouse, hiding in plain sight, kept a wary distance. As did the rainbow trout when we crossed the creek, flashing their shadows like shape-shifters among the shoals.

The truck lurched and juddered to a stop, at which point David repeated what he'd said under his breath a couple of times coming up from Fort Collins: "I'd rather push a Chevy than drive a Ford." He was as good as his word, as we put shoulders to the wheel to get it off the dirt road and closer to the cabin. David's half-ton bucket of bolts, which had rolled off a Detroit assembly line during the Berlin Blockade (before either one of us was born) and for all the years in between soldiered down America's asphalt highways and better back roads, would be motionless, or as David put it, at Parade Rest, for the next three months.

"Grub first," David said. "After that, we'll take care of the small stuff." He retrieved a coiled rope from the innards of the truck bed, paid it out, and looped it around the short but sturdy bough limb of a tall cottonwood. Together we hoisted the deer carcass—less the head and a hindquarter—out of reach of wolves, mountain lions, and vermin.

We found an aluminum box behind the cabin, washed it clean with creek water, and tossed the hindquarter inside. The ambient temperature would keep the meat fresh as winter set in. As with squirrels caching acorns for a long winter, we laid in stores of flour, spuds, and granola.

The stacked-log cabin was rigorously fitted out with a wide, native stone fireplace, a potbelly stove, a built-in wooden couch, wide bunk beds, and a small table with two sawed-off-log chairs. Elk, moose, and deer antlers hung randomly as coat racks. It smelled thoroughly of its headless trophies. A bare lightbulb dangled from the center beam at the peak of the ceiling and behind the couch we discovered a single socket—all that was necessary to air out those Klipsch Heresy speakers with some New Riders of the Purple Sage: "Panama Red, Panama Red… The judge don't know when Red's in town / He keeps well-hidden underground." We christened the cabin with a fog of deep lung exhalations no less than the liturgical three swings of the priest's thurible and danced a jig around the Crow Indian's sacred cottonwood tree to a hopeful prefiguring of things to come. Butterflies and four-leaf clovers were no better omens than Panama Red, 100 pounds of venison, and Big Al Yates's cabin hideout. We were young fools again, addled with the tidings of delight; surrendering to chance had never felt so right. Our "errand into the wilderness" had begun, living out John Wayne's pipe dream, in a cabin "…on a bend in the river where the cottonwoods grow."

Mid-afternoon Big Al pulled up in his new white Chevy pickup with a moose carcass in back. "Welcome, boys," he greeted us in a high Montana twang, stepping out and offering a hearty handshake to each of us. "I was expecting you tomorrow. How was the trip up from Colorado?"

"Piece of cake," David said. "That is, if you don't count that the transmission is out on that sucker," pointing to his '49 Chevy. "We got the dirt bike till I find some parts." Big Al shrugged, gave a wan smile, and said, "Those are good trucks. There's a salvage yard or two around." He added, "Might need new shocks, too—that front end is whomper-jawed," tapping the bumper with his foot to show the misalignment. "She's a wonky old beast," David replied. "It's all on the list. Thanks anyway."

Big Al, born in 1910 and now sixty-three years old, was still in the pink of health, fresh as a daisy. The "Big" in Big Al was because of seniority, not size. At 5'6 tall and wearing a size 6 shoe, he was a product of the pre–World War 1 gene pool of smaller body types. But body types in these parts didn't matter so much as what a man could do. On this morning Big Al had bagged the moose while hunting on packhorses with his youngest son Ron, who lived with his wife Mary Ann in a trailer fronting Big Al's house.

Ron stopped by as Big Al was leaving, and we finished unpacking the truck. David stepped his way, stuck out his hand, and fed him a bite of Arkansas tough talk. "You ain't never met a motherfucker like me. I'm David Huie." Ron perked up with a half laugh, adjusted his soiled orange baseball hat, and shook David's hand firmly while staring up at a southbound skein of trumpeting geese patterning the sky. He was a curly-headed, easy going fellow. As we all parted, Big Al invited us to dinner to share the best part of the moose, the heart. "Fresh, tender, and bloody," he promised, cracking a gnomish grin.

Back in Fort Collins, Alvin, who had been a naval officer for four years and was learning to be a sculptor at Colorado State on the GI Bill, had given David the skinny on the Yates ranch and the family story, which could fill a book. Or a fireplace. Indeed, Alvin and Al had transcribed parts of the family diaries and placed them in bottles like time capsules in the rocky fill of the cabin's fireplace.

As an adolescent Alvin thought of himself as a budding rancher on 500 acres with a cow-calf operation of registered Black Angus. The reality was they were salt-of-the-earth subsistence farmers in their 1,000-square-foot prairie Mansion de Xanadu with fifty cows and a bull. His dad, Big Al, worked derricks on a cable tool rig during the winter and ranched in the summer. It was a family enterprise, sunrise to sunset, cutting hay, slopping the hogs, shearing the sheep, feeding the chickens and horses, fetching ice from the ice house, milking the cows, working the creamer for resale in town. Life had it that they took their baths after a day's work, not before. Getting your hands dirty was the mark of a man.

In between bucolic white Christmases, prairie openness and endless skies, purple mountain majesties and Friday night barn dances, it was not an easy life. The monochromatic winters fostered steadfastness and family solidarity but also took their toll. The elemental, silo-like living in long spells of darkness was often short on fairy tales and screamingly boring, going to Red Lodge only for banking and courthouse business. Women did the same work as men, bore children like minks. Household chores were Sisyphean. The Rural Electrification Administration (REA) didn't show up till 1948. For all the greener pasture pleasure the pioneering Yateses enjoyed, their Red Lodge Creek ranch had its share of treacherous shoals. David and I were happily oblivious, though, living Hitchcock's definition of drama, life with the dull bits cut out.

We crossed the chuckling creek after dark and curled around a well-trodden path to Big Al's white clapboard prairie home. Smoke coiled from the fieldstone chimney. Juno, Big Al's half-Shepherd, half-Malamute, with the prey drive of a wolf, stood sentinel. Big Al had run his trapline that day. A bobcat, two red foxes, and three snowshoe hares hung by their feet from the barbed-wire fence running up to the barn. Four hundred pounds of skinned moose were hoisted nearby on gambrel hooks. Big Al's black stallion Missouri Fox Trotter neighed, and two buckskin trotters nuzzled the ground beneath the hay hood. A deep snow was falling. By sunrise there would be two feet on the ground. It was a flying start to what promised to be a harsh winter.

Wearing a blue-brown patterned flannel shirt and Wrangler jeans, Big Al awaited us on a small gray stoop. David and I both looked like Pigpen—and that begrimed aura would only ripen over the next three months. We had nowhere to bathe.

Big Al motioned us inside and seated us at his tidily set kitchen table. The rest of what I could see of the smallish house was spotless and simple and in apple-pie order as if the missus, who had gone to her reward years before, still had a hand in things. We could hear the ham shack crackling in his bedroom. The pleasant aroma of cooking meat hung in the air and mixed with a slight scent of cheerlessness. The four-seated table was centered with a mouthwatering, fresh-from-the-oven moose heart and a half-full bottle of Early Times bourbon. Big Al poured three small glasses, neat, and he began to talk while the meat cooled and the gravy simmered. As he finished one story, another would bubble up in his mind, each shot with an owlish caliber of wit. We drank it all in. Better than tossing a coin in a blind bard's cup.

"My father Joseph Rose 'Rowdy' Yates arrived in Montana before the fox. Dad's favorite saying was 'Goddamn Abraham Lincoln.' Said it till the day he drew his last breath. Couldn't get over the Civil War." Big Al took a sip, adjusted his glasses, paused to get his step with the story.

"Dad was the original 'Rowdy' Yates. A Southern Methodist. Hated Elmer Gantry-types and Catholics equally. Cussing gave him some kind of mental relief. Blasphemies and oaths were like punctuation marks to him. 'The goddamn cherry on the shit Sunday of my fucking day' was his way of responding to the most trivial event, a hole in a sock or a loose shirt button. Started and finished most sentences with 'motherfucking, cocksucking son of a bitch,' and was on best behavior if he just kept it to 'pass the goddamned potatoes.'"

"When open ranging was coming to an end," the Yates family arrival story began, "Rowdy signed on as the cow boss outside of El Dorado Springs, Missouri, for a couple of the final drives up the Bozeman Trail. The heyday of post–Civil War cattle drives taking cheap-priced Texas longhorns to beef-starved settlers in Montana's Gallatin Valley had run its course. Fenced cattle ranches were everywhere. The Yateses first wanted to homestead Gallatin, but Uncle Roscoe had settled on Crow land, which was plentiful and cheap.

A dream vision by Crow Nation Chief Plenty Coups (many scalps), of westering whites wiping out his people—children of the large beaked bird—inspired him to swap good milo-growing acreage around Red Lodge and Luther for a much bigger reservation in Hardin near Little Big Horn. Once the coal miners arrived, it was the best deal he could negotiate with the Great White Father. The singing lead of the hide men had littered the plains in buffalo carcasses. Plenty Coups' wolf medicine, from which he had derived his martial power, had gone the way of the Indians' walking grocery store, bleached bones glistening like ghosts up and down the white man's trail.

Rowdy knew Plenty Coups and respected him in spite of his conversion to Catholicism. After the land swap, born restless, he seized the opportunity to own a piece of the abundant grasslands. He left the sodbuster life in Missouri for the last time with mom (Ellen) and their worldly possessions on a train to Billings, Montana with the promise of a 160-acre-homestead two miles east of Luther. Named for the postmistress Grace Luther, the homesteader enclave had two blacksmith shops, Dude Linley's mercantile store, a dance hall, a one-room log school house, a Methodist church, two saloons and the office of Dr. Carl Koehn, who traveled to see his patients in a horse drawn buggy. It was 1902, Rowdy's days of cowpunching and bull-whacking for Texas cattle companies were history."

In the telling of his pioneer family story, Big Al colored the cattle-drive era with a certain glow, the picture of a cowboy golden age.

He also deeply connected to the 1953 movie *Hondo*, a Hollywood take on the oft-repeated chain of events that displaced Indians, breaking their golden rhythm. As the defeated Apache turned and rode away, Hondo Lane (John Wayne) lamented, "End of a way of life. Too bad. It was a good way.... Wagons ho."

Big Al swung around sideways in his chair and pulled a tray of roasted potatoes from the '40s vintage Maytag oven. He began slicing and serving the moose heart, the consumption of which Native Americans believed to imbue the hunter with the properties of the animal—stealth, cunning, strength.

"Let me know what you think of that, boys," he said, flashing his reluctant, tight-lipped smile. He then stood, fastidiously pouring brown gravy into a soup bowl, as he set a plate of white bread on the table.

At the height of the Space Age, David and I were mesmerized at the conspicuously old-fashioned elegance of it all. The ample western hospitality, the bloody tender moose heart, slugs of whiskey. Big Al's unvarnished frontier sensibility and larger than life simplicity hit the sweet spot between Red Lodge's past and the everyday doings of the present. Serene mannered trapper, hunter, horseman, cattleman, sheep shearer, backwoodsman who could fix or figure out anything, he had cut his teeth in another era in a land of little religion. Had he not been sitting across from us, his stare resolute and eyes radiant with owlish wisdom, it struck me that some worthy Hemingway might have invented him, a throwback character of tensile strength, a curio of another age. Hard to know a man's true essence in such a short time, but so far as we could tell, we had found a safe portal, figuring Big Al to possess all the hallmarks of the genuine article, someone who respected men of good intentions.

"Best flavor, most tender meat I've ever eaten," I said. In turn, David chimed in to agree.

"My favorite part of the moose," Big Al replied, whiffing his plate and wrinkling his nose in delight.

He then commenced to tell us more about his father. "Dad's best friend was a rancher named Harry Heare. Locals thought of the two together as the best elk hunters in the Beartooths. Ernest Hemingway seemed to think they knew where to find the elk. He hired them as guides on several hunts in the early '30s. Chub Weaver in Red Lodge ran their camp, cooking and guiding some too. Dad kept diaries and recorded those pack trips," he said, pointing across the room to a credenza containing black moleskins. "Harry and Dad were the first to take me bear hunting. We'd pack a rancid cow carcass in a tarp on the horses and head up high into the Beartooth forest, near the plateau and fresh water lakes. Once we found a good spot, we'd tie fishing line to the foul-smelling carcass and 100 or so yards downwind wrap it around my boot and wait for a tug. I taught the boys the same tricks. Ron and I go every fall."

We could have listened to Big Al's stories all night, but as we were tucking into second helpings he poked around gently with questions about our past, our work histories. David wasn't shy about selling himself, if not audaciously self-confident. I thought of his confidence as a virtue, a survival skill. He took no time to fire off a Gatling gun barrage of real and aspirational skills that would have made for a five-page résumé.

"Well, now that you asked," he began, with no shortage of self-regard. "I can weld anything. I've worked on engines my whole life and operated heavy equipment. I've been a carpenter, cook, woodsman, fireman, soybean farmer, deep-sea diver, iron worker, knife maker, and dynamiter. I jump out of airplanes, can sail any ship." He stopped just shy of yodeling and tap dancing and claiming to have turned a sow's ear into a silk purse.

Big Al pulled a deep breath, sobered, and arched his brow. He said nothing, bewildered, I assumed, as a dog trying to understand a new magic trick. I held back, as my résumé for the type of labor skills and derring-do David jawed on about was too lean to bring up, closer to a gofer than a greenhorn on the rise. Most of what David said about himself was accurate by degrees. He was a man who understood, and rarely shied away from, all things mechanical or technical. He only trimmed the truth when necessary, certain that sticking to your story is as good as anybody's version of reality. It was a fact that he had operated heavy equipment once at Independence Pass…and he took it off the side of the mountain. "Jumped on that sucker," he told me, "jammed it in gear but didn't know how to stop it."

It was also bona fide certain that David and Mark Stouffer had appropriated a cache of dynamite and blasting caps from a construction site near Wildcat Mountain. And together, the three of us, for shits and grins, over the course of two weeks, blew fish sky high out of the Arkansas River. A few days later, David had dropped me off at Pendell Lane after school in his dune buggy and proceeded to set a charge beneath a thick juniper stump two feet from my bedroom. It worked. Blew that fucker fifteen feet in the air. Shook the foundation of the house. When my dad swung into the driveway after work that day the stump and new trench in the front yard grabbed his attention. He was soon hotter than a billy goat's ass in a pepper patch. David didn't come around for a few weeks.

Big Al sat there that snowy winter evening chewin' on it all, laconic by nature, mopping up the last of the gravy on his plate. He did have a glint in his eye when he alluded to gussying up and going dancing and drinking the weekend before with Leota. "A widow lady in Red Lodge," he called her. Other than his satisfaction with the moose heart and the sparkle at the mention of Leota, his eyes had betrayed no emotion. They seemed to take in all things and nothing at once. This no-guff, not-to-be-buffaloed frontiersman had to have been thinking his son Alvin had palmed off on him a double handful of hard luck and Southern-fried horse hockey. Our reason for being there was our biggest whopper.

Before we torched it back to the cabin, Big Al said we could probably pick up some quick cash shoveling snow the next day in Red Lodge. He knew we didn't have two nickels to rub together. Rimed in frost on its rock-strewn edges, the shallow stream was clear and chill and slippery to hop across. The riffles would be frozen over and muted by morning. The last of the fiery fall foliage snuffed out, no different from a guttering candle extinguished into darkness.

At first light, the silence of winter enveloped us. The snow feathered down, pillowing the rooftop in knee-deep whiteness. I cussed my way out of bed, feeling aggrieved at having to go to work after just arriving. A few days to rest up and take the lay of the land would have done us good. Instead, we bundled up in everything we had. For me that added up to JCPenney long johns, patch-worthy Levi jeans, a threadbare Pendleton flannel, a pine green cable-knit sweater, a loaner pair of L. L. Bean insulated rubber boots, my trusty M-65 army field jacket with no lining, a set of woolen gloves, and no watch cap, only the thin hoodie on the field jacket, which I turtled into. The near zero-degree temperatures were tolerable until we hopped on David's Honda 300 dirt bike and began that thirteen-mile drive to Red Lodge, knuckles white on the black rubber grips, cheeks burning as if freshly raked by a cheese grater. Madmen or masochists, hard to say which as snowflakes as big as golf balls fell.

MT-78 had been partly plowed but several long stretches were, as we say in Arkansas, slicker than greased owl shit. And down we went, again, and again, and again, careening wildly, flying ass over elbow, but mostly sliding on our backs like human toboggans and not giving a flying flamingo. On one fall, David got up and said: "We could have lit a joint and smoked it by the time we stopped." A little road rash but not too bad—and gladly on our feet and back on the bike with the nonchalance of having stopped at a roadside strawberry stand. It took us over an hour and a half to make it to Red Lodge.

Pulling up in front of the Red Lodge Café, though we had no shovels, we decided to inquire about clearing their sidewalk. As we stepped just inside the front door, the café smelled strongly of bacon and coffee. David greeted Reba, the gum-snapping head waitress commanding the register that morning, with a "How's it going." All motion, she took off for the kitchen, shouting back, "Coal one day, diamonds the next. Never know." Two heavyset ranchers on their way to the co-op stood at the cash register, grousing aloud about fuel prices, above the buzz of background chatter and banging plates. "Goddamn Arabs are making out like bandits. Gas 55 cents a gallon. Sell the calves. We're in the wrong business." They galumphed off and Reba returned. After hearing David out, she made a call on our behalf, proclaiming aloud the first blizzard of the season to be "a real doozy." Ten minutes later, we were outfitted with long-handled steel shovels from the back of her husband's pickup.

It was no coincidence that we had mentioned Big Al Yates and were now on the receiving end of the town's goodwill. By the time we finished shoveling the café's sidewalk and collected our fifteen bucks from a cigar box beneath the register, word had spread. We were no longer lying doggo. KRBN-AM radio was broadcasting from a studio across Broadway and got wind that "David and Phil"—now publicly known sidekicks—were fresh arrivals in Red Lodge hankering to help out the community and take home a few bucks, too. The DJ, whose radio name was Benny B. (short for Bloom), encouraged the town's merchants, little old widows, and spinsters to phone in and he'd send David and Phil right over.

In a matter of an hour, Benny B. became our booking agent and one-man employment bureau. Two fugitives with deep drawling Arkansas accents had quickly become celebrities in Red Lodge. "Welcome, David and Phil," was not an uncommon greeting, perfect strangers easily picking up on our presence on the streets of Red

Lodge. My guess is we couldn't have attracted more attention with tin cans tied to our ankles, rattling down the sidewalks.

We finished three houses behind the Labor Temple, an impressive red brick structure built at the turn of the century by local members of the United Mine Workers of America, before trudging a short distance south of the Italian section to Mertie McMinn's white clapboard house at 301 North Platte. Mertie was Big Al's mother-in-law, his late wife Naomi's mom. She had sent word for us to clear her steps and sidewalk. Mertie was knocking on ninety years old, widowed half a century before when husband Harry was vaporized in a freak accident on a drilling rig. As a midwife for six decades, she had delivered all the Yates children and half the town of a certain age, charging clients the equivalent of $35 and staying with them for up to a week. In the '40s and '50s, she boarded the Yates girls, Juanita, Luanda, and Margo, after they finished primary school in Luther and came to Red Lodge to attend junior high and high school.

She was a rascally old lady, short and slightly humped, bluish veins marbling her pale pink skin, yet still spry of mind as the twenty-five-year-old I imagined her to be at the Billings train depot when she arrived from a hardscrabble farm near Hartford, Michigan, by way of Chicago. Stuck in Billings for days, Mertie and her family had finally caught the caboose of a freight train on to Red Lodge. She said it was "so slow that the brakeman went grouse hunting along the way." That first long, harsh winter, Mertie, her mother, and three siblings stayed above Jenny Ames Café in Red Lodge, working in the restaurant and doing other odd jobs to get by.

When the weather broke, Mertie's father, Ezra Beardslee, moved the family into a dirt-roofed, earthen-floor homesteader cabin on Willow Creek. Soon they became aware that the blood stains on the cabin door were from a shootout over a land dispute that had dispatched the former owner and his son. Otherwise friendly homesteaders surrounded them on every quarter section, and Mertie and the family savored the ritual gatherings with neighbors at grain threshing time or when butchering a hog.

On this day, she'd tottered out to check David and me out, passing along snippets of her pioneer story, while monitoring our progress so she could settle up promptly. "Fast pay makes fast friends," she told us, chortling at her own quip. We tricked old Mertie, though, snuck off and gave her a freebie.

Next on the hand-scribbled list Benny B. had given us was Robert Moran at the Red Lodge Carnegie Library, a hallowed civic sanctuary located across the street from the Northern Pacific depot and its hulking wooden water tower. We stuck our heads inside the library's front door and hollered to let him know we had arrived. It was a well-stocked library, with an antique scroll wheel that allowed a researcher to have seven books open at the same time. The carpeted floors and carrels handled the overflow of books that wouldn't fit on the shelves or circulation desk. Bennie B. had told us that folks could call in and Mr. Moran would hand deliver books to Red Lodge homes and businesses. As fastidious as Mr. Moran came off, carrying a newspaper on a stick as he greeted us, I felt sure the disarray of books lining the library floors had been properly categorized in the library's neatly numbered Dewey Decimal System card catalogue and would find a place on the oak shelves or in someone's home by closing time.

A good looking, dapper dressed man in his late forties, Mr. Moran was a local celebrity, a community bridge builder, and a font of Red Lodge lore and worldly knowledge. After serving in World War II, he had moved to Paris for post-graduate work at the Sorbonne. Once back in Red Lodge, he taught high school French and English and Alvin Yates and others described him as the finest teacher they ever had, gifted with an Oscar Wilde wit, playfully heretical, his mind as clear as the nearby trout streams he loved to fish. He started the Festival of Nations to honor the duke's mixture of nationalities that had settled Red Lodge in the mining days of the 1890s with little more than their long-shot hopes: Italians, Yugoslavians, Scots, Norwegians, Finns, Welsh, English, Irish, Germans and more than a few Crow Native Americans. Suspicion and green-eyed bitterness had greeted each wave of this caravan of culture, until the next arrived and there was a new ethnicity to kick around. Over time, Red Lodge's lines of social-ethnic division got shaken like a snow globe and the common causes of the miners, merchants, sodbusters, bankers, bohunks and small ranchers took precedent over the resentment toward someone's great grandfather Amario who was once a *contadini* from Abruzzi. Now, the winter of '73, in keeping with local (and universal) custom, long-haired hippies were the newest arrivals to pique everyone's suspicions.

Mr. Moran checked on us right along, hearing the drone of our shovels scraping the sidewalk. An hour on, as we were finishing up, he wanted to chat. He was enamored that we were a circle of veterans, and he wanted to know all about where we had been stationed, and our take on the Vietnam War. He expressed his disdain for Arkansas's former segregationist governor Orval Faubus and championed Arkansas's U.S. senator Bill Fulbright's stance against President Lyndon Johnson after the Gulf of Tonkin Incident. He then launched into telling us about the Northern Pacific depot and water tower by asking if we had ever read *For Whom the Bell Tolls*.

"No, sir," we said in unison.

"But I've read a few of his books. Just finished A. E. Hotchner's *Papa Hemingway*," I threw in.

"Well, you've missed his best," he stated knowingly. "The protagonist, Robert Jordan, is a fictional Spanish professor bred and raised in Red Lodge. His conscience compelled him to give up teaching in Missoula and join the fight against fascism in Spain."

Mr. Moran giddily recited the book's epigraph written by John Donne from which Hemingway took the title: *...any man's death diminishes me, because I am involved in Mankinde; And, therefore, never send to know* **for whom the bell tolls; It tolls for thee.**

Mr. Moran was gifted with some kind of thespian gene, given to the soliloquy. He had our undivided attention, as he pointed to the depot and tracks and effused about the daily arrival of a steam engine from Billings, clouds of steam smoke, whistles tooting till they were hoarse, wheels screeching, skidding to a stop, and passengers fleeing from their Pullman cars almost before the iron horse stopped.

As if he had lived this story and sifted it in his well-stocked mind and heart, Mr. Moran told us about the goodbye scene near the ending of *For Whom the Bell Tolls*. Robert Jordan, an expert dynamiter, and his guerilla comrades—war-wearied Pablo, wise old Pilar, Pablo's wife, Robert Jordan's lover, Maria—had gathered in the forest before embarking on a dangerous mission to blow up a bridge behind enemy lines.

Jordan was not filled with sadness or trepidation as they parted in various directions to take their posts, which could be their last. Instead, Jordan felt young again, like the day he stepped onto the day coach as he left Red Lodge to go off to school on the train to Billings. On that day his dad had wept and asked the Lord to take care of his son. Jordan found the prayer unnecessary and felt sorry for his dad. The *idea* of crying and praying for him he found hard to absorb. Yet he was strangely vitalized by the thought of being the older, mature one of the two.

At that point in the telling, Mr. Moran stood between us and the station and quoted verbatim parts or all of the passages from the book after Robert Jordan boarded, an allegory for noble, coming-of-age journeys of the soul:

> *After the train started he had stood on the rear platform and watched the station and the water tower grow smaller and the rails crossed by the ties narrowed toward a point where the station and the water tower stood now minute and tiny in the steady clicking that was taking him away.*

After watching the sagebrush and looking for sage hens, the brakeman said to Robert Jordan:

> *"You don't mind going away to school?"*
> *"No," he had said and it was true.*
> *It would not have been true before but it was true that minute and it was only now, at this parting [with guerilla comrades and lover], that he ever felt as young again as he had felt before that train left.*

This was the exact opposite reaction I had on the day I left for the army shortly after turning seventeen: I puked on my way to the bus station. The ending to the book— Mr. Moran insisted I take a copy, which I read cover to cover in a matter of days—was equal parts heroic, romantic, and epically tragic. A rational world of polarized ideas of left and right, fascism and communism degenerated into a proxy free-for-all of bloodlust on Spanish soil. What had Vietnam been to my generation? I asked myself. The momentous story of Robert Jordan taking up arms in the International Brigade hung with me like a fever dream, intense and unresolved.

In less than forty-eight hours, a gathering sense told me that I had landed on the mothership of agile-minded, keen-eyed, cast-iron characters, even if, like Robert Jordan, they were already partly fictionalized by Ernest Hemingway. Red Lodge, I came to think, was punching above its weight for a frontier town. We thanked Mr. Moran, the worthiest of village explainers, for the twenty bucks and the literary *tour de monde* and headed south on Broadway to the Yodeler Inn.

Along the way, we stopped at the City Bakery and admired Cindy-the-baker's warm-pie smile and apple-colored cheeks and enjoyed a cinnamon roll that was so big that David mused, "If you dug it out you could sleep in its soft interior."

We crunched in the Styrofoam-like snow back to the west side of Broadway, a wider than normal main street. During the mining days, we were told, Red Lodge was considered a six-track town, three on each side. When a rut got too deep, the horse-drawn carts would move over and start anew. The sidewalks were once wood-planked, which kept pedestrians above the mud. As we approached the front door of the Yodeler Inn, greeted by a sign lettered in a Fraktur font, David mused aloud that Red Lodge back in the day reminded him of our hometown, Fort Smith, "Hell on the Border," in which horses, cattle, carts, wheelbarrows, goats, and people once clotted the streets, letting loose an anarchy of human and animal sounds and smells.

A pleasantly plump Germanic woman by the name of Ursula worked the front desk. Her mood was far removed from Julie Andrews and 'the hills are alive with the sound of music." After a fifteen-minute pigeonholing on winter's harshness, she directed us to get started on the fifty yards of sidewalk paralleling Broadway. The former mining quarters had been renovated a few years before and confected Bavarian style in whitewashed veneer walls, chocolate-colored fachwerk (half-timber) panels, and shutters and steep gables strung year round in Christmas lights. As we broke apart and scooped and piled away the snow and ice, David whispered to me, "You wouldn't want to jump rope with Ursula. She'd never let you in," referring to her gabbiness.

We didn't wrap up with Ursula till around five and had two more houses to shovel in the Italian district near the cannery. The cannery was once occupied by the Yellowstone Distributors who made corn whiskey and barley rye during Prohibition. Keeping the illegal enterprise on the lowdown, the spirits were labeled as cough syrup.

We had to double-time it to finish shoveling our last driveway for the day by seven. We had done a gangbuster business, raking in over $150 and had more shoveling lined up the next morning. Shovels returned to the café, the sun well over the yard arm, we'd raised a thirst, practically chugging three Olympias at the Bull and Bear Saloon to muster some courage before heading back to the cabin. At the backside of the bar, several tag-team drinking locals—talking loudly, scratching and rearranging their nuts, and doing shots of tequila—coveyed around two cornfed cowgirls in a corral of ten-gallon hats. Toward the door, next to the boisterous bunch, ensconced at the bar, a prematurely gray-bearded cowboy, with pronounced cheekbones and deep-set gloomy eyes, threw back shots of Johnnie Walker Red as if a condemned man. Knocking at the gates of forty years old, pear-shaped with short alligator arms, he introduced himself to me as Chavez through a golf-ball-sized plug of chew. Tobacco juice dribbled out of the right side of his mouth. As we talked, Chavez relieved himself of the plug, placing it in an ashtray.

He had been drinking so long it appeared that his wavy white hair was drunk. A bowl of chili arrived, and he fired up a Pall Mall. Between slurping spoonfuls with one hand, Chavez smoked with the other by turning his head to one side and leaning into the cigarette. And, like a juggler, alternating both hands with more thingies and a rising tempo, he emptied more shots of Johnnie Walker Red. Hard to say what all that tasted like, or which direction he was headed; or for that matter what else he had on board. But there was a certain rhythmic madness to it all that suggested the cigarette might be headed down the hatch too. At times, I just nodded while he grunted over his shoulder in some vernacular of manic cursing and mangled metaphor. Friendly as he was, he may as well have been speaking Swahili.

On the other side of Chavez, David was talking to a gonzo named Simon from Hartlepool, England, by way of the West End Swinging London scene. Simon stood out for a number of reasons: his Midlands-Cockney accent; his lizard-skinned, lipstick-red winklepicker pointy boots; a trippy zebra-striped op-art shirt; and his lank blond hair falling out of a black woolen bowler. His well-worn get-up seemed to confer an essence of who he was, like a trademark, consecrated by countless coming-of-age memories.

Drawing me into their conversation, David poked at me, saying, "Listen, listen, to where this guy is from. He says his hometown's claim to fame is hanging a monkey from France." As I stepped in closer, admiring the illusion of black hole spirals created by his shirt stripes, Simon shed some light. Turns out, during the Napoleonic Wars, a monkey liveried in French military garb washed ashore at Hartlepool and was hung in the public square for being an enemy of the state. After explaining, Simon said to David—and in my direction—"Wouldn't you? He was French."

"No other choice when a monkey shows up in a Napoleon army uniform," David deadpanned, hee-hawing at the thought of hanging a monkey. Simon's origin story, which he swore to be true, made us think that we weren't the only ones in the room to be running from something.

One seat over from Simon, a thirty-something biker chick steadied a beer between her thighs. A leather jacket with an Outlaw-gang skull logo was draped over her shoulders and button-popping red blouse. Her black Greek sailor hat was cocked back at a devil-may-care angle, unloosing thick bangs of tousled hennaed hair. Her face was geisha white, matching her cleavage, which was lifted up and laced in black. "She cleaned up real nice," David observed, "the Miss Kitty of Red Lodge." Stealing a glance, I wanted to stroke her rapturous body to see if it felt as soft and sensuous as it looked.

After blowing a lung full of Marlboro into the hazy air and taking a slow, sexy sip of her beer through a straw, she stepped forward from her stool and, with a free and easy smile, introduced herself as Mountain Bird, born and raised in Chugwater, Wyoming. Easily drawn, we moved in closer. "You don't look like Sacajawea," David blurted, laughing at himself.

"She was a Shoshone like me," Mountain Bird said, while chuckling and explaining that the Shoshone name was given to her while she was a volunteer health worker at the Wind River Reservation south of Cody.

Then, without pause, in a rising smoky voice, she hazarded a guess about who we were: "I bet you are the two snow shovelers we heard about on the radio today. Phil and David, right?" We both beamed bright at the sound of our names rolling off the pretty pink lips of this complete stranger.

"Yes, ma'am, that's us. Be back at it tomorrow. Glad to help," David told her, with a practiced sincerity. "Folks are so nice here it makes my teeth hurt."

"Hell yeah, two days in Red Lodge and we're already *stars*," I added with a half-grin, basking in her sizzle.

"I guess you are. Benny B. talked about you all day on the radio. Must be true. But judging from your accents, you sure came a long way to shovel snow," she said, poking around, making sheep eyes at me.

"We're aiming for a career change soon," I replied, leaving it at that.

Mountain Bird had overheard our small talk with Chavez and wanted to let us know that we should catch him on the front side of his daily sousing; that he was a cowboy singer and told good stories about his clown days on the Pampas rodeo circuit in Argentina. "He's earned his spurs," she declared. "Saved more *gauchos* doing the 'suicide wrap' than Moses did Jews when he parted the Red Sea." We took her word.

In the back corner beneath a single bulb on a cord, a singer in a crushable gray cowboy hat, strumming an out-of-tune acoustic guitar, shouted the lyrics to Johnny Cash's "Folsom Prison Blues" above the crowd's din. It was like open mic night at Core's back in Fort Smith, where enthusiasm always counted for something.

Meanwhile, Chavez had started chugging glasses of water and licking his whiskers clean like a cat. When there was a break at the mic, as if the sky had cleared and the Red Sea actually was parting, Chavez careened off his stool, landed on his feet, wobbled cowboy-style, sideways and slightly spraddle-legged, squeezed through the ruck to the singer's corner, and unlimbered his own gut string

Gibson guitar from behind an empty stool. Mountain Bird poked me and said, "Watch this, watch this, he's playing tonight."

"I'd have taken the other side of that bet," I replied. "Thought he was headed the wrong way to vomit."

Soon, the hubbub of loud voices slowly died away. Next thing we knew Chavez was atop that stool, leaned over, hugging and strumming the guitar and singing like a poet songbird a new Steve Goodman tune, "Don't Do Me Any Favors Anymore":

> *I've been accused of being ragged and unholy*
> *I guess I've been called every name 'cept dead*
> *But it would take ten strong men*
> *A hundred years of running loose and wild*
> *To live up to all the stories you spread...*

As they say in showbiz, you had to be there. Don't know if I was more shocked at Chavez's cleaned-up face and sudden clarity of purpose or that the song he chose about an insufferable ex-girlfriend trashing him with lies struck a personal chord and surely had his name smeared all over it. "If they ain't talkin' 'bout you, you ain't livin', Mountain Bird said, before he started another song.

As if the town knew what time Chavez tumbled off his barstool, the saloon started filling with a younger, more bohemian crowd, braless girls with hairy armpits. Cindy from the City Bakery swanned her way in, more striking than ever without her fruit-smudged apron. David waved at her and got that apple-pie smile boomeranged back at him. You could feel the heat as he all but melted. Cindy's arrival had upped the number of women in the Bull and Bear to a grand total of eight among at least twenty-five men. This made the inside joke among Montana women a harsh reality: The odds are good, but the goods are odd.

We tucked a few of our fresh-earned greenbacks in the singer's tip box like a couple of newly minted Comstock Lode millionaires.

We were feeling the moment, pain free, loins girded; we'd be back. As I zipped up my field jacket and swigged the last of the beer, Mountain Bird and I exchanged a glancing smile and a finger gun farewell. About then, amid a few whoops and whistles from the new arrivals, a perfectly coherent Chavez announced his next song, Dylan's "You Ain't Goin' Nowhere."

At the bar, Simon, tall and thin as a rake and pop-eyed on something, began kicking up his red winklepickers in some kind of huskin' dance or Highland Fling while Mountain Bird shuffled solo to the dance floor, leading with her fleshy bosoms, showing and shaking her stuff and snapping her fingers like castanets as if she were the main act. Near the door, within earshot, I bellowed forth my best come on, "Say, baby, would you like to sleep under a 'star' tonight." Never missing a beat, she put a hand to her cocked ear, mocking a hearing problem and mouthing the sing-along verse: *Oooooee ride me high / Tomorrow's the day my bride's gonna come.*

David coughed out a belly laugh as we stumbled onto the sidewalk. "Hot diggity Philly Dog, look at you," he razzed as we straddled the dirt bike. "She got the message. If you hear that Harley pull up to the cabin tonight, it's probably her," I cracked back, pulling down my new wool balaclava and giving a soft kick to the chopper parked next to us. In darkness, with the wind prying tears from our eyes and loaded down as Balaam's talking donkey with a 100-pound sack of potatoes as cargo, the ride to the cabin was no less harrowing than the morning one. Didn't occur to me on that evening, as we howled like Comanches with each tumble to the ice, that Mountain Bird would be my last best chance of hitting pay dirt in Montana.

Those first days in Red Lodge, David and I worked out a cook and bottle washer division of labor that would become the pattern of our lives for the next three months. On most evenings, David would bread and chicken-fry venison backstrap and whisk together a brown gravy in his cast-iron skillet. If the mood hit, he'd doll up the venison, making lasagna, steak au poivre, stroganoff, or a single-meat burgoo. And, every week or so like the miracle of the loaves, he'd pull out his Dutch oven and bake cornbread, make biscuits, or knead dough like granny and whip up a fruit pie from scratch, with sprinkled sugar on the lattice. First guy I met who traveled with a spice rack and two cookbooks, *Mastering the Art of French Cooking* and *The Joy of Cooking*. His implacable chutzpah in all things in life also made him a kitchen badass.

As David's sous-chef, I started the fire in the potbelly and stoked and fed it fresh logs. The nights that he cooked, say, chicken-fried venison, I sliced and boiled the unpeeled red potatoes and whipped them into a salty, buttery mash—an army recipe I cribbed while a civilian KP at Fort Chaffee in high school. We packed away our weight in spuds alone. We may have been strapped and cabin-bound at night, but we metabolized that isolation with busy hands, bong hits, and a tendency to chow down like death row inmates, ready to explode like blood ticks when finished.

The dishes were on me. On most nights I had to thaw the pump handle outside by the woodpile and stroke it twenty or so times to get the water to boil for scrubbing the skillet. By the time the dishes were dried, I was ready to ladder up to bed and nuzzle with Wells's *Outline of History*, a sure cure for the rare onset of insomnia. If it didn't do the sandman's job, I worked on my memorization of the Geological Time Scales: ...**Cambrian** *period (500 million years ago, major animal phyla appear),* **Ordovician** *(450 mya, Ice Age, first major extinction),* **Devonian** *(360 mya, low oxygen, second major extinction)...* Whoosh. Sigh. Soft snowy owl hoot. Eyelids down. Lights out time.

David had chosen the bottom bunk. He would stoke the fire until late and throw on an extra log before the hissing and crackling coals helped put us into a nod. There would still be hot coals to start a fire in the morning. From the top bunk, I would swing over and pull the string on the single bulb at lights-out hour and he would close the draft. Beginning our first night, within minutes of my pulling the string, we could hear tiny mice feet skittering near the potbelly stove. The first time I registered the rhythmic patter, I shouted down to David to quit slapping his monkey. As it turned out, the furry fucks had discovered the grains, seeds, and Medjool dates in David's gunnysack of granola from Susie Seed's store in Fort Collins.

David wasn't putting up with the sneaky little bandits. On night five or six, he placed the granola bag in an open space and tucked into bed with a .22 automatic rifle that he took from above the fireplace. His cue to come up blazing was when I flipped the light. As the smoke cleared that first night of "Operation Save the Medjools," there were three furry splatters across the floor. And the next night two more and so on. We never celebrated a full *coup de grace* moment; mice in cabins in the woods don't roll like that. But David's large succulent dates did survive to wriggle down our gullets, and, thanks to his keen eye, neither of us caught a ricochet in the heat of ambush. It was all very Zen. A mousetrap would have been pure mindlessness. Our daily lives had not only taken on extra color but depth as well.

We had fallen into a work-a-day rhythm that first week, but we needed another blizzard. By chance, that first day of shoveling snow, David had run into a couple of home-grown wild asses, Chico Tanner and Deke Bronson. Both were competitive stunt skiers, hotdoggers of the highest order, who paid the bills working as carpenters refurbishing the '50s-era dilapidated lodge at Grizzly Peak. A few days later, he biked up Rock Creek to Chico and Deke's worksite at Grizzly Peak ski area. Atop the mountain, after sharing a thermos of mulled wine, David joined them in racing the two and a half miles down the mountain without poles. Chico and Deke quickly figured out that

David had balls that clanked too and hired him as a carpenter's assistant. For those guys, each work day thereafter ended the same: hot wine and schussing down the pillowed slopes of Grizzly Peak.

With David gainfully employed, the pressure was on for a dreamer like me who preferred a mental life to manual labor. Since my army days I had kept a dictionary by my side along with an ever-expanding word list of sixty or seventy pages that I reviewed as a memory tool weekly. On a whim one day, I walked into the *Carbon County News* office at 11 North Broadway and introduced myself to David Emil Henderson. He was ten to fifteen years older than me, and he looked the part of a prim, well-organized newspaper editor—which he was, having recently cashed out as the editor of a Chicago-area newspaper chain owned by Time, Inc. His move to Red Lodge with wife Darlene and pre-teen daughters Tammy and Karen was true to type at the time with a wider, hippie-driven, paradise-seeking migration to Montana. Along with a majority interest in the *Carbon County News*, D. Henderson had purchased a home near the golf course and ski slopes on Upper Continental Road. Word at the café had it that he had made a name for himself at the *Evanston Review* by interviewing the likes of Henry Fonda, Barbra Streisand, Charlton Heston, and other leading lights. At that time— in the '60s Midwest—celebrity exclusives with local and national news and other features were an untried model.

Spectacled, clean-shaven, side-swept blond hair, and accessorized like an Orvis model, D. Henderson appeared to be growing into the friendly fabric of Red Lodge. The receptionist offered me coffee as she escorted me into his office. D. Henderson stopped typing, stood, and greeted me, seemingly unfazed by my disheveled attire, cabin wood-smoke smell, and untamed beard and ponytail. As he shared the details of his family's decision to leave Chicago and move to Red Lodge, I was immediately struck by the virtuosic way he chose his words as a high-end jeweler sorts his gems. Never a throwaway sentence, all precisely cut back, yet granular and vivid in detail. I'd never met a fabled big city newspaper editor.

After the usual exchange of niceties, I got down to the business of laying out my case for being a staff reporter and perhaps having a feature column. I told him about the army, the dictionary fetish, the word lists, the curious compulsion of memorizing the *Geological Time Scales*, the books I'd recently read, my wise insights about the Vietnam War and worldly experiences, including some name dropping. As a point of pride, I threw in for good measure my meeting Neil Armstrong when he gave a can-do, rousing speech on Christmas Eve at a USO show in Korat, Thailand, six months after he walked on the moon. Armstrong was the vision of a dream, the ultimate adventure traveler who took the ultimate journey, astronaut, pilgrim, and Argonaut all packaged into one Super Hero. He had some creds and I wanted to leach a few, to touch the hem without actually meeting him.

I could tell, however, by D. Henderson's scrunched face and clouded eyes that all this had caught him cold and caused him to wonder what all I was saying had to do with the *Carbon County News*. Didn't matter. Other than prolifically penning love letters to six different girls while in the army, it was the sum total of what I had to offer. He responded slowly, fully conscious of not offending me. After a stroke or two of the neatly parted blond hair and a furrow of his brows, he thanked me for my interest in small-town journalism. He said, "Never thought of reading the *Geologic Time Scales*, much less memorizing them. Were you a science major?" "No, never majored in anything," I replied. "The tables are in the dictionary, somewhere between 'aardvark' and 'zygote.' They're just a memory aid to mark deep time up against Wells's *The Outline of History*. Both hefty books with a lot to unpack."

He nodded as if in agreement, and proceeded to metaphorically toss my spiel in the slush pile, explaining that the *Carbon County News* was a shoestring operation and that he didn't foresee any reporter openings of the nature I mentioned. But (long pause), giving me the eyes-over-the-glasses look, he said that he did have a moving van waiting to be unloaded in front of his new home on Upper Continental Road. If that works, when you finish up there, come back and see me.

He read me right. I was just fishing. Blazed up, fresh off a ritual bone in the morning, to boot. In my mind, reporters had it made, their notebooks a privileged passport to talk to anyone and explore everything. They did, however, have editors and bosses. And Thoreau's warning was spot on: Beware of enterprises that require new clothes. When I returned three days later, he hired me for the next two months to paint and hang the acoustical ceilings in the new home of the *Carbon County News*, a two-story office building, west of Broadway, on 13th Street and Hauser, across from the new post office. It was the first time one of my misguided ideas ever proved to be providential and landed me two jobs. It was the last time I ever let my inner-Hemingway out and solicited newspaper employment. Yet, those cub thoughts of writing were left to gestate like a seed pearl.

My new on-site bosses were a mixed blessing. Freddy, a runty man at 5'4 with a drill-sergeant-sized gruffness, was a finish carpenter and general contractor at the newspaper office. He had recently hired an assistant, Luke, who was learning the trade. Luke and his wife Bonnie were back-to-the-land fugitives from the East Coast, *Whole Earth Catalogue* disciples, and dreamers of a deeper utopian revolution. Luke had a psychology degree from Cornell, Bonnie had majored in sociology at State University of New York at Potsdam. Almost to a person, these college-educated, back-to-the-landers lacked knowledge, skills, and horse sense for a self-reliant life. Balancing the ledger were their resolve and resourcefulness to learn and succeed. While working together, in dribs and drabs, Luke unbosomed a few of the movement's patron saints: Henry David Thoreau (*Walden*), Aldo Leopold (*A Sand County Almanac*), Rachel

Carson (*Silent Spring*), and E. F. Schumacher (*Small Is Beautiful*). Luke and Bonnie were putting their former life on a potter's wheel and remolding it. They had both attended Woodstock but kept that cosmic fling on the lowdown around local folk—especially Freddy, a former non-wartime marine and wiry bundle of right-wing dynamite, ready to blow off at a millimeter's difference.

Luck was on our side with Luke: He lived beyond Al Yates's homestead in Luther and drove a ten-year-old blue Ford pickup into Red Lodge every morning. He offered that David and I could catch a ride with him to and from work if we didn't mind hunkering down under his tarp in back. We had to be at the pavement at seven each morning. For the next two months, at first light, David and I walked a few hundred yards to the highway, directly into the scattering pink-to-purple shadow of the Beartooth Mountains, and waited on Luke's truck to round the bend. We carried our lunches in David's Austrian army calf-skin-covered haversack, me with a potted ham sandwich and David with white bread sluiced in bacon grease and slathered in mayonnaise. Most days, on the ride in, we were plastered against the cold steel of Luke's battered tool box. With a subzero wind chill cutting to the bone, face and hands purpling with the sky, my musings often willed myself into a future that included tapping into two things: an easier way to start the day and a warm-blooded, apple-cheeked Montana hippie chick.

"I don't like work—no man does," wrote Joseph Conrad in *Heart of Darkness*, "but I like what is in the work—the chance to find yourself." Although I had come to think of punctuality as an overrated virtue, I was always on the dot each morning at the soon-to-be *Carbon County News* offices. Days were warm and welcoming, with central heat and convivial company. For a change, I was temperamentally suited to this job, relishing the quotidian mundaneness, shoulder to the wheel, no hands on the clock, staying late, establishing a Socratic equilibrium with myself. Menial labor took the edge off because there was no emotional plug-in like a career job. Nothing to impugn, honest work, every day a fresh vitality.

The offices of Stan Linde and Denny Neville occupied the upstairs, northeast corner of the pine-green concrete-block building. In 1958, Linde created the syndicated *Rick O'Shay* western comic strip. By the early '70s, he had an average worldwide daily readership of 15 million. Neville, Linde's trusted assistant, lettered and inked the cartoon strip. Most days, they arrived in separate pickup trucks, each stylistically attired in a cattleman's cut sheepherder, starched pleated jeans, polished chestnut Tony Lamas, earth-tone vests, pearl snap-button shirts, and wide Stetsons with a cattleman's crease that never seemed to find a hat rack. Linde wore a fresh-clipped moustache and often donned a pastel-colored cravat, the artist in Red Lodge affect. They came off as friendly, level-headed guys, if not a bit cranky about cowboys and their costumes.

To a ragtag wanderer like myself, their sartorial sensibilities seemed confected, when in fact I would later learn it was a big-city newspaper office tradition of performance for cartoonists to dress smartly. It also fit Linde and Neville's well-ordered personalities and the painstaking nature of their creative enterprise. One day's comic strip took up to twelve hours. Everything in their cheerfully fenestrated office had its place in sustaining the daily ritual of an artist: drawing tables, Bristol boards, cartoon blowups on the walls, easels, inks, pens, pencils, and a portable Empire AM/FM radio, playing country and western music all day long. Soundtrack, mood, and being in the zone struck me as vital elements in Linde and Neville's creative process, no less than Nobel Laureate Gabriel García Márquez penning the magical realism of *One Hundred Years of Solitude* while listening to the Beatles' *Magical Mystery Tour*.

Linde, almost twenty years my senior, was born and raised in Billings but had spent several years in Manhattan feeding at the golden corral of cartoonists, forging connections with newspapers, and syndicates. In 1962, once *Rick O'Shay* had gained success, Linde returned to Montana.

Neville was a Mormon from Byron, Wyoming. After his LDS (Latter-day Saints) mission in France and Belgium, he graduated with honors from the Art Center College of Design in Los Angeles. He stayed on in California for several years working as an illustrator for Hughes Aircraft and as an animator for Filmation Studios. Linde and Neville came together in Red Lodge when Linde reached out for an assistant—perhaps more of an understudy.

I had never been much on reading the funnies at breakfast, but my daily interactions with Linde and Neville piqued my interest in character development and the larger creative process. Set in the mythical western town of Conniption, *Rick O'Shay* featured composite characters out of Linde's past and from cowboy lore: Rick O'Shay the deputy sheriff, Hipshot Percussion the gunslinger, Deuces Wild the gambler, Gaye Abandon the dance hall owner, Dr. Basil Metabolism the physician, Ophelia Pulse the nurse, Mort Gage the banker, Horse's Neck the local Indian chief with his homely but nice daughter Moonglow and her relentless suitor Crazy Quilt. Linde held the artist's mirror up to a cowboy culture that was dying out in the production studios of Hollywood and New York and on the high plains ranches of Wyoming and Montana.

The radio background music to Linde and Neville's daily grind of creativity featured a cowboy, country-squire-attired contemporary of Linde's, Charlie Rich, the Silver Fox. In fact, Linde and Neville dressed so much like Charlie they could have been mistaken for band members if ever found in the same room. Rich was a crossover to the new generation of country music, a cultural movement defined by country rock, outlaw country, country pop, and traditionalists paying homage to a bygone era.

All day long, while Linde and Neville bent over their drawing boards and I stood on a stepladder hanging the acoustic ceiling or painting the walls in bright yellow sunshine, Bennie B. down the street at KRBN-AM announced each record, lauded the singer, and spun like clockwork Rich's two Grammy- winning hits, "Behind Closed Doors" and "The Most Beautiful Girl." It was the first time I put the face and the name with the music and the connection to Arkansas. Before then, I wouldn't have known the Silver Fox if I had tripped over him.

Locations have stories, real and imagined. Forevermore, when I hear Rich's songs I think about Red Lodge and the *Rick O'Shay* guys in the same way that I associate the Animals' iconic song "We've Gotta Get Out of this Place" with the Vietnam War and fellow vets. A gift of artists, writers, and musicians, intended or not, is that their work often sets up an illusion of place, the attitude of a situation, a tone poem. Red Lodge, *Rick O'Shay*, Big Al, "The Most Beautiful Girl" are thus harmonized.

Life went along swimmingly for our first two months of cabin living, hiding out. That is, until one Friday afternoon when we knocked off early. As we approached the cabin and squinted into the distance, we realized Rex Roden, a commune-living, costume-wearing Captain America, had found us. He and David had briefly lived in the same boarding house in Fort Collins. Rex knew that David had hightailed it to Red Lodge, but nothing more. We found out later that he had arrived that morning in town, asked around about us, and eventually got directions from Reba at the café out to Big Al's. The problem, among many other things, was that every square inch of Rex's '65 Chevy van was painted in an American flag motif. He had blown what little cover we had garnered in town, and now his van was parked to the side of our cabin, visible from Big Al's barn, conspicuous as any old razor-toothed giant green Martian.

As we drew closer, Rex, a dead ringer for a cult leader, his fierce falcon eyes wild as ever and coal black hair and beard as unkempt as Manson's, emerged from the van vestured in his trademark red, white, and blue buckskins, whooping with joy to have found us. Iron Butterfly's "In a Gadda Da Vida" blared endlessly from his tape deck out the open door and down the road to greet us. He was in the neighborhood, he said, and decided to stop in. There were no mirrors to check our mood, but we could not have looked (or felt) more dismayed. The object lesson of not upholding a cone of silence went without saying: *When on the lam do not tell unwanted company where you seek refuge.*

Because we had to earn a living, our variant of "on the lam" didn't include hunkering down in the woods, full of fear, like hunted rabbits. No one's mug was on the post office wall. But we did, on most days, keep a low profile and our guard up. At least one of us was one tipoff (or blunder) away from a very different life.

We had pissed in our own whiskey, as Uncle Scott liked to say, and were stuck with Rex for a day or two. We moved his Abbie Hoffman look-a-like van behind the cabin for those passersby who had yet to scope it out. We stayed to ourselves that weekend, and only brought Rex out at night to walk the cottonwoods along Red Lodge Creek and, even then, only after we had all taken an orange, barrel-shaped hit of acid. The new moon, Milky Way, weather, and orange pill conspired to turn the sour taste in our mouths over Rex's arrival into a finger-licking frolic in the woods.

Early on, David and I hammed it up by putting on James-Gang-era oilcloth dusters and twirling the Winchester like a pea shooter. Then the skies turned large and luminous, moisture-clean, touchable, definitely capable of being felt and followed along the star paths. Two feet of fresh snow covered the ground and traced the trees, which appeared like a ghostly birdcage against the sky and sharply silhouetted mountains. For the first time, treetops keening, I felt the warm winds of a Chinook rake down the western slopes of the Rockies and poof—a 50-degree rise in temperature, the exact opposite of a Norther. We stripped down to our tee-shirts while the Chinook blew for several hours. The farther we footslogged, the more the ground snow melted, the faster the trees dumped their hoary coats and the creeks thawed and then swelled and swirled by us. Afraid to blink, I thought the great woolly mammoth, frozen deep in time, might be the next to spring free of winter's ground.

As the waters quickened, I ogled like a lover the luminous sky that had glazed over in jeweled sashes of jade. Polaris and the Big Dipper overhead. Orion 45 degrees south. Felt but not touched, like the color plunges that finish a great painting, the jade mists gave off warm shimmers of saffron and smoky purple and pulsed like a cosmic poltergeist, pushing their weightlessness across the blackened canvas. Contemplating eternity came easy beneath the sublime splendor of those big skies. Conversing with the stars and they with each other. Sharing the vast rotunda and cosmically isolated at once.

Rex and David disappeared, not replying to my whoops. An hour or so later, after watching a shooting star split the sky, I circled back. A thin line of smoke rose from the chimney. Chunky icicles—frozen, thawed, refrozen, thawed—dripped like diamond daggers from the eaves. Peering through the partly fogged cabin window, lightly framed in frost on the edges, I could see David on the couch. He had thrown a couple of fresh logs on the fire and was reading Kahlil Gibran's *The Prophet*. The warm amber glow filling the room flowed out onto the woodpile. At times, David would turn up a bota bag of cheap wine and take a squirt. Beethoven's Ninth Symphony played softly against the susurrus of the stream and treetop breeze. I watched for ten minutes, not wanting to upend his poetic reverie, until I noticed David hadn't turned a page. The book was upside down. He was cooked, mooning into space, channeling John Lennon: "Turn off your mind, relax, and float downstream."

Rex trudged up an hour later with his tongue hanging out, wondering where we had been. He'd taken enough LSD to put Big Al's black stallion in orbit. He never slept that night and left at sunrise. We never saw or heard from him again and were glad to be free of his menacing spirit.

Big Al had gotten an eyeful of our fifth columnist caller. A few days later, he caught up with us splitting wood in front of the cabin. "Boys, the game warden stopped by an hour ago. He seemed to think you two might have been stalking a moose below Castle Mountain. Said he saw your motorcycle then you took off into the woods."

"I can't say he didn't see the motorcycle, sir. That's how we get around. But we hadn't been stalking any moose, I promise you." David gave up nothing while deflecting Big Al's steady gaze, knowing full well we had seen the game warden and had taken off like a shot, disappearing down an old logging trail.

"Be careful. He's watching you," Big Al warned, his temper cracking slightly, knowing a doozy when he heard one, and fully aware that we were the only ones in a 500-mile radius riding a pine green dirt bike in mid-winter and carrying a rifle.

He then told us about some good-paying coal-mining jobs he'd read about out in eastern Montana. Before leaving, he asked David if he'd like to make some extra money and skin twenty some skunks at five bucks a piece. The market price for skunk pelts had caught up with muskrats, he added.

"Darn tootin'," David replied. "Let me finish chopping this wood and we'll meet you at the barn."

Our socializing was limited to work and an occasional night at the Bull and Bear Saloon hitting on biker chicks. But they came closer to getting us roughed up than giving us a rough tumble in the sack. Mountain Bird had disappeared a couple of weeks after our first meeting. When I ran into Chavez one morning coming out of the café, he told me she'd taken off with the English dude, Simon, whose hometown was famous for hanging monkeys in French military uniforms. Without even a tallyho to the Bull and Bear crowd, they had taken flight to northern California. Rolling his eyes and shaking his head, he added that Simon had sniffed out a business opportunity in some place called Humboldt County. Mountain Bird's stock went up in my mind: a free spirit, emancipated, catching the back of a wind to anywhere but home to Chugwater.

David and I needed to pick up our game, no doubt, but our sanitary regimen of sponge baths hadn't been exactly robust, which may have accounted for the polite distance most women kept from us. On two Saturday afternoons over the course of our three months, Chico and Deke, David's hotdogger buddies who had rented a rundown Victorian in the Hi-Bug district where the Freemason coal barons had once lived like town squires, let us use their bathtub. In return we always brought along some venison backstrap and ribs.

As we were reeking to the bones, lathering up in the tub for an hour was nothing short of heavenly. Left me singing that old spiritual with a bar of soap in mind: "He's got the whole world in his hands / He's got the whole wide world in his hands..." We figured on those days that since we were at our cleanest, smelled the best (even our feet), and wore our freshest dirty clothes the girls would be most vulnerable. We were well positioned it seemed: Chico's and Deke's house felt like a revolving door of hippie chicks stopping by to get high on the best dope in town. We gave it our best, and, on those spruced up days, in our minds, it was their loss.

David did finally make a date with Cindy, the manager at the City Bakery. He had taken up a daily routine of buying jelly rolls while admiring her dimpled smile, her button nose, and the firm fit of her blue jeans. Other than the stray hippie chicks at Chico and Deke's and a few college girls coming home from Missoula on

Thanksgiving and Christmas break, we weren't dealing with a hot singles scene in Red Lodge.

When David showed up for a date at Cindy's parents' home off-Broadway on his dirt bike one winter-stricken evening, things began to chill. He was back at the cabin in an hour. He guessed that her parents had raised the expectations bar for their only daughter. Something better, he speculated, than a filthy cabin hideout with the unwashed.

David quit the jelly rolls after that dissing. At wit's end, one night he blurted out, "I'd fuck a pile of rocks if there was a snake in it." For me, I didn't like the dry spell, but, smelly or not, had gotten used to the old go-by from free-spirited hippie chicks. The explanation was obvious (but not true), I came to believe. My fellow peaceniks wrongly cast the blame for the mistakes of Vietnam to anyone who had worn a uniform, and it was hard for me to hide that past. My heaviest winter coat was an army field jacket.

Things purred along in the cabin as usual and after Thanksgiving, in early December, Mike Williams and Susie "Seed" McIntosh paid us a visit from Fort Collins. We were anxious to hear the latest news about David's bust and the status of the warrant. The feds and local police had rounded up and arrested Susie with the rest of the tenants in the Fort Collins farmhouse. She spent one night in jail and was released after Denver lawyer Joe St. Veprey bailed her out on a $10,000 bond. "The police seized several pounds of marijuana and large quantities of cocaine in the barn and the upstairs rooms in the house," she recounted to us. "My room was clean other than the residue in a couple of pipes. They didn't find anything in yours either," she said, pointing at David. "Joe got all charges dropped." This news augured well for David.

We told her about Rex-the-Captain-America blowing in like an ill wind. After a few minutes of cursing, she explained, "I let him stay at my place on Lowell Street a few weeks back while I was in

Denver for a night. When I returned the next day, he had stolen my pot stash, taken $200 from the jewelry box, and left town. Word had it he was headed for Oregon." David and I shook our heads, thinking we had dodged a bullet when he passed through Red Lodge, probably on his way to Oregon. "His pot sure was good, Susie," David said, laughing out loud and patting her on the back to calm her down. "He's not welcome around me again. He looks and acts like a vampire. He takes, takes, takes," she said with a pinched hiccup of laughter followed by a sneer.

Originally from Arlington, Virginia, Susie had many claims to fame, including owning the Seed, the health food store in Fort Collins and having been babysat in her Arlington, Virginia childhood home by neighbors, Shirley MacLaine and Warren Beatty. She hadn't laid eyes on either one of them since they left for Hollywood until he played Clyde Barrow in *Bonnie and Clyde*, one of my favorite movies. The outlaw in me. Susie was a great cook and had brought a peach cobbler and a fresh sack of homemade granola for David. She could sew anything and knew her way around an ax and chopping wood.

She was also delightful and a good-looking blue-eyed blonde who looked the part of a hippie mountain chick in her leather fringe jacket hand-made by her friend Diane Blackstone, the seamstress at Mellow Yellow back in Fort Collins. It wasn't clear for several days just who might emerge as Susie's suitor. We were all in the mix, with David holding the advantage...or so I thought. David had shied away from anything romantic back in Fort Collins because of an Arkansas love interest (who was still gnawing at him from afar). Two months of celibate cabin life might have changed that.

The open question of Susie's wooer was still not resolved (in my mind anyway) when David and I had to go to work on Monday morning. Mike and Susie stayed back and got us caught up on chores—splitting wood, deep cleaning the stove and pots and pans, and sweeping and mopping the cabin. On day two of that arrangement, Susie and Mike dropped the chores and took to staying in David's bed all day.

At first, disappointment set in. It certainly crossed my mind that sharing could work as an act of mercy. If "nothing but two-bit outlaws on the dodge" like Butch and Sundance could take in an Etta Place as moll and muse, why not a whiff or two of venereal fragrance for David and me? The bright side was that their pairing did cut the cat-and-mouse tension. To celebrate the obvious inflection point, we each took a hit of the chocolate mescaline, compliments of their care package. Our isolated milieu and the wealth of natural resources were perfect for an impromptu journey of the senses, tramping the asteroids and black holes of our perceptions. Together, we struck out to slog the eleven miles downstream to where Red Lodge Creek ran into the Yellowstone River and Cooney Dam. But the plan was way too ambitious, with no forethought about our return in the middle of the night. Events proceeded and redirected us, song dogs yipping away, a new moon, the Milky Way, the Big Sky, the whole cosmic fun house.

Soon, David goaded us to stop boring our way through the forest and to get a fix on Orion, the hunter, drawing his bow at Taurus the bull. "Look up high and south. Can't you mooncalves see the three stars that make up his belt?" he kept repeating, standing in a shadow thrown by a leafless cottonwood. "It's the spine of the bison. I can feel his breath on my shoulders."

"I see the belt, but that's not the way I've ever looked at Orion," Susie Seed said. "The Indians say the three stars represent antelope, bighorn, and mule deer. The wolf star Sirius is following, the fiery, bright one," she added, pointing to the east.

For hours, we rumpused in the crisp wintry woods, the snow crunching and creaking underfoot with each step. Never more than two miles from the cabin, we watched raptly, as the Big Sky's moods and expressions changed on its nightly voyage, always aloof and sparkling and taking its breath from a gazillion pricks of light. At some point, the talking and crunching and yipping of song dogs ceased and the soft-sighing breeze turned to a howling wind. We no longer cared about Indian or Greek names or celestial folk tales or trigonometric brushstrokes of the star charts. The moonless geometry of the wheeling firmament had coalesced. An indistinct veil of lustrous silver lit up our faces and washed over us clear and clean. Swirling and flaming and lasering with frosty ribbons of rich color. Like John Denver's night in the forest, we filled up our senses.

David and I knew our days in Red Lodge (and Arcadia) were a month or so from an end—and that sometimes things happen that are nothing short of serendipitous. Mike and Susie departed a few days later, married soon after, and eventually had a son and two daughters. The newest entry on my burgeoning dictionary list was an English slang term that fairly described my mounting restlessness when saying goodbye to Susie and Mike. *Coddiwomple*: To travel in a purposeful manner toward a vague destination.

Some briary old fella once said aloud "that the only sure thing about luck is that it will change." Around late December of that year, news floated in that the county sheriff had dropped the warrant for David back in Arkansas. The stool who dimed David out was busted for selling heroin, and the prosecutor reckoned the jury would likely find his testimony unreliable and throw it out. The Colorado warrant was still active, but Susie said lawyer Joe St. Veprey could get charges dropped if David would show up and give an affidavit. Further active intelligence gathering signaled that the real culprits were part of a larger cocaine ring based in Mexico.

The same lovely fellows, David and Susie told me, had drawn guns on me when I called on David my first day or two in Fort Collins. David had backed them off with the guns and met me in the front yard where, on their demand, their marksmen took our measure from the barn and upstairs bedrooms. David said he had thought they were dealing small quantities of pot, but after that day he sensed something bigger going down. Twenty-four hours later, the house was raided. Someone had spilled the tea.

All this news came just as my job at the newspaper office painting the walls was coming to an end. Although the rigor of Big Al's hospitality was impressive, in a different frame of mind he had started bringing up those coal-mining jobs more often. David and I had *snowbirding* on our minds as well—following the sun south after the solstice, and he had found a new transmission for his spavined old truck. On a sunny day in the high 20s the two of us installed it under the twisted cottonwood from which we hung our meat. At the same time, a friend in Florida, Tommy Horton, sent word that he had purchased a ticket for me to a Dylan and the Band concert in Miami in late January. It was the first Dylan tour since his motorcycle accident in 1966.

The crossroads beckoned. Settling debts, we fished out $125 for the cabin-size woodpile that we had reduced to a circle of sawdust. Before we said our fare-thee-wells, Big Al slipped us a contact number for the Rosebud Mine on the high plains near Colstrip, Montana. He said they were building a coal-fired electrical plant and that there was a mint of money to be made by young men like us. He should have saved his breath. On the lam, living the dream as temporary exiles in Montana for an early winter was one thing; hunkering down for the long hard winter of life in the state's newest Last Chance Gulch mine shaft was another. We respectfully shined it on, figuring we'd already made bank. Just as Thoreau advised, our accounts fit on a thumbnail: simplified, simplified, simplified.

We said our goodbyes to the oilcloth dusters and twirled the Winchester one last time like a pea shooter. We then ramped the bike onto the bed of the '49 Chevy pickup, drew the lashings tight, and split for Colorado.

The road from there back South was an easy one. Burglars in that wolf-moon night couldn't have gotten away with treasure as dear as our sunny thoughts of the warrant-free road ahead. On the calendar, our sojourn in Red Lodge had been short-lived, but spiritually it packed an enduring punch. As with the forebears, I wasn't in Montana to see the world change (though it was changing), I was there for it to change my world (and it did). As naturalist Aldo Leopold wrote so long ago, "Glad I shall never be young without wild country to be young in."

Native Americans say that the geographic environment is the mold into which the human race has been poured, that the spirit of a place is determined as much by culture and human imagination as landscape. Intuitions of space and time told me that Big Al's high-country tarns of the Beartooth Plateau, bounded by a rolling sea of diamond-tipped granite peaks, like rogue waves holding up the sky, awaited my return—popping with beautiful silences and cutthroat trout, refracting mirrorlike the gaudy summer meadows of peacock-bright larkspur, lupine, Indian paintbrush, and year-round ice-blue glaciers. Small wonder that unseen image, as if seared permanently into my retinas, would never melt away. Yet if ever a day came that I attempted to backtrack this adventure's mental meanderings, the old guy would likely not be inhabiting his white painted prairie house. Showing me the way atop his black stallion was more like an unfinished dream, a boon not so removed from Peter Mathieson's unseen snow leopard in his namesake book, *The Snow Leopard*: In the end it was the 'common miracles'…the 'hardships' endured and Himalayan aesthetic that defined his journey and grew his spirit.

In February of 1974, David returned to Colorado. Within months, he became a wildlife cinemaphotographer with the Stouffer brothers whose *Wild America* serial became PBS's longest-running program. On breaks from *Wild America*, David also worked with environmental activist Jacques Cousteau on the *Calypso* and with *National Geographic* deep-diving to World War II submarine wrecks on the *Mir* submersible.

At least for the time being, I continued to hurl myself at life, which flew by almost kaleidoscopically. Arrivals begat departures, beginnings blurred into endings and vice versa. Corners remained hard to see around. Bearing witness to where I stood on any given day was about as good as it got. Same spot as the future. Red Lodge and its wildness had surely been a kind of throbbing, lyrical web of natural fecundity and fertile solitude for me. Or as the unsentimental Hemingway would say, it's good country.

Swan Songs

Chapter Sixteen

CHECKY LISTENED TO THE BEATLES on the pride of the Camp Ramason's PX, a Sony turntable. Marvin was always headphoned up to a reel-to-reel listening to Miles Davis. Waltauvos played his Colorado-bought acoustic guitar and sang old country standards. Gene played nonstop Bob Dylan, mostly the free associative tunes of *Highway 61 Revisited*, on his cassette player.

In the army, Gene and I were separated by a couple of bunks at Camp Friendship in northeastern Thailand. A natural for the finance corps, with a degree in accounting from the University of Minnesota, Gene had been drafted upon graduation and had some solid Dobie Gillis creds going his way. His looks—clean shaven, nicely coiffed short hair, horn rims, and fatigue shirt always tucked in—fit the profession and square guy image to a T. He was also more than slightly Howard Hughes–like about staying fresh and clean every day.

Climate-wise, wintry Minnesota and the cloying swelter of the tropics were apples and mangos. On most mornings and evenings and when possible at midday, Gene could be seen in skivvies with a towel wrapped around his neck and dock kit in hand, latrine bound. So, it wasn't exactly an act of creative christening to nickname him "Clean Gene." After a few months, I just shortened it to "Clean." He was fine with that and responded warmly when greeted as such.

Clean hailed from Hibbing, Minnesota, the same hometown as Dylan, and the epicenter of the Mesabi Iron Range, way north, near the Canadian border. A town of fewer than 20,000 souls, Hibbing is surrounded by the world's largest open pit iron ore mine, which can be seen from the moon. The mine supplied the raw materials to U.S. Steel for twentieth-century America's industrial revolution. It was also the inspiration for Dylan's *North Country Blues*, an ode to the ups and downs of a mining community. Dylan's dad, Abraham Zimmerman, sold those miners appliances. Clean's father, George Bronson, kept the books at the U.S. Steel field office.

Clean's older brother rode motorcycles with Dylan (née Zimmerman) and his brother, Dave Zimmerman. Bleak, withering winters, a seasonal fashion of sixteen-year-olds with leather jackets, was about all the inside poop about Hibbing and Dylan that Clean passed along. He wasn't holding back. There just wasn't much to tell.

A few years before I met Clean, Bob Dylan's pungent lyrics and stark and edgy voice hit my radar. But I couldn't say I was a gung-ho fan or had any immediate sense that he was already a poet/rock 'n' roll avalanche. And I certainly wouldn't have given a flip about his hometown. But it mattered, that was for sure.

Woody Guthrie's authenticity as a folk singer owed heart and soul to his Dust Bowl roots in Pampa, Texas, and Okemah, Oklahoma, where my grandmother Fincher was born a decade before Woody. Experience was a vital thread of Woody's art and soul. Hibbing and the Iron Range were Dylan's Okemah and Dust Bowl.

Breaking out of the white-bread Ozzie and Harriet world of the '50s was a well-worn trail of the alienated and restless. My uncles had followed it to California and I wasn't far behind. In January of 1961, Dylan set out on a pilgrimage to meet Woody Guthrie. Before departing, and almost overnight, as if channeling the hospital-bound folk legend who was suffering from Huntington's disease, Dylan taught himself over 200 Guthrie tunes. Within eight months of his arrival in New York, the legendary talent scout and record producer John Hammond inked Dylan to a recording contract with Columbia records. By the time he turned twenty-one, he had penned "Blowin' in the Wind."

Then, bam, bam, bam, came a creative boom of iconic songs and lyrics, signaling the death knell of over half a century of Tin Pan Alley giving short shrift to the singer-songwriter. In August of 1965 alone, forty-eight different artists recorded his songs.

Dylan did not arrive in New York with evolved ideas of social justice, equality, or even art and theater. His lover, muse, and subject of many songs, Suze Rotolo, who was with Dylan on the album cover of *The Freewheelin' Bob Dylan*, helped raise the Iron Country boy's socio-political consciousness. She had learned what it meant to bootstrap life in a union organizing family, and, at an early age, she knew her way around Greenwich Village's hotspots of bohemian art, theater, and music.

His timing could not have been better scripted. In the late '50s and early '60s, New York City had been a brash melting pot of artistic self-exploration and spontaneous subconscious expression. Charlie Parker's jazz improvs. Marlon Brando's *On the Waterfront*. Jackson Pollock's *Mural*. Jack Kerouac's *On the Road*. Allen Ginsberg's *Howl*. William Burroughs's *Naked Lunch*. Harry Smith's *Anthology of American Folk Music*. Milestones of cultural change, all. The heavy slap of Cold War censorship stirred the ferment of creative democracy coming out of the McCarthy years and into the Kennedy era.

Voila, out of the Midwestern provinces and onto the Village folk scene stage bounds Bob Dylan—an energetic quick study and a natural-born rebel, a card-carrying Kerouacian character.

He spoke to our souls in the same way that Muriel Rukeyser described poetry as the art that relies on the "moving relation between individual consciousness and the world." Similarly, Dylan called it "the perpetual motion of illusion." Baby boomers such as myself have almost osmotically sponged up the biblical beauty of his stirring anthems and squeezed their essence into our worldviews: "Blowin' in the Wind" ('63 March on Washington), "The Times They Are A-Changin'" (revolution), "Masters of War" (attack on business of war), "A Hard Rain's A-Gonna Fall" (nuclear apocalypse), "Mr. Tambourine Man" (consciousness and drugs as muse), "Desolation Row" (loss of meaning; cultural collapse), "Maggie's Farm" (oppression; escape from conformity), and "Like a Rolling Stone" (disillusionment and freedom).

Arriving from Montana to Miami's Hollywood Sportatorium on January 19, 1974, for Dylan's Planet Waves Tour with the Band had the raucous vibe of being present for a prophet returning with The Word. Drugs were involved. Due to a motorcycle accident, Dylan had not toured since 1966, about the time he released two lyrically ground-breaking masterpieces, *Highway 61 Revisited* (1965) and *Blonde on Blonde* (1966).

The traffic leading in to the Sportatorium backed up for a mile along Pines Boulevard. I had traveled almost 3,000 miles, as the proud holder of a $9.50 general admissions ticket. I had no job, no car, no cash flow, and no destination when the concert was over. Treading water in Florida, in a state of perpetual penury, life was on hold for my pilgrimage to the Second Coming of Dylan.

The afternoon of the concert, my friends Tommy and Susan, an acquaintance of theirs named Blinkie Bates, and I drove to Miami from Tampa in the Blue Beast ('67 Ford Fairlane). I got along well in the back seat with Blinkie, a red-faced, curly-silk-haired rascal with a bawdy sense of humor who, looking back, was channeling the future Chris Farley (a ten-year-old at the time). For what he lacked in savoir faire, Blinkie came with assets, a couple of ounces of Mexican swag. We did our best to smoke it all, going to, during, and returning from the concert. The more PBRs we downed, the more we smoked, and the more we coughed, which was Blinkie's cue to egg us on: "The more you cough, the more you get off." Susan was having trouble keeping up and probably should not have tried.

Once we were inside, the Sportatorium whipped and buzzed with cries of chemically enhanced exhilaration. Arena bench seating but nobody sat. Susan disappeared before Dylan and the Band opened with the crisply played "Most Likely You Go Your Way and I'll Go Mine." The would-be prophet of peace was decked out in a casual white linen suit, and an untucked black-and-white checkerboard shirt. The rest of the package was pure Dylan: frizzy hair, an adolescent's growth of hair on his face, reflective sunglasses. He strummed the rhythm chords, stressing the ending to each verse.

As he began a semi-countrified version of "Lay Lady Lay," Dylan mumbled under his breath, "Good to be in Miami." He didn't speak again the rest of the show. No jokes, no bon mots, not a single anecdote to be told. No chance of pulling back the curtain with an instructive or inspirational backstory like, say, I wrote this song on the toilet at Gerde's Folk City on the Fourth of July the day after my daddy died and my girlfriend left me. Not a single crumb of that kind of stage patter for the Dylan-starved multitudes. As with all art forms, I came to understand that Dylan lets his songs, lyrics, and performance do the talking—leaving the audience to do their own conjuring. "If you are looking for a Maharaja…go to India," he once quipped.

Though he had for years plugged my head like a munificent earworm with lyrically inspired social commentary and rock 'n' roll attitude, my expectations were in retreat as he started his acoustic set. There would be no "return of the messiah" as Ethiopian emperor Haile Selassie had only a few years before pulled off by arriving into Palisadoes Airport in Kingston, Jamaica, to a rapturous multitude of 100,000-plus Rastafarian devotees. Just as Ram Dass never wanted to be a guru, Dylan never wanted to live up to the idea I had of him as more oracle than person, Mosaic instead of mosaic. Not only did he not have the answers, I wasn't too clear anyone knew the questions. With that realization taking hold, I stepped back and enjoyed the performance, each song having its own chemistry and gravity with no need for stage patter or magical thinking about a poetic prophet.

After a forty-five-minute set, Dylan left the stage and the Band's bass player, Rick Danko, sang lead on "Stage Fright." My homeboy Levon Helm, from Turkey Scratch, Arkansas, picked it up from there. He played the fire out of the drums and sang lead vocals on the Band's "The Night They Drove Old Dixie Down" and "Up on Cripple Creek" and then gave up the drums for the mandolin and played "Rag Mama Rag." The entire arena was dancing to that good ol' floor slamming rock music of the high '60s.

At some point, the Band took a break and Tommy and I left Blinkie to feed the crowd more joints. We ventured off looking for Susan. Thirty minutes later, we found her "being monitored" on a military-type cot in the Red Cross overdose tent. A heavyset cop, in full blue uniform, stood imposingly at the door. He told us Susan had fainted while standing in line for the girls' bathroom. Tommy looked at her pupils and quipped that she was sure enough pie-eyed. He whispered to me that the only thing wrong with Susan was that "she freaks out" in crowds, possibly provoked on this occasion by low-level paranoia induced by all of Blinkie's joints. "There was no bad acid or manic-depressive disorder, no Thorazine necessary," he told the two volunteer docs in tie-dyes and cutoff jeans. She was ready to leave, and the volunteers needed the army cots for a growing line of eyes-in-the-back-of-their-heads-folks on very bad trips. The brown acid, like Woodstock, someone opined.

When we returned to our seats, Dylan was playing an acoustic set with guitar and harmonica, his voice stark, penetrating and as edgy as his lyrics. He finished with "The Times They Are A-Changin'," "Don't Think Twice, It's All Right," and "It's Alright, Ma (I'm Only

Bleeding)," which had the Watergate-era crowd shouting back: *But even the President of the United States sometimes must have to stand naked.* The Band returned with Dylan and performed the fast version of his recently released "Forever Young," inspired by the 1966 birth of his son, Jesse. It's a song for everyone that evokes our oldest literature's (*Epic of Gilgamesh*) quest for eternal youth...*May you stay forever young!*

Poet Allen Ginsberg, said, in so many words, that "Forever Young" should be sung by every child in every school every morning in every country. The song was full of hope and encouraged people to find their own truth. "'Like a Rolling Stone' might be Dylan's masterpiece," Ginsberg said, "but 'Forever Young' is his national anthem."

Dylan and the Band brought it all home with "Like a Rolling Stone," the iconic 1965 rock 'n' roll chart topper. While Dylan sneers at "Miss Lonely" and her fall from grace with a confrontational *How does it feel?*, it's the final verse that struck a responsive chord with me: *When you ain't got nothing, you got nothing to lose / You're invisible now, you got no secrets to conceal.* So it goes that Miss Lonely's vulnerability becomes her path to liberation and freedom (and a beacon to those of us stranded in the wilderness).

Words matter. They don't just feel good when paired with melodies that make us shiver and shake and move us to shout out loud. They instruct, motivate, inspire, and, often, effect change—the aim of every artist. Timelessly, they spool memory and what could have been into the here-and-now emotional conditions of our personal lives. Dylan's song lyrics have been cited 186 times in U.S. court opinions and briefs, more than any other writer. The most common quote is of a familiar stanza from "Subterranean Homesick Blues": *Keep a clean nose / Watch the plain clothes / You don't need a weatherman to know which way the wind blows.* Much to Dylan's dismay, a militant '60s student group even co-opted the "Weatherman tag" and the last stanza as their slogan for violent revolution.

My road out of Florida in February 1974 was a tortured one, full of Dylan's tumbling words, restless images, and the false idol of financial security drawing a bead on me. Problem was I had too many voices talking to me, not least the cynical words of Lucas Jackson (Paul Newman) in *Cool Hand Luke*, six years after the movie was first released: "Sometimes nothing can be a real cool hand."

For me, the yin and yang of late adolescence to early adulthood had been, at best, a tenuous balancing act—from army conscript to aimless free spirit, from lost soul to sellout banker, from drugged-out bartender to fugitive in Montana. Life indeed had been rich with the accidental and incidental, the fruits of an appetite for improvisation and capitulation (to new cultures and ideas). For three years, nothing had been planned or rehearsed. A great life if you can get away with it. My idea of maturity as the art of living in peace kept getting hijacked by the necessary evil of financial security as a predicate for the art of living in peace.

Now at age twenty-three, having recently walked away from a three-month truck driving gig with Halliburton Company, the pressure was on to return to dependability. It was time to let that inner lion of experience swallow whole the free-roaming lamb of innocence that I cherished above all. It required coming out from behind my armor (kiss the bankers), embracing my own gifts (as a working stiff), taking the agency of my future away from the cops, duns, and druggies and consider aiming higher than prostitutes (tone down the fun). In Dad's world of pithy words, just straighten up and fly right, Phil. Which I did, after one last blowout.

North of Springfield, Missouri, the birthplace of Route 66 (some say), the traffic picked up. RC (Randy Cutting), with whom I'd been living while working for Halliburton, began laying on the horn, swerving from side to side, feigning lack of control in his pale green Pontiac Grand Prix convertible, a memorable boat-size machine that oozed a breezy, bad-boy heedlessness. Then, to announce our arrival at the Ozark Music Festival in Sedalia, Missouri, he let go of several earsplitting rally cries, "It's big, it's big, I'm losing it, I'm flippin'!"

It was RC's world in that car—hard to think of one without the other, like road and rubber, Cheech and Chong. With the wind at his face, shoulder-length hair aslant, he pleasured in giving it the full laid-back sprawl in the car's spacious white leather bucket seats. It was his personal pilothouse. Driving like a bat out of hell, he talked with his hands and curated the conversation (sports, poontang, Patty Hearst), punched the radio, periodically reached for a beer in the back seat, paid the gas station attendants without budging (pre-self-service), and on the whole kept alive his enfant terrible, perpetrator identity, a five-star general in the army of party hounds. He didn't have Tourette's syndrome, but for perfect strangers, when out of the blue he would do this maniacal scream—"It's big, Wolfman Jack, baby!"—followed by a fist in the air or the smashing of a glass, they might think something wasn't cricket.

Tickets for the festival, held July 19–21, 1974, were fifteen bucks for three days of rock 'n' roll. The featured acts were Aerosmith, Bob Seger and the Silver Bullet Band, the Eagles, Jefferson Starship, Lynyrd Skynyrd, Blue Öyster Cult, the Marshall Tucker Band, Joe Walsh, the Nitty Gritty Dirt Band, Bachman-Turner Overdrive, the Ozark Mountain Daredevils, America, Elvin Bishop, Boz Scaggs, Leo Kottke, REO Speedwagon, the Charlie Daniels Band, and the Earl Scruggs Revue.

As RC and I arrived, Sedalia's otherwise sedate streets of billowing Stars and Stripes had morphed into a busy gauntlet of hitchhikers and half-naked drug dealers. Openly occupying the street corners like some jackleg preacher selling salvation on any other day, the traveling merchants each peddled a different taste of divine glory: LSD, PCP, MDMA, 'shrooms, barbs, coke, weed, speed, black tar opium, blond Lebanese hash, white and brown heroin. Concertgoers had arrived from coast to coast a day early by the tens of thousands, like living waves of the sea, one rolling up on another, inundating every aspect of Sedalia.

Tags registered in far-flung states like New York, Alabama, Montana, and Arizona abounded. RC and I talked it up with the blind-drunk driver of a mint-condition, white-topped, metallic green '67 GTO, licensed in Edmonton, Alberta. Thirty hours and 1,600 miles before, he and three of his partying pals had set off from the boreal regions and boomed across the foothills of the Canadian Rockies and the Dakotas' desert badlands. Veering south, the night before, they blew hard as a Chinook gust down through the fruited plains of the American heartland.

And, presto…we were being funneled along together in a horn-blaring, ravening pageant of breathing-room-only VW vans, '60s-era heaps, prototypical motor homes, and packs of Hell's Angels-types. Donning colors, swastikas, and German iron crosses, airing out the armpits on polished chrome Harleys, the garish and grubbily garbed Wild Bunch seemed to revel in the reflected glory of their fabled California counterparts. Goosing the throttle with one hand, swilling beer with the other. Their peroxide-friendly "old ladies" on the pillion seat pressed a joint to their wet, puckered lips—pilot fish for a party. The rumble of anarchy was in the air. The four winds crossing had accumulated force.

That spring, the Kansas City concert promoters had decided to go big and took out a full-page advertisement in *Rolling Stone* magazine. For weeks, Wolfman Jack, the iconic Texas border station disc jockey and the festival's master of ceremonies, spread the word across the WLS (Chicago) airwaves to all corners of America. RC and I were carrying a canary yellow flyer etched in bold red with a jug of Ozark corn likker in the middle and the music lineup spelled out across the page. Professionally promoted, the festival's socko motto was "No Hassle Guaranteed." It sure got RC and me on board and probably was the plug that uncorked the broader lemminglike rush to Sedalia. If you missed Woodstock five years before, the savvy marketing hook suggested, Sedalia was your makeup event.

Promoters estimated 50,000 attendees—and printed tickets accordingly. They missed the mark by at least a factor of five. Well, hello 200,000, or more, party crashers. We were "boomers," always arriving in big numbers. All systems were soon on overload. Food, water, utilities, doctors, hospitals, police, and jails came under siege. The only commodities in plentiful supply were illegal drugs. In a matter of hours, local authorities and state police, in this mostly white-bread, overalls-friendly, former railroad terminus and stockyard town of 20,000 Bible-beating souls, had yielded control to the unwashed hordes of baby boomers. While stalled in traffic, already deep in the bag, bad boy Randy Cutting and I decided to get in touch with our inner-Sedalia-selves by dropping our favorite psychiatric medicine, Orange Sunshine.

An hour later, we parked at the backside of the fairground lot, laughing at the warning from the ticket takers that the gates would be closed until the festival was over. No chance we were checking out early. From the car, we threaded the tents and tarps and carnival cast of characters to the Ferris Wheel, and planted ourselves next to a couple of country cousins who had to be looking for the NASCAR track on the wrong weekend. A full-on assault to the eyes, they wore matching pink terrycloth halters and tiny shorts with beehive hairdos, blue-lidded eyes, and tattoos head to toe. Each muscled a jumbo ice chest with one hand while a cigarette dangled from their lips awaiting the other hand. After a rest, they lumbered on. RC sent them Rasta vibes. Jah, man. Jah, man.

The acid had kicked in, 100,000 million unused neurons cracking. The explorer and escapist in us channeling in equal doses. We were now consumed by the challenge of gravity, of doing basic things like walking and talking and standing upright. Inhabitants of a giant piece of Sunkist taffy sprang to mind. Apprehending the steady parade along the midway of bare-chested women, did, however, come to us trouble-free. Missouri's nickname is the Show Me State, a ministerial command for harmonic convergence worthy of goofing on. We'd fallen down a dirty ol' rabbit hole and come up in a pale reflection of Woodstock, Monterey, or Altamont.

Becky Abbott found me and RC spread eagled, eyes skyward. We were grabbing on for dear life, groping for purchase, our bodies acting all stoved up. The sky was a-poppin' with falling glitter even though it was mid-day, not the Fourth of July. Slo-mo, Becky coaxed us to our feet, which, as matters progressed, had the feel of standing up on a parking-lot-size banana peel. She then led us like six-year-olds on a hold-a-ring walking rope down makeshift lanes of scrofulous camps, with sizzling patches of fellow druggies.

By a stroke of blind luck, The Captain, Joey Schneider, a high school running buddy and our tried and true carnival ringleader, had landed a camp spot beneath the shade-friendly spread of a fine old oak tree. It was next to the swine barn and Junior Livestock Auction Hall on these state fairgrounds. The flyer had advertised crafts and commercial exhibits and farm-style amusements, but there were no tractor pulls, powdered sheep, 4H-ers, or jam makers in sight.

Circling up in lawn chairs, a convivial port in a heat wave, for three scorching days, we—those positioned in a certain camp next to the pig barn—were hard to extract. A committed cadre we were: Becky, Kathy, Harris, Jane, Vic, RC, Hal, Sach, the Captain. People changed chairs and the drugs changed people and we all changed drugs. It wasn't safe to just be yourself, melding into the milieu was the chameleon's mask we all put on ("...*coram populo*, our souls are not our own"). Sharing a ten strip of blotter counted for something in our group affairs and affects.

We did sporadically decamp and sally forth to catch a glimpse of steam-driven performances by the Ozark Mountain Daredevils, the Eagles, Jefferson Starship, Lynyrd Skynyrd, and Bachman-Turner

Overdrive, the official headliner. On each such outing, we were sure to be all but mugged in the gauntlet-like tunnel beneath the NASCAR dirt track, the only route into the concert. Tattooed, ear-ringed, faded-leather-vests-and-tattered-denim-clad bikers acted as strongmen for the even scruffier, hophead mood merchants, who guerilla marketed their products by displaying signs slung around their necks, painted on their naked bodies, or inscribed on their hats. Customers stood three or four-deep with round-the-clock lines. Hallucinogens, Quaaludes, and animal tranqs were the hotcakes. Hal, god love his bona fide bonkers ass, kept returning to the tunnel and the painted face clown for PCP, which he was shooting in the back of the van. In less than twenty-four hours, both his forearms looked like a hot red millipede had wriggled down to his wrists and rooted. Out of fear for his survival, the Captain handcuffed him to the pop-up trailer.

On day two, full of when-in-Rome audacity, RC and I doubled down on the blotter and black tar opium. Next thing I knew, the Captain and I were wheeling RC through the crowd passed out cold in a grocery cart. No one seemed to care. He was a human dishrag with a satisfied smile on his face and no more self-awareness than a dog licking his own ass in public. We were in search of ice, which was being sold for a tidy sum. Water sources had dried up. Dehydration was rampant. It was hotter than blue blazes, triple digits by early afternoon. We were one real fight song short, and as timely as could be, the Ozark Mountain Daredevils, playing like demons, delivered their hillbilly-inspired standard for those in need of (spiritual) slaking:

> *...if you want a drink of water*
> *you got to get it from the well*
> *if you want to get to...heaven*
> *you got to raise a little hell...*

We heeded all that. Still and all, the bad acid was poisoning many in this arena of bad choices. Stretchers of epileptic-like bodies, with twisted mugs and eyes that jiggled and jerked and rolled white as petit moons into darkness, didn't deter many. People were overdosing by the hundreds, with at least one death. Sedalia's Bothwell Hospital had maxed out. Patients—dehydrated, drugged, and sounding death's rattle—were being transferred seventy miles away to the medical center in Columbia.

Concert promotor Bob Shaw, the *Kansas City Star* reported, had a heart attack and on day two left town. Rumor had it that the local police were ready to call in the National Guard but thought better of it when they were reminded of Kent State. The Guard did, however, send down an armored personnel carrier from Kansas City. The *Kansas City Star* also reported that Jim Mathewson, a Sedalia resident and one-time state senator, took a ride with the county sheriff around the concert grounds. It didn't last long. Drug-addled merrymakers accosted them, all but dancing something akin to the teaberry shuffle on the hood of the patrol car. Mathewson, the article said, rushed home and had his wife and kids evacuate while he loaded all his guns. He then set up a concerned citizens hotline.

The music played on. Helicopters whooped overhead ferrying in the bands. When the Eagles dedicated "Already Gone" to Richard Nixon's imminent resignation they could have just as easily been alluding to the psychotropic flight most attendees had lifted off on.

On night two, in the dim grayish light, the normal hour of the crickets and frogs, the Captain and I surveyed the levitating ranks of the concert infield. Joe Walsh was ripping it apart on stage and the mosh pit of hairy domes was pogo-ing up and down, roaring in ecstasy. Panning away, as far as my blurry eyes could accurately focus, an outdoor orgy of revelers balled up and fornicated like farm animals in an opaque pasture of plenty. The Captain pointed thereabouts and drawled out in slow disbelief that out there a "man could get more pussy than a toilet seat." Steam rose from hot mother earth, a witches' brew of humanity, a free sex zone, the herd mind grinding away.

Beyond the free sex zone, the scrappy bivouac of the biker gangs—the Fourth Reich, Diablos, Scorpions—had laid claim to the northwest corner of the fairgrounds, a makeshift tollgate ringed by chopped hogs and clots of raw-assed renegades and their raunchy-acting old ladies (or perhaps "mamas"), demanding money, food, drugs, and whatever else for passage. But they had no monopoly on alienation or anarchic, criminal crudity, just a finer shade of defiance.

On Sunday morning, acting more like the Red Cross than Kent State aggressors, the National Guard did indeed show up and distributed bottled water and medical supplies and rousted catatonic bodies to consciousness. They were on to something, making sure those narcotized folks were alive. Hal caught their interest. He had collapsed athwart the camp circle. One of the boys in starched fatigues and polished boots appeared to notice Hal's hard-on peeking out from his jean cutoffs. Mouth agape, drawing flies, his face a mask of leaden gray, the pitch of his snore never changed while the boys-in-boots inspected. Blood was flowing, they must have concluded. After a snickering start, they moved on, leaving the priapic jackal be.

Sleep had been sparse for all of us. When it did intrude, it was usually drug induced. And, that predictably turned an animated circle of fools into a grab bag of uncovered bodies planted like twisted gourds on the bare ground or propped in lawn chairs like window dummies.

In the commonsense lull of morning at Sedalia, the pig barn was the only place to scrub off. The faucets were set low in the livestock washing stations so we had to sit on refuse-sated earth or the foul metal grating to capture a decent flow of water. The long lines of people talking to themselves almost made it too fussy a proposition.

Last afternoon of the festival, next to the pig barn, RC and I babbled to a buck-naked couple from California. It was as if our shirtless nonchalance and their full nudity was a natural happening on Sunday morning in this Bible Belt town. My eyes were—without much voluntary muscle restraint—raking up and down and all over the long-legged, copper-skinned body of the California maiden. Zombified, I hardly spoke while contemplating her sonnet-worthy, kind of beatific religious form, the uncropped Promised Land, her left golden globe, on which the word "Faith" was tatted, the piercing blue eyes, the sly smile, the full Venus package.

Thirty minutes on in that spell, a posse of archetypal Southern sheriffs arrived on horseback screaming down at us to "get the fuck out of here and don't come back." Buzzkill sons of bitches, I thought, not paying a lick of attention to them. Neither did the mesmerist, her main squeeze, or RC—who was talking to beat the band. The cops circled back, roaring louder, the raw hatred of a lynch mob flashing from their eyes. The heavy tanks and dive bombers were next. We snapped to, not unmindful of our contraband. The Californians, our newest best friends, threw on their Tarzan and Jane set of rags and scrambled for their vintage VW microbus. A blur of Wes Wilson psychedelia flashed by as they crashed through the gears, getting out of Dodge.

The cops had regained control. The whole place was in motion. You could see, feel, and hear the sucking sensation of sun-and-drug-fried flesh fleeing for fear of reprisal (and for some extended wound licking). Church bells chimed. It was a Sunday afternoon coming-down for the Woodstock Generation's last blowout in backwater Missouri. Several days would pass before my ears would quit ringing with Lynyrd Skynyrd's anthem, "Freebird":

> *If I leave here tomorrow*
> *Would you still remember me?*
> *For I must be travelin' on now*
> *There's too many places I got to see*
> *…And this bird you cannot change*

◉ ⊕ ⊕

Early one Saturday afternoon, jazzbo, blues man, rockabilly and country star Charlie Rich was playing Miles Davis's *Kind of Blue* on the cassette player of his butter yellow 450SL Mercedes. He was blowing it out down the delta back roads of eastern Arkansas, chain smoking Salems, and tapping out Miles's riffs on the steering wheel—ten and two, Harlem style, rhythm on the left, improv on the right. In the mood as well, I slumped back comfortably in the tan leather shotgun seat, holding in my lap a sack of sliced pork sandwiches from Craig's Bar-B-Q of DeValls Bluff, sipping Old Charter from a water cup with one hand, and burning a Winston with the other. Charlie wasn't one to talk your head off, but he was good company. He bullheadedly kept his deeper thoughts locked inside, if not in the private diary he kept in the old farmhouse in Colt. Raised among black sharecroppers, he picked up on their songs of freedom, the blues and spirituals they sang every day in the fields. When he was not in the studio or on stage performing, listening to Miles and goosing it down the pancake flat, familiar back roads of eastern Arkansas settled his soul, as only an ass-pocket of whiskey and a landscape muse can do.

Since his days with Sam Phillips and Sun Records, Charlie had frequented Craig's, which served a mash-up of poor blacks and whites, duck hunters, and wayfaring strangers traveling U.S. Route 70. Most customers, including the two of us, ordered Craig's sauced and sliced pork barbecue on a bun piled high with coleslaw mixed with chopped apples, every bite a panoply of flavors. The African American owner, Lawrence Craig, had played Charlie's music on the jukebox before he hit the big time. Indeed, as we stood in line to order, Charlie stepped over to the vintage Select-O-Matic, situated in the formerly black-only side of the shotgun shack, popped a quarter in, and punched his 1960 Billboard Hot 100 hit, "Lonely Weekends," followed by Al Green's chart-topper, "Let's Stay

Together." Thirty minutes later, we were at my home in Little Rock, smelling like bourbon and barbecue, trading tidbits about the Arkansas Razorbacks, awaiting the kickoff of Frank Broyles's Hogs against the Aggies of Texas A&M.

A year before, at the Rink dance bar in Fayetteville, Arkansas, on a warm summer night in July, RC and I were listening to Zorro and the Blue Footballs. A perfect stranger sitting at the table next to us asked me to dance, and so we did, twirling and whirling and shaking a leg till the wee hours. Turned out her name was Renee Rich, the oldest child of the Silver Fox, Charlie Rich. She was raised in a town not far from my Piney Woods roots. One thing led to another and we began an on-the-road, backpacker's romance: Key West, New York, Amsterdam, Paris, Munich (Dachau), Istanbul, Kurdistan, the Cradle of Civilization.

On March 15, 1975, we married at a sunrise ceremony in Memphis, Tennessee, at 196 West Cherry Street, known as Foxwood, home to Charlie and Margaret Ann Rich. The theme conceived by Margaret Ann, a songwriter in her own right, was Hemingway's eyebrow-raising novel *The Sun Also Rises*, which, ironically, was more about wandering souls and sexual freedom than traditional marriage, love, and fidelity. Sunny yellow designer wedding invitations embossed with a half-orb rising in the middle symbolized the commencement of a new cycle of life.

That day at 196 West Cherry Street when Charlie played "Behind Closed Doors" and "The Most Beautiful Girl," I had one foot firmly planted in Memphis, marriage, college, and a kid in the hopper, and the other splashing sunshine on the walls of a newspaper office in Red Lodge, Montana. Life in the Rockies and the vertical world of mountain goats and bighorn sheep went on, oblivious to my whereabouts. I was no longer a stranger to the winds. Women would come and go, but The Road would never end.

Epilogue

"EVERYONE GOES HOME in October," wrote Jack Kerouac, author of *On the Road*. "I always thought October was a kind old love-light."

Two score and eight years after my coming of age story ends, it's fall in Arkansas and I've been walking the Buffalo River trails, feeling profound gratitude to the Ozark Society for spearheading the fight to stop the dam builders from destroying this riverine paradise. On this foggy morning in October Jack's 'kind old love-light' shines like the dickens in a medley of colors, contours and sounds. Near Ponca's low water bridge a bull elk bugles exquisitely out of the white mists; the purling beat of the milky-jade river echoes in the background. Further on hiking the Steele Creek trail, the mist lifts and turns to dewy hues of honey yellow, fiery red, and vibrant orange, chipmunks chirp and bound among the moss-covered boulders, white tail deer jump from a bed of hickory leaves, passerines deliver a chorus of cheeps and alarm calls, and geese fly low along the mineral-streaked bluffs of the Buffalo, honking and quacking up a storm. Whether delighting in a ramble in the woods or stoking the peregrine spirit abroad, the more I take in the more alive and inspired I feel. Exploring. Experiencing. Marveling. Freedom.

My road-trip-of-life has been an abiding rebellion against status quo and the past (not history), playing catchup for the lost years of juvenile dementia, possessed with a voraciousness to be a globe-circling Phileas Fogg (without the valet or a clock). It's only when the departure whistle sounds and I'm in motion—a splendid sunrise summit of Mt. Kinabalu, or turning up at a midnight Candomble (Voodoo) ceremony, or standing in awe at the Saturn-like aspect of Aya Sofia's massive dome—that I am comfortable in my own skin, hitting on all cylinders, awash in the beauty and spirit of things.

Reinvention may be the most underused and underrated tool in the human stockpile. I've never put a number to my various incarnations, or the experiences on top of experiences that have opened doors to new perspectives, but they are many and multiplying. I've long admired Jack London, a rags-to-riches Zelig and true American spirit, who had the courage to take risks, to wander the world, to blaze new trails, and to embrace fresh beginnings. London, the product of a broken home and an unrepentant rulebreaker, made the most of his short forty years—as an oyster pirate, sailor, tramp, jailbird, Klondike gold digger, boxer, and rancher—and memorialized it in his novels, poems, war correspondence, and photographs. Absent John Barleycorn's intercession, he surely had more tracks to lay down.

London's brief but full-blown life makes me think it's a boring fool who lives in and mythologizes the past, and a royal buffoon who professes to have a clue about the vagaries and vicissitudes of the future. Morphing and migrating through time makes perfect sense—tadpoles become frogs, caterpillars turn into beautiful butterflies, boys and girls grow up, reinvent, evolve, and find their reason for being. There's no grand formula, whatever it is that sticks and grows, more like catch-as-catch-can, ups and downs, each to his own.

After finishing top of my class at the University of Arkansas at Little Rock in accounting, Ernst and Ernst (E&E), a "Big Eight" international accounting firm, recruited me. The job required shucking my tie-dyes and bell bottoms for two Stein Mart polyester suits, powder blue and beige, with reversible vests, solid on one side and checkered on the other, and extra pants to match the reversible vests. Do the math: According to the fundamental counting principle, those wild-and-crazy-guy suits provided eight work days of dress code compliance. Boy oh boy, had I leapt across a cultural abyss to a corporate world of geeks who thought it chic to holster their hand-held calculators to their belts, loaded for bear, come what may. Even more challenging was the love affair many of my colleagues had with big wig clients and all the swells that flocked like moths to the glow. It was the all-day regimen of Tab sodas, Winston Lights and the nuts-and-bolts audit and tax work and systems analyses that I found gratifying, telling stories with spreadsheets, with numbers and bits and bytes.

I couldn't help but laugh out loud at the irony of being one of the first CPAs in my orbit to get a personal computer and use Lotus 123. All because I could type. I'd taken typing for three years, beginning in junior high, because there was no homework to interfere with my after-school delinquency! Although I didn't have enough credits to finish the tenth grade, I could smoke the keyboard at more than eighty words a minute, 70 characters per line, ding, ding, tapping it out, "Now is the time for all good men to come to the aid of their country." The army rewarded my skills by bumping me up into the finance corps, eventually giving me accounting expertise, and making obtaining an accounting degree and passing the CPA exam a slam dunk. Many of my CPA colleagues were cyberphobes because they were mostly greasy grinds who passed on taking what was then considered a secretary's course with all the girls. My corner-cutting scheme that paid off.

During those years of my finishing college and working for E&E, Renee worked as a pediatric nurse (LPN) at Doctor's Hospital in Little Rock and gave birth to our two children, Maggie and Wes. For four busy years, we hunkered down to child rearing, slaphappy in love with our two miracles, sharing grocery shopping, cooking, feeding, washing clothes, changing diapers, and shuttling the rug rats to and from daycare, while feeling both the strain and joy of being two working parents.

A few years on, Grant Thornton (née Alexander Grant) offered me a supervisory audit and tax position in Memphis. I took it and we moved to Forrest City, Arkansas, an 80-mile, round-trip commute to my office in the NBC Bank building overlooking the Big Muddy. Renee was born in Forrest City, and her grandmother, Helen Rich (Nanny), with whom she was close, lived in a newish house on Chestnut Street off of North Washington. Aunt Stella and Uncle Raleigh Rich lived around the corner from Nanny, while Aunt Libby and Uncle John Armstrong had moved into the old Rich farmhouse at Colt a few miles north out Washington. After making the Sunday dinners and birthday celebrations with all the relatives and partying late on weekends at the former-commissary-cum-recording studio on the Twist plantation with friends, the reality of living in Forrest City, named for the founder of the Ku Klux Klan, started to settle in. Homebound with two young kids in conservative small-town Arkansas wasn't the nostalgic paradise Renee had imagined. She turned restless and adamant about not going back to pediatric nursing.

It wasn't like we didn't have options. Charlie had recently thrown out an offer for her to sing backup with him on an upcoming U.S.-European tour. It turned out to be a no-brainer, a cool gig for her, and a family affair: her brother Allan and sister Laurie were also in the band. She was a natural-born Darlene Love, twenty feet from stardom. I never knew.

We were pulling in some good dough and it felt only fair for at least one of us to be going abroad again. Given the extended absences, however, we grew apart, ships passing in the night. It wasn't uncommon for me to be on the road serving clients across Tennessee and Arkansas for monthlong stretches; home late Friday night and off again before daylight on Monday. A little hanky-panky on the side was not unusual. After a year with both of us on the road, one Sunday evening, with no warning, Renee didn't come home from a long weekend away, up to no good. There I was on Monday morning stuck in Forrest City, with two young ones needing attention, a power job in Memphis, the new Darlene Love gone AWOL, and no daycare options. Holy Fucking Jesus. Déjà vu all over again.

The kids were bereft, especially Wes, who was still in diapers. Charlie and Margaret Ann were none too thrilled either. Like me, they didn't see a little hanky-panky as a deal breaker. It was all-hands-on deck, rallying for a reset to work this crazy shit out. But Renee wasn't budging. It was as if she were under some decoder ring spell and her best option was to fly off in the opposite direction. I came to realize she wasn't just shucking me and the kids, she was lifting a page out of my former playbook and jilting responsibility. Period. For life.

Channeling Dad a decade and a half before, I faced the music and grabbed the bull by the horns. We sold the house. I gave up my only source of income in the world with Grant Thornton. Two friends drove a borrowed laundry truck from Fort Smith to Forrest City, and we loaded up my share of the furniture. Two days later, I packed up the Pinto wagon and moved with the kids to Fort Smith, where Dad and brothers John and Greg lived and could be of help.

In a matter of two weeks, five years of marriage was kaput and I was living jobless and homeless on my brother John's secondhand hide-a-bed sofa in his garage apartment with two toddlers. That cozy rollaway was a far cry from the glory of my fifteen minutes of fame: hailed by local newspapers as Country Music Royalty on my wedding day, appearing in *Photoplay Magazine*, father of the *Most Beautiful Girl* (Maggie), and on TV with *Good Morning America* as the father-with-a-golden-rod of the Silver Fox's first grandson, Wes. As the pixie dust wore off and the shit sandwich set in, every night when I passed out on that old rollaway I thanked my lucky stars that I was the one cuddled up with, feeling the warmth and love of our two precious miracles. Freedom's just another word for nothing left to lose…goes the "Me and Bobby McGee" song lyric.

Renee, Judge Warren Kimbrough, and I signed the divorce agreement, giving me sole custody of the children, in the same courtroom where my parents divorced. Golden Rod was on his own. My commitment to raising Maggie and Wes was rock solid. I never shook the dream, however, of returning to the wanderer's life, the adult version of running buck wild as a kid before the cuffs of classroom authority waylaid me. Being engulfed by the unknown in the far reaches of the planet would be my North Star for the next sixteen years.

Where there are risks there are rewards. Business is a powerful trump. A few years before, while taking a lunch break from a month-long audit assignment with Arkansas Best Freight, I had run into Jim Hanna at the Broadway Grill in Fort Smith. We had a nice chat, and as we were saying goodbye, he'd asked if I'd be interested in moving to Fort Smith and working as his CFO at Hanna Oil and Gas Company. Jim, my former probation officer, I had not laid eyes on him since that night he got in a shoving match with the bouncer at the Electric Flag and Greg and I were blitzed on LSD. I'd never thought mixing friends and business was a good idea and told Jim so. He assured me I would be working with him, not for him. That conversation continued for another four years until I split with Renee, moved to Fort Smith, and saw it his way.

With divorce having left me busted, facing a Himalaya of bills, including student loans and a hundred dollars a week for daycare and preschool, my outlook on money turned from a youthful abstraction to one of parental utilitarianism. Recognizing that Jim had a thriving natural gas exploration and production company, I agreed to become its first CFO. From day one he was as good as his word. He treated me with an unstinting generosity of spirit, like family, as a best friend, and I felt the same for him. It is a rare thing. At some point Jim and I were in each other's presence so often—at work, breakfast, lunch, happy hour, conferences across the country—we could all but finish each other's sentences.

Life was not without its challenges and bad choices on my part: a fondness for Peruvian marching powder comes to mind first. Still, the children grew up comfortably in a neighborhood of agemates (many of whom became lifelong friends). We backpacked, canoed, and slept rough on spring and fall weekends in the Ozark and Ouachita mountains and in winter they snow skied in Colorado and New Mexico. They joined me in running 10ks and on stretches of two of my three marathons. While coming of age, they got their travel mojo working and darted off to six continents, attended Outward Bound and graduated from the colleges of their choice. Although it wasn't Dr. Spock's script (way too unconventional and colorful), on Mother's Day they choose to call me the "Best Mom".

In the spring of '77, brother John who taught economics at the best liberal arts school in Arkansas, suffered a severe diabetic coma, no more scrawling out interest rate and money supply formulas on college blackboards. In fact, he could no longer write a legible sentence and had to take a remedial English course to re-learn basic grammar. He spent his last three years on dialysis, living by himself in the garage apartment, refusing to be someone's dependent in the face of his inevitable deterioration. One Sunday evening after stopping by my house that day, he went into another diabetic coma. Dad and I found him the next morning after he didn't show up for dialysis. He was thirty-four years old. We stood over his lifeless body sprawled on the shag carpet as two carloads of policemen pulled syringes out of drawers and insulin bottles from the refrigerator, before they figured out he was a diabetic and not a junkie and allowed the Edwards brothers from the funeral home to take him away. His heroic struggles from early childhood as a diabetic were over.

Dad, also known as Grandpa John, never rebounded from the divorce, and doubled down on his booze intake after John died. In his later years, we enjoyed many father-and-son country drives to

Alpine, small-mouth fishing the lower Caddo River, chatting it up and nipping on some Charter 10 along the way in a Cheech and Chong smoke-filled car. We had a kind of catechistic routine with me recasting the same questions about the inflection points of his early years and him filling in the blanks with old stories that sometimes took on new twists; e.g., he did actually bed down the Atkins girl in the hay shed. Dad lived to be a month shy of seventy-four years old with his Homeric drinking routine and, on December 10, 1993, after spitting projectiles of blood across his hospital room for two days, he died of cirrhosis of the liver. Flawed as he was, my earliest understanding of the moral and ethical goodness of humans had come from Dad's big-hearted soul. As he wished, with full military honors, Major John Morgan Karber took his place in the fallen soldier formation of white marble headstones in the national cemetery. Ave atque vale!

Less than two years later, Charlie Rich, or Papa, died at age sixty-two of a blood clot in his right lung in Hammond, Louisiana. He and Margaret Ann were on their way to see Allan Rich and his band open for Freddie Fender. Charlie and I had remained friends after the divorce. There was no reason not to be. He loved his grandchildren, and was heartened that Renee had eventually picked up her game by spending more time with the kids, deepening their bond. Over the years, I had enjoyed many a long night of Charlie playing jazz and blues in his studio and shared a few escapades out and about in Memphis.

The funeral at Memorial Park in Memphis was a small affair, family and a few friends: Sam and Knox Phillips of Sun Records; LeAnn White and her singer/songwriter husband Tony Joe; and Prince Mongo, a perennial Memphis mayoral candidate, who wore a faux crown and was always barefooted, avowing it connected him to the earth's energy.

Tony Joe, Knox, Mongo, and I served as pallbearers. Tony Joe said a few kind yet drearily familiar words before we ritually tossed handfuls of dirt atop the lowered casket. All low key, no fanfare, the anti-Icarus, Charlie's soul now resting somewhere near the Arkansas Delta and Beale Street.

"Money is numbers, and numbers never end," said reggae legend Bob Marley, evoking the long-ago dilemma of a wealthy young prince named Siddhartha Gautama. "If it takes money to be happy, your search for happiness will never end."

After sixteen years working with Jim at Hanna Oil and Gas, I married a kindred spirit and sweetheart, Joellen Lambiotte, who was head of Planned Parenthood for Africa. She had pushed back against the worn path for women of the day in favor of grass roots nonprofit work in family planning and reproductive health. I'd known her from crayons to perfume, as Lulu would say. At age forty-four, I moved to Nairobi, Kenya, bidding farewell to the bondage of the eight-to-five, work-a-day world forever. The kids were off to college and I had a chunk of change burning a hole in my pocket. Hanna had made that happen. Randomness, an abundance of luck, coincidence, and improvisation are more than just words in my life, they are the coin of the realm, the invisible hand, the higher power, the road not taken that I more often than not chose.

One of the hardest conversations I ever had was to tell Jim Hanna I was packing it in. As the years piled up, he watched me take off a few weeks over Christmas or for a month in the summer: climbing and whacking my way in hot pursuit of an eastern lowland gorilla family, up the jungle slopes of the Congo's Kahuzi-Biega National Park; train riding on the Trans-Mongolian and Trans-Siberian railways across ten time zones from Beijing to Amsterdam; sailing in a century-old river boat from Leticia, Colombia, up the Amazon floodplains to the Iquitos jungle region; donning all whites in Pamplona, neck cinched with a red handkerchief and running and shouting "Ole" and "San Fermin" with six 1,200-pound bulls breathing down my ass; summiting Lowe's peak in Borneo and tracking orangutans in Sabah and Sarawak provinces; pitching a pup tent on the Mara River in Kenya as the wildebeest migration made its annual crossing of the crocodile-infested waters; boarding the *Akademik Ioffe*, a Soviet polar research ship, in Ushuaia, Argentina, and, escorted by a squad of wandering albatrosses, the world's largest bird, transiting the rough seas of the Drake Passage to the wildlife rich (penguin, seals, whales) white continent of Antarctica; trekking in the Simien Mountains of Ethiopia among the rare walia ibex and the gregarious gelada monkeys; and four-wheeling up the Niger River in Mali from Bamako to the mythical ancient city of gold, Timbuktu. "Traveling," as the peerless wanderer Ibn Battuta said, "makes you speechless, then turns you into a storyteller."

Hanna knew that someday the kids would grow up and I would leave and not return. I scratched out diaries of my travels, read avidly about my destinations, and was in high demand to give slideshows for classrooms and social gatherings. Recounting travel stories and deconstructing stereotypes often took on the feel of a higher calling to bring a corner or two of the World to life and ease folks away from their comfort zones and personal pieties, like loosening earth around a lodged rock.

As time went by, Hanna would say to me, "Karber, you don't look, dress, talk, or act like any CFO I've ever met." He meant it as a compliment. I was successfully deprogramming my ephemeral identity as a business type while leaning into a full reinvention as a global soul. When I told Hanna of my plans to resign one Monday morning before things got humming at the office, he fell back in his chair half-shocked and in silence. He then rose up, rested his elbows on the desk, looked me dead in the eye, and said, "I get the marriage, but Africa!!!

Shortly after arriving in Kenya, I started a three-month course in Swahili at the Peace Corps training center. In a life of travel, it was the only time I attempted to become a proficient speaker in a foreign language. I must say Swahili spoken like a six-year-old in a piney woods twang down the roads of East Africa drew some laughs and more than a few good-hearted imitators. Those fast-talking, multilingual locals never suspected me of being a born-and-bred white Kenyan, but they understood me.

Before long I was traveling with Joellen to her project sites: Khartoum, Sudan, working with obstetricians/gynecologists to reduce female genital mutilation; Dire Dawa, Ethiopia, facilitating the distribution of condoms to Somalis; and Kisumu, Kenya, on Lake Victoria, partnering with private physicians to incorporate contraceptive services into their practices. Getting in the groove, I started using her work destinations as jumping off points for my travels, chronicling them in long emails to friends, often peppered with Swahili words and sayings. It swarmed from there. Soon, I was galivanting all over Africa and beyond to the world's far reaches and had developed a loyal following of readers.

By then, Joellen and several old pals put the bug in my ear to turn the travel stories into a book. I think I was looking for a shove, and it worked. The farther I ventured, the more I wrote, my timidity about identifying myself as a travel writer melted away. Buoyed with newfound confidence, as impecunious as professionalizing a passion like travel can be, I became the person I always should have been and never looked back.

Home in a sense had become the road, living somewhere between escape and quest, my daily bread as a cultural carnivore being movement. When asked about my favorite country, which often happens, I respond: "The places I've never seen. Picking a favorite country is like choosing your best-loved child. (Okay, Bhutan blew my mind!) Each country (and region) is a unique encounter, right down to the stews and soups endemic to all cultures.

J. R. R. Tolkien was on to something when he wrote "not all those who wander are lost." Being restless and manic, which I confess to, are only faults when not accompanied by some form of discipline.

Funneled properly, it is a means to an end, passkeys to a Valhalla of discovery and experiential eye-openers.

While living in Hanoi, Vietnam's French Quarter for five years, a festering case of pent-up itchy feet took me to the wild blue yonder so often I needed two passports to keep up with visa requirements. As I would return for a pit stop from a month-long trip, a DHL package with a freshly stamped passport from a visa service in Bangkok or Washington, DC, would await me at my Hanoi residence. I'd then stick my just-used passport and new visa applications in a DHL package for yet another journey. Repeat that process over and over. Made Forrest Gump proud, gulping up life with a big spoon.

During that time, one passport had 125 extra pages and the other had fifty. It wasn't, however, passport stamps I was chasing: I felt an existential urgency to go see, to smell deeply, to leave no stone unturned—down rivers, up mountains, across continents and oceans. As my mind coughed up new ports of call, and the oracle of mother nature beckoned, a Damoclean sword hung darkly in the air. The planet convulsed before my eyes, more people, less wildlife, higher temperatures, melting sea ice, and unchecked habitat destruction.

From late 2001 through the fall of 2002, I traveled on occasion with Joellen and friends, but more often on my own: boating and tracing the Mekong River, from the Tibetan Plateau to Ho Chi Minh City and the South China Sea; camping in Namibia, tracking desert rhino and elephant, and discovering six thousand-year-old cave art in the Brandberg Mountains; riding the rails from Hanoi, across China to Kashgar and the Pakistan border; driving and busing from Havana to Santiago and back in Castro's Cuba; scuba diving in the plankton-rich Galapagos with Darwin's penguins, interminable schools of barracuda and big-eye jacks, and sea lions playfully nuzzling my mask; visiting North Korea twice, once on a Hyundai-owned boat with reunification-minded South Koreans and the second time on a black market visa with the first group of American tourists to enter the Hermit Kingdom in half a century; motorcycling on Russian Minsk bikes along the Chinese border, traversing the trails and dirt roads of the exotic hilltribe mountainous regions of Northern Vietnam; float-planing into the McNeil River in Alaska and viewing the largest congregation of brown bears in the world (forty-eight in one day); and training across Canada, from Vancouver to Halifax with a weeklong detour to Churchill, Manitoba, on the southern shores of Hudson Bay to see the largest gathering of polar bears in the world (eighty-two in one day). Strapping on seven league boots, however, doesn't fully describe my restlessness.

Travel is also about connection. If possible, I would make company with every creature on earth, including humans and all the grit and gratifications of their lives. Pulitzer Prize winner Forrest Gander's poem-essay *Core Samples from the World* speaks to a traveler's will to surrender, to be displaced and to encounter: "I was looking for bonds. I wanted to break a mirror. I wanted to render myself accessible, available. I wanted to borrow eyes from another language. I was looking for the words to come."

Stepping out of one's comfort zone and increasing the personal threat level by crossing a lawless border into a gauntlet of hungry hustlers and bribe-thirsty boys with AKs, or bedding down with relief agencies in conflict zones (Afghanistan and Iraq), gives rise to sharper senses, unmediated awareness, and more attention paid to cultural cues. There is strength in surrender and humility and when all works out it's as if your parachute has popped open for another safe landing. Traveling at the mercy of others is not so much about masculine derring-do as connecting for a brief moment in time with the benighted who because of birth happen to be living in challenging circumstances. Accepting that your life is in someone else's hands and trusting the golden thread of humanity enough to make yourself encounterable and come out the other end knowing more about the vulnerable and voiceless and yourself—is a pilgrim's bargain of the heart.

Some of the most somber roads I have traveled have been to old battlefields and genocide memorials. Bearing witness, making a connection, listening to horrific stories about the gas chambers, crematoriums, and killing fields of the Holocaust and Tuol Sleng Genocide Museum (S-21) in Phnom Penh, a former secondary school where photos and clothes of those tortured to death by the Khmer Rouge, led by Pol Pot, are displayed. The Gettysburg National Military Park testifies to the bloodiest battle of the Civil War; in three days, 51,000 from both armies killed, wounded, captured or missing. The list goes on, Rwanda, My Lai, Hiroshima, Ukraine…, but each time I connect with such historical force fields I find myself reflecting on what an American psychologist concluded at Nuremberg after interviewing dozens of garden-variety Nazis about their beliefs and motivations: to a person the common thread was that they lacked Empathy! The opposite of empathy is demonizing and dehumanizing, a necessary tool in war, genocide, and often in everyday politics.

Expatriate communities on foreign soil are generally small, accessible pools of people who cover the waterfront occupationally. While living in Asia and Africa, Joellen and I were blessed to sit at the table and enjoy friendships with many trial-by-fire, world-shaking artists, writers, CEOs, aid workers, idealists, doers, and donors including the inimitable women's activist Susie Buffett. On three occasions we were in the presence of the extraordinarily charismatic Nelson Mandela. It's awe-inspiring and enriching to find yourself present and in sync with those doing the grunt work as well as leading the frontal assault to reshape the world.

After more than three decades of steering clear of all things military, life deposited me in Hanoi with a small squad of vets set on making their peace with a long-ago war. It couldn't have been a more serendipitous moment there in the bosom of the former beast; the past, present, and future all seemed to be happening at once. Suel

Jones (Marine), Chuck Searcy (Army), John Lancaster (Marine), David Holdridge (Army), Eric Herter (Army), I and many others fussed around about the merits of putting together a VFW in Hanoi, but after several meetings and blowups with the Kansas City brass, thought better of it and formed instead the Veterans for Peace Chapter 160, named Hoa Binh, meaning Peace. This community of vets were not only spade-shovelers for world peace, they were down-in-the-dirt activists, courageous to the core, capable of moving ships over mountains, shaking it up with governments and advocating creative solutions to lift up the underdogs.

Suel Jones—who'd been shot in the back in '69 near Dong Ha, medivaced to Okinawa, and redeployed in combat within a month—devoted most of his energy to raising money for the Friendship Village, which houses Vietnamese veterans and children with disabilities. Chuck Searcy, who worked in military intelligence in Saigon, dedicates all of his time to the removal of unexploded ordnance and to educating children about the dangers of cluster bombs in Vietnam, Laos, and Cambodia. Eric Herter, who spent a year as a military advisor near Can Tho in the Mekong Delta, returned to Vietnam as an Associated Press video producer of news stories and documentaries on social and environmental topics. David Holdridge, who as a young infantry lieutenant was gut shot near Chu Lai, negotiated the first joint agreement between the U.S. and Vietnam Departments of Defense to remove unexploded ordnance. John Lancaster, who was critically wounded and paralyzed in an effort to rescue a wounded Marine on May 5, 1968, in the second wave of the Tet Offensive, took up the disability cause, became legal counsel for Paralyzed Veterans of America, was instrumental in getting the Americans with Disabilities Act of 1990 (ADA) passed, and was present in the Rose Garden when President George H. W. Bush signed it. In 1995, President Bill Clinton appointed him to be the executive director of the President's Committee on Employment of People with Disabilities. As Clinton left office, in the spirit of reconciliation and friendship, John returned to Vietnam on a Department of Labor contract to advocate for the passage of a similar law to the ADA in Vietnam. Which he did, changing the lives of up to ten million people with disabilities.

After a decade of expatriate life, one of the toughest decisions Joellen and I ever had to make was to move back to the States. The pressure was building from Joellen's aging parents, the kids and our first grandchild to repatriate. It was May 2005 and we had been living in Bangkok on the Chao Phraya River for two years next to the historical Oriental Hotel and across the water from Wat Arun. The debate turned serious when Joellen was offered a corporate-leadership position in international health in Cambridge, Massachusetts. We knew we'd be returning to an America much different from the one we'd left. Friends, family, politicians, and policies had been shuffled and reshuffled until so many of the familiar hole cards were either turned upside down, in reverse, or replaced by jokers. States were now divided among red and blue, foreign nations were either with us or against us, and leaning toward the latter. In the end, family won out. Joellen traveled ahead of me and began her new job while I stayed behind to finish a manuscript. As with many returning expatriates, an inner voice had been playing a familiar message: "You can't go home again."

A month later I trained into Port Kelang, Malaysia, and took a room at a hole in the wall hotel full of seafarers. Rather than flying, I'd chosen to hop a freighter, to measure every degree of longitude and latitude between Bangkok and Beantown. Perhaps out of caution, which is not always my first instinct when traveling or otherwise, I felt the need to acclimate, as one does when going to extreme altitudes. The next morning two Malaysian shipping clerks escorted me dockside to the *Hanjin Madrid*, a German freighter, which glistened with fresh paint, as if just out of dry dock. The seven decks of whitewashed superstructure, projecting up like a prairie grain silo, would be my home for the next 7,000 miles and 25 days. All around me gantry cranes whizzed by like daddy longlegs on steroids, whining, screeching, crashing. Greeted by Filipino able-bodied seamen, I groaned my way up the gangway, loaded down to my own Plimsoll marks with duffel bags full of books and clothes. It seemed the Pilgrims might have traveled to America with fewer personal belongings.

Late in the afternoon we sailed south toward the Malacca and Singapore Straits where fog horns blew in frantic bursts between the Raffles Lighthouse and Buffalo Rock, only five to eight miles wide, an area some have described as a pirate's toll way. Through this "global choke point" a thousand ships sail each week, carrying one-third of all seaborne trade and half the world's crude-oil shipments. I glanced out at the glittering sky-line of tropical, Victorian Singapore, a paragon of global commerce and arguably the safest, most law-abiding city on the planet, while at the same time, surveying the pirate-infested waters of Indonesia's impoverished Riau Archipelago.

Intense tropical light awakened me the next morning as we turned north into the South China Sea, tracing the contours of Vietnam's thousand-mile coast and, amid squalls and dense fog, on to the congested East Asian ports of Yantian, China, Hong Kong, Kaohsiung, Taiwan, and Pusan, South Korea. Loaded to 90 percent of the *Hanjin*'s 5,000-container capacity with cell phones, computers, semiconductors, the whole tech inventory, from Pusan we turned east, crossing between the Japanese islands of Hokkaido and Honshu, where Shinto shrines stood like beacons. It was all Pacific in front of us for the next eleven days.

Wednesday, June 28, was a special day because we got to celebrate it twice. Early one evening, as the chief mate played Strauss's *Waltzes*, we crossed the international dateline—180 degrees longitude, 49 degrees north latitude. All clocks were retarded by twenty-four hours (not making the mistake of Phileas Fogg). Tangential to

Alaska's Aleutian Islands, we were now sailing south, into the Western Hemisphere, east giving way to west. In this northern Pacific netherworld of thick fog and rain, the ocean, however, was unmarked by the curves and infidelities of date lines and time.

On the afternoon of July 5, we entered the Santa Barbara Channel—a postcard visage of California sunshine, shimmering blue waters, and rugged islands. The dun-colored Sierra Madre drew closer by the second. Froth curled around the bow, gulls gathered in our wake, pelicans streamed by, flocks of ducks lighted in the clear water of the Channel Island littorals; schooners and light craft tacked the cobalt sea and the foghorns of work boats wailed. I never thought returning to America could feel so right, its familiar beauty slapping me silly, fond memories flushing through me like a numbing truth serum, the warmth of its bosom welcoming me in.

Los Angeles was ringed in a rust-colored cloud, the city's linear shapes blurred in a sepia fade—inviting nonetheless. Once berthed at the Port of Long Beach, the custom agents arrived and within seconds my passport was stamped, bags inspected, and I was gleefully sprinting down the gangway. A fortysomething, blinged-out black dude with gold necklaces, bracelets, and earrings, who talked with my accent and said he was originally from New Orleans, gave me a golf cart ride to the gate. Once there, he dropped me beneath a lone streetlight to wait for a taxi and said, "Welcome home, man."

Arriving in Boston's North Station in a coach seat a month later, having crossed Thomas Wolfe's "…wild, bizarre, unpredictable, Hog-stomping, Baroque America" by car and train, coordinates measured, I had acclimated.

In the introduction to *Postmarks from a Political Traveler*, I wrote: "Spurred, in equal parts, by chasing dreams and chucking demons, travel, often undertaken as a political act, is now the closest thing to an identity to which I would admit." The sentence begs some revision and unpacking. First, I'd be remiss to not also garb myself in the cloth of a family man, proud-as-punch husband, father of two, father-in-law of two, and grandfather of four girls. As a family, we are fortunate to have and to know deeply the eternal value of affection. I believe as Albert Camus once wrote, "The older I get, the more I find that you can only live with those who free you, who love you with an affection that is as light to bear as it is strong to feel." The "chucking demons" allusion is more darkly complex, tinged with a host of divorces, untimely deaths of loved ones, and deeply flawed family members.

After Charlie checked out the Rich clan's behavior resembled a runaway train with no conductor in sight. They took a deep dive into all-day regimens of getting buzzed, baked, and pickled in a sprint to the graveyard. Between Christmas day of 2006 and December 22, 2012, Margaret Ann Rich and children Renee, Laurie, and Jack gave up the ghost. It wasn't just disturbing for Maggie and Wes to watch their mother and the Rich side of the family die off before their time, it was gut-wrenching to internalize that your own flesh and blood could so utterly forsake the joy of living.

My brother Greg, Maggie's and Wes's favorite uncle, trailed close by on the heels of the Rich family demise. He made several trips to see Joellen and me in Nairobi. Greg loved East Africa's game parks and colonial artifacts such as the Mount Kenya Safari Club and the Norfolk Hotel. And I still smile at the thought of an afternoon at Tanzania's Ngorongoro Crater when we ran into fellow Arkies Hillary Clinton, daughter Chelsea, and Brady Anderson, the American Ambassador to Tanzania. More than a little tipsy and loaded to the gills with chutzpah, Greg spent an hour trying to put the make on the First Lady of the United States, convinced she had the hots for him. It sent him over the edge a few weeks later when he received a signed photograph of our gathering at the Serena Lodge, saying, "Where will we meet next?"

The last night I spent yarning about world travels with Greg at his home in Fort Smith, eleven unopened bottles of Bombay Blue Sapphire lined his bar. Greg had become an unapologetic dipsomaniac. He was my Irish twin, and in a close heat with my oldest brother John as the cleverest and best educated of our tribe. The visage of a brain-soaked Greg cut me to the bone.

He left this mortal coil into the white light of peace on the Ides of March in his own bed and blood full of too much drink but only after writing the most elegantly humorous memoir, the free associative insights of a world-weary Southern lawyer. With a black dog breathing down his neck, his memoir was a big middle finger to the judicial system and federal judges he'd argued First Amendment cases before. No amount of money, or love of family, or friends, or his brilliant author/screenwriter son and namesake, or a double line of sporting girlfriends at the front door of his country club address could convince him that growing old and gray was a good idea. He travels with me wherever I go just as I nightly put on John's pale leather camping moccasins.

My mother kicked the bucket four months after Greg, following a long battle with Sjogren's syndrome, an immune system disorder. I, the dutiful son, grateful for the gift of life and for the nurturing that forged me as an avid reader and traveler, schlepped to Oklahoma City throughout her illness.

With all these family passings, before long, as the grief ebbed, trumpets sounded in my head. Demons and deceptions chucked, I felt liberated from the Garden of Good and Evil.

Time marches on. In late January of 2020, Joellen and I busted out of our second-story condo in Cambridge, Massachusetts, for warmer climes. We traveled in El Salvador for a week, chilling on the black (volcanic) sand beaches of El Zonte, a world-class surfing destination. We then caught a sail/dive boat for five days from

Panama around the San Blas Islands, an archipelago of over 350 islands and cays, and home to the indigenous Kuna people. Captain Goeran ran a tight ship, the *Quest*, without imposing too many pesky rules on us and our fellow passengers, all millennial backpackers.

They say you can't stay forever young, but you can be forever childlike. Hands down, my favorite rule the Captain rattled off was the first: put your sandals in a box in the hold and go barefoot until Cartagena. For five days, there was no more friction on the feet than dappled turquoise waters, gleaming white sand beaches, fins donned for snorkeling, or a toe stubbed staggering to the head in the middle of the night. On a couple of evenings, anchored beneath the coconut palms of some uninhabited islet, perfectly positioned between a rising moon and setting sun, Guna divers paddled up to deliver us fresh lobster. And like all modern-day pirates, our soundtrack was Jimmy Buffett and Bob Marley, accompanied by our spirit of choice: rum and Coke, rum and coconut (Cocoloco), rum out of the bottle, cheap rum, premium rum, more rum.

The open-sea sail from the San Blas to Cartagena wasn't for the faint hearted. After getting our step back, we wandered the cobblestones of Cartagena's walled Old Town, a UNESCO World Heritage Site and inspiration for the magical realism of Nobel laureate Gabriel García Márquez. A few days later, we made our way, mostly by bus, to Medellin and Bogota and then down the Magdalena River Valley to the pre-Inca archaeological site of San Augustin and the bird-rich Tatacoa Desert. From the ochre-tinted canyons of Tatacoa, it was onward across the Andes to Ecuador by overnight bus, a thrill-a-minute ride, often careening around hairpins as if a Formula One entrant at Monte Carlo. A week later, we left Quito and returned to Cambridge. It was mid-March 2020.

The world turned. The jig was up. Heck of a journey, but the Covid pandemic and shelter-in-place protocols were upon us. In short order, I canceled a June trip to Saudi Arabia and Turkmenistan.

Those early weeks back in Cambridge were hard to process as some kind of new normal. But as I read about the burials of people in Guayaquil, Ecuador, in cardboard boxes only two weeks after we flew out of Quito, I had a flashbulb moment and buckled down for the long haul. Abiding by the strictures of the quarantine, social isolation, and a firehose of news about infection and death rates defined our days and weeks. The new abnormal in our Covid hot zone included Zoom happy hours, binge-watching Netflix and Prime Video, booze and grocery deliveries, drive-by birthday parties, telemedicine, and jumping like cats when someone sneezed a block away. We felt our privilege and thanked our lucky stars as we watched the news from black, brown, and other less advantaged communities. As the Boston area racked up 4,000 new cases and 200 deaths a day, businesses shuttered, hospitals filled to capacity, highways emptied, second home prices soared, and vaccines were a pipe dream. Suddenly we were a world without plans or plane tickets, and for a rabid traveler, that was *terra incognita*. It would be a year before I was liberated by a second vaccine.

Our plan had been to sell our Cambridge triple-decker condo upon our return from Ecuador and move to Fayetteville, Arkansas, to be closer to the kids and four granddaughters, a 'house with a crowded table' redux. Problem was, there was zero chance our condo mates or anyone else would allow an open house, and we wouldn't have done it anyway. But after three months, *voila*, real estate agents adapted and came up with Zoom open houses.

On a Sunday morning in late May 2020, we hightailed it out of Cambridge before daylight, packed to the rooftop in our ten-year-old Hyundai, and wheeled across the Charles River and onto the Mass Turnpike. Proper goodbyes, dinners, and hugs and kisses would have to wait. We felt like cat burglars stealing our way out of town in the darkness, and carried with us sheets and pillows for motel stops somewhere out there in the mutant wasteland.

Across the U.S., all fifty states were reinventing the wheel as if we were not connected as humans. The communal, science-minded, data-driven approach to the pandemic that we experienced in Massachusetts was vastly different from the deeply familiar libertarian, every-man-for-himself culture to which we were moving. My family had settled in Independence County, Arkansas as yeoman farmers circa 1810 and Joellen's in Fort Smith as immigrant glass cutters a century later.

In the words of Ray Midge, the narrator of *The Dog of the South*, written by *True Grit* author Charles Portis, "A lot of people leave Arkansas and most of them come back sooner or later. They can't quite achieve escape velocity." I had been away twenty-five years and Joellen fifty-one. After wandering the world, I was returning to the only place on the planet where, upon hearing my piney woods/Caddo River accent, no one asks me where I'm from. My transmutation from born-and-bred native to outsider laying down a track record of fresh truths on foreign soil and then bringing it all back home is as close I'll ever get to time travel.

Mission accomplished. Two global souls return home, as T.S. Elliot wrote, arriving where we started and knowing it for the first time. It feels good to be on our ridgetop in Fayetteville, cocooned by photos, books, diaries, maps, art, and artifacts of a life of travel, checking out the migrating birds at the feeders outside my office, spending evenings kicked back on the front porch, watching the sun spin golden on its solstice-to-solstice journey, and plotting our next transit abroad. Movement, I'm certain, is in our nature. The journey is all.

Acknowledgments

HEMINGWAY ONCE SAID, "Writing at its best is a lonely life." If I'm not reading, taking notes, or pecking away at the keyboard every morning, the story will never see the light of day. But I'm fortunate to have my wife, Joellen Lambiotte, two rooms away to bounce things off of and to be my first line of editing for structure, content and proofreading. With her West Coast and Ivy League pedigrees, she makes me look better than I am.

I'm also blessed to have several literary friends who have pitched in untold hours to review and edit the manuscript. Chief among those is Mike Boulden, a retired tall building lawyer and my pal since primary school. Mike read the manuscript four times and gave me valuable feedback, often in long phone conversations over the course of a year. He helped shape the book as more travelogue than memoir. Billy D. Higgins, a retired history professor and old family friend, not only put the red ink of a professor on the proof pages, he advised me on several occasions about tone and content in various chapters. My son Wes read the book with feelings of pathos and glee, not knowing where or what was coming next. Thus, he suggested the title, *Vagabond Memoirs*.

Bad behavior on my part while zigzagging the country and beyond, is not an uncommon theme. I asked Randy Cutting, Dennis Bearden, and Tommy Horton, my accomplices on several escapades to read the proofs and point out anything that might embarrass them or their families. They were all okay with the material as written.

Two Arkansas-based writers provided helpful insights with their stories of road trips around the piney woods of my ancestors: Rex Nelson of the *Arkansas Democrat-Gazette*, and the late Charles Portis in his book, *Escape Velocity*. Ali Welky, of the *Butler Center for Arkansas Studies* and by coincidence the editor of *Escape Velocity*, put her editorial touch on *Vagabound*, enhancing its flow and making it immensely more readable.

I am deeply grateful to the Yates family of Red Lodge, Montana, for their generous hospitality in allowing David Huie and me to stay in their cabin the early winter of 1973. Big Al Yates had long since passed when I returned to Red Lodge four decades later, but I connected with his sons Ron and Al. Al has since unstintingly provided me with many details of the Yates family story. Until this day, David and I reminisce about those months on the lam and count our stay in Montana as pure sustenance for the soul.

I chose to change the names and personal circumstances of a few characters in the book, which contains a stockpile of ideas, dates, names, places and events. In the end it is only me who can vouch for all the details.

About the Author

PHIL KARBER is a two-time Lowell Thomas Award–winning travel writer. He has journeyed to all continents and 155 of the 193 UN-recognized countries, lived in Africa and Asia for fourteen years, and has authored the following books: *Postmarks from a Political Traveler*; *Fear and Faith in Paradise: Exploring Conflict and Religion in the Middle East*; *The Indochina Chronicles: Travels in Laos, Cambodia and Vietnam*; and *Yak Pizza to Go: Travels in an Age of Vanishing Cultures and Extinctions*.

www.ingramcontent.com/pod-product-compliance
Lightning Source LLC
LaVergne TN
LVHW041654060526
838201LV00043B/435